Francis G. Kaput

At Peace With
All Their Neighbors

Catholics and Catholicism in the
National Capital 1787–1860

John Carroll, first Catholic bishop in the United States, founding president of Georgetown College / Portrait (detail) by Gilbert Stuart, ca. 1803-1805.

At Peace with All Their Neighbors

Catholics and Catholicism in the National Capital 1787–1860

WILLIAM W. WARNER

GEORGETOWN UNIVERSITY PRESS / WASHINGTON, D.C.

Georgetown University Press, Washington, D.C.
© 1994 by Georgetown University Press. All rights reserved.
Printed in the United States of America
10 9 8 7 6 5 4 3 2 1
THIS VOLUME IS PRINTED ON ACID-FREE OFFSET BOOK PAPER   1994

Library of Congress Cataloging-in-Publication Data

Warner, William W.
    At peace with all their neighbors : Catholics and Catholicism in
    the national capital, 1787–1860 / William W. Warner.
        p.   cm.
    1. Catholic Church—Washington (D.C.)—History—18th century.
    2. Catholic Church—Washington (D.C.)—History—19th century.
    3. Washington (D.C.)—Church history—18th century.   4. Washington
    (D.C.)—Church history—19th century.   I. Title.
BX1418.W37   1994
282'.753'09033—dc20
ISBN 0-87840-557-7   94-9699

for
John and Andy

Contents

List of Illustrations

Introduction

Small beginnings in the study of history often do not remain so. One discovery leads to another, until the researcher finds himself compelled to consider a much larger portrait than he originally envisioned. So, at least, it has been with this book. What began as a simple parish history took on greater dimensions as a wealth of records gradually revealed itself.

The reader will have no trouble recognizing the parish in question as Holy Trinity of Georgetown, the District of Columbia's oldest. The baptismal and marriage registers of this church, virtually complete from 1795 onwards, carry certain names that anyone familiar with Maryland history will recognize. They are the family names of Maryland's first Catholic settlers, who lived under the proprietary regimes of the Lords Baltimore in the seventeenth century. In the case of the author, this finding immediately framed a larger question: what role if any had these descendants of North America's first English-speaking Catholic settlers played in the creation of the national capital? The answer as it proved is a large one. In such spheres as the building, early government, and financial development of the capital, the area's Catholics made major contributions, out of all proportion to their small number.

The purpose of this book is a modest one, namely to bring to light these contributions and the generally good relations and respect they engendered between Catholics and the area's Protestant majority.

To do so adequately it has proved necessary to shed some light as well on the church that nurtured the District's first Catholics. The Catholic church in the United States following the Revolution was a small one. Often described as an orphan body, its clergy numbered twenty-one priests, all former Jesuits whose parent order had been ruthlessly suppressed throughout the world by Pope Clement XIV by 1773. Nationwide the church counted an estimated 24,500 adherents; approximately 15,000 of them and nineteen of the twenty-one priests were concentrated in Maryland, not far from the future capital. Thus it happens that the history of the early American church was in a sense local history, shaped by strong traditions from Maryland's colonial era. Some of these, too, must be treated.

For many readers colonial Maryland is remembered as "the Catholic colony" which passed landmark acts of religious liberty in 1639 and 1649. It may come as a surprise, therefore, to learn that Maryland did not long remain a haven of religious tolerance and freedom. Shortly after England's Glorious Revolution of 1689, the proprietary reign of the Lords Baltimore was overthrown and with it went all semblance of religious freedom. By 1703 the Maryland Assembly's Act to Prevent the Growth of Popery ushered in a seventy-two-year period of anti-Catholic penal laws during which time Catholics as a class were deprived of communal worship, religious education, eligibility for public office, and other basic human rights. I have therefore thought it essential to cast a backward glance at some aspects of this history, not only because they are so little known even among informed Catholics, but also because they had such perduring effects on the emerging American church. It was in the colonial period, after all, that an ecumenical outlook—the determination "to live at peace with all their neighbors"—was born of the second Lord Baltimore's wise (and politically prudent) policy of religious freedom in the face of an overwhelming Protestant majority. It was in the colonial period, too, that a strong tradition of public service and close business and social ties with the Protestant community, especially through interfaith marriages, had their beginnings. And it was during the period of proscriptive legislation that there arose among Maryland Catholics a spirit of independence and self-reliance, stemming from the necessity of home worship and the lack of a hierarchical church structure. So, too, with a belief in the necessity for the separation of church and state, impressed upon Maryland Catholics by the experience of living under a hostile government. All these attributes—ecumenism, self-reliance, belief in church-state separation—remained very much in place in forming the character of the native American church and its first followers in the District of Columbia.

Trinity Church, as it was simply known for so long in its history, was at the center of the first Catholic presence in the national capital area. Born in the shadow and of the substance of Georgetown College, Trinity was the pastoral proving ground for a generation of church leaders and the base from which many of its pastors and priests served missions or stations—in effect, proto-churches—throughout the neighboring Virginia and Maryland countryside. Happily for the historian, there is a relative abundance of records concerning Trinity. These come as much from diaries, correspondence, and other forms of records in the Archives of the Maryland Province of the Society of Jesus, the *Woodstock Letters*, the Georgetown University Archives, and the Archives of the Archdiocese of Baltimore as from the Trinity Church records themselves, although the latter are invaluable in determining the nature and composition of Trinity's congregations. By comparison St. Patrick's of Washington, which had its beginnings almost as early as Trinity, unfortunately lacks definitive records of its origin and early years. This is counterbalanced to some degree, however, by the rich history surrounding St. Patrick's second pastor, the remarkable Father William Matthews, which has been well researched and interpreted by his biographer, Reverend Joseph T. Durkin of Georgetown University.

To repeat, the central theme of this book is a modest one. But behind it runs a subsidiary theme of greater significance. It concerns what I have chosen to call the first face of American Catholicism. As congressmen, senators, journalists, government officials, merchants, and distinguished visitors from all over the young republic descended on the nascent capital city, they did not find an alien "immigrant church" so often ascribed to urban Catholicism in the United States. Rather, they found well-to-do, educated, and generally tolerant fifth- and sixth-generation American Catholics not very different from themselves. These Catholics, moreover, were working with their Protestant counterparts in the difficult task of building up and governing the capital city, which in its early years was constantly threatened by failure or removal to Philadelphia. In this role some of these Catholics moved easily in high circles, from the White House and cabinet departments to the city's first drawing-room salons. The result of this interaction was remarkable.

"That upright gentleman is a Catholic? Is that the teaching of the Catholic church? How different from the idea I had formed of it!" Such was the typical reaction, as described by Father John Grassi, ninth president of Georgetown College, among Protestants first coming to know Catholics in the District of Columbia. What was happening was the erosion of deep-seated prejudices, of the cultural legacy of anti-Popery and Guy Fawkes Day brought from Europe by so many English-speaking settlers. What was happening was the beginning of understanding, a mutual understanding that withstood in large measure even the extremes of the American nativist and Know Nothing era. It would not have happened, we must stop to think, had the capital been elsewhere. Thus its significance.

PART I

Georgetown and the Maryland Tradition

.

1

A Chapel for Worship

Near the residences of the clergy, and on lands belonging to them, small chapels were built, but few elsewhere, so that it was necessary to say mass in private houses.

-JOHN CARROLL
Report to the Roman Congregation, 1790

In the spring of 1787, at a time when dogwood and redbud begin to bloom in the great oak forests of the Potomac Valley, we may imagine a small group of Catholics making their way to the high ground west of Georgetown. George Fenwick, an aspiring young surveyor, might be leading the way. With him would be his uncle, Captain Ignatius Fenwick, a former ship owner and man of substance; the brothers George and Adam King, merchants of Georgetown; and Alexander Doyle, a local property owner. Wives, children, and friends may also have formed part of the excursion, given its celebratory purpose.

Walking slowly and looking carefully for tree slashes, hardwood posts, or other marks of the surveyor's trade, Fenwick would eventually guide the group to their destination—a small plot on a wooded knoll, next to which lay a rustic cemetery guarding the few graves of the area's first Catholic settlers. The countryside around it, long known simply as the Heights, was already famous for its salubrious air and its unrivalled views of the "silvery and majestic Potomac," which one contemporary author confessed "neither the pen nor the pencil can discharge . . . [by] the most animated description."[1]

No one in the group, we may be sure, would have disagreed. From where they stood they could take delight not only in their view of the river, but also in the small settlement rising along its eastern bank. Below them would be a cluster of tall ships, warehouses, shops, wooden dwellings, and a dozen or so brick houses. This, but for a few upland estates, was Georgetown in the spring of 1787.

Well satisfied with the view, the men in the group would soon have turned to the business that had brought them there. This was to determine the exact boundaries of Lot 72 in what was then called Threlkeld's Addition to Georgetown. At the time there were no less than five such "additions" beyond the original limits of Georgetown. They had become necessary because of the town's rapid growth; each of them had generated some confusion over titles, boundaries, and streets, the latter often existing only on paper. Our group, to

4 be sure of their ground, would therefore have carefully examined the deed they possessed to Lot 72. At approximately 60 by 120 feet, the lot might prove small for the use intended. That was some cause for concern, to be sure. But the deed was unequivocal, and Lot 72, they could easily see, was ideally situated. With such reassuring thoughts the group might have disbanded. Or, had the day been especially fine, lingered to enjoy the scenery which then as now all but defied the most animated description.

We do not know if such a scene ever occurred. But the possibility that something like it took place is very strong, given the existence of the deed to Lot 72 and the significance it held for the persons mentioned above. Their goal, in fact, was nothing less than to build the first Catholic church within what would soon be the ten-mile square of the District of Columbia. Not coincidentally, it would also be the first place of public worship for the Catholics of the area, a right that was denied throughout the colony of Maryland from 1704 until 1776. The deed that would make this possible, well preserved at the Maryland Hall of Records, reads in part as follows:

> Ex D^d
> A Doyle
> At the Request of the Rev. Dr. J. Carroll the following Deed was Recorded this 24th Day of April 1787 . . . between John Threlkeld of Montgomery County . . . and the reverend John Carroll Doctor of divinity, superior of the Roman Catholick Clergy in the united states of america. . . , WITNESSETH that for and in Consideration of the sum of five shillings . . . the said John Threlkeld . . . doth grant . . . and confirm unto the said John Carroll . . . and his successors, . . . forever, . . . Lot Number seventy two, with all the appertinances thereunto . . . for the purpose of erecting and maintaining thereon a Chapple or house for divine worship.[2]

The document called for what in effect would be the first visible symbol of a Catholic presence in a place that was already being considered for the future capital of the United States. This Catholic presence, we will see, was rooted in a multi-generational tradition of ecumenism, public service, and strong social and commercial ties to the Protestant community. In this sense it was unique. Nowhere else in the young republic, nowhere else in the towns and nascent cities of the Atlantic seaboard would the nation's early Catholic communities have such a place in civic affairs.

The key points of the deed are easily explained. First, the token payment of five shillings leaves no doubt that the deed was in effect a gift. (At the time nearby lots in western Georgetown sold for anywhere from £20 to £50, Maryland currency, or approximately $35 to $53, while commercial property along High Street (now Wisconsin Avenue), the town's main thoroughfare, might go for two or three times as much.)[3] Second, the notation "Ex D^d A Doyle" in the upper left-hand margin of the deed means that Alexander Doyle, an important figure in the Catholic community to whom we will presently return, had a third-party interest in the transaction. Third, the language "a Chapple or house for divine worship" may have been purposefully cautious or, if not, at least an accurate reflection of Catholic practice of the day. Throughout the long years of prohibited public worship, those Catholics of rural Maryland who lived near Jesuit missions might celebrate mass and other sacraments at the Jesuits' manor chapels. Those who did not either practiced home devotions or attended mass while visiting the great houses of the landed gentry, many of whom had private chapels occasionally served by the nearest priest. In towns the same arrangement obtained in the homes of leading Catholic residents. Thus Catholics quite literally had their chapels and mass houses, not churches. The word church, even after independence and Maryland's 1776 Declaration of Rights restored religious freedom, still smacked of the establishment—of the Church of England and the Maryland Assembly—whose more zealous members had imposed the most odious restrictions on Catholics throughout most of the eighteenth century. For the time being, therefore, it might be prudent to avoid using the word and its still-suspect connotations. Lastly, it is only necessary to add that all existing maps and land records of Georgetown clearly show that Lot 72 is the exact site where the first Trinity Church was built and where it stands now as the parish center of today's Holy Trinity Church.

Of the lot's donor, John Threlkeld, a Protestant, we know almost everything except precisely why he chose to make this gift. Threlkeld was a second-generation Marylander whose parents' estate, "Berleith," at one time occupied much of western Georgetown. As parts were sold off to form the various additions the growing town required—the "Beatty and Hawkins Addition," the "Threlkeld Addition," the "Peter, Beatty, Threlkeld, and Deakins Addition"—John Threlkeld as an only son became a prime beneficiary of Georgetown's short-lived boom period. From the accounts of his contemporaries he was a man of commanding appearance, a good horseman, and a Latin scholar who might often "rein in his steed, until he quoted some Latin epigram to any one liberally educated, and then he would wheel suddenly round and be off on a tangent."[4]

From other sources we know also that Threlkeld and his wife Elizabeth kept a fine table and frequently entertained their wide circle of influential friends. Sir Augustus John Foster, an early British envoy who was both an astute observer and a demanding critic of American society, confessed in his memoirs that he occasionally enjoyed pleasant evening parties at the homes of the Threlkelds, the George Masons, the Thomas Lees, and a few other Georgetown families, which he considered "to much advantage . . . compared with the society of many an English provincial town."[5] From the picture that emerges, therefore, it is obvious that one reason the staunchly Anglican John Threlkeld chose to give a small piece of land to a Catholic church is that he could easily afford it. Another is that he risked no opprobrium in doing so. In pre-Revolutionary times such a gift might have aroused suspicion among the Protestant majority in Maryland who favored a strict enforcement of the law prohibiting

6   Catholics any place of public worship. By 1787, however, religious differences were fast giving way to Georgetown's soaring commercial ambitions. Indeed, by then Threlkeld's gift was neither unique nor uncommon.

To understand this development it is necessary to remember that although Georgetown in 1787 was a small tobacco port of less than four thousand souls, its leading citizens dreamed of nothing less than national stature and unlimited prosperity. They had every reason to do so. The fierce competition for the site of the nation's capital was still the talk of the day, but Congress was already narrowing the choice to the banks of the Delaware, meaning Philadelphia, and the Potomac, which was generally understood to be Georgetown itself. Moreover, the prospect of becoming the national capital was not all. To seagoing ships the Potomac at Georgetown offered the deepest inland penetration of the entire Atlantic seaboard. Georgetown was thus the nearest port to the overland route across the Alleghenies and down into the Ohio and Mississippi River systems. More to the point, two years earlier George Washington himself had organized a limited stock company to link the two river systems. Known as the Potomac Company, it would seek to make the Potomac navigable—by locks wherever absolutely necessary, but mostly by "improvements" in the river course itself—to the point where cargos could be transferred over the relatively short land route to the Ohio River.

Little wonder, therefore, that Georgetowners of 1787 fancied themselves at the commercial as well as political epicenter of the nation by virtue of their favored position as "the gateway to the West." If anyone had doubts they need only consider General Washington's obsessive interest in the project. Not only did he talk about it to the point of boring his dinner guests, but he himself had also hosted the Mount Vernon Conference to lay the groundwork for the precedent-setting interstate cooperation that would be vital to this and future projects. The Mount Vernon Conference had in turn engendered the Annapolis Convention of September 1786, which had more states in attendance and more issues to consider, and now, in the very spring of 1787, a conference of all thirteen states at Philadelphia that came to be known as the Constitutional Convention. Throughout its deliberations and in many newspapers across the land, the natural advantage of the Potomac River received occasional mention. Invariably, the Potomac route was described as the gateway to opening up the West and the riches of the continent. To the little town at the head of its navigation, everything seemed to be falling in place.[6]

Everything, that is, except some of the public institutions necessary to a well-ordered community. Georgetown in 1787 had neither schools nor much in the way of religious institutions. Education was the province of private tutors for those who could afford them, and public worship existed only for Presbyterians in a church on Bridge (now M) Street. Given their expectations of prosperity, the leading citizens of Georgetown were undoubtedly eager to lend the town increased stability by encouraging more such respectable public institutions, whether churches, centers of learning, or well-appointed taverns. Thus arose the civic spirit—one wants almost to say ecumenism—that prompted a

degree of interdenominational participation in church and civic projects virtually unknown to previous generations. Examples are many. Bernard O'Neill, a
prominent Georgetown Catholic, served on both the board of lottery managers
raising money for the Rock Creek Episcopal Church and the first board of commissioners superintending construction of Georgetown College.[7] When
Colonel Charles Beatty, an early landholder who had Catholic descendants,
first offered land for sale in the two-hundred-acre "Beatty and Hawkins Addition," he and his partner Hawkins set aside four lots "to wit: one for building
on, a church for the use of the Church of England, one of a Calvinist church,
one for a Lutheran church, and the other for a market house." Beginning in
1794, Georgetown Episcopalians were invited to share use of the first Presbyterian Church on Bridge Street, while they patiently waited some eight years
for the completion of a church of their own. Catholics contributed to the build-
ing-fund campaigns for Protestant churches. Protestants returned the favor. In
short, for Georgetown in the last quarter of the eighteenth century, business
growth and a stable society, not sectarian differences, were the order of the
day.[8]

The recipient of Lot 72, as every Catholic reader must know, has gone
down in history as "the architect of the American Catholic church." It is tempting to place John Carroll in the role of the founder of Trinity, as some historians
have and as the language of the deed would itself seem to imply.[9] There is,
however, no documentary evidence for such a view. Among the more than 350
letters of John Carroll preserved in the archives of the Archdiocese of Baltimore, many of which concern the beginnings of other churches, there is not one
about Trinity.[10] Rather, what Carroll's considerable correspondence does suggest is that he considered a chapel in Georgetown, if at all, as incidental to a
larger objective. This objective was to create an academy "for every Class of
Citizens [where] Reading, Writing, Arithmetic, the easier Branches of the Mathematics, and the Grammar of our Native Tongue will be attended to, no less
than the Learned Languages." To this end Carroll wrote incessantly to his closest friend and most faithful correspondent, the British Jesuit Charles Plowden.
The proposed academy was "the object nearest my heart now, and the only
one, that can give consistency to our religious views in this country." More, to
Carroll it was the very foundation of "all my hope of permanency, and success
to our Holy Religion in the United States."[11]

But many obstacles over a long period of time had stood in the way of the
object nearest to Carroll's heart. He had come to the United States in 1774 after
long years of study and teaching in Europe, deeply distressed by Pope Clement
XIV's world-wide suppression of the Society of Jesus the year before. Awaiting
him was a clergy of former Jesuits who for the most part were content to man-
age their rural estates in southern Maryland in which they had invested from
the earliest days of the colonial period, as they patiently awaited a new day for
the Society. During his first years in America, therefore, Carroll lived with his
mother, the widowed Eleanor Darnall Carroll, and reacquainted himself with
his many relatives as he travelled the countryside on rural missions, using the

John Carroll as a young man, variously attributed, circa 1774.

family chapel at Rock Creek, Maryland (between today's Kensington and Silver Spring), as his base. But soon, whether he wished it or not, Carroll found himself caught up in affairs of church and state at the highest levels. In April 1776 he formed part of the unsuccessful mission to Quebec sent by the Continental Congress to secure French Canadian support for the Revolutionary cause. With him went Benjamin Franklin, Samuel Chase, and his wealthy cousin by marriage Charles Carroll of Carrollton, who had played the chief role in convincing Carroll to go by putting aside his doubts about "ministers of Religion who leave the duties of their profession to take a busy part in political matters."[12]

But in the years that followed, John Carroll's grief over the suppression of the Jesuits gave way little by little to a realization of the unique challenge of serving in a nation in the very act of creation. On the one hand, he saw an enormous opportunity for the church. ("The prospect before us is immense," he would soon write Plowden, as he began to receive requests for priests and offers of property for new missions "from every part of the U. States, North, South, and West."[13]) On the other, he could look with dismay at the pitiable state of the orphaned Catholic church in America at the close of the Revolution.

As he surveyed the general scene, Carroll could count but twenty-four priests—nineteen in Maryland and five in Pennsylvania—in the United States. Two or three at most were able men who shared his views on the sensitive and difficult task of building the American church. The remaining were nearly all elderly ex-Jesuits whose chief concern was how or in what form the Society might be reconstituted in the United States. What was more troubling, these former Jesuits had neither organization nor leadership except for a distant and inattentive vicar general in London who was nominally the superior of all ex-Jesuits in America.

Carroll, always of a practical mind, set himself the task of putting things in order, first by writing "A Plan for Clergy Organization," entirely on his own initiative, in 1782. The "Plan" in turn gave rise to the historic meetings at Whitemarsh, Maryland, in 1783, which gave the American Catholic church its first framework of incorporation and hierarchical administration. But barely had the meetings at Whitemarsh begun when James Talbot, the vicar apostolic in London, refused to grant faculties to preach and hear confessions to two priests bound for America. Talbot claimed that America was no longer under his jurisdiction. If doubts about playing too political a role in church and state affairs still troubled Carroll, they must now have vanished before this ill-conceived ruling from London.

To Carroll and his colleagues of like mind it was patently impossible for the church to rise to the opportunities from every part of the country if the American clergy were to be limited in their priestly functions by regulation from abroad. Boldly, therefore, and with a keen sense of emerging American values, Carroll and four other priests wrote to Pope Pius VI to inform him that "because of the present arrangement in government in America, we are no longer able as formerly to have recourse . . . to bishops or vicars apostolic who live under a different and foreign government." With the agreement of the Whitemarsh conferees, he proposed instead that an aging priest who had served as Maryland's superior before the suppression be named so again and given the episcopal powers then vested in London. But Rome, after obtaining the advice of Benjamin Franklin in Paris, responded in the summer of 1784 by naming Carroll himself as "Superior of the Mission in the United States." Faster than he realized or wanted, Carroll was on the road to becoming America's first bishop. There was no one else.[14]

By the time of the deed to Lot 72, therefore, Carroll was deeply engaged in building the foundation of a uniquely American church. The Whitemarsh

10   meetings that would eventually produce a "Constitution of the Clergy" were not yet concluded. The applications for new missions from north, south, and west continued to pour in. So, too, did uninvited priests from abroad who often pursued individualistic ministries with no regard for the particular sensibilities common to the new republic. At Holy Trinity Church in Philadelphia, the citizen trustees of the German congregation had engaged a German-born priest of their own choosing in the first of many independent trustee actions that would sorely trouble Carroll and his successors for generations to come. Worst of all, Carroll had found his dream of an academy for every class of citizen firmly opposed by the conservative Maryland clergy who feared (not entirely without reason) that some of their faltering estates might be sold off to finance such a radical new undertaking. In summary, we may forgive John Carroll if in the spring of 1787 he gave little time or thought to a small chapel for the relatively few Roman Catholics of Georgetown on the Potomac.[15]

Thus the question remains of where to look for the founders of what was first known as Trinity Church. (It was so called, without variations or exceptions, until 1845, when from one year to the next the name was changed to Holy Trinity in the *Metropolitan Catholic Almanac and Laity's Directory*.[16]) As in the case of so many of our early Catholic churches, the answer in general appears to be congregational grass-roots demand, rather than the result of any systematic plan by an emerging hierarchy. Within this context one man, Alexander Doyle, stands out.

A native of Port Tobacco in southern Maryland, Doyle had come to Georgetown in the early 1780s. He is best known as the publisher of the *George-Town Weekly Ledger*, which he and his brother James took over from its first owners in 1791. The Doyle brothers also published *A Pious Guide to Prayer and Devotion Containing Various Practices Calculated to Answer the Various Demands of the Different Devout Members of the Roman Catholic Churches*. Printed in 1792, the *Pious Guide* had more to recommend it than its prolix title. Typical of the spiritual manuals that first became popular for home devotions and study while public worship was prohibited in Maryland, the *Guide* was a runaway best seller of its kind, going through some twelve editions between 1792 and 1852. It also had the distinction of being the earliest Catholic imprint in the District of Columbia. But well before joining his brother in publishing, Alexander Doyle had established himself as a grain and general merchant on Georgetown's High Street. He also soon became a major property owner in the western part of Georgetown, in the course of which he must have known John Threlkeld, whom land records show as involved at some point in nearly all land transactions in that part of the town.[17]

Exactly what role Doyle played in the establishment of Trinity Church is difficult to determine. Some earlier historians have incorrectly cast him as the actual builder of the church. Others believe he paid for the lot, not without reason. What we do know, however, is that Doyle's will, written one month before the deed to Lot 72, directed that "any benefit or anuity which may arise from the rent of the Pews in the Georgetown Chapel . . . is to be divided between

[his] male children, namely James, Alexander, Joseph and John Doyle." Such a provision, of course, implies foreknowledge of the deed and some part in its origin. How large a part, however, remains uncertain. In any case Doyle claimed the chapel's pew rents for whatever he may have done to secure the deed and later asked to trade the rentals due on pews reserved by Georgetown College for its boarding students in exchange for tuition and board at the college for his four sons. That some such arrangement was accepted we know from the account books of the college, which by 1796, or two years after Doyle's death, acknowledge that the sons were still entitled to an aggregate of "12 years Board & Tuition in College gratis for [Doyle's] expenses in building the Church." But what direct building expenses Doyle may have contributed cannot be determined. Either he or his wife Elizabeth, who came from Stafford County, Virginia, could easily have been major contributors. Well after Doyle's death, however, when his heirs were seeking further compensation from the college insisting that Doyle had purchased the lot and "built the Church out of his own pocket," Leonard Neale, Trinity's first pastor, indignantly refuted these claims. He himself had paid the construction bills, Neale maintained, and he knew the money had come by subscription from the good citizens of Montgomery, Prince George's, Charles, and St. Mary's counties. Any claims to the contrary were merely "an attempt to obtain charity from the college by appearing under the dust of old papers."[18]

An early Washington newspaper, *The Impartial Observer and Washington Advertiser*, once characterized Alexander Doyle as "the projector and principal agent of Trinity Church," and this may be as accurate a description of his role as any. Doyle may well have made some donations to the church, but it is much more likely that his principal contribution was to exert his good offices with Threlkeld to acquire the church plot and with Carroll to lend the prestige of his name to its acceptance. Carroll for his part could scarcely have been expected to do more. He might approve and encourage the Georgetown Catholic community's effort to build their first place of public worship, but he had neither the priests nor the money to advance it. Carroll not only had the college to build. There were also all those other demands for clergy and churches from every part of the nation. If, as it appeared, more ground was required for the Georgetown chapel, if funds were needed to launch construction, the community for the time being would have to look to itself.[19]

What happened next in the history of the District's first Catholic church is veiled by a singular gap with no written record. Not until 1792, or five years after the original deed to John Carroll, is there documented evidence of progress on construction. The intervening years may have seen some efforts at fund raising—slow, difficult and unaccustomed efforts, we must add—since the practice as we understand it was then all but unknown to both the Catholic and the Protestant laity. Among the latter this was especially true of the Episcopalians, who had suddenly to adjust to the loss of public revenues granted them as the established church of colonial times. With Catholics the opposite

12   was true. In the colonial period they had become accustomed to receiving from the church as much as or more than giving. This was because the Maryland Jesuits, who had some degree of financial independence through their country estates, supported the laity, more than vice-versa, through religious observances at private homes and chapels, education in the form of family tutors, and even provision of libraries.

But if progress towards raising the Georgetown chapel moved slowly, various events that would have lasting and profound effects for its future parish and the Catholic community at large came very quickly during the five-year gap in which there are no written records. In July 1790, after prolonged debate and a rash of compromises, the United States Congress passed the so-called Residence Act directing "that a district or territory not exceeding ten miles square, be located as hereafter directed on the river Potomac, at some space between the mouths of the Eastern branch [the Anacostia River] and Connogochegue [Conococheague Creek at Williamsport, Maryland] . . . for the permanent seat of the Government," with the final choice to be left to President George Washington and three commissioners of his appointment.[20]

The first battle with Philadelphia for the site of the national capital had been won. But the provisions for the choice of the exact location were much too ambiguous for the prominent Georgetown landowners who confidently expected the capital city to rise right around their wooded heights. Accordingly, Robert Peter, Georgetown's first mayor; Benjamin Stoddert, the town's wealthiest tobacco merchant; John Threlkeld; and other eminent landholders sought Washington's ear with tempting offers of their lands at whatever price the President thought reasonable.[21] At a humbler level aspiring citizen-poets filled the pages of John Fenno's *Gazette of the United States* with tributes to Georgetown in rolling doggerel and dubious rhyme. Among them one unknown bard saw both great strategic and moral advantage in Georgetown's inland location:

> *O! What a charming thing and pretty,*
> *To have a noble, Federal City!*
> *Surpassing in few years to come,*
> *All that history says of Rome;*
> *That ancient seat of arts and wars,*
> *The mother of eternal jars!*
> *Not near old ocean's margin built,*
> *Where blood by hogsheads may be spilt;*
> *Where ships which vomit smoke and fire,*
> *May force the people to retire;*
> *May set a scampering our patricians,*
> *Cursing all maritime positions.*
>
> *Besides, all seaport towns, we know,*
> *The floods of horrid vice o'erflow;*
> *There business, noise, and dissipation,*

Distract the rulers of the nation!
There morn, and noon, and midnight revels,
With a long list of Syren devils—
Balls, treats, and visits—arts cajoling,
Will set their wits and senses rolling,
Till on the rocks of tempting beauty,
They shipwreck honor, truth, and duty.
No, let us to the woods repair,
For peace and innocence dwell there. . . . [22]

But neither the best offers of Georgetown's landholding aristocracy nor the poetic effusions of its anonymous moralist had the desired effect. Although President Washington had chosen the ten-mile square of the Territory (later District) of Columbia within one year of the congressional directive, the local battle over where the capital city should rise within the one hundred square miles of the District dragged on for months thereafter. Finally, in June 1791, Washington succeeded in reconciling the differences of competing groups of landowners and chose an area of 6,100 acres for "the Federal City." It did not include Georgetown.[23] Rather, the City of Washington, as it was officially named three months later, was to be centered three miles to the east on Jenkins Hill, "which stands as a pedestal waiting for a monument . . . [where] no situation could stand in competition . . . [and] none would ever be made so grand," as the French city planner Pierre L'Enfant enthusiastically described the site. The final decision was a bitter disappointment to the many Georgetown landowners who had fought it to the end, to say nothing of the even more embittered Philadelphians who would continue to press for retention of the capital until well into the nineteenth century. But Georgetown at least could look forward to the consolation of being near if not itself the seat of government.[24]

Chief among those *not* disappointed was John Carroll. On the contrary he had long foreseen the advantages of having his proposed academy near to, but not part of, the future capital city. Carroll first got word of the victory over Philadelphia, or the preliminary decision in favor of the Potomac, while still in England, shortly after his consecration as the first Catholic bishop of America in August 1790. Immediately he wrote Plowden:

My letters from America as well as the public prints, inform me that the district, now settled for the future capital of the United States, . . . is on Potowmack river. Commissioners under direction of the President are to determine the particular spot . . . The knowledge, I have of the Country, makes me confident, it will be either at George Town, or, what would answer better for our school, within four miles of it.[25]

When the better solution indeed came to pass, Carroll redoubled his efforts to open the college nearest his heart as soon as possible. For reasons we will examine in the next chapter, these efforts greatly accelerated the pace of

14   events leading to the construction of Trinity Church. In what might be called the first manifestation of the symbiotic relation between the two institutions that exists to this day, as the college advanced, so, too, did the plans for Trinity. In fact, at about the same time the first students entered the college, ground was being broken on the small knoll in Lot 72. The structure that would rise there was modestly planned, both in design and dimensions. But it would have salubrious airs and a splendid view of the Potomac.

2

The College and the Church

There is a little Presby. Church partly finished and a plain brick Roman Chapel at the W.[est] End with a clumsy steeple to it. They have an Academy here under the Direction of a President and a Vice-President who are Romish Priests. . . . Tho' the Academy is but of two years old they have now between 80 and 90 scholars drawn from all quarters and principally from Roman Catholic families. . . . The Academy contemplates to give degrees. It gives great attention to the scholars. A Physician visits them daily, and it is growing rapidly.

-JAMES KENT
"Observations on the River Potowmack," 1793

Early in November 1791, or some five months after the creation of the Federal City, a young student from North Carolina named William Gaston arrived in Georgetown. The college he expected to attend was not quite ready to receive him. He was therefore temporarily lodged at the Green Tree Tavern of Joseph Semmes, a southern Maryland Catholic whose family would later be prominent parishioners of Trinity. On November 22, 1791, Gaston began a program of solitary studies. A month later he was joined by Philemon Charles Wederstrandt, a boy who like many other Georgetown students would one day have a distinguished naval career. By the following April some twenty-nine more boys—nine boarders and twenty day students—had entered to form a class. A three-story brick building, later known as "Old South," had been readied for them. The nation's first Catholic college, the College of Georgetown on the Potomac, was a reality.[1]

Within two years of breaking ground in 1789, John Carroll had overcome the Maryland Jesuits' opposition, raised funds both at home and abroad, and personally assembled the nucleus of a faculty for the college he so ardently desired. In so doing he contributed far more to the successful growth of Catholicism in the Washington area—and, indeed, the nation at large—than anything he might have done to help local parishes. Fundamental to his success were Carroll's founding principles for the college, especially his insistence that it "be open to students of every religious profession." To fellow clerics critical of this policy Carroll posed a simple question: since Catholics had so recently been granted equal toleration in the new republic, would they not be taking a backward step, even risking eventual isolation, if they did not offer the same to others?[2]

One immediate result of Carroll's open-door policy was that Protestant parents were quick to send their sons to the new institution on the Heights. Benjamin Stoddert, Jr., whose father was soon to be first secretary of the navy; Augustine and Bushrod Washington, great-nephews of the President; Richard Claggett, a relative of the first Episcopal bishop of Maryland; and George and David Peter, sons of Mayor Robert Peter of Georgetown, were among the Protestant students enrolled during the first three years of the college.[3]

To be sure, Georgetown parents had few other choices for their high-spirited adolescent sons. Since Georgetown was initially a "college" only in the European sense, offering classes to students from eight to fifteen or sixteen years of age, the prospect of getting young boys out of the house and into a well-disciplined school, no matter its religious auspices, was undeniably attractive. Still, it represented an enormous break with tradition. As a boy John Carroll had himself grown up during an era when Catholic schooling in Maryland was completely proscribed. By the time he was a young man, Protestant zealots in the Maryland Assembly were even attempting to forbid Catholic education abroad, with periodic tirades against students like Carroll who were "sent from here to St. Omer's and other foreign Popish Seminaries out of His Majesty's Obedience . . . return[ing] here as Popish Priests, or Jesuits."[4] Yet here was the same John Carroll founding a college where students of all faiths were taught by the very Jesuits who had once been the most suspect of "Popish priests."[4]

That such a change could take place in one man's lifetime was due in no small part to the influences of John Carroll himself and his extended family. His older brother, Daniel Carroll II of Upper Marlboro, who had represented Maryland at both the Continental Congress and the Constitutional Convention, was a member of the first United States Congress, where he took an active part in the drafting of the Bill of Rights. He would later become one of the three original commissioners for the District of Columbia. His cousin by marriage, Charles Carroll of Carrollton, a signer of the Declaration of Independence, was widely regarded both as the wealthiest citizen of the land and one of the intellectual fathers of the Revolution. Another cousin, Daniel Carroll of Duddington, was a major landowner who had a prominent role in President Washington's negotiations for the Federal City. All together they represented one of the most respected families in the United States. Moreover, the Carrolls' commitment to the emerging American principle of separation of church and state was already well known. Thus, to doubting parents John Carroll's name alone was an assurance of education dedicated to "the diffusion of liberating and tolerating principles" he so often proclaimed.[5]

Still another founding principle—that of emphasizing "useful branches of knowledge" and "the grammar of our native tongue" as much as the classics—also did much to gain immediate acceptance for the college. From the first day of classes, students were entered either as "English scholars" or "Latin scholars." The college account books for the first years also show that students might at a slight extra cost receive specialized books (and presumably the tutoring to go with them) for what today would be called vocational training. There are records, for example, of a student who had completed both the English and Latin scholar core curricula moving on to *Moore's Navigation, Morse's Geography*, and *Fr. [French] Grammar*, in obvious preparation for a career at sea. Or, similarly, *Gibson's Surveying* and additional texts in mathematics, for an aspiring civil engineer. Given early Georgetown's mercantile character, such offerings must have been very well received.[6]

For these and other reasons Georgetown College had an auspicious beginning. Although beset by many internal problems, the college in its early years seems always to have been favorably viewed by its immediate constituencies. It is little wonder, for example, that in 1797 a just-retired President Washington gladly accepted the college's invitation for a quiet visit in celebration of the Muses. Georgetown College was and would continue to be a respected community asset for generations of Georgetowners and Washingtonians.[7]

More to the point of our inquiry, the successful establishment of the college had immediate effects on the church to be known as Trinity. These effects came about because in the eyes of John Carroll and other of the college's founders "the chapel in Georgetown," as it continued to be called for some time, would have to come under the spiritual care of the college (but not the fiscal, as events would prove) if for no other reason than a general shortage of priests. This being so, the search for the initial college faculty was also in effect a search for the chapel's first pastor and clergy. If there were any discussions or debates on this point at the time, we do not know of them. It seems simply to have been taken for granted that the chapel would initially be served by priests of the college faculty. The fact that the clergy-faculty would be mainly former Jesuits presented no problem. Should the Society be restored, as all hoped, it could be argued that "collegiate chapels" near to or associated with educational institutions were a traditional Jesuit apostolate.

At first glance these developments, which would eventually result in a permanent union of Trinity and the Society of Jesus, may seem somewhat casual. (Not until 1845, in fact, was the question of Jesuit control of Trinity parish even brought up at meetings of the Maryland Province.)[8] In reality the search for the clergy-faculty, which John Carroll himself conducted, was anything but so. Understandably, Carroll took some pride in the native Marylanders like himself who had endured the long rigors of study and ordination abroad. As early as June 1785 we find him imploring his friend Charles Plowden in England for the return of Charles and Francis Neale, Leonard Brooke, John Mattingly and Joseph Semmes, Marylanders all, who were then studying or teaching at the Jesuit academy at Liège. All too often, however, many of Carroll's first choices were retained for service in England or the continent. Three years later, therefore, in a somewhat more discouraged tone, Carroll was still reminding Plowden of his promises of assistance and continuing to express the opinion that, among others, "Mr. Francis Neale will be a favorable opportunity," although not as the college's president.[9] For the latter office Carroll finally had to settle for Robert Plunkett, an English-born missionary not long in the United States, only months before the college was scheduled to open.

But the need for more native-born clergy was never far from Carroll's mind. When Francis Neale eventually returned from Liège in November 1788, Carroll duly noted the date in his correspondence and wrote to Plowden "I am much pleased with and promise myself great assistance from him."[10]

Sadly, these were among the few appreciative words Bishop Carroll would ever write of Trinity's first pastor. Almost immediately the two men, so opposite in temperament and outlook, had their differences. Assigned after his arrival to St. Thomas Manor near Port Tobacco, Francis Neale soon fell in with the rural clergy who opposed Carroll's plans for an academy. What is more, Neale did not hesitate to make his views known directly and in writing. He must have done so in an especially forceful manner towards the close of 1789, for we find Carroll testily answering Neale in January of the next year with what proved to be the first in a series of admonitory letters. Carroll expressed great disappointment over the misunderstandings that had arisen between them and told Neale, "You evidently show that you have been exceedingly misinformed, since you came to America." To Neale's complaints about the many neglected congregations in rural southern Maryland, Carroll answered that he would never relent "in my endeavors to procure fresh supplies to the Country missions." Then, turning the tables, Carroll let loose a broadside of questions about Neale's own efforts. Was he attending the mission at Mattawoman? Had he been actively promoting subscriptions to the newly published American edition of the Douay Bible? Carroll was ashamed when he looked over the list of subscribers. There were too many prominent Catholics in Neale's congregations who were not on it. And where were the payments for the spiritual retreat readings written by his brother Leonard, which like the Douay Bible had been printed by Matthew Carey in Philadelphia? Such was the tone of their early correspondence. Unfortunately, it would continue.[11]

Although Francis Ignatius Neale, the object of this censure, was in Carroll's own words a model of piety, he was also a man accustomed to having his own way and using his influence in both church and lay circles to get it. Neale and his brothers were the scions of an old Maryland family of some wealth, which may well be one of the reasons for the outspokenness with which he addressed his superior. Neale's great-great-grandfather was Captain James Neale, a bold entrepreneur, sea captain, and sometime confidential agent of King Charles I, who had first come to Maryland around 1637 in the service of Governor Leonard Calvert. Although once indicted on allegations of aiding the escape of the ship *Reformation* and its notorious master, Richard Ingle, "the plunderer of St. Mary's," Captain Neale nevertheless contributed enough servants and performed enough good services for the Calverts at home and abroad to merit a manorial grant of two thousands acres near what would later become Port Tobacco in Charles County. Here the family of Captain James and

Anne Gill Neale prospered. Their children married well, as often to Protestants as Catholics, to such a degree that the Neale family genealogy reads much like a colonial Maryland and Virginia peerage.

In the first generation, for example, the sons and daughters of James and Anne married into the families of Leonard Calvert, first governor of Maryland; Richard Bennett, one of Cromwell's first commissioners for Virginia and Maryland and later governor of Virginia; Sir Edward Digges, who succeeded Bennett as governor of Virginia; Colonel Philemon Lloyd, a wealthy landowner of the Eastern Shore; and the aristocratic Robert Brooke, the first in a long line of Brookes to hold prominent public office in Maryland. Succeeding generations did no less well. (There would be four more intermarriages with the Brooke family, to give but one example.)

As with so many Maryland Catholics families, the Neales also sent some of their sons abroad for education at the English Jesuit colleges in French Flanders, the Netherlands, or Spain. None, however, did so with such spectacular result as William and Anne Brooke Neale, fourth-generation descendants of Captain James. Of the thirteen children of William and Anne seven were boys. All seven crossed the Atlantic to study at the English colleges at St. Omers, Bruges, or Liège. Two were not to come back, dying as students, but four of the five surviving sons became priests. Francis Neale was the youngest of these. Preceding him were William Chandler Neale, who remained with the Jesuits returning to England after 1794; Leonard Neale, later president of Georgetown College and second archbishop of Baltimore; and Charles Neale, who is mainly remembered for bringing the first Carmelite sisters to America. In addition, the Neale brothers had three sisters. Clare, the oldest, married Henry Brent, member of a prominent Virginia and Maryland family that had thrice intermarried with the Carrolls. Eleanor, the youngest, married first John Holmes and then Raphael Boarman, while Mary, the middle sister, married William Matthews, great-grandson of an early doctor and attorney of Charles County. Their son, also named William, was destined to be one of the first and most highly respected priests to serve in the City of Washington.[12]

All of this, or Francis Neale's long and impressive ancestry and the prominence of his immediate family, may have had much to do with Bishop Carroll's decision to bring him to Georgetown in 1792. Neale's acquaintance and relationship with many of the old-line Maryland families who had descendants living in Georgetown would make him welcome as pastor of the proposed chapel. Needless to say, it would also serve him especially well in the initial task of fund raising.

Then, too, from Carroll's point of view there was much to be gained by removing Neale from St. Thomas Manor, where he appeared to be at the center of continued opposition. Georgetown College was no longer an issue, but the rural clergy of southern Maryland were still resisting any change in the administration of their country estates and also pressing Carroll harder than he thought prudent for restoration of the Jesuit order through affiliation with a remnant province in Russia under the protection of Catherine the Great. (Much to Carroll's annoyance Neale had even written him a nagging letter on this subject while Carroll was in England awaiting his consecration as first bishop of the United States.)[13] Carroll had in fact tried to transfer Neale from St. Thomas two years earlier, when Governor Thomas Sim Lee requested a priest for the fast growing frontier town of Frederick, only to have Neale come down with one of his periodic bouts with ill health. Now Neale was well and there was the opportunity of the Georgetown chapel.[14]

"Francis Neale arrived January 13, 1792 . . . one year's salary proceeding this day at £35." So read the notes in the fly leaves and balance columns of Georgetown College's earliest account book. Neale's arrival coincided with the first group of students. The nominal pastor of Trinity was therefore immediately put to work for the college as well, since it was the sole source of his board, lodging, and salary. Judging from an occasional account book entry in his hand, Neale seems to have been made the college treasurer pro tempore.[15] If so, it was the first of many administrative duties for the college he was only too willing to accept. In any case Neale promptly began raising funds for the chapel with an energy that belied his occasional illnesses and a generosity that was rare in his day.

Neale was remarkably successful. Within seven months of his arrival he had cast a wide net and brought in enough money "by subscription presented to the people of Montgomery, Prince Georges, Charles and St. Mary's Counties," as he described his campaign, to build the foundations of the chapel on Lot 72. This we know from a letter to Captain Ignatius Fenwick, written in August 1792, in which Neale asked Fenwick's assistance in managing the subscription effort. After a complimentary opening with frequent reference to mutual friends, Neale came right to the point, summarizing the extent of previous support and what he hoped Fenwick would do "to solicit and receive donations and contributions, either by subscription or any other way you judge best, toward the finishing of the Roman Catholic chapel of Georgetown."[16]

In describing the task at hand as finishing the chapel, Neale appears to have erred on the side of optimism. But not by much. An itemized billing by the chapel's builder for the work done the next year lists the principal materials costs as bricks, lumber, scaffolding, nails, and lime. The principal labor charges, by far, are those of bricklayers and carpenters. Notably absent from the billing are any charges for digging, the drayage of earth, and the placement of field stones that were typical of foundation work at the time. From all this it is reasonable to assume that the chapel's foundation was completed in 1792, Father Neale's first year, and most of its bricklaying, roofing, and possibly interior woodworking, by the close of 1793.[17]

How well Captain Fenwick may have done as leader of the campaign we do not know, since the records of his efforts have not been preserved. But what we do know is that he was a person of considerable enterprise who had all the right credentials for the job. Fenwick's forebears, like Neale's, traced back to the beginnings of colonial Maryland. Although he suffered occasional reverses in his long career as a sea captain and trader, his personal wealth by the time of his retirement in the 1790s was considerable.

During the Revolution Fenwick had bought a commission as captain of the Maryland state ship *Lydia*, then engaged in the overseas tobacco trade. (Wartime though it might be, trade had to be vigorously pursued to offset heavy drains on the state treasury.) Fenwick, however, had the misfortune to run into a British fleet ascending the Potomac that promptly captured him and the *Lydia* on his maiden voyage aboard her in January 1778. Some measure of Fenwick's influence and importance can be judged by the fact that Maryland's governor and council secured his release within a matter of days through an exchange of prisoners. It was well that they did, for Fenwick was soon back on his feet after a few years of privateering to such an extent that by 1780 he could easily afford to loan the state 17,350 pounds of tobacco. In that year, too, he married the widow of Charles Carroll of Duddington II and Carrollsburg, who had been a major landowner in what would soon be the District of Columbia.

Following this match, which allied him with the more affluent Charles Carroll of Carrollton branch of the family, Captain Fenwick put aside his sea roving for a business career and began to acquire property in both Georgetown and the future Federal City, where we will hear of him again. By 1792, or approximately four years before his death, he realized the sailor's dream of retiring to a farm, from which he supplied Georgetown College with fresh pork, beef, mutton, and choice sides of veal.[18]

The zeal of Pastor Neale and the influence of Captain Fenwick evidently made a good combination. Although the founding of Trinity may seem to have proceeded at tortoise pace by modern standards, we must remember that the progress made after Francis Neale's arrival—from almost nothing to near-completion of the church building in two years—was something of a record in comparison with other Georgetown churches. (St. John's Protestant Episcopal Church in Georgetown, for example, was ten years in the building, from 1796 to 1806, even though its subscribers included such prominent figures as President Thomas Jefferson, architect William Thornton, and the affluent John Threlkeld.)[19]

Even so, Fenwick's and Neale's joint efforts were not enough. For the Catholic laity, church support remained an unaccustomed and difficult role. When the completed church proved to be as wide as Lot 72, Neale evidently tried to safeguard the pre-existing cemetery and acquire protective strips of surrounding property by another subscription. In December 1794 Captain Fenwick donated twelve pounds and ten shillings to this purpose, not a princely sum for a man of his means.[20]

But by June of the next year Neale had given up further subscription efforts and dug into his own pockets for £65, or approximately $160, to buy parts of six lots immediately east and west of the church. This sum is greater than it appears to modern eyes. Construction costs for the church incurred in 1793 totalled £314 or $830. Thus Neale's personal contribution was more than twenty percent of the major building cost. It was also almost twice Neale's starting salary at the college and only ten pounds less than the £75 the college paid for its original campus tract of one-and-one-half acres. Fifteen years later Neale again had to use his own funds to buy the remainder of the lots west of the church, presumably as a further safeguard, in order to acquire the complete corner property on which Holy Trinity's Lower School now stands. He got this for $500 of "his own money, with the positive intention that it should serve the Church," as his archbishop noted. Nor was this the last of his generosities.[21]

Trinity Church was built by Leonard Harbaugh, from whom we have the detailed construction bill for 1793.[22] Although probably not a Catholic, he deserves more than our passing attention because of his close family and professional ties to the Catholic community and his prominent role in George Washington's Potomac Company and the building of the capital city, subjects that are treated in later chapters.[23] Originally a resident of Baltimore, Harbaugh had gained a reputation there as an engineer and builder by saving a historic courthouse from slipping into Jones Falls.

Harbaugh was first invited to the Washington area in March 1792 by the three-man Board of Commissioners responsible for the creation of the capital city. The commissioners, one of whom was Bishop Carroll's older brother Daniel, were beginning to feel "much anxiety . . . to see business of some sort conducted here," as they expressed it in a letter to Thomas Jefferson asking the latter's help in securing President Washington's approval to engage Harbaugh as soon as possible. Their concern was not unjustified. The act of Congress of July 16, 1790 that created the District of Columbia required the commissioners to provide suitable buildings for the President, the Congress and the executive branches of government within ten years. By the spring of 1792 almost two years had passed, and the commissioners did not yet have one public building to show for their efforts.[24]

Harbaugh's first assignment was to build a bridge over Rock Creek at the eastern boundary of Georgetown. The only requirements were that it be capable of carrying both horse and carriage and be so positioned as to connect with the post road to Washington and Bladensburg. Although he had not before built a bridge, Harbaugh approached the task with considerable flair. He designed a triple-arched stone structure with a central section that spanned the broad lower reaches of the creek in a single arch. He then engaged and supervised all labor, invented an ingenious horse-drawn stonecutting machine, and even provided the commissioners with a script for the ceremonies marking the laying of the cornerstone.

What was more important, Harbaugh finished the bridge within the five months stipulated in his contract. But in June 1793, or less than a year after the cornerstone ceremonies, the commissioners ruefully reported to President Washington that "the Center Arch of the Bridge, much to our sorrow is in a very ticklish state." In fact they believed—wrongly, as time would prove—that it might soon collapse. Not surprisingly, the commissioners gave no more business to Harbaugh for some time thereafter, even though they recognized his worth and had found him "a modest well-tempered man [who] seems equally disposed and able to be very useful to us."[25]

The District Commissioners' loss was the Georgetown Catholic community's gain. Harbaugh's temporary freedom from government contracts gave him the only period in his career when he was not engaged in multiple public and private projects. From 1793 through the first months of 1794, by which time he was president of the Georgetown Architects and Carpenters Society, he was free to devote his full attentions to finishing the District's first Catholic church. This he accomplished by March 1794, if not earlier, in which month the Georgetown College ledger books show the first "seat rents at the Chapel" charged to boarding students at seven shillings and sixpence a year.

Thereafter, or beginning in 1795, there is considerable evidence to suggest that Harbaugh was also the architect-builder of Georgetown College's second building. Known as Old North, it stands today as Georgetown University's oldest. By the close of 1795, when John Carroll was proudly calling Old North "nearly completed," Harbaugh had moved on to supervise the Potomac Company's difficult attempt to build locks around the Great Falls of the Potomac.[26]

The church that Harbaugh built was judged plain by some and modestly handsome by others. Chancellor James Kent of Columbia College in New York, who visited Georgetown in 1793, called it "a plain brick Roman chapel . . . with a clumsy steeple to it." Reverend Aloysius Roccofort, S.J., Trinity's first historian, thought the church "neither grand nor assuming in its style and proportions, but . . . of a neat and becoming appearance." Whatever the verdict, we may say with certainty that Leonard Harbaugh built well, with good bricks. The proof of his work is with us today. It is the oldest church in the District of Columbia in its original form and in continuous use since the day it was built.[27]

Surprising as it may seem, there is no record of any consecration or other formal ceremonies celebrating the opening of Trinity Church. If indeed none occurred their absence was neither an oversight nor a rare occurrence. Throughout the Federal period the growing number of Catholics without regular places of worship was the church's most urgent problem. Many newly built churches and chapels therefore simply "opened their doors" as soon as they were ready, or even before. The formalities of consecration or blessing would have to wait. An interesting case in point is St. Mary's of Alexandria, the first Catholic church in Virginia, which was a mission of the Trinity pastorate attended by Trinity priests until 1818. Here the first chapel structure was begun in 1796 and continuously used in an unfinished state until 1809. By that time Pastor Neale, discouraged by its out-of-the-way location and shabby condition, had seized the opportunity to buy a Methodist meeting house in central Alexandria for $900, notifying Archbishop Carroll after the fact and asking that it "receive the title of St. Mary's."[28] Much the same may have happened to the "chapel in Georgetown." From Harbaugh's billing the building appears to have been roofed over in 1793, in which case it may have received its first congregations in that year.

Georgiana Warner.
First Trinity Church, Georgetown, now the Parish Center of Holy Trinity Church.

Whatever the answer, Trinity Church had no problems attracting parishioners. Through its doors came a much larger and more geographically varied congregation than Francis Neale or the provincial authorities had reason to expect. Catholics throughout the countryside—from Bladensburg to Great Falls in Maryland, from Alexandria to Dumfries in Virginia—traveled difficult roads or sailed the fickle winds of the Potomac to celebrate long-denied sacraments at Trinity. The evidence comes from the church's first baptismal and marriage register, which runs from January 1, 1795, to April 1805, written entirely in Father Neale's hand.

In making his register entries, Neale nearly always took care to list the towns of residence of parents or married couples. Outside of Georgetown these were mainly Alexandria and, after 1800, the City of Washington. Unfortunately, Neale gave less detail on the places of residence of his rural parishioners. More often than not, he lumped them together under such broad headings as "of Mungummery County" or "living near Bledensbourgh." (Even in an age of permissive orthography, Neale was a notoriously bad speller.) Nor did he leave any exact records of the total number of his parishioners.

Nevertheless it is possible from a number of sources to postulate a rapidly growing congregation, which undoubtedly reached several hundred or more communicants within the first twenty-five years of the church's existence. There is, first of all, the comparative data that can be extracted from the first register itself. Annual baptisms rose from seventeen and eighteen in 1795 and 1796, respectively, to fifty-three in 1801.[29]

Soon, therefore, or as early as 1806, there occurred the first of a number of enlargements to the church. Some were rather bizarre, such as makeshift lateral sheds, gained through arches cut in the church's side walls, and outside stairways for the African-American congregants to ascend directly to their gallery seats.[30] Even so, there are constant references in the ensuing years to overcrowding, along with the observations of visiting priests who invariably found the church too small for the congregation. But not until the arrival of Trinity's first diarist, Rev. John McElroy, do we have any hard figures. In the Easter season of 1818 McElroy, by then assistant pastor, happily noted the confirmation of 250 persons by Archbishop Maréchal. By Christmas of the next year McElroy found himself giving communion to approximately 200 persons in one of three masses celebrated that day, noting that "the morning was fine and the church tolerably full."[31]

Meanwhile, in another part of the District, somewhat similar events were beginning to unfold. In January 1794, or the same year Trinity was finished, Father Anthony Caffry, an Irish Dominican newly arrived from Dublin, began a ministry for the growing number of Irish laborers engaged in building the capital city. Before the year was over he was holding services in rented quarters while he negotiated the purchase of two lots in what is today downtown Washington. Caffry's efforts would soon take shape as St. Patrick's Church, the first Catholic church within the original boundaries of the City of Washington. Both the church and its second pastor, William Matthews, the nephew of Francis

Neale, would play significant roles in the formative years of the national capital.[32]

In Trinity's earliest years Father Neale had no regular assistants and was hindered in the development of his parish by other heavy demands on his time. Some came as a result of his college duties, which Neale himself appears to have favored. But others came directly from Bishop Carroll, whose differences with Neale never seem to have diminished. Eventually the disputes between the two men, so often seemingly trivial, almost embroiled Carroll in the most serious form of trusteeism. This was the American phenomenon of laity control of parishes, including attempts to select priests and pastors, that so shocked the European clergy and troubled the conscience of their more democratically inclined American confreres. In the spring of 1797 Bishop Carroll tried to involve Neale in the first of many difficult transactions for the sale of rural estate properties. Neale responded by insinuating that such matters were more properly the concern of the Reverend Charles Sewell, Carroll's trusted assistant and agent for the Corporation of the Roman Catholic Clergy. At about the same time Carroll continued to hold Neale responsible for the regional sale of the Douay Bible and his brother Leonard Neale's retreat meditations, the accounting of which caused further frictions.[33]

The differences between the two men culminated in late April, when Bishop Carroll seized an opportunity to have Francis Neale removed from Georgetown. Shortly before then, a meeting of the clergy at St. Thomas Manor had recommended the transfer of Neale to the Jesuit manor at Whitemarsh. Neale thought this assignment would be the subject of further deliberations, but Carroll evidently moved very quickly to approve the recommendation. For this reason we find Neale indignantly telling Carroll, in a letter dated April 26, 1797, that he had hoped to demand a private conference with the bishop "before I ultimately could give my consent to live at the Marsh or attend the Congregations adjoining." But, he pointedly added, "As you have given *your consent*, I presume I must acquiesce. . . . " This being so, he would try to bring his affairs with Trinity Church to a close as quickly as possibly and otherwise prepare for the move to Whitemarsh. As a parting shot Neale also informed Carroll that he was appointing an attorney to receive monies he had advanced to Trinity Church. He supposed this action would give no offense, since any examination of the books would show what large amounts were due him.[34]

Meanwhile, however, the brothers Adam and George King, influential Georgetown merchants who were married to sisters of Alexander Doyle, and George Fenwick, soon to become Georgetown's official surveyor, told Carroll they had heard of the possibility of Neale's removal. These gentlemen, along with one James Simpson, constituted Trinity Church's first board of trustees. Both they and the congregation, they claimed, sincerely wished that Neale remain. At the very least the trustees hoped that the bishop would "not at any rate decide on his removal before you come to this place, when we shall lay down before you reasons which we make no doubt will have weight with you."[35]

Bishop Carroll received the trustees' letter by the end of May 1797. At the time Carroll was at the height of the long-standing dispute with the German-speaking congregation of Holy Trinity of Philadelphia, which would soon lead him to declare it in schism. Lesser problems had already occurred in New York and Boston. He can scarcely have wanted to take on another battle in Georgetown, much less offend such as the Fenwicks and the Kings. Francis Neale remained.[36]

Three months later a special committee of the Maryland clergy resolved that Georgetown College would thenceforward be run by a five-man board of directors chosen from among their number. Although the move was primarily directed at ousting the Sulpician Father Louis William DuBourg, the college's third president, it also had the effect of removing Bishop Carroll from direct control of his beloved academy. Francis Neale was among those chosen by the committee to serve on the five-man board. At its first meeting in October 1797, a quorum of three—Robert Plunkett, John Ashton, and Neale—elected Neale vice-president of the college. Shortly thereafter the board defined the respective duties of the president and the vice-president. The latter were to be largely those of an administrator and treasurer, with emphasis on the control of expenditures, disbursements, and receipts. Thus did the college make formal what Neale had apparently been doing all along. And thus did Francis Neale gain a lasting foothold in Georgetown.[37]

Thereafter, if little help or encouragement might come to him from Carroll, Neale could and did look to Georgetown College for support. Throughout its early years the college received a steady stream of foreign clergy, especially Sulpicians fleeing the French Revolution, who came either to serve as faculty or to learn English and absorb American ways as they awaited further assignment. Many of them came to Neale's aid, especially to help with Trinity's swelling tide of marriages and baptisms. In this capacity the church's first register records among others the names of Ambrose Maréchal, Louis William DuBourg, and Benedict Joseph Flaget. Maréchal, who studied both law and theology in his native Orleans, was to become the third bishop of Baltimore. DuBourg later became bishop of New Orleans and St. Louis. Flaget is best known as one of the pioneers of the church's westward expansion and "the first bishop west of the Alleghenies" at Bardstown, Kentucky. All had their first American parish experience at Trinity.[38]

The same was soon to be true of native-born clergy. Before John Carroll died in 1815 he was deeply gratified to see a new generation of American-born priests graduated from the college and already part of its faculty. Like their foreign predecessors they lent generous help to Trinity. Among them were two sons of George Fenwick, Enoch and Benedict. Enoch, called the best scholar of his day, became the college's twelfth president. Benedict, who served as Trinity's pastor for one year following Francis Neale's retirement, was twice president of the college and later bishop of Boston. In the years that followed, more faculty priests served as mass celebrants, when Trinity's growing congregation made necessary multiple mass schedules on Sundays and feast days. Even

Georgetown University Library/Special Collections Division.

"Southeast End View of the G.T. College from the Trinity Church Steeple. . .1831," by James Simpson. Today's Old North building is on the right. Directly across from it is Old South, the College's first building, demolished in 1904.

after he became president of the college, Benedict Fenwick is known to have preached at Trinity on almost every Sunday. Others who offered occasional help were John Grassi and Anthony Kohlman, both presidents of the college in their time, and the talented Roger Baxter, professor of languages and polite literature. To this day, in fact, the relationship continues, with some of Georgetown University's leading theologians keeping up their pastoral practice at Holy Trinity.[39]

In return the first Trinity Church served for many years as the place of Sunday worship for Georgetown College students, crowded though it might be. The church was also the scene of all the college's exhibitions, as graduation and other academic ceremonies were then called. (Trinity Church continued in this role until 1833, when the newly finished Mulledy Building offered the college a hall large enough for the purpose.) The earliest of such exhibitions at Trinity to attract significant attention from the Georgetown community was a memorial service for President Washington on February 18, 1800. The *Centinel of Liberty* reported that a large assembly gathered to hear both religious services and eulogies by students Robert Walsh and Dominick Lynch "delivered with profound propriety, and spirit, in an ingenious and eloquent academical eulogium."[40]

The students attending Sunday mass were not only a large element in Trinity's first congregation, but also its most colorful. Uniforms were the order of the day—blue coat, blue pants, and red waistcoat with yellow buttons for special occasions—in which the students marched the short distance from the college to the church in strict procession. How this quasi-military exercise appealed to the students we do not know, except that it probably became quite popular by 1831, when jovial President Thomas Mulledy allowed "a weak mint sling" to be served them while they formed ranks.[41]

The number of students making the Sunday march to Trinity varied in direct relation to the up-and-down fortunes of the college in its first thirty years. In 1795, or the church's second year, they totaled a respectable ninety-one, of whom forty were boarders. After the turn of the century the student population declined to an average of fifty-one students, day and boarder combined, for the years 1801-1807 during which Leonard Neale, Francis's older brother, was president. In the final year of the elder Neale's presidency, in fact, a low of thirty-seven students almost forced the closing of the college. Francis Neale, elected president for two years thereafter, did little better.[42]

Two factors contributed to this alarming development. First, St. Mary's Seminary in Baltimore, established by French Sulpicians who arrived there in 1791, was by this time a growing institution with a talented faculty that was drawing potential students away from Georgetown. Second, as Bishop Carroll did not hesitate to point out, the Neale brothers imposed such a monastic disciplinary regime at the college that many parents became unwilling to send their sons there. But after the restorative administration of Rev. John Grassi, often called "the second founder," the college could count more than one hundred students by 1814.[43]

A more interesting variance, if not so pronounced, occurred in the number of Protestant students who also made the Sunday march to Trinity. It seems reasonably clear from the founding principles of the college that Protestant students whose parents had made special arrangements for them were free to go to their own churches. But what to do with Protestant boarders for whom no arrangements had been made was a question that long troubled the college. In the prospectus for 1797 the college advertised a separate boarding house for non-Catholic students under the direction of "a widow lady of the most reputable character." However, not much seems to have come of this.[44] But by 1814, when the college was again on a good footing, parents were being advised that "the object of the institution is principally for the education of those who profess the Catholic religion, which is the religion uniformly practiced by the boarders . . . ," a statement that at least suggests the possibility that non-Catholic boarding students were being required to attend mass.[45]

The experiences of architect Benjamin Latrobe's son John, who entered as a boarder the next year, appear to confirm this requirement. Young John Latrobe claimed that he was "the only Protestant boy in the college who stuck to his faith," adding that his coreligionist classmates seemed to have no objections to going to mass or even serving as acolytes. Latrobe found that he was never treated unkindly because of his Protestantism. Instead, he was the object of the priests' special attentions and "petted rather than otherwise."[46]

Although some faculty priests were deeply disturbed by the practice of admitting non-Catholics to mass, others who favored it (and, not incidentally, the opportunities that went with it for special attentions and possibly conversions) clearly won the day. By 1820, under the presidency of Rev. Enoch Fenwick, there was no more doubt. The prospectus for that year announced that as always the college would receive non-Catholic students, of "whom it is only required that they respectfully assist at the *public* duties of Religion with their Catholic companions."[47]

But, as was so often the case, these and other growing pains were hardly noticed outside the college walls. In the eyes of the Georgetown community the college's auspicious beginning and the aura surrounding its founder and the Carroll family in general were enough to give it enduring respectability. Leading citizens bought or borrowed books from its growing library. Later they might attend demonstrations at its observatory and museum. And, following Washington's example, presidents of the United States would continue to visit the college or receive delegations from its student body.[48]

From all this, of course, the small church almost in the college's shadow derived much benefit. From the beginning the same Georgetown newspapers that indulged in ill-disguised anti-Catholicism by publishing unsigned "letters from abroad" attacking the Jesuits or other religious orders in Europe took care to avoid unfavorable comment on the local scene. Rather, in both Washington and Georgetown newspapers, one hopeful editorial after another promising a bright future for the national capital dutifully listed Georgetown, its college, and sometimes even its new Catholic church as community assets. As early as 1793 Chancellor James Kent—the same who had dismissed Trinity Church as the plain brick chapel with a clumsy steeple—was moved to write that even though "the Protestants don't relish it . . . the Academy nearby under the direction of a President and Vice Presidents who are Romish Priests . . . gives great attention to the scholars . . . and is growing, rapidly." The respect might be grudging, but it was nearly always there.[49]

Like the college, Georgetown itself had its share of growing pains. Trouble signs were already on the horizon even as James Kent and many other visitors endlessly praised the town's commercial prospects. In 1793 the dissolution of the Farmers General, or the French tobacco purchasing monopoly that had offered the steadiest market for Maryland tobaccos, signalled the beginning of the end of the Chesapeake's traditional tobacco trade. Already flour was replacing tobacco as Georgetown's principal export.

In that year, too, the Potomac Company's much-heralded gateway to the West had progressed no farther than the first lock at Little Falls three miles upstream. Meanwhile a less dramatic but much more practical alternative—a system of toll roads west to Frederick and beyond—was being built by the merchants of a small town at "a more centrical location," as John Carroll called it when choosing his episcopal seat forty miles to the northeast. This was Baltimore, soon to be the fastest-growing city in the United States. But the citizens of Georgetown can scarcely be blamed for ignoring these troubling telltales. After all, the permanent seat of government was about to be transferred from Philadelphia. And a new Rome would rise within their sight, but one short league down the Potomac.

Unlike the town or the college, Trinity's growth was free of serious problems. In this respect it stood virtually alone among the early Catholic churches of the towns and cities of the young republic. At the time of Trinity's founding, St. Mary's of Philadelphia already had long experience trying to accommodate a congregation of German immigrants, French Acadians, and a handful of prosperous Irish merchants, only to see the Germans, by far the largest immigrant group, march off to form their schismatic Holy Trinity. In New York St. Peter's harbored a congregation that was for the greater part Irish and "very poor" in the words of its first pastor. Even John Carroll's pro-Cathedral, St. Peter's of Baltimore, was plagued by a German priest who attempted to make a separate and independent congregation of his countrymen in imitation and with the help of Holy Trinity of Philadelphia. Boston, Norfolk, and Charleston all had their troubles with unruly pastors, divided congregations, or a combination of both. The list was long.[50]

By contrast no one ethnic or nationalist group would ever come to dominate Trinity Church of Georgetown. The extreme diversity of its first congregation, unique in its time, was its best protection. Viewed as a whole this congregation was scarcely "the immigrant Church" so generally associated with urban Catholicism. Nor could it lay claim to a concentration of prosperous Catholic merchants and bankers, as St. Joseph's and St. Mary's of Philadelphia once had. Rather, the Trinity congregation mixed both these elements—immigrant and elite alike—along with representatives of every social level in between.

At the lowest economic stratum was a large number of African Americans, slave and free, constituting thirty percent of the congregation in its first ten years. We will see that their bonds to the church were both old and strong, and that many converts were brought in by the remarkable efforts of one free black woman. Irish immigrants were present from the start, as when James and Alexander Doyle's *Georgetown Weekly Ledger* advertised, "Just arrived . . . from Cork . . . a number of healthy, likely, Men and Woman Servants and Redemptioners" or "an healthy Irish Indented Servant man . . . an excellent Hair

Dresser, being bred to that business."[51] Soon to follow, but still a small fraction of the great numbers yet to come, were the Irish laborers engaged to dig the Potomac Company canals or work on the roads and streets of Washington City.

Germans there were also; although never so strong as in Philadelphia or Baltimore, they were sufficient in number for Georgetown newspapers to advertise for printer journeymen able to spell and write in German. There were French, too, witness a scattering of French names in the church's baptism or marriage registers and the account books of the college, representing for the most part refugees from the slave insurrection at Cap François, Santo Domingo, in 1793. Some few Spanish came, too, for the same reason.

But for many years the largest single element in Trinity's early congregations had neither strong ethnic nor social affinities. Generally speaking its members were of English and Irish descent and their stations in life varied from farmers and innkeepers to high government officials and the richest landholders of the area. Their one paramount bond was a common heritage. They had all come from another part of Maryland and they were all members of old Catholic families. As such they represented an element not to be found in urban parishes outside of Maryland, for the simple reason that in the years following the Revolution no other state in the union could lay claim to a significant population of fifth- or sixth-generation Catholics.

For much of the colonial period, in fact, "old Catholic" and "old Marylander" were synonymous. In Georgetown they bore such names as Boarman, Brooke, Fenwick, Lee, Mudd, Neale, Semmes, Sewall, and Slye. In the Federal City and beyond they were Brent, Carroll, Digges, Matthews, and Young. Their contributions to both the church and local government were out of all proportion to their relatively small numbers. Indeed, it is impossible to understand the successful growth of Catholicism in the national capital area without some knowledge of who they were, how they came to Georgetown or the Federal City, and what they did thereafter. To this purpose we must first journey some ninety miles down the Potomac, as the crow flies, and a century and a half back in time.

3

Terra Mariae

It is surprising that, notwithstanding all these difficulties, there were still so many Catholics in Maryland who were regular in their habits, and at peace with all their neighbors.

-JOHN CARROLL
Report to the Roman Congregation, 1790

In the late autumn of 1638, after one of the long and frightful sea voyages common to Atlantic crossings in the seventeenth century, a Gloucestershire country squire named Giles Brent arrived at the infant settlement of St. Mary's City on the shores of the lower Potomac. With him came his brother Fulke and their two maiden sisters, Margaret and Mary. The land they intended to settle was formally known as *Terra Mariae*—the Land of Maria, so named by Sir George Calvert, the first Lord Baltimore, in order to please King Charles I and his French wife, Queen Henrietta Maria.

Like most of the gentlemen adventurers of Lord Baltimore's colony, Giles Brent had been attracted by the generous land grants offered to men of quality like himself. But Brent and his siblings were also moved—perhaps more than most—by the prospects for the free and unprejudiced practice of their faith in the only English-speaking colony in North America under Catholic proprietorship. They had good reason to be so. Earlier, in England, all eleven of Giles Brent's brothers and sisters had converted to Catholicism, following the lead first of their oldest sister and then of their father. This action cost their father nearly all of his estate, since he refused to conform in any way to the Church of England. Later all of his children remaining in England would lose much of their land for the same reason.

By contrast the four Brents who journeyed to Maryland received a most propitious welcome. As happened almost automatically with men of their stature, Giles and his brother Fulke were both invited to serve on the Governor's Council, the members of which also sat as judges of the Provincial Court. Their sister Margaret, well known for her business acumen, soon found herself the most trusted agent of Governor Leonard Calvert. In addition Giles, who evidently shared some of Margaret's fiduciary talents, was appointed treasurer of the colony. Their first land grants totalled more than two thousand acres. With such advantages did the Brents settle comfortably into the life of the province.[1]

It comes as a surprise, therefore, to learn that six years after their arrival Governor Leonard Calvert issued a warrant to his high sheriff "to arrest the Body of Giles Brent, Esq. and keep him in safe custody . . . until I shall call him to make answere to several crimes against the dignity and dominion of the right honorable the Lord Proprietary of this Province."[2]

Incredibly, the governor's peremptory order had its origin in a lengthy dispute over the administration and ownership of the first Catholic chapel in English-speaking America. The dispute began when the first Jesuits to come to Maryland in 1638 built a chapel close to their residence and the town's fort in St. Mary's. But Cecilius Calvert, the second Lord Baltimore and brother to Leonard, insisted that "a house with a chapel adjacent for the seate of his Lordship or his Governor" be among the first structures raised in the new settlement.[3] The argument over the chapel's location and, more important, its administration eventually caused the Jesuits and their supporters to sue Governor Leonard Calvert. Giles Brent, as judge of the case, ruled in favor of the Jesuits. He soon found himself at odds with his superior, or, more specifically, the object of a counter-suit by the governor demanding the considerable sum of 30,000 pounds of tobacco as compensation. Thus came the warrant for his arrest.[4]

Behind the chapel controversy, often seemingly petty in character, lay deeper roots of misunderstanding between the colonizers, the Jesuits, and the Lords Baltimore about what the Maryland experiment was meant to be. For most general readers early Maryland is the "Catholic colony" of the Baltimores, known for its toleration. In the popular mind Maryland remains the place "where in a remote corner of the world . . . the mild forbearance of a proprietary adopted religious freedom as the basis of the state," as historian George Bancroft once so ebulliently expressed it.[5] Such, of course, was the intention. But in practice it was a long, hard, and costly experience for many of the Catholic families of colonial Maryland to stand firm in their faith, even in the regime of the Calverts.

It is not within the bounds of this work to chronicle all the misunderstandings and problems of the early settlers, much less to offer a comprehensive history of colonial Maryland, since in recent years both the church-state dispute and early Maryland history in general have received the careful scholarship they have long deserved.[6] But what is paramount to this study is some knowledge of the Catholic families whose later generations played a prominent role in the establishment of the national capital. Stated another way, it is difficult to account for the latters' prominence without some understanding of the history of their forebears. More specifically, we must examine how the earlier generations managed to live in comity with the colony's overwhelming Protestant majority, how some among them rose from indentured servants to community leaders, and how nearly all kept their faith during an era of harsh anti-Catholic penal codes.

The Brent family offers a good example on most counts. Giles Brent, who served as the colony's second-in-command in the governor's absence, strongly favored the royalist cause in England's developing civil war and generally opposed the proprietor's attempts to control the religious practice of the Catholic colonists of St. Mary's. As the chapel and other disputes heightened, Brent had more in common with Thomas Cornwallis, one of the colony's leading investors, than with the Calverts he served. For Cornwallis and some other of the Catholic gentlemen adventurers, the free exercise of their religion was the cornerstone of their presence in Maryland. "Security of Contiens [conscience] was the first condition I expected from this Government," Cornwallis had declared in 1638, adding that he would sooner leave Maryland than "willingly Consent toe anything that may not stand with the Good Contiens of A Real Catholick."[7]

The Lords Baltimore, by contrast, held no such singular view. To them the commercial success of the Maryland venture was as important as its religious foundations, if not more so. In their view matters of church were certainly not to outweigh or take precedence over the colony's prospects for trade. For this reason the proprietors went to considerable lengths—the chapel incident was but one of many—to govern the religious life of their fellow Catholics. Indeed, if their policy toward the church and the Jesuits' mission in the New World could be reduced to one word, that one word would be caution. In the case of the first Lord Baltimore it was caution born of his experiences as a Catholic colonizer amid a small band of suspicious Protestant settlers on the rock-ribbed coasts of Newfoundland and his subsequent difficulties in obtaining the charter and sufficient investors for the Maryland adventure. This caution he passed on to his son Cecilius, the second Lord Baltimore, who enjoined the first colonists aboard the *Ark* and the *Dove:*

> that in their voyage to Mary Land they be very carefull to preserve unity & peace amongst all the passengers on Shipp-board, and that they suffer no scandall nor offence to be given to any of the Protestants, whereby any just complaint may heerafter be made, by them, in Virginiea or in England, and that for that end, they cause all Acts of Romane Catholique Religion to be done as privately as may be, and that they instruct all the Romane Catholiques to be silent upon all occasions of discourse concerning matters of Religion; and that the said Governor & Commissioners treate the Protestants with as much mildness and favor as Justice will permitt. And this to be observed on Land as well as at Sea.[8]

If the tone of these often-quoted instructions seems to reflect a completely conciliatory or even submissive attitude toward Protestants, that is just what the Baltimores had in mind. They understood that if the promise of their new colony was to be realized, their everyday commerce, their trading ventures, and their neighbor-colony relations would be conducted almost totally with Protestants. Even among the approximately 130 passengers who first disembarked in Maryland from the *Ark* and the *Dove* in 1643, Protestant servants and freemen far outnumbered the Catholic gentlemen investors. Thereafter, or for the remainder of the seventeenth century, it is doubtful that Catholics ever constituted more than one-sixth of the colony's total population. Thus Maryland,

ANNO Dñi 1657

Ætatis 51

36   *Cecilius Calvert, second Lord Baltimore, first Proprietor of Maryland, mezzotint by*
        Abraham Blooteling, 1657.

"the Catholic colony," began with a fragile minority of its putative religionists. It would remain so, moreover, throughout its history.[9]

The Lords Baltimore also understood as well as anyone the delicate position of the Catholic church in the mother country. At the time of Maryland's settlement, Cecilius Calvert, who remained in England trying to attract more colonists, Catholic or Protestant, found his efforts hampered by constant accusations that he was turning all of Maryland into a vast and seditious Papist seminary. In addition, by this time English Catholics had resigned themselves to the realization that the Church of England was there to stay, and they would be one among a number of dissident sects allowed their faith, within limits. Among the latter was permission to have private chapels in their homes, but under no circumstances any place of public worship. From such restrictions there arose among the English Catholic gentry a private and highly personal approach to their faith, an inherent caution in its practice, and a tolerant attitude towards others. The Calverts' religious policy was thus in many ways a reflection of the culture and society of which they were part in England. It was one to follow in the New World as well, they had no doubts.

The Jesuits, however, could hardly be expected to agree. Hunted down and exiled from England at the time of the Maryland settlement, English Jesuits burned with the missionary zeal of Edmond Campion, Robert Parsons, and all the English Martyrs of generations before them. Maryland to them was a long-awaited opportunity to assert their rightful place in society and to pursue the traditional Jesuit apostolate of missions to indigenes of faraway lands. The results of such conflicting views were entirely predictable. In the first years of the colony Governor Leonard Calvert and some of his Council members attempted to curb the energetic Father Andrew White's missionary forays among the Piscataway Indians, ostensibly because of concern for his safety, but more because they thought his success might interfere with their expectations for a far-ranging fur trade. Matters grew worse in 1639 when the chief of the Patuxent Indians made a gift to the Jesuits of a large plantation at Mattapany on the Patuxent River, about seven miles north of St. Mary's. To the Proprietor this struck at the very heart of his land-granting powers. He refused to recognize the Jesuits' title, even though they had improved the land and were successfully farming it by the time he heard about it.

To European Jesuits ownership of landed estates was an accepted and traditional practice. Within some of these estates, moreover, they had grown accustomed to a high degree of independence and freedom from taxation by civil authorities. Thus when Lord Baltimore dismissed the Maryland Jesuits' demands for self-government and the right to accept the Patuxent Indians' gift as totally inappropriate, the Jesuits responded by threatening to excommunicate him and any of his allies who were thus violating the divine rights of the church.[10]

As these and other disputes developed, Giles Brent found himself more and more in trouble. While serving as acting governor in 1644 he made the mistake of dismissing John Lewger, secretary to the Council and a wealthy settler who happened to be a friend and Oxford classmate of the Lord Proprietor.[11] There was also the matter of Brent's marriage to Mary Kittamaquand, the orphaned daughter of the *tayac*, or emperor, of the Piscataway Indians, who had been entrusted to the care of his sister Margaret. By this union Brent hoped to inherit vast lands from the Piscataways, only to be thwarted by both Governor Calvert and Indian laws of descent.[12] This was not all. A year earlier Brent had used his authority as acting governor to seize the trading ship *Reformation* and her master Richard Ingle, who was in the service of William Claiborne, a Virginian of the Puritan faction whose trading post on Kent Island was a source of constant dispute with the Calverts. But Brent's action was foiled by some colonists who were more concerned with maintaining peaceful trade than with Puritan-royalist differences. Taking matters into their own hands, they helped Ingle recapture his ship and escape by dead of night.

One year later Ingle returned to St. Mary's "to assault and beate down the dwelling house of divers the inhabitants," as he had been heard to vow. There followed what colonists for years thereafter called "the plundering time," as Ingle laid waste to the principal houses, took some prominent citizens and servants prisoner, and seized a Dutch merchantman anchored in the harbor. The *Reformation* and her Dutch prize thereupon set course for England. Among the unwilling passengers, deep in the hold of the Dutchman, were Giles Brent and the Jesuit fathers Andrew White and Thomas Copley.[13]

Two years later, after entering a suit against Ingle and regaining his freedom, Brent returned to Maryland to find a ravaged St. Mary's. Moreover in the minds of many of the settlers, Brent was to blame for the town's plight because of his earlier attempt to seize the *Reformation*. He was thus more than ready to shake off the dust of the sadly depopulated capital and make a new start. So, too, were other of the principal colonists who had already moved to lands up the Potomac River near where Father Andrew White had been allowed to establish a mission among the Portobaggo Indians. (By coincidence this new area came to be called Port Tobacco, a corruption of the Indian tribal name that accurately reflected the principal commercial function of the town and county seat that would later be at its center.) But Giles Brent went much farther. He ventured up the Potomac some fifty miles by river course from St. Mary's and, what is more remarkable, across the river into hostile Virginia. His spirited maiden sister Margaret, whose services to Leonard Calvert had previously earned her a non-voting seat on the Council, soon followed.[14]

The Virginia the Brents entered had a daunting array of anti-Catholic penal laws based on the Acts Concerning Popish Recusants of 1641 and 1643. Catholics and other recusants who failed to attend Anglican church services were subject to a monthly fine of £25. Nor were they permitted to travel more than five miles from their homes without permission of the local courts, on pain of risking all their property. Worst of all Catholics were explicitly prohibited from saying mass and were required to take oaths of supremacy and allegiance that forced them to deny key tenets of their faith. Failure to comply meant facing life imprisonment and loss of all property. Nor could Catholics hold public office, practice law, or educate their children as Catholics. To be sure, a number of these laws were irregularly or seldom if ever enforced. Nevertheless they represented a continuous threat, a dark cloud ready to rain down at any moment on all who refused to conform to the Church of England.[15]

Faced with these conditions, the Giles Brent who had little taste for Lord Baltimore's cautious religious policies while he was in Maryland was now quick to adopt them once he had cast his lot in Virginia. The reason that he, his sisters, and various relatives who followed him lived successfully and rose to some prominence over the years in colonial Virginia must in the first instance be ascribed to the fact that none ever made a cause or an obtrusive display of their Catholicism. Rather, they would get along by going along, as the modern expression has it, both in their approach to religion and to community affairs in general.

Working in Giles Brent's favor, it must also be noted, was the fact that he arrived at a politically opportune moment. By 1650, the year Brent left Maryland for good, the Cromwellian government in England was still cautiously attempting to gain the allegiance of a resistant Virginia dominated by Cavalier gentry. To the Virginia Cavaliers a strong royalist and wealthy Catholic like Brent, especially one who bore a grudge against the Calverts, was more to be welcomed than any radical Puritan.[16] But such circumstances alone cannot account for the Brent family's successful beginnings in Virginia. Far more important was the course the Brents generally followed after their arrival. This course comprised three basic elements: private worship, the cultivation of social and professional ties with the Protestant community, and a strong commitment to public service. It is worth examining, in brief, since it offers some parallels to the course followed by Maryland Catholics half a century later when it was their turn to survive a hostile and repressive government.

For his first country seat Brent chose a large tract bordering Aquia Creek in what was then part of Westmoreland (now Stafford) County, about eight miles south of present-day Quantico. He named his estate "Peace," either to express his good intentions to the Virginians or, what is more likely, what he hoped to achieve by leaving St. Mary's. But if the latter were indeed the case, it was not to come without effort. As one of the northernmost white settlements in Virginia, "Peace" was an outpost on the fringe of the wilderness. Indian attacks, provoked either by white colonists or by shifting allegiances among warring Indian tribes, were a constant threat.

Characteristically, Brent did not wait for attacks to come to him. Rather, he rode out with such prominent neighbors as Captains George Mason and Gerald Fowkes to guard the frontier. Brent himself captured and imprisoned a Potomac chief who had previously been tried and acquitted of a murder charge. This earned Brent and his colleagues a stern rebuke and revocation of their militia commissions from the House of Burgesses and Governor William Berkeley, who had long attempted to build a system of treaties and reserved lands for friendly tribes. But Jamestown was far away, and different values held sway on the frontier. Brent's neighbors rewarded him with the rank of captain in the local militia, used his son Giles' knowledge of Indian languages learned from his mother to good advantage, and otherwise applauded his efforts. In the eyes of the frontier landowners, in short, fighting Indians was a high priority public service. Indeed, by 1668, after a fiery Anglican parson named John Waugh and some disaffected neighbors successfully brought suit against Giles Brent before the Stafford County Court because of his religion, the Governor's Council and General Court summarily reversed the lower court's decision, claiming to have had "21 years experience of his [Brent's] fidelity in not seducing any person in the Roman Catholic religion." By then, quite clearly, word of Brent's military service, his efforts to attract more colonists, and his friendship with such as Mason and Fowkes had been heard and welcomed in the capital.[17]

Before he died in 1672, both Giles Brent's sisters and two of his nephews had followed him to Virginia. The family holdings soon stretched from the lower course of the Potomac to Hunting Creek near present-day Alexandria. By this time, too, his son Giles II was soon to marry a cousin, Mary Brent, and serve with Captain George Mason in the Indian fighting that led to Bacon's Rebellion, all of which earned him not rebuke, but a captaincy in the militia and the position of collector of taxes on tobacco exports.[18]

With the arrival from England of the brothers George and Robert Brent, nephews of Giles I, the family's commitment to public service gradually moved from Indian fighting to colonization schemes and the practice of law. George, first to come in 1673, settled at Woodstock near Aquia Creek and formed a law partnership with his neighbor William Fitzhugh, by all accounts Virginia's most able barrister. In 1681 Seneca Indian raids from Maryland momentarily interrupted their work; Fitzhugh and Captain George Brent of Woodstock, as he came to be called, therefore joined to command a troop of horse known as the Stafford Rangers. Shortly thereafter Brent was appointed receiver general for regions north of the Rappahannock. In 1686 his younger brother Robert arrived in Maryland to join him in his law practice; the two were soon taking prominent cases throughout the colony. In that year, too, Captain George of Woodstock was appointed the King's attorney general in Virginia. Thus it came about that for the years 1686 and 1687 the colony's highest judicial office was held by a Catholic lawyer who by the letter of the law should never have been allowed to practice, let alone enjoy public office.

One year later his Stafford neighbors voted George Brent their representative in the House of Burgesses. Since this occurred in the short reign of the Catholic King James II, during which the anti-Catholic penal codes of Virginia were briefly suspended, Brent took his seat in the House without taking the customary test oaths, which were then administered on a voluntary basis. Later, after the Glorious Revolution of 1688 in England brought an end to James II's reign and a return of the anti-Catholic penal codes to Virginia, political enemies of George Brent used the unsettled times to spread rumors that the

Catholics of Maryland were joining forces with the Seneca Indians to sweep across the Potomac and annex Stafford County.

These events encouraged an attorney named Richard Gibson who had lost a number of cases to the Brents to bring them to court in 1691, demanding to know why such well known Popish recusants as they should not be forced to take the test oaths if they wished to continue the practice of law. The Stafford County Court, however, studiously ignored Gibson's complaint. He and others tried again two months later, adding a charge of "severall wicked crimes" of unspecified nature. On this occasion the Stafford Court allowed the Brents to appeal the charges to the Governor's Council, which promptly dismissed them. Finally, in 1693, Richard Gibson went again to court with a summation of his previous charges, noting that "of all which there seems to be little or no notice Taken, but they [the Brent brothers] suffered to go on."

Gibson's weary complaint proved both accurate and prophetic. The Brent family was indeed suffered to go on unmolested, to the point that by the eighteenth century their private chapel was regularly served by Catholic priests from Maryland. Although the unfortunate half-Indian Giles Brent II died at an early age after his wife left him charging cruelty, succeeding generations continued the Brent tradition of public service and large families. Giles II's grandson William founded a new estate called Richland about four miles north of Aquia Creek. He had but one son, also named William, who served in both the House of Burgesses and the Virginia Convention of 1776 and married Bishop Carroll's younger sister Eleanor. William and Eleanor had seven children, some of whom we will come to know later as a militia colonel during the Revolution, an early marshal of the District of Columbia, a United States senator, and the wife of the largest landowner in the city of Washington.[19]

Initially the line of Captain George Brent of Woodstock advanced the family fortunes more through opportune marriages, at first to the leading families of Bermuda and later to such well-known southern Maryland Catholic families as the Sewalls, Mudds, and Neales. By a coincidence that was not uncommon among Maryland Catholics, Robert Brent of Woodstock, great-grandson of Captain George and a cousin of William of Richland, married Ann, another sister of Bishop Carroll, in what proved to be the second of three interlocking marriages between these two families. Their children were eight in number. We will meet some of them again as well, one as a career official of the State Department and consul in Paris, another as a longtime Washington City Council member and valued friend of Thomas Jefferson, and a third as the first mayor of Washington.

Not only judicious marriages but also interfaith or "mixed" marriages with Protestants were an important factor in the social acceptance of Catholics in colonial America. So much was this the case in Maryland, in fact, that it is difficult to find a prominent Catholic or Protestant family of the early settlement period whose descendants in one generation or another did not engage in mixed marriages. Some Maryland families, it is true, went to extraordinary lengths to avoid them. Others took strong or unusual measures to express their disapproval. A prime example is Major William Boarman, a strict Catholic and a close friend of the third Lord Baltimore, who apparently found it so difficult to find an eligible Catholic partner after the first of his three wives died that he settled for the younger sister of one of his sons-in-law, thus making Boarman both father-in-law and brother-in-law to his young bride's brother. Boarman also stipulated in his will that his principal plantation should pass to the next in line if his oldest son did not properly maintain the family chapel.

The marriage of Henrietta Neale, a daughter of Captain James and Anne Neale, to Colonel Philemon Lloyd provides a milder example of disapproval or, better said, the misgivings that sometimes accompanied mixed marriages. Lloyd, a wealthy Talbot County planter, willed that their children "be brought up in ye Protestant religion . . . and carried to such and such churches where it is preached and to no others." His executors, moreover, were to remind her constantly of this obligation should he predecease her.[20]

But, much as the Catholic church might try to discourage them, interfaith marriages continued to take place and were for the most part accepted. Not infrequently they proved advantageous to one or the other of the participants, if not both. An instructive example is the Brooke family, whose members served in the Maryland Assembly for four generations. At its head was Robert Brooke, a one-time Anglican parson whose father was a member of Parliament. Brooke, his wife, and ten grown children arrived in Maryland in 1650 with a retinue of twenty-eight servants, a pack of fox hounds, and other appurtenances of the landed English gentry. A year before, Cecilius Calvert, the second Lord Baltimore, had successfully urged passage of Maryland's celebrated Toleration Act, which promised that no person in the colony who believed in Jesus Christ would ever be "in any waies troubled, Molested, or discountenanced for or in respect of his or her religion nor in the free exercise thereof."[21]

Although a true landmark of tolerance in its time, the act was also a conscious effort by the Proprietor to attract just such prominent and wealthy Protestants as Brooke, the better to mollify the rising Puritan element both in the colony and in England. But far from establishing a solid Protestant presence in Maryland, succeeding generations of Brookes made a practice of interfaith marriages with attendant conversions—back and forth between Catholicism and Protestantism, that is—to a surprising degree. The line of Thomas Brooke, second oldest of Robert Brooke's eight sons, provides the most interesting case in point, among many.

Thomas married Eleanor Hatton, the daughter of a Protestant planter of St. Mary's County, but he later converted to Catholicism. Unlike his brother Baker Brooke, who converted upon marrying Anne Calvert, Lord Baltimore's niece, and thereafter held a lifetime seat on the Council, Thomas Brooke's conversion brought him no apparent reward. Instead he served in various local offices before being elected to the Lower House of the Maryland Assembly for a span of eight years. (From 1646 onwards the Maryland Assembly met in two houses, or the governor's appointed Council, also known as the Upper House, and a Lower House, whose members were freely elected.) But Thomas and Eleanor Hatton Brooke's first son, also named Thomas, chose to convert back to Protestantism at a time when the proprietary regime of the Lords Baltimore had been replaced by direct royal rule, for reasons we will presently examine. Accordingly, Thomas Brooke II was appointed to the Upper House of the first Royal Assembly of 1692, there to serve on and off for thirty-seven years.[22]

But almost as if to defy family tradition, three of Thomas's five brothers turned their backs on such worldly attainments and became Jesuit priests. Robert, the oldest of the three, was the first of many Marylanders to go to the English Jesuit academy in St. Omers, where he became the first American-born Catholic ordained a priest and was commended as "yielding to few Europeans for being the first in their class."[23]

In the next generation Thomas Brooke II's daughter Sarah married the Virginian Philip Lee, thus uniting the Brookes with the powerful and largely Protestant Lee family of Maryland and Virginia. Among their grandchildren was Thomas Sim Lee, the future governor of Maryland who himself would later make an interfaith marriage. By contrast, Sarah Brooke Lee's eight first cousins, or the family of Thomas Brooke's brother Clement and Jane Sewall, remained staunchly Catholic. Among their children was Elizabeth Brooke, the future wife of Charles Carroll of Annapolis and grandmother of Charles Carroll of Carrollton.[24]

There were others. The Protestant Diggeses, descendants of one of Virginia's early governors, became Catholic after intermarriage with the Sewalls of Maryland. The Neales of Charles County, through one of their early interfaith marriages with the Brookes, established a Catholic family that in four generations included Chief Justice Roger Brooke Taney, the first American-born Catholic to achieve cabinet rank. The list is long, the reader will see in future chapters, extending well into the nineteenth century.[25]

But it is doubtful that any of these alliances produced such an extraordinary family confrontation as that which befell the above-mentioned Robert Brooke, oldest of the three Jesuit Brooke brothers. Four years after his return from Europe, or in September 1704, Father Brooke found himself brought to trial before the colony's Provincial Court on the charge of celebrating mass at the St. Mary's chapel. With him was his superior, Reverend Robert Hunter, charged with consecrating the chapel's altar. Sitting in stern judgment by virtue of his seat on the Governor's Council, whose members also served as the Provincial Court, was his Protestant brother Thomas Brooke II, who appears to have held a lifelong enmity towards the Catholic church and his Jesuit brothers.[26] The newly appointed royal governor John Seymour—one of the most bigoted and surely the most pompous ever to hold office—presided over the court. Seymour, along with his predecessor Francis Nicholson, had shown every sign of wanting nothing less than the total eradication of Catholicism. Nicholson had three times sent unsuccessful proposals to the Maryland

44   Assembly questioning the right of Catholic priests to perform marriages. Now Seymour, even as he was preparing more sweeping measures, was determined to make a showcase of the trial.

Accompanying the defendants was a lawyer, Charles Carroll, the first of his name to come to the colonies. Carroll asked if he might be allowed to represent the priests. The court unanimously refused his request.[27] The trial itself was quickly resolved. Brooke freely admitted to saying mass in the St. Mary's chapel, pleading only that "others had formerly done so." Father Hunter denied having consecrated the altar, since this was a function reserved only to bishops. The Council, upon being advised that this was the defendants' first offense, recommended no more than a severe reprimand. This Governor Seymour took upon himself to do. He first warned the two priests not to be deceived by clemency. But, should he find that they continued "at publick times and in publick places your gawdy shows and Serpentine Policy to amuse the multitude," he would not hesitate to banish them to a place where they would be dealt with under the severest of laws. "Pray take notice that I am an English Protestant Gentleman and can never equivocate," Governor Seymour thundered, as he concluded his reprimand. Noting that a Protestant church had recently been built in St. Mary's, the governor and the Council then proceeded to order the high sheriff to lock up the Catholic chapel and keep the key "so that no Person may presume to make use thereof under any pretence whatsoever."[28]

So ended the first chapter in the history of the St. Mary's chapel—"the cradle of American Catholicism," historians have called it—which the first Lord Baltimore had so wished to control. In the same month, September 1704, the Maryland Assembly passed Seymour's "Act to Prevent the Growth of Popery." Its most sweeping provision simply forbade Catholic priests from saying mass or exercising any other priestly functions, with a fine of fifty pounds and six months imprisonment for the first offense and banishment to England for the second.[29]

The dramatic reversal from a Maryland of the Toleration Act of 1649 to that of a harshly anti-Catholic regime can be traced to a number of circumstances, both in England and in the province. In the beginning was the fact that Maryland was a colony populated mainly by Protestants in which a minority of Catholics held much of the power and a large share of the land. (The earliest Catholic gentlemen adventurers received manorial grants of two thousand acres for every five manservants transported to Maryland.) A potential for conflict, in other words, existed from the start. That it did not quickly develop was largely the result of the second Lord Baltimore's prudent policies. Among these, the policy of attracting Protestant investors with the same generous land grants Catholics received, appointments to the governing Council, and a legislative guarantee of equal standing, may have been sound and far-sighted, but it also carried the danger of creating a new class of Protestant leaders who might threaten the status quo.

In fact, trouble from this source first came shortly after the Toleration Act when word of the execution of Charles I and the successes of Cromwell reached the colony. Buoyed by these developments, William Claiborne, the Calverts' old nemesis, incited some Protestant settlers near present-day Annapolis to a rebellious skirmish known as the Battle of the Severn that ultimately caused a twenty-eight-year interruption of proprietary rule.[30]

But in the longer run it was the changing attitudes of Charles Calvert, the third Lord Baltimore, that ultimately brought about the downfall of the Catholic Calverts. A governor of the province in his younger years, Charles Calvert became proprietor after the death of his father Cecilius in 1675. Although he supported religious toleration, he chose not to continue his father's cautious course of balancing Council appointments. For Charles Calvert the way to tighter control and a more effective government was to dispense Council seats among Catholic friends and relatives while at the same time trying to mold the freely elected Lower House more to his liking.[31]

How Calvert went about the first objective is best shown by his treatment of the Catholic Sewalls (sometimes spelled Sewell) of Calvert and St. Mary's counties. First to cast roots in Maryland in 1661 were Henry and Jane Sewall, who had come as close friends and at the personal invitation of the then Governor Charles Calvert. Henry Sewall was immediately appointed a member of the Upper House and secretary of the province. Unfortunately, he was to serve no more than four years, or until his death in 1665. Less than a year later Charles Calvert married Sewall's widow Jane. As a stepfather Calvert saw to it that Sewall's son Nicholas and his four daughters' husbands were all rewarded with seats on the Council or well-paying administrative posts.

The Sewall daughters for their part married mainly within the small and select community of Maryland Catholics, if not always easily and sometimes on the second try. Jane, the youngest, was wed at the age of seventeen to Philip Calvert, the youngest son of the first Lord Baltimore who was three times her age and uncle to her stepfather Charles. Of the other sisters, who seem to have had a marked propensity for outliving their first husbands, Mary first married William Chandler, a Protestant, and second, Catholic George Brent of Woodstock; Anne, first Protestant Benjamin Rozer and second Catholic Edward Pye; and Elizabeth, first Jesse Wharton, a Catholic, and second William Digges, a Protestant and the son of Virginia Governor Sir Edward Digges. All their spouses, with the exception of the Virginian George Brent and William Chandler, were named to the Council. To repeat, neither Digges nor Rozer were Catholics, but both became council members as a direct result of their marriages to the Sewall girls. To make sure of their fealty, Charles Calvert also made them collectors of revenues.[32]

By 1688 Charles Calvert had carried his policy so far that the Council was entirely Catholic, with the rare exception of William Digges, his step son-in-law. Far from creating the strong and loyal government he envisioned, Calvert's concentration of power and privilege proved to be a major irritant that led to the quick collapse of the proprietary government following England's Glorious Revolution a year later. Less than three months after the news of William and Mary's accession to the British throne reached Maryland,

46   angry Protestants, led principally by a quondam Anglican minister named John Coode, marched on St. Mary's. Although William Digges, now a colonel in the militia, gathered some eighty to one hundred men in the St. Mary's state house to oppose the "rebels," his troops refused to fire on Coode's larger force. Similarly, on the shores of the Patuxent River seven miles to the north, Henry Sewall's son Nicholas and Henry Darnall could raise no more than 160 men in defense of the proprietary government and thus quickly saw the wisdom of surrendering to a Protestant force of seven hundred laying siege to Sewall's estate at Mattapany. Thus the reign of the third Lord Baltimore—he was away in England at the moment—came to an abrupt end without the firing of a shot.[33]

By the spring of 1692 the colony had its first royally appointed governor—Lionel Copley—and both houses of the Maryland Assembly had been totally purged of Catholics. Two years later the capital moved to Annapolis. The Lords Baltimore, as it happened, would have another chance. But religious freedom, as defined in Maryland's Act of Toleration of 1649, was no more.

Not long after the turn of the century came Governor Seymour's previously mentioned "Act to Prevent the Growth of Popery." Besides prohibiting Catholic worship, the act also decreed that no "Papist or Person making profession of the Popish Religion shall keep Schoole or take upon themselves the Education Government or Boarding of Youth in any place within this Province."[34]

But, as happened so often in Maryland's Protestant-Catholic disputes, the results of these extreme acts were not always what their perpetrators intended. The principal provision of Seymour's act was too much for the Maryland Assembly, upon reconsideration, not to mention Queen Anne and her councilors in England. Less than three months after its passage, the Assembly temporarily suspended the clause prohibiting the celebration of mass as long as it was done "in a private family of the Roman Communion"; two years later Queen Anne ordered it suspended indefinitely, under the same proviso.[35]

Thus, by supreme historical irony, the kind of restricted and private worship that the first Lord Baltimore hoped would placate and make more tolerant the Protestant majority was vengefully codified as the law of the land a century later by those it was specifically designed to please. In 1715 proprietary rule was restored in the person of Charles Calvert, fifth Lord Baltimore, who had conformed to the Church of England. But neither he nor his son who succeeded him did much to redress the many wrongs that were now being heaped on Maryland Catholics. In 1717 the Assembly reluctantly yielded to the urgings of the British government and repealed the Act to Prevent the Growth of Popery of 1704. But this was no more than a token action. In the two preceding years the Assembly had passed laws that strengthened some previous legislation barring Catholics from holding elective office, doubled the tax on the importation of Irish servants, and deprived Catholic widows of Protestant husbands of custody of their children. These remained in force, as did the provisions against public worship and Catholic education.

Nevertheless, in 1718 the Assembly sourly noted that notwithstanding its previous efforts "it is very obvious that . . . professed Papists still multiply and increase in number." It therefore passed a strongly worded law prohibiting all Catholics from voting in any provincial or county elections unless they first took a test oath denying the validity of transubstantiation and subscribing to such purposely confusing language as swearing to "detest and abjure, as impious and heretical, that damnable doctrine and position, that princes excommunicated or deprived by the Pope, or any authority of the See of Rome may be deposed or murdered by their subjects, or any other whatsoever."[36]

Although this act of disfranchisement may have been seldom applied, it was always available for intimidation, at the whim of local sheriffs. Indeed, much the same could be said of many of the Assembly's anti-Catholic laws. Their application, especially in arrests and trials, may have been rare, but the effect of most of the laws was comprehensive. From 1689 to 1776 no Catholic held any public office, civil or military, nor were there any Catholic schools in the province except for an academy close to the border with Delaware, ready to move there at a moment's notice. But, as in Virginia, all the statutes remained very much on the books, ready for zealots to bring up against anyone who might disregard them.[37]

In the long years that followed, the Catholics of Maryland maintained their private worship and did indeed multiply and increase in number. In 1708 they were no more than three thousand, or slightly less than one tenth of the population. But by 1765 there were approximately twenty thousand Catholics in Maryland, and their rate of growth was higher than that of the population at large.[38] Their faith, moreover, seemed to grow all the stronger in the face of oppression. To be sure, the prohibition of public worship and an extreme shortage of priests made difficult the celebration of mass, let alone other sacraments. But the Brookes and other large landowners had house chapels, to which circuit-riding priests came for visits of a week or more. Then, too, persons living close to the large Jesuit manors—St. Thomas Manor in Port Tobacco, Newtown near St. Mary's or Whitemarsh in Prince George's County, for example—might regularly attend mass at the Jesuits' chapels. These chapels thus became proto-parishes, where Maryland Catholics might enjoy their first sense of congregation. But for the majority, simple prayers around the fireside aided by guides or manuals for home devotions were the norm on any given Sunday.

Ironically, the ban against Catholic education helped bring forth what some historians consider the most noble testament of Maryland Catholics to the preservation of their religion. This was the significant number of sons and daughters sent to European schools and convents, often at considerable expense and with the personal anguish of long years of separation. Sending a boy abroad for five to ten years to have him return a man was the common experience of the many Marylanders who sent approximately 130 sons to the English Jesuit colleges at St. Omers, Bruges, and Liège from 1681 to the time of American independence. Smaller numbers attended various Dominican and Benedictine colleges in northern France and Germany, while those studying for the priesthood might go on to Valladolid in Spain or the English College of Rome. Beginning with Mary Digges in 1721, some thirty-three Maryland girls also went abroad to convent schools in France and Flanders.

The results of this phenomenon were scarcely what the Maryland Assembly's Protestant lawmakers had in mind, for at least two reasons. First, Catholic education abroad meant that the Catholic gentry who could afford it would remain among the best-educated people in the American colonies. This was especially true of the young men at the Jesuit colleges, where the well-known *ratio studiorum* with its emphases on philosophy, rhetoric, and other humanistic studies gave them an excellent preparation for public life. As personified by Charles Carroll of Carrollton, to cite the best-known example, graduates returned to America to become some of the country's most articulate defenders of religious and civil liberties.[39]

The second unintended effect was to incline more Maryland youths toward the priesthood. Vocations increased, as might be expected, as the well-established Catholic families whose members were now denied public office were only too pleased to have sons pursue alternative careers in the ministry. So it was, for example, with some of the later generation Sewalls. After the Protestant rebellion, Nicholas Sewall's children could no longer count on the lucrative Calvert patronage that he and his sisters had enjoyed, but his daughters seem to have made up for this deficiency to some degree by marrying well, if not always within the Catholic community. (One daughter married a member of the distinguished Tasker family of Protestant Annapolis; another, a wealthy Cecil County planter with the splendidly implausible name of Peregrine Frisby.) However, it remained for two of Nicholas' grandsons, Charles and Nicholas Lewis Sewall, to maintain some of the family's prestige through eminence within the church. Both were educated abroad, first at St. Omers and then at the Great College at Bruges. Charles returned to this country as a priest and attended the historic Whitemarsh meetings on church organization, from which he emerged first as secretary and then as agent, or treasurer, of the Corporation of the Roman Catholic Clergy. It was at these meetings also that he must first have attracted the attention of John Carroll, who made Sewall one of his most trusted aides.

"My good brother and companion," as Bishop Carroll often referred to Charles, executed some of the more complex sales of Jesuit properties, served as Carroll's eyes and ears on the board of directors of Georgetown College in its earliest years, and undertook various delicate missions to help Carroll contain some of his most vocal opponents.[40] For these reasons, in order to keep him close at hand, Carroll made Charles Sewall his first resident pastor in the city of Baltimore and later rector of its Pro-Cathedral of St. Peter's. His brother Nicholas became part of the faculty at Bruges and then chose to be among the priests returning to join the restored Jesuit province in England. There he remained for the rest of his life, serving the English mission with distinction. He was twice rector of Stonyhurst, the first Jesuit college to be established in Great Britain. During his later years, Sewall was named provincial of the restored

English province. This was a signal honor for a "colonial," although it is doubtful that Nicholas Sewall, described as more British than the British, ever thought of himself as such.[41]

Other families who sent more than one son or daughter abroad include the Boarmans, Brents, Diggeses, Semmeses, Neales, and Boones. The record, however, must go to the Catholic Brookes, who sent no less than thirteen boys to St. Omers and Bruges, followed by the Diggeses with nine. Overall, from the approximately one hundred and thirty who went to the men's colleges, there came forty-three Jesuit vocations and three secular priests. Twenty-one of the Jesuits returned to active ministries in America, mostly during the second and third quarters of the eighteenth century.

The importance of this phenomenon can scarcely be exaggerated. The number of priests in Maryland and Pennsylvania, which is almost to say in the American colonies, reached a high point of only twenty-three in 1773. Thus the small but steady stream of Jesuits returning from the European colleges and academies in the eighteenth century proved a main source of supply. With them, in effect, lay the foundations of an American clergy. Much the same can be said of America's women religious. Thirty-three Maryland women entered contemplative orders in European convents in the eighteenth century. At least fifteen more followed their steps on these shores to be among the first twenty professions at the Carmelite convent established in Port Tobacco in 1791.[42]

Another factor that helped Maryland Catholics maintain status throughout the period of oppression was economic growth, much as Protestant governors and assemblymen sometimes tried to impede it. Although Catholics were barred from public service, they were not denied the opportunity to advance in more material terms. This advancement was not only the prerogative of the wealthy, who in many cases increased what were originally large and generously granted estates by reasonably good management, participation in government (until it was prohibited), and family associations. From the earliest days of the colony, upward opportunity also existed for white indentured servants and free laborers. Aiding the growth of all, rich or poor, was the basic respect for private property that was an inalienable right of all English subjects.

When in the 1750s the Lower House of the Maryland Assembly proposed a number of bills affecting property rights—one would have confiscated all the Jesuits' manorial properties, for example—the bills were nearly always rejected by the Governor's Council, or Upper House, after intense debate. This was not the case, however, following the onset of the French and Indian War. As had happened before and would happen again, rumors quickly spread that Maryland Catholics were conspiring with the Catholic French for the overthrow of the colony. Consequently in a rush of nervous patriotism after General Braddock's stinging defeat at Fort Duquesne in 1755, both houses of the Assembly passed a tax bill on property to provide Maryland's overdue share for supplying his Majesty's forces. Incredibly, the act doubled the tax on all Catholics on the grounds that they were not serving in the militia from which, as the Assembly conveniently chose to forget, they had been excluded by law eleven years

50   earlier. The double tax law remained in force for four years, although never applied, as Charles Carroll of Annapolis and Father George Hunter, superior of
the Jesuit mission, argued eloquently against it. By 1760, however, the Council
found time to give the offensive measure more sober consideration and prevailed on the governor and the Lower House to rescind it.[43]

It is not difficult to understand why. Of the twelve all-Protestant Council
members all but one were themselves large property owners. In addition seven
of the twelve had Catholic relations and two were partners of the Baltimore
Iron Works, one of the principal sources of the Charles Carroll family wealth.[44]
They undoubtedly reasoned that since the more radical members of the Lower
House were so often tempted to transgress the property rights of their Catholic
associates, the day might come when similar actions would be directed against
them.

In any case the defeat of the double tax marked the last serious attempt of
its kind. Private property remained secure. Jesuits never suffered the loss of
their manors. Nor was worship in their manor chapels ever curtailed, since
these were within the Jesuits' properties. With the exception of an order to turn
over their militia arms in the years before the French and Indian War, the
Catholic gentry never lost any real or personal property. Nor did the humblest
of indentured servants, who after working off their usual four-year contracts
received "one good Cloth suite of Keirsey or broadcloth a Shift of white linen
one new pair of stockins and shoes two hoes one axe, 3 barrels of Corn and fifty
acres of land whereof five at least to be plantable."[45]

Some of these servants, it is gratifying to note, were to become heads of
families that contributed as much to government or the church as their landed
peers. With none of the initial advantages of the Brookes or the Brents, such
families as the Fenwicks, Boarmans, Mudds, and Semmeses played large roles
through succeeding generations in the church and state affairs of Maryland,
the District of Columbia, and the nation at large.

Marmaduke Semmes, for example, progenitor of the numerous Semmeses of Georgetown, began life in America as a doorkeeper to the Maryland Assembly's Upper House. After receiving his fifty acres in 1666, he soon acquired
many more by marrying a widow with the felicitous (and apt) name of Fortuna
Mitford.[46] Their second son James purchased land in Charles County at an opportune moment—he is among those credited with founding Port Tobacco and
making it live up to its name—married well, and became a successful planter
and shipper. We will come to know his direct descendants in Georgetown and
Washington as distinguished merchants, lawmakers, doctors, innkeepers,
shipowners, and naval officers. But it remained for Marmaduke's grandchildren, the issue of James' second son, Joseph Milburn Semmes, and his wife
Rachel Prather, to offer the contribution that seems to have become a *sine qua
non* of Maryland Catholic families of the eighteenth century. Seven of their
eight daughters professed at Benedictine and Sepulchrine convents in France.
Their only son, Joseph, entered the Society of Jesus at St. Omers, going on like
Nicholas Sewall to be a founder of the Jesuits' Stonyhurst College in England.[47]

Not all indentured servants or free adults first worked the land. Those who were literate might serve as secretaries or overseers to the wealthier settlers who had paid their ship passage. Such was the case with Cuthbert Fenwick, first of many Fenwicks, who came to Maryland around 1634 as the indentured secretary to Thomas Cornwallis. Within one year of completing his service to Cornwallis, Fenwick was an attorney in his own right and a member of the Assembly. He appears always to have sided with the Jesuits in their initial difficulties against Lord Baltimore, serving as their attorney in the suit brought by Cornwallis against Leonard Calvert in the St. Mary's chapel dispute. As a result Father Thomas Copley appointed him trustee of the Jesuit manor of St. Inigoes, when the proprietor would not allow the Jesuits title in their name to any of their lands. By this and other means Fenwick was able to leave his family an estate of at least two thousand acres. It is unnecessary here to chronicle all the achievements of his descendants. The reader will soon hear of them, especially in the fifth and sixth generations, as priests, consuls, ship captains, bishops, and college presidents.[48]

Major William Boarman—he of the three wives—came to Maryland in 1645 as a youth of no more than fifteen. He spent long years exploring the Chesapeake, trading with Indians, serving in the militia, and speculating on land. Such services and a good sense for property values earned him the friendship of Governor Charles Calvert, a captaincy in the militia, and estates that eventually totalled more than ten thousand acres. As he rose in status Boarman was elected to the Lower House of the Assembly for the years 1671-1675 and also served as justice, coroner, and sheriff of St. Mary's County.

A strict Catholic who objected to marrying out of the church, it was Boarman who in the second of his three marriages wed Mary Matthews, daughter of a prominent Catholic doctor and planter of St. Mary's and the younger sister of Thomas Matthews, Jr., who was married to Boarman's daughter Sarah. Something of Boarman's sense of religious adherence must have passed on to his descendants, since the family's most remarkable contribution by far was to the church. Beginning with the fourth generation, at least six Boarman boys were sent to Jesuit colleges at St. Omers and Bruges. Two were ordained as priests and a third served as one of the first lay professors at Georgetown College. Three great-granddaughters of Major William Boarman were among the contemplatives at the Carmelite convent of Port Tobacco, the first of its kind in America, established by Father Charles Neale in 1790. Later generations saw Catherine Boarman profess as Sister Mary Francis with Elizabeth Seton's Sisters of Charity in 1824 and no less than ten Boarman girls as early students of Georgetown's Visitation Convent. From this number two took vows together as Visitandines in 1817 before then-Archbishop Leonard Neale, along with two of their first cousins.[49]

The Mudd family presents an almost equal example of upward economic mobility, with at least one Jesuit priest and two nuns also within its ranks. Its founder, Thomas Mudd, first settled in Virginia around 1655 at the age of eighteen "bound to Anthony Noakes for three years." By the time he moved to

Maryland twelve years later he had not only worked off his indenture, but was also prosperous enough to bring eight servants with him. At the time this gave him head rights to 450 acres, 200 of which he improved to create "Mudd's Rest" plantation in Charles County. Mudd then increased his acreage and personal fortunes by marrying well and outliving two of his three wives. The first was Julia Gardiner of an established Catholic family of St. Mary's; the second, from whom he received an exceptionally large dowry, was Sarah Boarman Matthews, Major William Boarman's daughter and widow of Thomas Matthews, Jr.; and the third, Anne Matthews, who was his second wife's sister-in-law. Among other advantages deriving from these unions Thomas Mudd rose to the stations of justice of the peace of St. Mary's county and advisor to an Assembly committee for the increase of trade. Historically, the best known of his many descendants was the unfortunate Dr. Samuel A. Mudd, who treated the fleeing John Wilkes Booth in 1865. But there were many others. We will find them as early members of Trinity Church, faculty and students at Georgetown College, and merchants and civil servants of the Federal City.[50]

So lived some of the representative Catholic families of *Terra Mariae*. During its first century "the land of Maria" was for the most part a haven where Protestant and Catholic lived and worked together in the unity of Lord Baltimore's vision. Granted the occasional periods of strife (often inspired as much by events in Europe as anything of purely local origin), Maryland of the seventeenth century attempted to provide a government which would tolerate persons of all faiths, give equal rights to all Christians, and keep church and state separate. In the eighteenth century all this was overturned and replaced by governments bent on eradicating Catholicism. Given the relatively low number of Catholics at the time, the wonder is that the new Protestant ruling class did not succeed in its stated aim of completely ridding the province of "the damnable doctrines . . . of Popish recusants."

But as we have seen, Maryland Catholics of the eighteenth century, no less than their forebears, preserved their faith and survived oppressive regimes. While it is true that some few abandoned their religion for political or social gain, the majority were united in their determination to stay in Maryland (although even the Carrolls sometimes thought about leaving) and keep to their faith. This they did in large part by worshipping and "cause[ing] all acts of religion to be done as privately as may be," to borrow the words of the second Lord Baltimore's constant injunctions to the earliest settlers. Throughout the period of prohibited public worship, as a recent historian has correctly noted, "the symbol of Catholic religion was a book, the ever-present manual of prayers."[51] Indeed, the necessity for frequent home worship without priests, aided only by devotional manuals, caused Maryland Catholic families to develop what has been well described as a very personal and inward piety. In time, with Rome and the church's hierarchical structure always far away, this self-reliance built up a strong sense of individualism that would leave its particular stamp on American Catholicism. Among its hallmarks was an appreciation of the importance of freedom of religion and the separation of church and state.

Other steps to preserve the faith, as we have noted, were the extraordinary measures some families took to marry their sons and daughters only into other Catholic families. If others permitted or even encouraged interfaith marriages, a majority of the children of these marriages appear to have been brought up as Catholics. In addition to this net gain to the church, the frequency of mixed marriages between prominent Catholic and Protestant families of the colony led to a high degree of business and social associations. These associations later became an important factor in the acceptance and successful growth of Catholicism in Georgetown and Washington.

In these ways, in short, the Catholics of colonial Maryland survived and prospered. The Catholics of America survived and prospered, we can as well say, since by mid-eighteenth century, eighty percent of all Catholics in the American colonies still lived in Maryland, with the remainder largely concentrated in Pennsylvania.[52]

In recent years the Catholic historian Thomas Spalding, himself a descendant of one of southern Maryland's oldest families, has best brought the Maryland Catholic colonial experience into historical focus. After first noting that the church that John Carroll shaped in the new republic had as its building blocks the Catholic Calverts and their vision of tolerance and the necessity for church-state separation, Spalding has also pointed out:

> There were other building blocks. As important to Carroll as to the Calverts was the broad ecumenism that persuaded Catholics and Protestants (Jews would be encompassed later) to live in peace and to their mutual benefit. An expression of this ecumenism was a civic sense that found an outlet in public service, a community spirit that brought the religious and public spheres into a productive relationship. With its roots in the Calverts' concept of a Catholic elite, however, it was a community spirit born of an aristocratic sense of noblesse oblige and of a belief in the leadership of those born to lead. In no diocese would the Catholic families of wealth and power persist with such self-assurance. In a changing church they would become the most dependable guardians of that ecumenical outlook and sense of public service that Carroll had inherited from the Calverts.[53]

Indeed. When in 1776 both Maryland and Virginia passed their acts of religious freedom, John Carroll was among the first to understand the enormous opportunity that lay before Roman Catholics in a land where they would no longer be persecuted or considered less than full citizens. With slightly premature enthusiasm he wrote to his British friend Charles Plowden during the

54   height of the Revolution, "the fullest and largest system of toleration is adopted in almost all the American states: publick protection and encouragement are extended alike to all denominations."[54]

If much more time would have to pass before these statements were completely true, we must forgive Carroll his ebullience. He understood what was most important. The Roman Catholics in the Revolutionary ranks—Brents, Brookes, Boarmans, Diggeses, Fenwicks, and Semmeses among them—were proving that it was possible to be both good Americans and good Catholics. But Carroll also understood that to secure their new rights, to banish forever the specter of discriminatory laws, Catholics would have to re-enter in force the political life and the civic posts from which they had so long been barred. "Roman Catholics are members of Congress, assemblies, and hold civil and military posts as well as others," he added excitedly in his letter to Plowden of 1779. (*Carrolls* are members of Congress, he might better have said, since at the time only his cousin Charles Carroll of Carrollton had been elected to the Continental Congress, to be followed by his brother Daniel Carroll in 1781.)[55] Twenty years later then-Bishop Carroll was making the same point in a far different context.

In a sermon on the death of George Washington, Carroll reached a peak of eloquence, not so much in recounting the general's military career, but in a powerful evocation of the personal sacrifices Washington had made "in venturing on the agitated ocean of national responsibility" and taking "into his hands the helm of the State."[56] The message was clear. Even though Catholics had proved themselves in the Revolutionary War they must, like Washington, continue to do so in the forging of the new republic. How well the Catholics of Georgetown and Washington would respond to this call we will soon learn. But here we may be sure of the audience Carroll had particularly in mind. He was calling out to those who remembered the long years of suppression and had kept the faith alive. He was calling to his kinsmen, the multi-generational descendants of the oldest families of *Terra Mariae*. No one else could so well understand the urgency of his message.

4

For Nation and Town

There are few towns which would not be willing to receive such benefits and avail themselves of every opportunity to reward the exertions of these humane and public spirited people.

-GEORGETOWN CITY COUNCIL
Debate, aid to Trinity Church Free School for Boys, 1832

Late in the harsh winter of 1792, while Baltimore's harbor was locked in ice, Bishop John Carroll put aside his daily diligences to write a difficult letter. Certain of Maryland's staunchest Federalists had asked Carroll to urge Thomas Sim Lee, governor of the state of Maryland from 1779 to 1782, to come out of retirement and run again. Who better than the bishop, they must have reasoned, to influence Lee toward their design? Carroll had played a large part in Lee's conversion to Catholicism four years earlier and was now both his good friend and spiritual advisor.[1]

> I may embrace the opportunity of writing to you, that I may communicate the wishes of some Gentlemen, who last week solicited me to employ all my interest with you, to prevail on you to profess your acquiescence in their using their endeavors in your behalf....[2]

So the letter began. It was uncharacteristically awkward for a writer who was, when he wanted, among the best prose stylists of his day. Carroll stumbled on, making sure to name the gentlemen whose wish it was that he write. He himself would of course understand if Lee thought the request inconvenient or disagreeable. It was almost as if Carroll were struggling with himself in an anxious interior dialogue over the propriety of his actions. If so, the struggle was not an unfamiliar one. He had first experienced it in 1776 when he accepted the Continental Congress's invitation to form part of Benjamin Franklin's unsuccessful embassy to secure French Canadian support for the American Revolution. On that occasion, as previously noted, Carroll's doubts and self-criticism centered on ministers like himself who might be tempted to put aside their normal duties, however briefly, and take a busy part in political matters. Would he now be violating one of his own precepts once again?

But after John Carroll had brought himself to ask the question—that is, would Lee accept—he could no longer hide his true feelings. All doubts, apologies, and the cumbersome prose quickly vanished. The letter ended simply and sincerely. Carroll was sure that should the governor forsake his beloved farm near Frederick and rejoin his many friends, they would rejoice "that you will be more in the heart of them, more accessible to them." No one, the bishop concluded, would enjoy this advantage more than he.

Three weeks later Lee accepted. Shortly thereafter the Maryland Assembly easily elected him to a second term. Within a month of the election Carroll was proudly telling his friends in Europe about it "as proof of the decay of religious prejudice here."[3] A little more than a year later he was routinely passing on intelligence to Governor Lee about certain rival factions who were out to unseat him. They would never succeed, the bishop added, as long as the governor were to "act, as you always do, on right principle."[4]

Carroll's change in attitude in this case, if indeed it was that, was neither an isolated nor insignificant event. Rather, his role in the re-election of Lee was but one more manifestation of Carroll's strengthening conviction that American Catholics must play their part in the building of the new nation. His earlier and overly optimistic views on the state of religious freedom, cited in the previous chapter, had by now given way to the cold fact that two years after the Treaty of Paris the constitutions of seven of the thirteen states included statutes that either barred or impeded Roman Catholics from public office. Seven years later, or early in 1790, Carroll was forced to admit to Charles Plowden that Catholic political rights were still not as he secure as first thought. "This unjust exclusion [from public office] has always hurt me," he wrote. He planned to bring the matter to General Washington's attention, in fact.[5]

Although these barriers to public office eventually disappeared from most state constitutions, Catholics could scarcely be blamed for not wanting to step forward everywhere and immediately take advantage of the corresponding opportunities. That John Carroll understood this is quite clear. Much of his effort to persuade Catholics to re-enter public life must have been by private meetings, given Carroll's sensitivity to anything that might be interpreted as meddling in politics. Still, as in the case of Governor Lee, circumstances were sometimes strong enough to impel him to write. In other cases, especially if they concerned lesser offices or involved members of his family, Carroll found some pleasure in the task. Thus in 1792, when his young nephew Daniel Carroll Brent took his first job as a clerk in Alexander Hamilton's Treasury Department in Philadelphia, Carroll wrote to him with great warmth, noting how he and all the family were "all longing to see you, my dear Daniel, and proud of your conduct." This, however, was not the chief purpose of the letter. Rather, the bishop hoped that his nephew would recommend the bearer, one Robert Walsh of Baltimore, to Mr. Hamilton for a preference in the Treasury Department. Lest young Daniel have any misgivings, Carroll took pains to present Mr. Walsh as "perhaps my best friend in this town . . . and [a man] of great integrity with a perfect knowledge of business."[6]

As it happened, Carroll's efforts on behalf of Lee, Brent, and Walsh were all amply rewarded. In each case, in fact, the rewards spanned a number of generations.

Thomas Sim Lee successfully completed his second term as governor in 1794 and again sought to retire. While still in office President Washington had asked Lee to serve as one of the three Commissioners of the District of Columbia charged with making ready the national capital. Lee was also asked to consider a unanimous vote to fill a vacant seat in the Maryland Senate as well as numerous entreaties to serve a third term as governor.[7] All these requests he resolutely turned down, however, in favor of a winter residence in Georgetown, where he wished his children to be educated, and the continued management of Needwood, his beloved estate in Frederick County. If Bishop Carroll was disappointed by this turn of events, he could at least take satisfaction both in Lee's steadfast Catholicism and his continuing influence, even behind the scenes, in national affairs. During the last ten years that he lived in Georgetown, the governor and his energetic wife, Mary Digges Lee, were strong supporters of Trinity Church. They also helped to re-establish the pastorate of the Church of St. John in Frederick, which had long been without a resident priest, and make provision for a rural church next to Needwood.[8] During this time, too, the Lees made their spacious Georgetown home a meeting place for the leading Federalists of the day, who were then beginning to organize themselves into a political party. When not so occupied, the former governor moved easily (if not always profitably) in the highest financial circles, alternately investing in the business schemes of Robert Morris of Philadelphia, the Potomac Company of General Washington, and real estate of the Federal City and Georgetown.[9]

During this period also the Lees could watch with pride as their eight children grew up, married well, and in some cases, entered the political arena their father had left behind. In April 1799 Mary Christian Lee, oldest of the two Lee daughters, married Tench Ringgold, a Protestant who would later serve as marshal of the District of Columbia, with the Reverend Leonard Neale, then president of Georgetown College, attending. Thirteen years later, or in April 1812, the Trinity Church register recorded the marriage by Archbishop Carroll of Eliza, seventh in line of the eight Lee children, to Outerbridge Horsey, United States senator from Delaware. Horsey was a Protestant whose forebears were among the earliest colonizers of Bermuda and Virginia's Eastern Shore. According to family tradition Eliza soon converted her husband to Catholicism, a task that may have been made easier by the fact that the Virginia branch of the Horsey family had a history of disputes with the Church of England. In any case it is known that Outerbridge and Eliza's first son, Outerbridge Horsey III, married Anna Carroll, the great-great-granddaughter of Daniel Carroll II of Constitutional Convention fame, and that their ten children remained staunchly Catholic, as have all subsequent generations of Horseys, down to the present time.[10]

Had he lived longer Bishop Carroll surely would have been pleased to see both families—the Horseys as much as the Lees, that is—continue the tradition of public service. Outerbridge Horsey II served for eleven years in the United States Senate and was also attorney general of Delaware. Outerbridge Horsey III practiced law in Baltimore and alternated between state politics there and the management of Needwood. Governor Lee's youngest son John was elected to Congress as a Democrat in 1823. Educated at both Georgetown College and Harvard, he was the second Maryland Catholic to hold a seat in Congress since the time of Charles and Daniel Carroll forty years earlier. In the next generation, the governor's granddaughter, Mary Digges Lee, married Charles Carroll of Doughoregan in what proved to be the second of some four intermarriages between the Lees and the Carrolls. Their son, John Lee Carroll, would serve in another age as governor of Maryland, from 1876 to 1880.[11]

Such, in brief, were some of the attainments of the first generations of the Maryland Lees. Like the Brookes of the colonial period, to whom they could also claim kinship, the Maryland Lees successfully balanced the various demands of public office, plantation stewardship, and commerce. Only a son to enter the priesthood seemed to be missing from the typical Maryland Catholic family picture. But this, too, would come in time. On May 3, 1866, Thomas Sim Lee, the youngest of the governor's eight grandchildren, was ordained a priest at the American College in Rome.[12]

History does not record what success young Daniel Brent may have had in placing the Baltimore merchant Robert Walsh with the Treasury Department, as Bishop Carroll requested. But some unsuspected fruits came of his efforts in any event. Brent and Walsh must have found some degree of compatibility, since Brent soon became a firm friend of Walsh's son, also named Robert, in spite of being fourteen years his senior, and later married Walsh's daughter Eliza.[13] Bishop Carroll in due course shifted his attentions to the son, who entered Georgetown College in 1797. Sensing the young Robert Walsh's promise ("he is the equal in extent of litterature to any youth I have ever known"), Carroll helped plan a European grand tour for him, writing letters of introduction to friends in England and France. The bishop's early assessment of the young man's literary talent was well founded. Walsh soon proved himself an accomplished editor, essayist, and critic. In 1811, after gaining a reputation in France and England, he founded America's first literary quarterly, *The American Review of History and Politics*, and quickly became a leading literary figure of his time. Although he only occasionally returned to Georgetown, he held influential salons in Philadelphia and himself wrote essays that moved Edgar Allan Poe to call Walsh "one of the finest writers, one of the most accomplished scholars, and, when not in too great a hurry, one of the most accurate thinkers in the country."[14]

Meanwhile Daniel Brent rose rapidly from the role of a minor functionary in the Treasury Department to the higher ranks of the executive branch of government. After leaving the Treasury in December 1793 with a letter of appreciation from Alexander Hamilton, Brent transferred to the State Department. In

1800 he moved from Philadelphia to Washington as one among the first government contingents moving to the new capital. Brent first served as clerk, at that time an administrative position of much more importance than the term implies today. By 1817 he had risen to the coveted position of chief clerk, then the second-in-rank in all executive departments. In the course of his long service in Washington Brent became the State Department's veteran professional. Before leaving for Paris as consul in 1833, he logged some thirty-three years of service to nine different secretaries of state, from the administrations of John Adams through Andrew Jackson. During much of this time he routinely served as acting secretary when his superiors took their summer vacations or left Washington on extended trips. Henry Clay claimed he would have often been embarrassed during his term as secretary except for the help of Brent, whom he characterized as "diligent and always obliging, perfectly conversant with the archives of the office and possessing great experience as to the course of public business." President John Quincy Adams used Brent to fill out the White House dinners of which he and Mrs. Adams soon grew tired. Bishop Carroll, as might be expected, continued to write his nephew about other job applicants.[15]

The fact that Daniel Brent could move so easily between Hamilton's Treasury and the Jefferson administration's State Department was undoubtedly due to his family connections, especially two of his first cousins who, unlike most of the Catholic gentry, were staunch Jeffersonians. One was his exact namesake, Daniel Carroll Brent, the second son of William and Eleanor Carroll Brent of Richland. Daniel Carroll Brent was a member of the Virginia House of Burgesses who stood as Thomas Jefferson's elector for northern Virginia in 1796 and ably defended Jefferson against some Federalist mudslinging in the nation's first truly political campaign. Among other charges, the Federalists accused Jefferson of lack of personal fortitude for removing himself from Williamsburg fifteen years earlier while he was governor of Virginia and British troops were invading the Lower Peninsula. (Overlooked in the Federalist charges was the fact that the legislature, including the firebrand Patrick Henry, thought it prudent to flee the capital well ahead of Jefferson.) The Virginian Daniel Carroll Brent refuted the charges in such detail and with such abundant documentation that historians today consider Brent's defense one of the best sources for the corresponding period in Jefferson's career.

In addition, Brent went on to defeat the opposition's elector in northern Virginia, the only Federalist stronghold in the state, and thus added to the electoral vote that gave Jefferson the vice presidency. For these and other services Jefferson later appointed Brent marshal of the District of Columbia.[16] Brent's older brother Richard, the only one of William and Eleanor's seven children not to marry, was the other Jeffersonian Republican. He proved to be one of Virginia's most durable legislators and a trusted friend and political advisor of James Monroe, serving continuously in the Virginia Assembly, the United States Congress, and the Senate during the years 1793-1814.[17]

Another Georgetown Catholic in the early State Department was Joseph Fenwick, a cousin of Captain Ignatius Fenwick. His career offers an interesting

60   example of how being a Maryland Catholic, far from constituting an obstacle, was sometimes an advantage in seeking appointive office. Joseph Fenwick was a member of an especially cosmopolitan branch of the numerous Fenwicks; his close relatives included a brother, John Ceslas, the first American-born Dominican priest, who spent much of his career in Europe; another brother, James, a successful sea captain in the transatlantic service who numbered Bishop Carroll and other notables among his clients; and a nephew, Edward, also a Dominican who in 1821 became the first Catholic bishop of Cincinnati. As a young man Joseph Fenwick was apprenticed to Georgetown's leading tobacco traders, the firm of Benjamin Stoddert, Uriah Forrest, and William Murdock. But by 1787, when he was barely twenty-one, he had established his own business in association with his cousin Ignatius, his seagoing brother James, and John Mason, the son of the Virginia statesman George Mason of Gunston Hall. Fenwick had also by then taken up residence in Bordeaux, the better to serve as the firm's European agent.

Two years later, when Fenwick saw that it would be to his advantage to serve concurrently as the American consul in Bordeaux, he had but to speak to his junior partner. John Mason dutifully asked his father to write to Thomas Jefferson, then secretary of state. The senior Mason seems to have been pleased to do this, pointing out to Jefferson with some pride that his son's partner was "a native of Maryland, of an old and reputable family there, and of the Roman Catholic Religion (a circumstance which will add to his respectability in a Roman Catholic Country)."[18]

Although Jefferson at the time was laying the groundwork for a more professional consular service and had another candidate very much in mind, Joseph Fenwick got the appointment. Happily for Jefferson, however, the new consul measured up well to his official duties. Fenwick became the chief contributor of commercial dispatches that Jefferson found good enough (and therefore useful enough for the pro-French cause) to have published in Philip Freneau's *National Gazette*. The young consul at Bordeaux also proved to be a good wine taster. Jefferson, always appreciative of such gentlemanly attributes, used Fenwick to order the finest French wines for himself, President Washington, and select friends.[19]

Still another Georgetown student in whom Bishop Carroll found much promise might also have had a rewarding career in the State Department but for his untimely death. This was Henry Carroll, the first son of Charles Carroll of Belle Vue (now Dumbarton House) in Georgetown. Both Henry's father and his uncle, the Washington landowner Daniel Carroll of Duddington, had cultivated the friendship of Henry Clay when the latter first came to Washington as the junior senator from Kentucky. (Their interests may have been mutual; Kentucky was the scene of pioneer Catholic settlements led by Marylanders.)[20] Thus when President Madison named Henry Clay to serve as one of the five commissioners to carry out peace talks with Great Britain in 1814, Clay responded by asking Henry Carroll to serve as his private secretary.

Carroll evidently made the most of what was an excellent opportunity to begin a career in diplomacy. When the peace treaty was finally signed on Christmas eve 1814, the five American commissioners agreed to have Carroll carry the news and the official text to President Madison. This he did with dispatch, aided by a fast winter passage aboard the British sloop of war *Favorite*, reaching New York and Washington by mid-February amid wild celebrations. Among his papers Carroll carried a letter from Clay recommending that he be given the post of first secretary at the American legation in either Paris or London. But Henry Carroll's father, who had already begun some of the ill-advised western land speculations that would make him a constant burden to his relatives, urged Henry to serve in his place as acting register of lands in Howard County, Missouri. There Henry Carroll was shot to death at the age of twenty-eight, a victim of frontier politics and prejudices. Far more fortunate was his younger brother William Thomas Carroll, for whom Clay secured the position of clerk of the United States Supreme Court in 1827. There William Thomas served with distinction for thirty-five years.[21]

If, as we have seen, the Maryland Catholics' commitment to public service found ample expression and opportunity in appointive office, the same was scarcely true in the larger arena of elective positions. Here the ever-present undercurrent of prejudice—"the deepest bias in the history of the American people," as one noted historian has called it—might often come to the surface. Demographics as well remained a barrier, since Catholics in Maryland during the early Federal period still probably constituted no more than one-tenth of the state's population.[22] A case in point is Captain James Fenwick of Pomonkey, Charles County, a nephew of Joseph Fenwick and older brother of Edward Fenwick, bishop of Cincinnati.

In 1808 Fenwick became the first Maryland Catholic to run for Congress since Charles Carroll of Carrollton and Daniel Carroll of Upper Marlboro had served in the Continental and First United States Congresses two decades earlier. That prejudice was a factor in Fenwick's campaign seems obvious. In an unusual letter to the Roman Catholics of southern Maryland that occupied all the front page of the *National Intelligencer*, the nation's first national newspaper, a Fenwick supporter with the nom de plume of Theophilus urged his co-religionists to seize the opportunity of "a man who offers to represent your district, from which a Roman Catholic never was sent to Congress, and never will be, unless you exert yourself." He also reminded the *Intelligencer*'s readers that the seeds of bigotry had not entirely vanished from the landscape, even in the cradle of American Catholicism. Theophilus therefore posed a challenging rhetorical question to his fellow Catholics in southern Maryland. "Will any man object to your having a representative once in an age," he asked, "to let the world know that you are not extinct?"[23]

Many voters, however, did object. The congressional district that Fenwick sought to represent embraced Calvert, Charles, and St. Mary's counties. Fenwick captured no more than 774 of the 2,600 votes cast, losing heavily even in his home Charles County. The message seemed obvious. However much Catholics gained in civic, social, and business circles, however much their connections might serve them in the executive departments of government, they nevertheless faced the daunting obstacle of their still-small number whenever they ran for higher elective office.

To James Fenwick's credit he continued the struggle at the state level, eventually winning election to the Maryland Assembly for five years. But it was not until 1819, or eleven years later, that another Catholic, Raphael Neale of St. Mary's, about whom very little is known, won a seat in Congress from the same district in which Fenwick had lost. Then, in 1823, two more Maryland Catholics gained the halls of Congress. One, William Leigh Brent of Port Tobacco, should perhaps not be so credited, since he won his seat after moving to Louisiana, a not-uncommon destination for ambitious Marylanders. The other was the aforementioned John Lee of Frederick County, the youngest son of Governor Thomas Sim Lee, who won a narrow victory by 52 votes out of 5,949 cast only to suffer defeat by an almost equally narrow margin in his first bid for re-election two years later. To his credit, he, too, was not above re-entering the more local political scene, winning terms both as a delegate and a senator in the Maryland Assembly.[24]

As might be expected, with such examples in mind, not all members of the older Maryland Catholic families were eager to enter the fray of either national or local politics. Of those who did not, some nevertheless held considerable influence during the early Federal period through close associations with President Washington. These associations they valued highly, since they recognized in the President a man singularly free of religious prejudice. (Best remembered by Catholics were General Washington's stern refusal to allow his troops laying siege to Boston in 1775 to celebrate Guy Fawkes Day, then fast becoming an anti-Catholic folk holiday, and the fact that Washington had twice visited St. Mary's Catholic Church in Philadelphia.)[25] These associations might be purely social in character, as with neighbors from nearby plantations, or with friends from military days. But more often than not they were entrepreneurial, as with investors in the Potomac Company or, what was most important to the President, with the so-called "original proprietors" of the lands essential to the planned city that was to bear his name.

Chief among the original proprietors was Daniel Carroll of Duddington II. Among other relationships he was the stepson of Trinity Church's first fundraiser, Captain Ignatius Fenwick, to whom he often turned for business advice, and the first cousin once removed of Charles Carroll of Carrollton.[26] Daniel Carroll of Duddington owned a large piece of land around and to the south of Jenkins Hill, which had come down to him from the pioneer settlers of the upper Potomac. Its ownership traced back to an 1800-acre grant of 1663, one of the first such by the Lords Baltimore in what is now greater Washington. By the time it passed to Daniel Carroll of Duddington, it is said to have included all but four hundred acres of the original grant. This latter acreage went to his half-uncle Notley Young, another of the original proprietors.

In June 1791, when President Washington succeeded in settling differences among the proprietors and announced the approximate boundaries of the Federal City, Daniel Carroll of Duddington's estates—New Troy, Duddington Manor, and Duddington Pasture—made him the largest single landowner in the newly defined capital. By modern delineation Carroll's holdings and Notley Young's four-hundred-acre portion of Duddington Pasture embraced all of Capitol Hill and considerable areas to the north, south, and west of it; all of Southwest Washington; and that part of Southeast Washington that lies west of the Navy Yard.[27]

Thus when President Washington favored Major Pierre Charles L'Enfant's recommendation to place "the Congress house" atop Jenkins Hill and make it the center of his plan for the capital city, Daniel Carroll of Duddington became the one landowner whose cooperation President Washington most needed. At the same time Carroll also came to be viewed as an unwelcome rival by the Georgetown proprietors who wanted the city much closer to them. Contrary to some earlier views, which portray Carroll as a profit-motivated obstructionist, modern scholarship has revealed him as a civic-minded proprietor who like a number of others suffered considerable loss for his role in the founding of the city of Washington. Carroll's entrepreneurial contributions to the Federal City, which included not only land but also capital investment and developed properties, are treated in Chapter 9. It is enough to note here that under the terms of President Washington's "half-and-half" agreement Carroll made the largest cession of land to the city of any of the original proprietors.[28]

By this agreement the proprietors conveyed all their land in trust to the federal government. The government then took half of their lands to be sold at auctions, which it hoped would finance the construction of the capital city. The half not taken by the government reverted to the proprietors; they were then free to sell it—in uneven competition with the government, as events would prove—once it had been divided into appropriate squares and lots. For land that the government had designated as reserved for public use or public improvement—squares, the Capitol and other government buildings, the Mall—the proprietors were reimbursed at the low rate of £25 (approximately $67) an acre. For lands used for streets and avenues, they received nothing. Daniel Carroll's conveyance was not only the largest; it also included a substantial amount of non-compensated land in the form of avenues and streets radiating from the Capitol.[29]

Thus, *ipso facto*, Daniel Carroll of Duddington cooperated to the full in an arrangement that the President and all concerned thought highly advantageous to the city. In the years that followed, President Washington remained a respectful if not close friend, always treating disputes between Carroll and L'Enfant or Carroll and the Georgetown proprietors with an even hand. Accordingly, although Daniel Carroll of Duddington was a very private person—

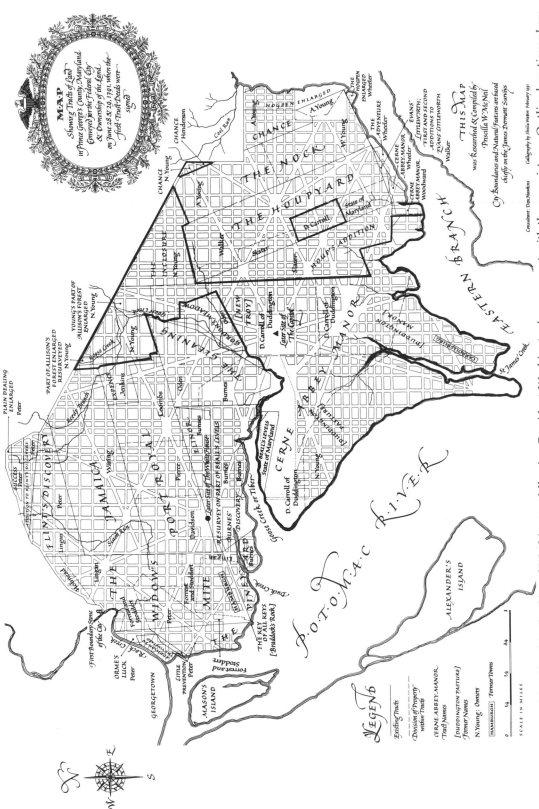

Map showing ownership of land in the City of Washington following President Washington's agreement with the proprietors. Outlined portions show the combined holdings of Daniel Carroll of Duddington and his half uncle Notley Young. The map also shows the boundaries of the city of Washington within the District of Columbia. Research and compilation by Priscilla W. McNeil, design by Don A. Hawkins.

"he saw no company," the British envoy Sir Augustus John Foster once said of him—he welcomed President Washington as one of a few visitors to Duddington Manor. Family records have it that the President enjoyed his brief stays there, usually while traveling to or from Mount Vernon. The President also occasionally did the same at Notley Young's. In this Washington showed his consummate good taste. No less a critic than Augustus John Foster called Duddington Manor and the Young mansion two of only three private gentlemen's houses worthy of mention in all of Washington.[30]

Among other Catholics with whom George Washington had close ties was his long-time friend and aide-de-camp Colonel John Fitzgerald, later mayor of Alexandria, and the Digges family of Warburton, whose country seat lay across the Potomac from Mount Vernon. Described as "an agreeable broad shouldered Irishman," Fitzgerald was a devoted aide to whom Washington entrusted such sensitive tasks as gauging the intentions of Thomas Conway, leader of the opposition forces at Valley Forge that came to be known as the Conway Cabal, or sounding out congressional support when the cabal might have seemed to be gaining force. After the Revolution, Washington rewarded Fitzgerald with what the President undoubtedly thought the boon and privilege of organizing the first subscriptions to the Potomac Company, chartered in 1785 to make the Potomac River navigable as far as Cumberland.

Fitzgerald responded dutifully, serving first on the company's original board of directors and later as its fourth president. He also himself bought three shares at £100 sterling each and persuaded such other Catholic notables as Charles Carroll of Carrollton, Thomas Sim Lee, Daniel Carroll II (the bishop's brother), Daniel Carroll of Duddington, and Notley Young to take greater or lesser amounts of the company's stock.[31] In return Colonel Fitzgerald may have persuaded the President to pledge a subscription to the first Catholic church in Virginia. Washington's diary carries a notation that he dined with Fitzgerald at the colonel's residence in Alexandria on St. Patrick's Day of 1788; there is a tradition that the possibility of building St. Mary's on land donated by Colonel Robert Hooe, Fitzgerald's successor as mayor of Alexandria, was discussed at this dinner and that Washington later contributed to the church.[32]

Whatever the answer, neither Fitzgerald nor Washington lived long enough to see either project come to fruition. Both died in December 1799, within two weeks of each other. At that time the Potomac Company was deep into one of its periodic crises, facing fiscal collapse and the seemingly impossible task of excavating canal locks in the deep bedrock on the Virginia side of the Great Falls. And the first Catholic church in Virginia was no more than an unroofed chapel on a bad road too far from the center of town. Another ten years would pass, in fact, before Father Francis Neale was able to buy the abandoned Methodist meeting house that became the first St. Mary's Church, on the present site, in the heart of Alexandria.[33]

Proximity to Mount Vernon and the American tradition of being neighborly were mainly responsible for Washington's long friendship with the

66   Digges family. Warburton Manor, the family's principal plantation, was situated on a bluff overlooking Piscataway Creek on the Maryland shore of the Potomac, almost directly across from Mount Vernon. During George Washington's time the chief occupant and family patriarch was William Digges, who lived from 1713 to 1783. William Digges was the grandson of Protestant Colonel William Digges, who moved to Maryland and became a Protestant member of the nearly all-Catholic Governor's Council by virtue of marrying Elizabeth Sewall, a step-daughter of Charles, third Lord of Baltimore. This mixed marriage, mentioned in the previous chapter, launched one of the fastest-growing Catholic families of the late colonial and early Federal periods. The grandson William Digges of Warburton, who was George Washington's approximate contemporary, continued the Digges tradition of large families. He and his wife Anne Atwood had four sons and five daughters who among others married Brents, Carrolls, and Colonel John Fitzgerald.[34]

If George Washington had any reservations about visiting such a nest of papists, as his critics would surely have called it, we do not know of them. On the contrary all records of social visits across the river to and from the Diggeses are among the most frequent in Washington's *Diary*, beginning in 1768 and lasting until the end of his life. To add proper circumstance to the crossings, William Digges had a large and ornate barge imported from England, in which, according to Washington Irving, "he always received Washington . . . , rowed by six negroes arrayed in a kind of uniform of check shirts and black velvet caps." With such stately appurtenances the exchange visits were made, in all seasons. (Only rarely were the river crossings halted by cold, wind, or ice.) Still, one wonders if Washington enjoyed them all. Despite the terse and almost impersonal style of most of the *Diary*'s social entries, a suggestion of weariness occasionally surfaces, as for example:

> January 6, 1775. Mr. George Digges and three of his sisters-to wit, Tracy, Nancy, and Jenny, and Mr. Danl. Carroll and Nancy Peake came here and stayed all Night.

Or, more noticeably:

> December 19, 1772. Mr. William Digges and his four Daughters came, as also a Mr. B. Buckner, who bot. flour of me.
> Dec. 20, 1772. All of the above company here all day.
> Dec. 21, 1772. The whole went over to Mr. Digges's. Mrs. Washington, myself &ca., went over with them and stay'd all Night.

Much more to the liking of the squire of Mount Vernon were the times when he "went out a hunting with Mr. George Digges," oldest of the Digges sons, and could record with satisfaction, "Found a fox but did not kill it." So, too, were occasional excursions to Annapolis, scene of some of the best theater, fancy balls, and race meetings of the Atlantic seaboard. Washington might typically begin the journey with a ritual lunch at Warburton and then ride on to Melwood, home of Ignatius Digges near present-day Upper Marlboro, to spend the night. (Ignatius Digges was a nephew of William of Warburton and the father of Mary, wife of Governor Thomas Sim Lee.) Thus refreshed, Washington could easily reach Annapolis the next day.[35]

For Catholics, George Washington's close and continuing friendship with the Digges family undoubtedly represented a valuable channel of communication. For some, like Bishop Carroll, it meant entrée to Mount Vernon and the opportunity to know the Washingtons in relaxed and convivial circumstances. For others, like William Digges's wayward second son Thomas Atwood Digges, Washington's friendship could even mean a way out of trouble. As a young man Thomas Digges was forced to live abroad because of some unknown scandal that dishonored the family. (Bishop Carroll described him to correspondents abroad as someone with the most respectable family connections who "in his early youth . . . was guilty of misdemeanors here, indicating rooted depravity.") Digges first settled in Lisbon where in 1775 he wrote *The Adventures of Alonso,* a lachrymose romance that literary historians now consider the earliest novel written by an American citizen.[36]

But by the outbreak of the Revolution, Thomas Atwood Digges had moved to London, where his flair for the dramatic led him into becoming one of America's first secret agents. In this role he provided valuable intelligence to Benjamin Franklin and John Adams, then the American commissioners in Paris. He also successfully smuggled munitions to the United States in third-country vessels and helped arrange the escape of many American prisoners, especially captured sailors who had been jailed in the notorious Forton Prison in Portsmouth Harbor. All these feats were accomplished only a few steps ahead of the British authorities with whom he was ostensibly working, until the latters' growing suspicion forced him into various disguises and constant changes of address. Joseph Gales, Jr., later a pioneer reporter and co-editor of Washington's *National Intelligencer,* remembered how his father, a British printer who had sold outlawed copies of Thomas Paine's writings, left England with his family in the nick of time "on the friendly warning of Mr. Digges, whom we next met on the banks of the Potomac."[37] Similarly, the Reverend Thomas Wren, a Presbyterian minister at Portsmouth, was extremely grateful for the safe havens in London provided by Digges, to whom he sent many of the destitute sailors he helped to escape from Forton Prison. Yet it was precisely this charitable activity—Digges never received any compensation for his troubles—that led him into deep trouble.

Although Reverend Wren later received the formal thanks of the Continental Congress, Digges got nothing but contumely from a penny-pinching Benjamin Franklin who suspected that Digges had pocketed some of the relief funds that were promised, after many unheeded requests, for the Forton prisoners. Franklin's accusation, which recent investigations have shown to be unjust if not completely false, dogged Digges for many years after the peace.

Even after returning to America, Digges found that his rightful inheritance of Warburton was threatened with confiscation "as the property of an alien." It was at this point that he sought the help of his friend and neighbor, George Washington. The President recalled certain intelligence Digges had sent him, as well as many favorable comments from the persons Digges had helped in England. Washington also praised Digges' post-war efforts to export industrial machines and their inventors to the United States. In sum there was no doubt where the President stood. "I have no hesitation" he wrote, "in declaring that the conduct of Mr. Thomas Digges towards the United States during the War... has not only been friendly, but I might add zealous."[38]

Thomas Atwood Digges had no further problems in claiming Warburton Manor. He settled there, in fact, for the last twenty-three years of his life. These may have been lonely times—all his brothers and one of his sisters had died before his homecoming—but they held certain comforts. Blissfully unaware of what John Carroll had once said of him, he gave the chapel his father had built and some adjoining land to the Archbishop "for the full benefit and use of the Roman Catholic Congregation of Piscattaway." For many years he gave refuge to an ageing and largely forgotten Pierre L'Enfant whose last assignment, never completed, was the strengthening of Fort Warburton, later Fort Washington. ("The old Major is still an inmate with me. . . , " Digges wrote of him to President Monroe in 1816. "I fear from symptoms of broken shoes, rent pantaloons, out at elboes &ca. &ca. that he is not well off—manifestly disturb'd at his getting *the go by* . . . ") Digges also corresponded with Presidents Jefferson and Madison, mainly about inventions and agriculture. And, like his father, he occasionally had the pleasure of quiet moments at Mount Vernon, almost directly across the Potomac.[39]

But for many of the area's Catholics there were no associations with President Washington nor any of the advantages of being a Digges, a Carroll, or a Brent. For them the surest road to public office and peer-group associations was highly localized, or at the level of municipal government. The City of Washington as a planned community in the process of creation offered the greatest possibilities. Accordingly, as we will see in later chapters, Catholics played their most significant role in its foundation. But even the older community of Georgetown—still overwhelmingly Protestant, relatively liberal in outlook, and always dreaming of itself as the gateway to the riches of the West—opened some few doors to Roman Catholics.

Chartered by the Maryland Assembly as a township in 1789, the Corporation of Georgetown, which consisted of a mayor, the ten-member Common Council, the six-man Board of Aldermen, and a host of appointive officials, exercised its own municipal government until well into the nineteenth century, even as it remained part of the District of Columbia. (So, too, did Alexandria, until Virginia "retroceded" or took back its portion of the District in 1846.) Its first mayors—Robert Peter, Thomas Beall, Uriah Forrest, John Threlkeld—were all staunch Presbyterians or Anglicans, drawn from Georgetown's first families and elected annually by a joint ballot of the incumbent and the members of the Board of Aldermen and the Common Council.[40]

Breaking this hegemony, at least for a single term in 1794, was Peter Casanave, a Spanish merchant from Navarre. Casanave, who was the nephew of Juan de Miralles, the Spanish agent to the Continental Congress, arrived in Georgetown in 1785 with £200 in his pockets and many problems with the English language.[41] He apparently first acquired a large stone warehouse on the waterfront from which he sold "salt . . . at the lowest Baltimore prices" for the Potomac's spring herring runs, rum and sugar by either the barrel or the hogshead, Baltimore-inspected pork, and many more exotic items such as "Sweet oils, Spanish sole leather, Hair Powder and Pomatum, fresh and well scented." Five years later he announced the establishment of Georgetown's first nail manufactory, promising nails in many sizes at lower prices than any European imports. Ever the entrepreneur, Casanave in the same year advertised the opening of "a Night Dancing-School for the Reception of Gentlemen who are not at leisure to attend in the Day-Time." (His hair powder and fresh pomatum sales, we may imagine, increased accordingly.)

These various initiatives soon grew to the point where Casanave could join the ranks of Georgetown real estate agents. Beginning in 1790 he was offering such choice properties as the City Tavern on Bridge (now M) Street, the Beall estate in northeast Georgetown (later Charles Carroll's Belle Vue and today's Dumbarton House), and the Robert Allison house on King Street in Alexandria. By the spring of 1791, moreover, Casanave was ready to marry into one of Maryland's oldest Catholic families. To this purpose he wrote his prospective father-in-law Notley Young:

> You Sir as a good prudent & tender Father I make no doubt you will wish to know whome I was before you knew me in George Town & my present Situation in Live for the support of the State I have So long wish to enter to with your Daughter. . . . [42]

Whether the letter's simple conviction or its author's heroic struggle with English syntax was the convincing factor, we do not know. But Notley Young gave his daughter Ann in marriage to the Spanish immigrant. The two were married in September 1791, most probably in the Young family chapel and with the good wishes of Bishop Carroll, who was Ann Young's uncle. The union gained Casanave kinship with many of Maryland's first families, not to mention such gifts as Notley Young's grist mill. (Like so many other fifth- or sixth-generation Maryland Catholics, the Youngs were related in varying degrees to the Brents, the Calverts, the Diggeses, the Fenwicks, and both Carroll families, to mention a few.)

Thereafter, as was customary for a man of his station, Casanave gave due attention to civic pursuits. One was to serve as the sponsor, agent, and banker for a host of Georgetown College's first boarding students. This meant that he received money from parents—there were no commercial banks in Georgetown until 1795—and paid all the students' tuition and boarding charges, down to the last extra bar of soap or broken dish. But since he also played the same role for virtually all foreign students and adults needing instruction in English, some of them destitute refugees from Santo Domingo, his services must often have been provided as a charity. By January 1793 Casanave felt secure enough of his standing in the community to run for the Georgetown Corporation's Common Council. He was duly elected and voted by the other Council members to the Board of Aldermen, as was then the custom. One year later, or some nine years after arriving in the United States, he was elected mayor of Georgetown.

Not much else is known about Peter Casanave. It is recorded that he fathered two children, including a son who attended Georgetown College, and that he died in 1796, less than a year after serving his term as mayor. But the fact that he attained the post at all—as a foreign-born and Georgetown's only Catholic mayor in its first half-century—speaks well enough for Peter Casanave, merchant of Navarre.[43]

More celebrated, perhaps, and certainly better known to more Georgetowners than most mayors or councilmen were the two Maryland Catholics who successively owned the City Tavern, a commodious three-story brick building located near the busy intersection of High (Wisconsin Avenue) and Bridge Streets, where it still stands today. First to occupy it in 1796 was Clement Sewall of the St. Mary's County Sewalls. Sewall had previously owned and operated the better-known Suter's Tavern, famous as George Washington's hostelry and the meeting place for his definitive agreement with the District's proprietors. After a brief interval under Charles McLaughlin, the City Tavern was purchased in 1801 by Joseph Semmes. Semmes, himself the son of an innkeeper and the great-great-grandson of Marmaduke Semmes, also had previous experience as the owner of the Green Tree Inn. Among his guests were William Gaston and others of Georgetown College's first students, before the college was ready to receive them.[44]

Under both Sewall and Semmes the City Tavern became one of Georgetown's finest. In their time, we must bear in mind, the role of a taverner was much more important than it is today. In fact, a late eighteenth-century tavern operator often served his community as a kind of unofficial chief of protocol, since he greeted important visitors, played host to major banquets, provided stage coach and other transport services, acted as postmaster, and frequently gave over his best meeting rooms to serve as city halls. Certainly this was true of both Sewall and Semmes. Sewall, who ran the tavern for three years from its opening in 1796, hosted the meetings of the Georgetown Corporation, as the municipal government was properly known, and the Mayor's Court, for which services he received $40 a year provided "that the said Clement Sewall is to furnish a competency of wood during cold weather and every other necessary when the corporation or Mayor's Court are sitting, or an election is held." Others using the tavern for business meetings included the directorate of the Georgetown Bridge Company and the trustees of the Bank of Columbia, the District's first, which was located in a building next door to the tavern.

During the brief tenancy of Charles McLaughlin, the City Tavern hosted a major banquet for President John Adams when the President came in June 1800 to inspect progress in the construction of Washington. A year later Joseph Semmes purchased the tavern, re-naming it the Indian King. He greatly extended the stagecoach services, begun in Sewall's time, which soon encompassed regular runs to Annapolis, Baltimore, Frederick, and Port Tobacco.[45] The Georgetown Corporation and the Mayor's Court continued to meet at the Indian King, as did volunteer fire companies and "Georgetown inhabitants. . . [wishing] to consult on the proper steps to be taken for the completion of the Pt. Epis. Church in George-Town." Semmes Tavern, as it was just as often called, was also a focal point of Georgetown's commerce. Auctions or sales of houses, ships, commercial buildings, land parcels, horses, and household furnishings were often held there or transacted through the offices of the tavern. So, too, were the sales of slaves, who for the most part were individual household servants.

Semmes's most novel contribution, however, may well have been his efforts to introduce some artistic élan to a busy and mercantile Georgetown. In October 1804 newspapers announced the presence of one Professor Mauro, "lately arrived at Mr. Semmes Tavern," where he was prepared "to teach the German, French and Italian languages . . . [and] to play on the Piano Forte and the Flute . . . having finished his studies in Europe under the tuition of the most eminent masters in this Art." Less than a year later, perhaps with Professor Mauro's arpeggios still ringing in their ears, Georgetowners could go to the Indian King to observe a collection of wax figures "including the late duel between Burr and Hamilton" with organ music accompaniment, all for the sum of fifty cents (half-price for children). Then, in the autumn of 1805, Semmes proudly presented "a Dramatic Performance at the Indian King . . . of the much admired Comedy of the Child of Nature with the Musical entertainment of Rosina." Of how the *Child of Nature* played or Semmes's various cultural initiatives were received, we have no record. But it is clear that if a traveller in the early 1800s wanted to know what was happening in Georgetown, the man to see was Joseph Semmes.[46]

Not many Catholics tried the more formal route to Georgetown's public affairs, or election to the Common Council or Board of Aldermen. The relatively low number of those who did attempt it appears to have been more a by-product of economic status than any deep-seated religious prejudice. For both the elected and appointed officials of the Georgetown Corporation a major qualification was property ownership. Thus it is not surprising to find one of early Georgetown's more prosperous Catholics as the first after Casanave to serve on its council. This was Adam King, brother-in-law of Alexander Doyle and one of Trinity Church's original lay trustees.

King was elected to the Common Council in 1794, or the fourth year of the Council's existence and the same year as Casanave's mayoralty. He subsequently served six terms as an alderman. In 1798 his brother George, also a brother-in-law of Alexander Doyle and a Trinity trustee, joined him on the Council.[47] As mentioned in a previous chapter Adam King was a general merchant and property owner, as was his brother George. Although their holdings might have been slight compared to those of Georgetown's tobacco and shipping aristocracy, the King brothers together owned a respectable number of small houses and lots appraised at approximately £1,000. Their joint service on the Council totalled thirteen years, with much the larger share contributed by Adam, the older of the two. Throughout these early years the King brothers' colleagues on the Council—Robert Peter, John Threlkeld, Ninian and George Beall, Benjamin Stoddert, and Richard Forrest—were nearly all the founding fathers of Georgetown or their next-generation descendants.[48]

Not until 1814 did another Catholic appear on the Georgetown Council's electoral rolls, in the person of Francis Fenwick. Fenwick's qualifications were not so much as a man of property as a member of the old and respected Fenwick family, mentioned in the previous chapter, that had close social and professional ties with the Georgetown Protestant establishment. His father, George Fenwick, had come to Georgetown from St. Mary's County as a surveyor at a time when there was much work to be done in resurveying the original town and its constantly growing additions; among his early clients were John Threlkeld, Thomas Sim Lee, the Beall Family, and Uriah Forrest. The senior Fenwick also found time to write *Fenwick's Arithmetical Essays, or a Plain and Concise Mode of Acquiring in a Short Time a Complete Knowledge of Arithmetic, the Whole Adapted to the Present Time*, which was as good as its promise and a popular and practical textbook of its time. Fenwick also served on Andrew Ellicott's surveying team as it was laying out Washington City according to L'Enfant's plan.

George Fenwick must have been pleased, therefore, when Francis, the only one of his four sons not to enter the priesthood, elected to follow in his footsteps as a surveyor. (Francis's three brothers were Benedict, second pastor of Trinity Church and later bishop of Boston; Enoch, president of Georgetown College from 1820 to 1822; and George, Jr., one of the college's early prefects of studies and professor of classics.) Thus when Francis Fenwick took up his father's local practice he probably had more than enough in the way of family background and professional associations to win the favor of Georgetown's propertied voters. He was elected twice to the Council, in 1814 and 1815. Thereafter, as the Georgetown Corporation seems to have required, he stepped down to accept appointment as the town's surveyor, a position he held for eight years.[49]

Next to be elected to the Council was Joseph Brooks (or Brook, Brooke, Brookes, as the name was interchangeably spelled) one of Georgetown's master carpenter-architects. Brooks, whose seventeenth-century forebears included Baker and Ann Calvert Brooke, married Letitia Boone, herself a member of an old and established Catholic family who were early settlers of Prince George's

County and the builders of the historic Boone Chapel near present-day Rosaryville. The couple settled in Georgetown in 1799, where they raised seven children and Joseph gained a reputation as a builder.

As his father had done before him, Joseph Brooks built some of Georgetown's outstanding residences. His most notable example is Cox's Row, or the five brick town houses on the north side of N Street between 33rd and 34th, which then as now are among Georgetown's most handsome. Brooks was first elected to the Common Council in 1818 and 1819, and again for the years 1825 through 1827. Making good use of his talents, his colleagues named him head of a committee to contract for a fireproof municipal warehouse and other public structures. He also served on the Board of Visitors for Georgetown schools receiving municipal aid.[50]

Other Catholics elected to the Georgetown city government in its earlier years included Charles King, Thomas Wright, John Holtzman, Raphael Semmes, and Bennett Clements. The first three were a lumber merchant, an auction-house manager, and a tax collector, respectively, whereas Semmes and Clements were both descendants of older Catholic families from southern Maryland. Raphael Semmes, a first cousin to Joseph the innkeeper, was one of six sons of Joseph and Henrietta Thompson Semmes of Port Tobacco. After marrying Matilda Jenkins in 1818, he moved to Georgetown with his bride and outdid the Semmes family talent for procreation by having eleven children. Like his father, who bequeathed him considerable acreage in Fauquier County, Virginia, Raphael Semmes engaged in property sales. But he also greatly strengthened his inheritance through such diverse enterprises as shipping, warehouses on Georgetown's Water Street, and a whiskey distillery near Mount Vernon, not to mention directorships of the Potomac Insurance Company and the Farmers and Mechanics Bank.[51]

An active supporter of Trinity parish, Semmes served only two terms on the Board of Aldermen, in 1828 and again in 1830. Quite possibly his family obligations, to say nothing of his business interests, stood in the way of greater participation in Georgetown's government. There was first his own family—six daughters to enroll at Visitation Academy and five sons to send to college—to whom were added some young offspring of his brothers. One, also named Raphael, was the son of Richard Thompson and Catherine Middleton Semmes, both of whom died before he reached fourteen. Young Raphael then spent two years with his namesake uncle before gaining an appointment as a midshipman in the United States Navy in 1826; later generations would know him as a Confederate admiral who won worldwide recognition as a bold and brilliant naval tactician. Another was the son of another brother, Alexander, the owner-master of a Georgetown coasting fleet who is said to have given young Raphael, the future admiral, his first taste for the sea. Four days before Christmas of 1826 and one week after the birth of his third child, Capt. Alexander Semmes set sail on the pride of his fleet, the *Eleanor H. Semmes*, 122 tons burden, named after his wife, the former Eleanor Harrison Beatty. Neither he nor the *Eleanor H. Semmes* was heard of again, victims, no doubt, of a winter storm.

74   Left without a father were three small boys, who appear to have been cared for by both Raphael Semmes and his brother Benedict Joseph, at least until Eleanor Semmes remarried. (By coincidence and in contrast to his more famous first cousin, one of the boys, Alexander Anthony, grew up to have a distinguished naval career in the Union navy, attaining the rank of commodore. Ironically he would meet his cousin Raphael as the two led opposing fleets in the Civil War siege of Richmond.)[52] But if all these obligations weighed on Raphael Semmes and did indeed keep him from a more active public life, he at least had the satisfaction of observing his younger brother Benedict's career and some early signs of promise in two of his sons at Georgetown College.

Benedict Joseph Semmes entered politics at the age of thirty-two, after serving as a respected country doctor in Piscataway, Prince George's County, for over a decade. He first won a seat in the Maryland Assembly in 1821. Four years later he was elected speaker of the House of Delegates, in which office he played a leading role in the passage of a bill abolishing religious tests that since 1776 had barred Jews and other non-Christians from holding elective office. Then, in 1829, running as a Democrat of the anti-Jacksonian faction, Semmes was elected to the United States Congress by a comfortable margin. After serving in the 21st and 22nd Congresses, Semmes stepped down by his own choice and returned to the Maryland Assembly. All this Raphael Semmes must have watched with pride, as well as his son Thomas's graduation from Georgetown College as class valedictorian. (Thomas, who became an outstanding trial lawyer of his time, was elected ninth president of the American Bar Association in 1886; his younger brother Alexander Ignatius was a well-known doctor and an early officer of the American Medical Association.) His later years were divided between a summer home in Virginia and his Georgetown residence, still standing today at 3257 N Street, where he enjoyed companionship and card-playing with such as Henry Clay and Franklin Pierce. There he died in 1846 at the age of sixty.[53]

Bennett Clements, by contrast, gave most of his productive years to Georgetown's government. A ranking clerk in the Treasury Department and a descendant of another large Charles County family, Clements was a member of the Common Council for twelve years, the Board of Aldermen for two, and as a concurrent appointment, a member of the Board of Visitors for seven. His total service, spanning the years 1828-1842, was exceeded by very few.[54] Among those who did was Thomas Corcoran, an Irish immigrant shoemaker who came to Georgetown in 1788. Corcoran was elected to the Council for twenty-two terms and mayor of Georgetown for five, as he progressed from making and repairing shoes for most of the Georgetown College faculty and student body to dealing in commercial properties. Although not a Catholic, Corcoran and his son William Wilson, who became a well-known banker, gave to Catholic cemeteries, the Baptists' Columbian College (later George Washington University), Holy Trinity Church, and both St. John's and Christ Episcopal Churches of Georgetown. Such ecumenical attentions, not altogether unknown in Corcoran's time, cannot but have helped their careers, Thomas as an elected official and William Wilson as a financier.[55]

Catholic or Protestant, the council members generally served with a sense of responsibility and worked diligently when the occasion demanded. Local historians have tended to emphasize their quainter achievements, citing ordinances to prevent "the going at large of Geese and Swine" or requirements that members be eligible to serve only "for so long as they shall behave themselves." But in truth Georgetown's municipal government faced many serious problems. Deprived of the capital they thought would be centered right on their "salubrious heights," Georgetowners were beginning to understand that their future rested with serving as a support community to the grander neighbor that was slowly taking shape to the east of them. Merchants still held to the vision of the Potomac River and the gateway it offered to the west "as the bright prospect before us . . . full of strong assurances that all will yet be well with us."[56] But many of the wiser among them could already see that Baltimore, busily building its national turnpike to the west, was clearly winning the race. Thus Georgetown's early mayors and councilmen had not only to grapple with property assessment, tax rates, public works, and other issues common to most municipalities. In a very real sense they were also constantly addressing the problem of the town's survival. What Georgetown had to do, they soon came to realize, was to make sure the town at least remained a strong commercial center with quality goods and services for the capital.

Examples of efforts in this direction are many. When private warehouses along the waterfront proved too old or potential firetraps, the Council voted for new fireproof public wharves and warehouses at considerable expense. If inns and rooming houses were not clean and well kept, the Council could and did revoke the licenses of offending owners lest the town lose its commuting residents or the numerous travelers coming to view the progress of the capital. (Many federal government executives preferred commuting from Georgetown over early Washington's primitive accommodations, and some congressmen, who had a longer journey, chose to ride the three or four miles to Capitol Hill.) When the Long Bridge and causeway built across the Potomac River in 1809 gradually caused river-borne silt to back up into the ship channels approaching Georgetown, the Council, ever mindful of its rivalry with the port of Alexandria, was more than willing to experiment with a newly invented "Mud Machine" dredge.[57]

Similarly, in recognition of Georgetown's new role as merchandiser to the nation's capital, the Council kept a sharp eye on the quality, measurement, and standards of most of the town's goods and commodities. To this end the Georgetown Corporation appointed an unusually large number of official inspectors. Heading the list was the inspector of tobacco, a post created well before Georgetown's incorporation in 1789. Next in time and importance was the position of inspector for flour, the establishment of which reflected the shift in Georgetown's prime export from the "Maryland yellow fine" that once commanded top prices in European tobacco markets to flours and grains from the upper Potomac Valley farmlands. Then came gauger of spiritous liquors, sealer of weights and measures, weigher of hay, straw, and fodder, measurer of plank and corded wood, inspector of salted provisions (an important post during the Potomac's bountiful spring runs of shad and herring), market master, superintendent of streets, and many others. For the town's greater security there were added captains of the watch, constables, policemen, fire chiefs, and, last but not least, powder magazine keeper.

Many of these positions attracted the town's growing Catholic population, especially for the period from 1820 through the 1840s. During this time a comparison of Trinity Church parish records and a list of corporation jobholders reveals what was soon to become a hallmark of American urban Catholicism—the increasing participation of Catholics in city government. At the upper end of the Georgetown hierarchy were John Holtzman, collector of taxes for more than ten years, and Lewis Carbery, the youngest son of a politically prominent family, who served as a justice of the peace, judge of elections, and the Georgetown Corporation's surveyor. But more typical were John D. Clarke, superintendent of fire engines; Ignatius Newton and Ignatius Clarke, both of whom served as weighers of hay, straw, and fodder; John Moore and Thomas Nowland, as inspectors of salted provisions; Joseph Nevitt, powder magazine keeper; Henry Trunnel, John B. Gray, Zechariah Goddard, and Daniel Ragan, as constables or police; John Connelly and William Dawson as chimney sweeps; and George Mahorney, scavenger (street cleaner) and later superintendent of streets, among those who can be positively identified as Catholics. Their salaries ranged from $400 and $225 a year for inspector of tobacco and clerk of the market, respectively, to $150 and $100 for the police and the town scavenger.[58]

For all its preoccupation with commercial viability the corporation did not neglect social issues. Here its most notable achievement was financial aid to privately operated free schools. Beginning in 1815, when Georgetown was already starting to feel the effects of the post-War of 1812 depression, the Council voted the relatively large sum of $1,000 for the annual support of Georgetown's one Lancaster School. (Lancastrian schools, then gaining acceptance throughout the country, used students to teach other students and to make their own teaching materials, often with no more than one paid teacher.) Then, in January 1832, the council received a petition for aid from the Trinity Church Free School for Boys, which was then experiencing difficulty in providing for its eighty students and two teachers.

At the time of which we speak, it is doubtful that a request for subsidizing a Catholic school would even have been considered by the governing bodies of most major towns and cities of the Atlantic seaboard, since the early 1830s was precisely the time when the era of good feelings of the Federal period was fast giving way to the virulent anti-Catholicism inspired by Protestant tract societies and the nativist movement. Indeed, the time was already at hand when New York City's Common Council had voted to help support Protestant bible studies and religious instruction that denigrated Catholics and Catholicism in the city's public schools. The controversy that would begin there culminated a decade later in Philadelphia with one of the bloodiest riots in American urban history.[59]

To its credit the Georgetown Corporation did not reject the Trinity petition. Rather, Mayor John Cox and the council debated the request on and off for three months, always with civility and often with intelligence. Working in the petitioners' favor, as Mayor Cox pointed out in his opening statement, was the fact that the Trinity Free School received "children of various denominations. . . , a discrepancy of religious creed forming no objection." Those opposed, among whom was Thomas Corcoran, argued that the generous appropriation to the Lancaster School was more than enough to provide a good education for the children of parents who could afford little or no tuition and that a diffusion of funds among several schools would tend to diminish the Lancaster's good effects. Reporting on the Trinity request, Henry Addison of the Board of Aldermen and Bennett Clements for the Common Council spoke of the Free School's ten-year record of educating destitute children and squarely confronted the religious issue by posing a searching question:

> If any portion of our citizens are excluded from a just participation of any investment of the public funds in consequence of a peculiarity of religious faith, a case presents itself which demands the exercise of a tolerating spirit. Such is now the case before us. The real question is, whether a religious sect which has been taxed more than seventeen years to support a free school of whose advantages they could not avail themselves, can now be allowed a small sum of money to assist in defraying the expenses of their one free school, established and supported for more than ten years by their own individual contributions.[60]

The debate was resolved when Alderman Samuel McKinney suggested that as a compromise $200, a sum first suggested by Mayor Cox, be taken from the Lancaster School's annual appropriation in favor of Trinity. Thus, on April 27, 1832, the Georgetown Corporation voted a donation of $200 from its municipal funds to the Trinity Church Free School for Boys. Small as it was, the subsidy was nevertheless something of a landmark. "A remarkable event," Trinity pastor Stephen Dubuisson, confided to his journal. In Rome Father Anthony Kohlmann, a former president of Georgetown College, reported that the world-wide leader of the Jesuits, Father General Jan Roothan, was "highly gratified" upon hearing the news.[61]

That same summer the cholera epidemic that had swept south from New York and Philadelphia reached Georgetown and Washington, taking a heavy toll. By then Georgetown had already struggled through one nationwide depression in 1819 and would soon face another in 1837. The town nevertheless kept itself alive, mainly as a satellite community to a Washington that was now growing much faster and being spared the full brunt of such depressions by its large federal government payroll. In addition, even though the time was one that historians have marked as the return of "Anti-Catholicism . . . as a fixed feature on the American landscape," there is little evidence of such feeling in Georgetown or that the early manifestations of the nativist movement had much effect.[62] Rather, there is more evidence to suggest the contrary, evidence to the effect that Catholics and Protestants worked largely in harmony to maintain their handsome "city on the hill," as Georgetown liked to call itself. "Georgetown is still a *very good place*," Father Steven Dubuisson, pastor of Trinity Church and later president of Georgetown College, wrote to a colleague in 1827, even as he bemoaned Washington's new primacy in population and commerce. What consoled him was the friendly spirit, the almost total acceptance of Catholics in Georgetown, which he linked to the good reputation of Trinity Church, the newly established Visitation Academy, and Georgetown College. The college, he liked to remember, only two years before had seen both President John Quincy Adams and Secretary of State Henry Clay attend its commencement exercises.[63]

There is more. During the same year that Father Dubuisson was convincing himself of Georgetown's basic goodness, an equally telling comment came from Anne Royall, then one of America's most caustic (and widely read) social critics, whose observations of some early Washingtonians eventually brought her to a court trial for being a "common scold." "How much I have heard said about these Roman Catholics!" Mrs. Royall exclaimed after a lengthy tour of Visitation and Georgetown College. "I have heard them stigmatized by every harsh name and accounted little better than heretics. But, I must confess, I never was amongst people more liberal, more affable, condescending or courteous. . . ."[64]

Mrs. Royall, for all her bombast and instant likes and dislikes, was as much on the mark as Father Dubuisson. Although relatively few in number, the public servants among Georgetown's first generation of lay Catholics probably did fully as much to ensure themselves a respected place in society as the town's imposing array of Catholic institutions. Certainly the civic contribution of lay Catholics helped carry the day in the debate over aid to Trinity's Free School. "There are few towns perhaps which would not be willing to receive such benefits and avail themselves of every suitable opportunity to reward the exertions of these humane and public-spirited people," the Board of Aldermen's committee report had concluded, as it attempted to summarize the Catholic contribution to Georgetown.[65] In short, civic participation—of the Mahorneys, Connellys, and Ragans as much as the Semmeses, Brookes, and Fenwicks—was winning for the church an early and remarkable acceptance.

It would continue, we will see, through good times and bad.

PART II
The Church

5

"A Church So Crowded . . ."

He added to the building two lateral wings, or chapels, which though very little in harmony with the original plan were nevertheless indispensable to accommodate the affluence of people coming from every part of the country.

-ALOYSIUS ROCCOFORT, S.J.
"Essai on the History of Trinity Church"

In August 1804 a young Irish immigrant named John McElroy was making his first trip to Washington by stagecoach from Baltimore. McElroy, later destined to be the assistant pastor who found it necessary to build Trinity Church's unsightly lateral-wing chapels, wondered about the length of the trip as the long summer day wound down into the cool of the evening. With still no sight of the capital he asked the driver when they might reach the City of Washington. "Why, Sir," the driver is said to have answered, "you have been riding through it for the last two miles."[1]

There was reason enough for young McElroy to ask. In 1804 the City of Washington could show little to warrant its formal name. To be sure, some progress had been made to meet the minimum requirements set by Congress in 1790 as necessary to the transfer of government from Philadelphia. The President's House, as the White House was first called, gave reasonable comfort to the widower Thomas Jefferson, although its roof sometimes leaked. One wing of the projected Capitol building on Jenkins Hill was all that was ready to shelter some thirty-four senators and one hundred and forty representatives. To the east of the President's House was the Treasury Building, housing both Treasury officials and most of the State Deparment's still-small staff. To the west was a barely finished War Office. Surrounding these structures, for the most part, was a mosaic of open farmlands, meadows, and forest, spread over the gently rolling hills of the piedmont and the adjoining flatlands bordering the Potomac River. Only here and there was there visible evidence of the city's painfully slow growth as a place of homes and people—a row of houses on Capitol Hill, a block along F Street to the east of the Treasury, or the so-called Seven Buildings of Pennsylvania Avenue. For the rest Washington was the "city of magnificent distances," in the words of its many critics. Magnificent and empty, to be more accurate.

No such problems hindered neighboring Georgetown, however, much less its new Catholic church. In the first quarter of the new century Georgetown's population grew from an estimated three thousand in 1800 to more than eight thousand in 1827, by which time the Georgetown Corporation seems to have thought the town might be suffering from overcrowding. The Corporation's annual report for that year complained of the difficulty of keeping current the count of the town's taxable dwellings since "many of the lots have from five to ten houses" on each. "We may reasonably suppose," the report nevertheless concluded, "that there are between 1100 and 1300 houses."[2]

But during the same approximate period, all available evidence suggests that Trinity's congregation grew at a faster rate than Georgetown's population. Although there are no total parish counts from Trinity's early years, as noted earlier, the increase in the number of baptisms and marriages in the church's first ten years was more than threefold. By March 1806, in fact, Pastor Francis Neale found the crowding in the small church reaching an intolerable level. Moreover, the college was beginning to complain about the continued use of its chapel in Old South for confessions and weekday masses, let alone the possibility of receiving overflow parishioners from Trinity who could not be accommodated there on Sundays. Neale therefore proposed that "two convenient confessionals be built adjoining the Church, which at the same time may serve as proper recepticals for the church Vestments and ornaments of the altar." Typically, Neale ordered most of the building materials, apparently paid for them out of his own pocket, and then told the congregation of his plan, even as he solicited the help of one and all to complete it.[3]

There are no records of an immediate response to Pastor Neale's plea. We may be certain, however, that the congregation continued to grow with an "affluence of people coming from every part of the country," as Trinity's first historian correctly described the expanding parish.[4] In the church's first decade the number of baptisms and marriages recorded for out-of-town parishioners almost equalled those for Georgetown residents. To these must be added the families of students at Georgetown College, many of whom also came from great distances to see their young. In Trinity's early years the Diggeses of Warburton and Melwood, the Brents of Woodstock, the Semmeses of Piscataway, the Fenwicks of St. Mary's County, and the Boarmans of Charles County all had sons, nephews, or other young relatives studying at Georgetown. It would be surprising indeed if these families, inheritors of the best traditions of colonial Maryland Catholicism, did not include worship at Trinity with every visit to the college.[5]

The reasons why Trinity initially grew so quickly and had such a broad geographic appeal are not hard to find. First, Georgetown and Washington grew steadily after the turn of the century, when construction of the capital city and an expanding federal government quickened the pace of population increase. Add to this the fact that St. Patrick's of Washington was still housed temporarily "in a little frame building," as one contemporary account described it, where it would remain until 1809. Thus for the first decade of the nineteenth century, Trinity was the principal center of public worship for Catholics over a large part of what we now designate as greater Washington. Regular *public* worship, we should perhaps emphasize, since a survey of the area in 1800 would also have revealed various country estates with private chapels that occasionally served as mass houses for nearby neighbors whenever a priest was available. These were in effect proto-churches. The oldest of them was Queen's Chapel, located on present-day Queen's Chapel Road in the suburb of Langdon about a mile-and-a-half east of Catholic University. This chapel may have been built as early as the 1750s on the one-thousand-acre estate of Richard Queen, an early settler of Prince George's County who, among other distinctions, was a great-grandson of Giles Brent and his Indian princess Mary Kittamaquand.[6]

At some distance to the northwest in Rock Creek, Maryland, was the private chapel of the widowed Eleanor Darnall Carroll to which her son John, the future bishop, returned in 1774. Some time between the outbreak of the Revolution and 1787—it is impossible to be more precise—the popularity of Carroll's itinerant ministry in rural Montgomery County and neighboring Virginia caused him to build a separate frame chapel about a half-mile from his mother's chapel.[7]

Much closer to St. Patrick's and within the limits of the original City of Washington were the manor chapels of Daniel Carroll of Duddington and Notley Young. The former, on the slopes of Jenkins Hill, was first used in 1794, but not completely finished under Benjamin Latrobe's direction until 1797. By contrast, the Young mansion may have been built as early as 1756. By the turn of the century it had grown into what was probably the most popular and accommodating of early Washington's mass houses. The mansion itself was spacious, with a number of parlors and great halls that might be used for Sunday services. It was also beautifully located on a bluff overlooking the Potomac "which furnished a view up and down the river as far as the eye could reach." Then, too, the Young family customarily invited communicants to eat in "the servants' dining room, where the commonality dined after Mass in the mansion, while the gentry dined above."[8]

Many of these mass houses continued to serve as such long after the prohibition of public worship by Catholics was repealed by the Maryland Declaration of Rights of 1776. But the friends and neighbors who frequented these houses considered themselves fortunate to be able to celebrate mass more than once every one or two months. Not even Duddington or the Young mansion could count on an assigned priest who might be expected to make regularly scheduled visits. Thus the early attraction of Trinity, St. Patrick's, and the other churches that were to follow them. They were the only places where the area's Catholics might be sure of regular public worship, where they might first experience a true sense of congregation. Small wonder, then, that they grew so quickly. Indeed, it is tempting to try to visualize what Trinity's parish comprehended in the first years of its existence. Certainly a bird's-eye view high above Georgetown on a fine Sunday morning would have revealed many small

84   clusters of coaches, wagons, and riders travelling along dusty country roads towards the "salubrious heights" to the west of the town. Once there we may picture them converging on the plain brick church of Lot 72, like iron filings to a magnet.

But, few as these first churches may have been, fewer still were the priests to serve them. As nearly as can be ascertained from church records, Father Francis Neale had no regular assistants from 1795 to 1807. But even though this was a period of critical growth for Trinity, Neale had also to serve—to make "stations" it was commonly called—at some of the outlying house chapels mentioned above. John Carroll's chapel in Rock Creek, for example, was first served by priests from Trinity and Georgetown College, often as a way station en route to Frederick. The Carroll chapel itself became a center from which other stations were made to attend smaller congregations in upper Montgomery County. Queen's Chapel survived three burnings and reconstructions over the course of most of the nineteenth century, attended all the while by priests from Trinity, Georgetown College, and later St. Patrick's of Washington. St. Mary's of Alexandria was by Bishop Carroll's direction a "mission" of Trinity from its inception in 1794 until 1818, at which time it received its first resident pastor. From Alexandria, moreover, attempts were made to attend congregations in Fairfax and Falls Church. Thus did the network expand.

Thus, too, did the first churches of the capital area evolve, as the fast-growing congregations at the various stations themselves built small chapels, which in time might become permanent churches. From its humble beginnings in Eleanor Darnall Carroll's home, the Carroll chapel two centuries and three buildings later has become today's St. John's the Evangelist at Forest Glen, Silver Spring, Maryland. From the ashes of the thrice-burned Queen's Chapel has risen present-day St. Francis de Sales.[9]

Seldom was this expansion easy, however, or the orderly progression that the simple telling of it suggests. Unfortunately, the greatest difficulties occurred at St. Mary's of Alexandria, which as the first Catholic church in Virginia was Trinity's most challenging mission. For all the time it remained in an unfinished building too far from the center of town, St. Mary's appears to have proved too great a discouragement for the priests who were supposed to visit it at least once a fortnight. Among these was the Reverend John Thayer, the Boston-born and Yale-educated Unitarian whose conversion in Rome in 1783 caused a national stir. Bishop Carroll had promised him the congregations of St. Mary's, Boone's Chapel, and the Digges chapel at Piscataway, but Thayer's vaunted missionary zeal was not strong enough to cause him to leave Georgetown and live anywhere near his congregations, much less give them his exclusive attentions. After some among them complained, a deeply disappointed Carroll told Thayer he had fully "expected opposition to your residence on the side of the river opposite to that on which much the greater part of your flock live."[10]

After Thayer's departure in 1796, Reverend Notley Young, Jr., the son of Notley Young by his first wife Jane Digges, gave Carroll similar concern.

Young, of whom it was said he never wished "to be out of hearing of the Capitol bell," claimed that he was so discouraged by the lack of congregational support at the out-of-the-way and "dismantled" chapel at Alexandria that he notified Carroll after the fact of his resignation and his resolve "to leave the Congregation to meditate on its own blindness and folly."[11]

The problem even appears to have continued well after Pastor Neale purchased the former Methodist meeting house in the heart of Alexandria in 1809 and the subsequent assignment of a resident pastor in 1818. As late as 1830 the trustees at St. Mary's complained to Archbishop Whitfield of Baltimore that they had "been subjected to a variety of Priests, one presenting himself one week, another the next &c, and for some weeks none at all." Given such difficulties at Alexandria, we may assume the stations at Fairfax and Falls Church suffered even greater neglect.[12]

A somewhat better situation prevailed in the rural missions of Montgomery County, thanks largely to the British-born Jesuit Robert Plunkett. It was he, the reader may remember, who was Carroll's choice as a temporary first president of Georgetown College. But Plunkett's expressed desire in coming to America was to be a missionary. Although he was retained at the college in one capacity or another after his two-year presidency ended in 1793, his missionary fervor was given some scope when he was permitted the management of congregations at Rock Creek, Rockville, Seneca, Barnesville, and Holland's River. These places he visited as often as he could on long rides from Georgetown. Plunkett's successor James Redmond, a young priest both newly ordained and newly arrived from Ireland, was able to do much better by establishing his residence at what became St. Mary's of Rockville in 1813. From Rockville Redmond was much closer to the center of all his other congregations. Even so, however, he calculated that he once traveled 1,972 miles on horseback over a ten-month period in an effort to give regularity to some of his visits.[13]

But Redmond's circuit was relatively short and well-defined compared to the vast region assigned to Father Francis Malevé, a Belgian-born priest who had come to Maryland by way of the Jesuit novitiate at Dunabourg, Latvia. In 1817 Malevé was reported to be attending six large congregations in between his base in Frederick and the frontier town of Cumberland 110 miles away, as well as four smaller congregations scattered over what are now the states of Maryland, Virginia, and West Virginia. Though he rode the circuit hard and without complaint, Malevé, like so many other priests, was deeply disturbed by the number of unchurched Catholics he could not possibly reach and the thought that many might forever be lost to the faith. Unlike the others, however, Malevé came up with an entirely original solution to the problem. In a report to Archbishop Maréchal he told how a "great many families are gone and are going every year from Virginy and Maryland to the Western Countries I encouraged them to go from Virginy, because great many Catholics have losed their relligion about Winchester and in other places."[14]

What Father Malevé expected those he encouraged to find farther west in the forests of Appalachia, he did not say. Unless, perhaps, he was dreaming of the pioneer Catholic settlements in Kentucky, half the known continent away.

All these difficulties in meeting the challenges of the expanding network were in fact but a local manifestation of the church's most pressing national problem. As the reader has surely surmised, this was a serious and chronic shortage of priests. Wherever John Carroll looked there were more "applications from every part of the United States, North, South & West, for Clergymen, and considerable property . . . [offered] for their maintenance," as he had first written Charles Plowden in 1785.[15] Fifteen or more years later, after the turn of the century, the situation was no better. There might be far more congregations forming, but the number of priests qualified and ready to serve them was proportionately less. The supply, as modern business terminology would have it, was not keeping pace with the demand. Under the circumstances the church's heavy reliance on foreign-born clergy is entirely understandable as a stopgap measure born more of necessity than design. Many foreign priests would bring luster to the church: Louis William DuBourg, Benedict Flaget, and Peter DeSmet in western expansion, for example, or Anthony Kohlmann and John Grassi in higher education. Others simply "washed up on these shores," as critics said of the uninvited priests, not a few in number, who came on their own to America to look for greener pastures. As it happened, many of the latter gravitated towards urban parishes where they played a disproportionately large role in the factionalisms that so plagued Carroll's efforts to build an American church.

In addition, if these common problems were not enough, there was also one of a particularly local and unique character. Historically, it stemmed from the fact that Maryland, as the only pre-revolutionary "Catholic colony," emerged as the one state in the new republic with a significant native priesthood. Small though their number may now seem, the American-born priests residing in southern Maryland were virtually the only domestic resource Carroll and other church leaders could tap to help them achieve their priority task of creating a national clergy. The southern Maryland priests, however, for the most part preferred to remain where they were.

Where they were, almost without exception, was on their great manor farms and estates, which dated from the time of the Lords Baltimore. Thus began what was to be a long-lasting dispute within the church over rural-versus-urban concentration of effort. (Within the Jesuit order, after its restoration, the dispute also engendered debates over whether or not its Maryland members who were no longer either missionaries or educators should continue in their roles of rural parish priests and slave-holding landholders.) It was not an easy question, even for Bishop Carroll. "It is impossible and cruel to abandon the Congregations already formed to go in quest of people to be established in new ones," he had first written to Plowden. Then, when the first waves of Irish immigrants began coming to the cities, it was almost more than Carroll's preoccupations and his Anglophile predilections could bear. ("The new emigrants from foreign parts introduced a licentiousness of manners," he later wrote of them, "which exposed the Catholic Religion to the reproach of its enemies.")[16]

But to his credit John Carroll knew where his duty lay. Not Georgetown, not Philadelphia, but Baltimore, the fastest-growing city of the day and the focal point for all Irish and German immigration to the mid Atlantic states, was his unquestioned choice for his episcopal residence. Unfortunately the same cannot be said of Carroll's first bishop coadjutor, Leonard Neale, who balked at going to Philadelphia and instead persuaded Carroll to let him serve as regional bishop for Washington and the nearer counties of Maryland and Virginia. Within this small area, Leonard Neale strongly supported the southern Maryland priests and their desire to remain on their rural manors. In fact, by 1813 the British missionary Robert Plunkett complained that there was but one pastor in the whole of suburban Montgomery County and half of Frederick County, whereas the southern counties of Charles and St. Mary's had no less than fifteen pastors. With exquisite sarcasm Plunkett wrote his friend and colleague Benedict Fenwick: "Verily Bishop Neale in the *singleness* of his eye to discharge of his duty and the best interest of his small share of the Diocese has done well. Too well, I think."[17]

Yet the network held. It held mainly through the steadfast convictions of lay Catholics who gathered together their resources, built small churches, and waited patiently for the day when a hard-pressed hierarchy might assign a resident pastor. "If it be asked how these churches are built and supported," John Grassi wrote of the countryside in general in a thoughtful report on the state of the church in the United States in 1818, "I answer, that it is generally done by the voluntary contributions of the faithful who subscribe a certain amount for the building. When the church is built all who wish to have the exclusive right to a seat pay a trifling amount, which helps to support the church and pastor."[18]

More often than not, however, the pastor might be years in coming. Meanwhile, the faithful had to be satisfied with the attentions of circuit riders who often arrived on short notice. It is difficult today to imagine the intensity of a circuit-riding priest's typical Sunday visit. Each might last seven or eight hours, during which time mass was said, infants and converts baptized, penitents confessed, couples married, the dead buried, and, if time permitted, the young instructed. If some in the congregations had died between visits or at distant points, their families were given handfuls of consecrated earth to take home and scatter over their graves. The long day done, the priest was nearly always asked to venture out into the night to administer extreme unction to the seriously ill.[19]

But, eventually, resident pastors were found, souls were saved, and churches took root, from Fairfax and Falls Church to Rock Creek and Barnesville. It would be hard to say who was more relieved, the congregations who suffered "one priest one week, another the next and for some weeks none at all," or the priests themselves, so weary of travel.

Hard as the lot of the country priest may have been, however, it would be wrong to assume that urban pastors had any easier time of it. If in the country the difficulty was how to bring the church to the faithful, in the cities it was how to keep the faithful, who soon came in overwhelming numbers, from turning away from the church. These sudden numbers, as every reader of Catholic history knows, were the result of urban immigration, or more specifically the first waves of what John Carroll early foresaw as the problem "of the [immigrant] Catholics who pour in upon us in large numbers from various European countries." Even in Georgetown, relatively small though it was, Pastor Francis Neale had to concern himself with the town's swelling Irish and German Catholic populations, as well as an unusually large number of African Americans, both slave and free. The vanguard of the latter, who might better be termed involuntary immigrants, had come to Georgetown as part of the households of the older Catholic families who had moved up from southern Maryland. From the relatively large number of baptisms and marriage meticulously registered by Father Neale—there were 111 black marriages and baptisms against 254 for whites in the church's first decade—we may assume that slaves and free blacks constituted approximately one-third of Trinity's first congregation. They remained at this level, moreover, until the middle of the nineteenth century.[20]

"Charity to negroes is due from all, particularly [from] their masters," Francis Neale reminded his parish. "As they are members of Jesus Christ, redeemed by his precious blood, they are to be dealt with in a charitable, Christian, paternal manner, which is at the same time a great means to bring them to their duty to God and therefore to gain their souls. . . . "[21]

In these few words Pastor Neale distilled the essence of what the church at large had to say about slavery in America at the beginning of the nineteenth century. If on the one hand the church basically condoned the institution (or collectively did little to do away with it), on the other it always urged its members toward charity and a paternalistic concern for blacks. And, although genuinely moved by black spirituality and a desire to improve the conditions of slavery, some priests and lay Catholics alike saw mutually beneficial effects in the church's concern for slaves. Their view, in fact, approached the purely pragmatic. Good Catholic blacks, some maintained, made good slaves. Even such a progressive as John Grassi exhibited this duality, quite common in his day, when he wrote:

> I ought not to pass over in silence the very great consolation which the negroes bring to the missionary; for amongst them, although they are poor slaves and so abject in the eyes of the world, are found chosen souls filled with such beautiful sentiments of true piety, that they move one to tears, and the missionary himself is encouraged to work for the glory of God. The frequent offering of their labors to the Lord, patient endurance of ill-treatment from hard masters, obedience for the love of God, the recitation of the beads when it is possible, these are the devotions chiefly

recommended to them, and which they chiefly practise; consequently, Catholic slaves are preferred to all others, because they are more docile and more faithful to their masters.[22]

However strange, however alien to the rights of man such a mixed statement may now seem, the paternalism that inspired it was none the less real and, in its limited way, an effective force for better treatment and the religious instruction of slaves. As with so many forces in the area's history, the roots of this paternalism began in southern Maryland on the great Jesuit estates. Recent studies of the subject now generally conclude that throughout most of the colonial period the Jesuit fathers showed more spiritual concern for their slave charges and gave them somewhat better treatment than was the norm in the Maryland planter culture of which they were part.

Among the principal differences on the Jesuit farms were days off during which the slaves might tend their own garden plots (and in some cases sell the produce thereof), cash payments for digging ditches or other hard labor not part of the normal plantation rounds, and strong encouragement to observe the sacraments of baptism, marriage, and extreme unction. (Never allowed, for example, was the rustic marriage ceremony in which couples jumped over a broomstick, condoned and sometimes encouraged on other plantations.) At St. Inigoe's Manor, the Reverend Joseph Carbery, a brother of Washington Mayor Thomas Carbery, allowed slave families to rent larger plots of land at the low fee of $1.25 an acre. The families were then free to work the land for their own profit.

Above all, the Jesuit managers made strong efforts to prevent married slaves and family members from being separated by sale or exchange. At Whitemarsh, in fact, managers pledged that no slaves would ever be sold from the manor "except such as shall shew themselves disobedient to the overseer, rebellious and incorrigible." Although not entirely successful, these efforts often meant that the Jesuit manors might buy slaves they did not need or sell others that they did solely to keep families together.[23]

The Jesuits' treatment of their slaves did not go unnoticed. Much of what was done on the Jesuit farms had some influence on the practices of Maryland Catholic slaveholders. Peter Guilday, the nineteenth-century Catholic historian, considered this influence one of the Jesuits' most significant achievements, since "in a splendid degree they accomplished something . . . perhaps unique in our colonial annals: they aroused, created and made firm in the hearts of Maryland Catholic colonists, men and women, their supreme duty of teaching the Negroes by word and example the doctrines and discipline of our Faith."[24]

Whether or not later ages would agree with Guilday's encomia, there is little doubt that the faith acquired by southern Maryland black Catholics stood firm through succeeding generations and their transport to Georgetown or Washington. It is not unusual, in fact, to find strong echoes of the southern plantation culture in the records of Trinity Church, as in:

May 2 1797   Married Edward Butler a free negro to Bett a slave belonging to Mr. Clement Sewall at the special request of Mr. and Mrs. Sewall in the presence of Miss Susana Sewall, Miss Mary Sewall, Mr. John Carbary & many others

Or:

1797 30 April   Gave the rights of the Church to Richard having rec'd Baptizm about 15 months old born of Sarah slave of Mr & Mrs Peter of Georgetown God Mother Lucy Butler

The first entry is reminiscent of the plantation wedding in which an owner celebrates the marriage of a particularly valued slave who has been "like a member of the family." In this case owner Clement Sewall, whose City Tavern was then at the height of its popularity, had more cause to celebrate than usual, since as we will see his slave Bett was marrying a free person from a notable black family. Sewall and his wife therefore apparently made an occasion of it by inviting their daughters, who typically might have grown up with Bett; friends such as John Carbery, older brother to both Georgetown's surveyor and a future mayor of Washington; and, as the entry has it, "many others." The second entry records the baptism of a child born of a Catholic slave belonging to a Protestant family, in this case of Robert Peter, the first mayor of Georgetown.

There are many such instances of black Catholics in servitude to well-known Protestants—to the Benjamin Stodderts, the John Threlkelds, the Charles Worthingtons, for example—in the Trinity baptismal and marriage registers. They occur in such number, in fact, as to suggest that Georgetown's black Catholics, like others of their time, made strong efforts to stay with their original churches. For slaves this was not only a matter of conviction; it was also one of the few ways available to them to strengthen both their individuality and their sense of cultural identity.[25]

Helping to do this, in great measure, were two remarkable African-American women. Even a casual reader of Trinity's early records will be surprised by how many times the names of Lucy and Liddy Butler appear as godmothers at the baptisms of both slave and free blacks. They and other Butlers appearing in the registers were members of a large but tightly knit family with a history that is unique in the annals of Maryland slavery, if not all the colonies.

Lucy and Liddy Butler's earliest forebear was Eleanor Butler, better known as Irish Nell, a white indentured servant brought to Maryland in 1661 by Charles Calvert, third Lord Baltimore, and engaged by Calvert's good friend Major William Boarman. By 1681, well free of her indenture, Nell Butler announced her intention to marry one Negro Charles, a "salt water" slave from the West Indies, who was the property of first the Boarman and then the Sanders families of Charles County. It is on record that Lord Baltimore came to Irish Nell on the day of her wedding and "said to her what a pity, likely a

young Girl as you should fling herself away so as to marry a negro" and, according to the same witness, warned her that by marrying Charles she would
make slaves of her children. "My Lord asked her how she would like to go to
Bed to a Negro," another witness to the event reported, "[but] she answered
him that she rather go to Bed to Charles than his Lordship."[26]

Nell Butler thereupon married Charles—with the ill wishes of both Major
Boarman and Lord Baltimore, we may well imagine—and settled down to a
long and useful life serving the various communities in which she lived as a
cook and a midwife. Little more might have been heard of her and Charles but
for the fact that their children and grandchildren always held their parentage
in mind and kept aware of the changes in laws affecting slaves. After some seventeenth-century legislation was amended to allow freedom to the children of
free white women married to slaves, William Butler, a grandson of Charles and
Irish Nell, and his wife Mary sued their owner, Richard Basil Boarman, a
grandson of Major William, for their freedom. John Hall, a prominent Annapolis lawyer with long service in the Maryland Assembly, represented the Butlers
and won a favorable decision in the autumn of 1770, after a long and drawn-
out trial. But the following spring Richard Boarman appealed. The appeals
court overturned the decision on legal technicalities.

Nothing daunted, the next generation took up the case in the person of
Mary Butler, a daughter of William and Mary, who brought suit again seventeen years later. Arguing for Mary Butler on this occasion was Jeremiah Town-
ley Chase, another distinguished Annapolis lawyer who often represented his
better-known cousin Samuel, a signer of the Declaration of Independence and
later a Supreme Court justice. For the first time Chase invoked Nell Butler's individual rights as an English subject and the injustice and cruelty of passing on
penalties to innocent generations of offspring. The court decided in favor of
Mary Butler on October 3, 1787, but in 1791 the case was appealed yet again.
This time Chase's previous eloquence and changing attitudes towards slavery
carried the day. The decision, finally, was upheld.[27]

By the time Trinity Church opened its doors two years later all the Butlers
who could prove descent from Charles and Nell were eligible for freedom.
Among them were Lucy and Liddy Butler. Everything in Trinity's records suggests that these two women did more to bring together a strongly committed
black Catholic community than the combined efforts of the church itself or the
white laity. In the course of the church's first twenty-five years Lucy Butler,
clearly identified as a free woman in the Trinity registers, served as godmother
to twenty-seven children and Liddy Butler for thirty-eight. Adding other members of the extended family, the Butlers accounted for more than thirty percent
of all black baptismal sponsorships during the same period.

Other black women also exercised a strong leadership role, whether in
observance of the sacraments or in joining Trinity's first sodalities. Following
the Butlers closely were George and Patience Siboure, both identified as free,
who served as sponsors for more than thirty children during the same time.
They and the Butlers obviously cast a wide net, since many of the families

whose infants they sponsored were slaves of distant owners such as Notley Young at the opposite end of the District or others from upper Montgomery County. They also gave as much attention to the children of slaves as they did to children of free blacks, with no trace of any of the elitism that contemporary historians claim to have found among free blacks vis-à-vis their slave brothers. Similarly, the Butlers and the Siboures did not shy from sponsoring "natural children," as illegitimates were called, lest they be lost to the church.

Nor were the Butlers, Siboures and other African Americans alone in their efforts. A number of slaves—Rebecca of Thomas Sim Lee, Susanna of William Digges, Sarah of George Fenwick—also served repeatedly as baptismal sponsors in Trinity's early years. Some few whites, too, appear in the sponsorial role, although they seem to have been preferred as witnesses at weddings.[28]

In sum, the impression is one of a mixed congregation with white members who were apparently much concerned with the spiritual welfare of the blacks, even as they appear to have insisted on separate facilities for them. Among the latter was the upstairs gallery for "the colored," probably dating from Francis Neale's time, which could be reached only by an outdoor stairway. Then, too, even though pastor Joseph De Theux encouraged African Americans to join Trinity's first confraternity from its inception in 1822 (known as the Confraternity of the Living Rosary, it numbered 130 blacks or thirty-four percent of its total membership in its first fifteen years), the fact that separate membership lists were kept and separate white and black presidents appointed strongly suggests that this and succeeding confraternities and sodalities were segregated from the start. Even so, black commitment to these and similar organizations was always strong. Strengthening this commitment, no doubt, was Trinity's regard for the religious education of the young, witness one of the area's earliest Sunday schools for black children started by Father John McElroy in 1819.[29]

Against such a background the black congregation continued as a prominent part of Trinity Church. It grew in proportion to the church's growth, but no more than that, remaining at the same level of approximately thirty percent of the whole from the 1790s until after the Civil War, when it started to decline. Whether this was more the result of post-war dislocations or dissatisfaction with the long history of segregated facilities, we do not know. In any case by the first quarter of the twentieth century no more than 357 African Americans were counted as regular parishioners of Holy Trinity Church, as it was then called. These 357 apparently left en masse in 1923 when the Josephite Fathers offered them a church of their own, to be known as Epiphany Catholic Church, in the eastern reaches of Georgetown. Thereafter, to all practical purposes the black congregation of Holy Trinity was no more.[30]

No such decline or exodus ever affected the Irish at Trinity. Although outnumbered by descendants of the old-line Catholic families of southern Maryland when Trinity first opened its doors, the early Irish of Georgetown and Washington—early in the sense that they came well before the great waves of the 1830s and 40s—soon became the congregation's largest national-descent group. Not all of them, moreover, conformed to the traditional stereotype of the uneducated Irish immigrant. Some came as respected professionals. Others had the means to establish themselves as merchants and traders. Outstanding examples include James Hoban, a classically trained architect of whom we will hear much more in the next chapter, and the previously mentioned Doyle brothers, Alexander and James, who combined property sales with printing, newspaper publishing, and general merchandising.[31]

The professions were even better represented by second and third generation Irish-Americans whose parents had come to Maryland before the Revolution. Not untypical was the family of General Thomas Carbery, Sr., an officer of the Revolution and a Georgetown resident who became a principal supplier of heavy timber and other construction materials for Washington's first government buildings. Among his five sons were a naval architect, a justice of the peace who was also a surveyor, an army captain who later became a mayor of Washington, and a Jesuit priest.[32]

But far more typical of the swelling tides were the indentured household servants so often advertised as "just arrived from Cork" in the Doyle brothers' *Georgetown Weekly Ledger* or the laborers for some of Washington's most ambitious public works projects. The demand for laborers was so great that in 1792 the District of Columbia Commissioners anxiously asked the captains of ships bringing Irish immigrants to the busy port of Baltimore to be sure to let the latter know that "as they may be at some loss for employment, we think it would greatly promote the Interests of the City if they could be informed of the Prospect[s]. . . ."[33]

The prospects were not always as advertised, however. The uncertain nature of Washington City's growth, whether from the failure of property auctions or irregular funding by Congress, caused many of the earliest laborers and artisans to face long intervals of idleness and consequent impoverishment. Their condition appears to have gone unnoticed or at least unrecorded by most of the city's officials, whose overriding preoccupation was getting the capital built on schedule. The exception was architect Benjamin Henry Latrobe, whose social observations on early Washington are among the best written and most perceptive we have. In particular, one strange incident moved Latrobe to write his most poignant and compassionate portrayal of the plight of the capital's labor force. It is so described, in his journal for August 12, 1806:

> Bishop Carol (*one of the best Men in the world*) being here, I walked a little before Sunset to Mr. Brent's to see him. As I passed over the uninhabited part of the town between the Capitol and his house, which is a low swampy piece of ground covered with Bushes, a tall middle aged woman popped out upon me from a cross road with a Gun in her hand. As I was then thinking, certainly not upon a *Gun* in the hand of a woman, I started a little back. "Sir," says she, "pray for god's sake buy this piece of me." There was a wildness in her look, which induced me to think her crazy. I

therefore took the Gun from her, and putting the Ramrod into it, found it was loaded.

The woman, it turned out, was genuinely frightened to discover her gun in such condition, and Latrobe, after setting her more at ease with a pleasantry, found her explanation neither wild nor improbable. She was the widow of a worker who had come to Washington with some means, but now she was left in destitution with several small children. A long summer drought had prevented her from growing any meal, and her money now gone, she was forced to sell her furniture, clothing, and any other articles of value. At this point one of Latrobe's superintendents came upon the two at the lonely crossroads. He knew the woman, vouchsafed her story, and bought the gun from her. Latrobe added what he called some trifling relief in cash. But then the thought of what might eventually happen to the widow and to so many like her began to haunt him. The journal entry concludes:

> The City abounds in similar cases. The families of Workmen whom the unhealthiness of the city and idleness arising from the capricious manner in which the appropriations for the erection of the public buildings have been granted, giving to them for a short time high wages, and again perhaps for a whole season not affording them a weeks work have ruined in circumstances and health, are to be found in extreme indigence scattered in wretched huts over the Waste which the law calls the American Metropolis, or inhabiting the half finished houses, now tumbling to ruins which the madness of speculation has erected.[34]

Obviously, the immigrant labor force presented the church with a difficult challenge. Initially, in the case of Trinity Church, it is only fair to say that the challenge simply could not be met. First, we must bear in mind that Trinity did not exist when the earliest contingents of Irish Catholic immigrant laborers arrived in the Georgetown area. These were mainly indentured servants who had come to work for George Washington's illusory Potomac Company. Their first tasks of clearing obstacles from the Potomac River bed and excavating the locks of Little Falls began in 1792, or at least a year or two before Trinity opened its doors. Some indication of the difficult conditions under which these first workers labored may be drawn from the fact that the Irish, described as "especially troublesome," frequently ran away, even though as indentured servants they ran the risk by so doing of arrest, jail, and leg irons.

Then, by the time Trinity was in its second year, the Potomac Company's main work had shifted to the Virginia shore of the Great Falls. This location was then so inaccessible from Georgetown or any other settled area that the company was eventually forced to provide housing for the work gangs in a village of slapdash huts and barracks that came to be known as Matildaville. There the Irish lived, labored, and sometimes died without any ministrations of church or clergy as they struggled to cut five locks through deep bedrock. (It is gratifying to note, however, that at a later date, or by the time the successor Chesapeake and Ohio Canal Company's excavations were well under way in the 1830s, Trinity priests could and did visit the canal workers' camps far up the river for baptisms and marriages.) With the completion of the Great Falls locks, many of the laborers resumed a transient life, going where the ready work was, whether in Washington or other cities up and down the Atlantic seaboard. But some few remained, as we will see, to find a better life in Georgetown.[35]

Other public works that employed sizeable numbers of Irish immigrants included the President's House (it was not commonly known as the White House until 1820), the Long Bridge over the Potomac, the Washington City Canal, and the first turnpikes to such places as Baltimore and Frederick, Maryland, and Staunton, Virginia. True to Benjamin Latrobe's observations, all of these projects suffered to a greater or lesser degree from capricious funding and consequent stops and starts. Inevitably, the work gangs laid off from one project would roam the District desperately looking for another. Meanwhile, more immigrant laborers were constantly arriving or being brought to the capital.

But in time both government construction and private enterprise in Washington and Georgetown began to offer more stable employment. In the latter category, beginning in 1818, Georgetown College itself became one of the more notable employers of recently arrived Irish immigrants. In fact receiving station might better describe the college's role, since it hired many single males as carpenters, cooks, cobblers, tailors, and farm workers for what appears to have been temporary employment while they looked for better positions.[36]

Little by little, as these and many other opportunities opened up, Irish Americans everywhere began their spectacular rise up the economic ladder for which they would be so well known by the beginning of this century. In the Washington area at the time of which we speak, the indications of their upward mobility were slight and relatively few. But they were there nonetheless, indicating at least a beginning. In the Trinity baptismal register there is for example this entry in the hand of assistant pastor Stephen Dubuisson:

> Supplied ceremonies to John, the son of Philip Gormley and Margaret O'Reilly, his wife from Ireland, baptized last year on the canal, born September 12, 1831 Sp[onsor] Mrs. Ann O'Reilly.

Nine months later Philip Gormley was a cart driver living on Georgetown's busy Water Street. Eighteen years later, or by the time of the mid-century census, Gormley appears as a grocery merchant.[37]

Again, in the same baptismal records we find many entries from the 1820s onward for Patrick and Dennis Donoghue, two brothers who raised large families. Their forebears were said to have come to Maryland as canal workers, but by the time their children were being baptized at Trinity, the Donoghues had established Georgetown's principal tallow chandlery. Other Georgetown members of the family included Peter Donoghue, a cloth merchant and tailor, and Timothy Donoghue, a grocer. In time the brothers Patrick and Dennis opened a second chandlery for soap and candles in Washington City.

Other members of the clan soon followed. One, Thomas Donoghue, was a clerk at Gales and Seaton's *National Intelligencer*, while two more were grocers, one near the Navy Yard and the other at the junction of the Washington Canal and New Jersey Avenue. The family remains prominent in Trinity records throughout the nineteenth and into the twentieth century, with but one difference. No longer were the Donoghues primarily tallow chandlers or small storekeepers. Now the sons, grandsons and great-grandsons were entering the white collar professions as teachers, clerks, and lawyers.[38]

Much the same can be said of the German immigrants, approximately thirty percent of whom were Roman Catholics, who came in numbers second only to the Irish in the late eighteenth and early nineteenth century. Kaldenbach, Harbach, Finck, Wiesner, Kellenberger—these are among the surnames in the earliest Trinity registers that are almost surely of German origin. Generally speaking, however, the Germans arrived in America with more education and artisanial skills than the Irish and thus moved more quickly into middle-class occupations. Also, since many German-speaking Catholics came from the predominantly agricultural regions of southern German, as well as Austria and Switzerland, they were more attracted to farming communities such as Frederick than to Georgetown or Baltimore. From Frederick, moreover, they might more easily move farther west in search of new lands. (As a true "gateway to the West" Frederick was sufficiently populated by German immigrants from the 1780s onwards to have supported two German-language newspapers, the *Marylandische Zeitung* and the *General Staats-Bothe*.)[39]

Of those who did come to Georgetown and Washington, some few were domestic servants. But far more typical were the Kellenbergers and Harbaughs (originally Harbach), to name but a few. Trinity parishioners George and Joseph Kellenberger were busy coopers on Cherry Alley, not far from the Georgetown waterfront, while John Kellenberger appears in the earliest Georgetown directory as a school teacher. Among the relatives of Trinity Church builder Leonard Harbaugh, nearly all of them Catholics, were a wheelwright, a grocer, and what the first Washington directory listed as a "Measurer of Carpenter's Work," which at the time meant a building inspector and cost appraiser.[40]

Such were the forces that would shape the character of American Catholicism for a century or more to come. The successive waves of European immigration set in motion what Catholic historians consider the church's greatest achievement of the nineteenth century. It is easy to see why, looking simply at numbers. Whereas at the time of the first national census in 1790 there were an estimated 35,000 Catholics—still largely concentrated in Maryland and Pennsylvania—by 1870 some 4.5 million Catholics were spread across the nation as members of what was already the United States' largest single religious denomination.[41] By great effort the church managed to keep pace with these growing numbers, at least in the cities. It was never an easy task. But, by stretching both human and material resources to the limit, parishes were founded and schools were built for most of the newcomers.

If Trinity did not at first play an active role in this great effort, we must bear in mind that it was mainly because Pastor Francis Neale had very little help. Unlike his successors, Neale had no regularly assigned assistant pastor. With only occasional college faculty assistance he could do little more than supply the pastoral needs of those who crowded into his church. Ministries to laborers' camps on the canal or in nearby Washington would have to wait.

Even had it been otherwise, Neale's own interests lay so strongly with the administration of Georgetown College and the restitution of the Society of Jesus that it is doubtful he would have focused much effort on the extension of his parish. In fact, much as Neale might complain of some of the extra-curricular tasks Bishop Carroll assigned to him, he seems always to have wanted to play a larger role in the administrative affairs of the college and in the rebirth of the Jesuits.

Neale's activities in the latter sphere began in earnest when word was received in 1801 that the newly elected Pope Pius VII was willing to receive petitions from former Jesuits to associate with the Russian Province. (When in 1773 Pope Clement XIV decreed the worldwide suppression of the Society, Catherine the Great directed that the decree be treated as "non-existant" and issued orders instructing all Jesuits in Russia to remain and carry on their ministries as usual.)[42] Carroll, though as eager as anyone to see the restoration of the order, was uneasy with what he called a *viva voce*, or only verbal authorization from Rome to affiliate with this remnant province. But by 1803, when the former Jesuits of England re-established themselves through the Russian nexus, Carroll yielded to the mounting fervor of Neale, his older brother Charles (then chaplain of the first Carmelite convent in the United States, which he founded at Port Tobacco), and seven other Maryland priests who asked to be postulants to a restored Society. When after a long delay in communications the Father General of the Society in St. Petersburg assured Carroll and the Maryland petitioners that the Holy Father saw "no obstacle whatsoever in the way; . . . no need of the petition or of insisting thereon; [and] that anyone at all, no matter how far from Russia he dwelt, was free to become affiliated to the Society," Carroll could scarcely have opposed such papal encouragement. Although he still harbored misgivings about the canonical basis of such a procedure, he nevertheless went ahead with plans to begin a Jesuit novitiate and, with authority from the Russian Father General, appointed Robert Molyneux as superior of the Maryland "mission" of the Society.[43]

This much established, Francis Neale quickly applied for the position of novice master. To strengthen his application, Neale offered a house directly across the street from Trinity Church, which he had purchased with his own money, to be used as a retreat for the novices. Molyneux, a jovial British Jesuit more interested in the grand design than in any details of such matters,

Rev. Francis Neale, S.J., first pastor of Trinity Church; visiting pastor of St. Mary's Church, Alexandria; procurator of the Maryland Mission of the Society of Jesus; president of Georgetown College.

Georgetown University Library Special Collections Division.

approved. No sooner did he announce his appointment, however, than objections to Neale came from many quarters. The newly arrived Anthony Kohlmann, one of five priests sent by the Russian Province to answer Carroll's urgent requests, was deeply disturbed by the choice of someone who had never had formal novitiate training. (Francis Neale was only seventeen at the time of the suppression and thus had not been able to enter the Society.) Kohlmann also expressed concern about Neale's pastoral responsibilities at Trinity, since "the flock entrusted to his care is constantly increasing, and he is busily occupied in many other affairs." John Grassi, another recent arrival who had been rector of the Russian Jesuit College at Polotsk, soon said much the same. So, too, did Bishop Carroll. But Molyneux stuck with his choice. Kohlmann, for his troubles, was named *socius*, or assistant novice master.[44]

On this note the first Jesuit novitiate in the United States began at a celebratory mass held in Trinity Church on October 10, 1806. Francis Neale as both pastor and *Magister Noviciorum* welcomed some ten novices, five of whom were descendants of old Catholic families of southern Maryland. On the following November 13, after thirty days of prayer and meditation in the house across the street, the ten novices were again honored at Trinity. This time, at a high mass, Bishop Carroll, Superior Robert Molyneux, and Father Charles Neale were all in attendance.

Whatever Carroll's lingering doubts, he must surely have viewed the occasion with joy and pride, given his love of the Society and his ardent desire to found a strong native clergy. So, too, Pastor Neale, who could point to three of the novices—Enoch Fenwick, Benedict Fenwick, and John McElroy—as members of his own congregation. Another who took great joy was Francis Malevé, the Russian-trained Belgian who was later assigned the Frederick-to-Cumberland circuit. Malevé was so moved by the occasion that he rose to deliver an impromptu Latin homily. His Latin pronunciation was so deficient and his peroration so rapid, however, that Carroll is reported to have whispered, perhaps half humorously, "What language is he speaking?"[45]

But nothing could dim the significance of the moment. Anthony Kohlmann, so often critical, spoke for all when he praised the novices as "young men of great promise, far above the average in personal appearance and mental endowments." Indeed, from among their number would come a future bishop, a president of Georgetown College, and the founders of both Holy Cross and Boston Colleges. Small troubles aside, the Society of Jesus was well restored in America.[46]

As the first novitiate neared its end, Francis Neale might well have turned his full attentions to the growing Trinity congregation. But such was scarcely the case. Rather, by the time the first novices had completed their studies in 1809, Neale was listed in the Jesuits' Maryland mission catalogue as vice rector of the college, master of novices, procurator (treasurer) of mission, and *Excurrens ad Alexandriam*, meaning visitor pastor, of St. Mary's of Alexandria. By November of the same year he was vaulted into the position of acting president of the college. A year later Francis Neale was confirmed as the seventh president of Georgetown College, even as he continued to be pastor of Trinity and St. Mary's, as well as treasurer of the Maryland mission.[47]

It was too much. At the college student enrollment dropped off sharply, albeit more from competition with St. Mary's of Baltimore and Neale's determination to run the college as a seminary rather than from any neglect of his office. At Trinity the congregation remained relatively static. There we will leave it for another time, when a dynamic young assistant pastor would give the church new life. Meanwhile, other resources were coming to the fore, in another part of the District.

6

St. Patrick's, St. Peter's, St. Mary's, and More

The increasing congregation of this city are at a great loss for a place of worship . . . not only to the purpose of inculcating the holy maxims of the gospel into the minds of citizens at large but . . . also [to] hold out a great encouragement for immigration from the Old World. St. Patrick's Church would make the town exceedingly pleasing and familiar to a great number of my countrymen and persuasion.

-FATHER ANTHONY CAFFRY
to the Board of Commissioners of the District of Columbia,
April 14, 1794

With the above words, Father Anthony Caffry addressed the three Commissioners of the District of Columbia in the hope of acquiring land for a church in the capital city. One of the three commissioners, as it happened, was Bishop Carroll's older brother Daniel. The commissioners promptly responded by offering two choice lots not very far from the President's House at reduced prices. So began St. Patrick's, the oldest Catholic church within the original confines of the City of Washington.[1]

Although much about the origins of St. Patrick's remains obscured by a scarcity of records, the church is said to have been the inspiration of the Irish-born architect James Hoban. A long-held tradition credits the dynamic and civic-spirited Hoban with personally inviting Dominican Father Anthony Caffry from Ireland to attend the spiritual needs of the Catholic workers engaged in building the capital, many of whom labored under Hoban's direct supervision. Although no documentary proof of such a role has been found on either side of the Atlantic, it would be entirely in keeping with Hoban's character. What we do know is that Father Caffry was settled in Washington and had begun his efforts to establish a church for the nascent capital's labor force by January 1794. His request to the commissioners "hold[ing] out a great encouragement for immigration from the old world" was both cleverly phrased and timely, since the commissioners were then anxiously attempting to attract a labor force and not worrying about an oversupply, as would later be the case.[2]

Not so successful were Caffry's efforts at fund raising or gaining the continued good will of his superior. Soon after the grant of the church lots Caffry complained that they had been conveyed in trust to Bishop Carroll and not to him, only to find that Carroll, although obviously annoyed by the complaint, was entirely amenable to whichever arrangement suited Caffry best. Six months later, or by December 1794, Caffry found it necessary to ask Carroll to intercede in his behalf once again with the District Commissioners. This time it was to continue the deferment of the first payment on the lots because his congregation "being tradesmen and labourers, struggling under the difficulties incident to new settlers," could not raise the sum.[3]

During these early years the first St. Patrick's congregation probably worshipped in what one contemporary source described as "a large room merely" in a building somewhere on the church's property, which was bounded by Ninth, Tenth, F, and E streets, Northwest. Next, or sometime shortly before the turn of the century, St. Patrick's gained a home of its own in the form of a modest wooden church building on F Street. Margaret Bayard Smith, the wife of Washington's first newspaper publisher and a careful chronicler of the city's events, has so described the church and its historic place: "For several years after the seat of government was fixed at Washington [1800], there were but two small churches: The roman-catholic chapel in F Street, then a little frame building, and the Episcopalian church at the foot of Capitol-hill; both very small and mean frame buildings." The latter, according to Mrs. Smith, was a virtual benefaction of the Catholic landholder Daniel Carroll of Duddington. "It had been a tobacco-house belonging to Daniel Carroll," she noted, "and was purchased by a few Episcopalians for a mere trifle."[4]

The first St. Patrick's Church may well have attracted some of the land-owning Catholic gentry who lived nearest to it from the beginning, but it was apparently much more patronized by Washington's Irish-born workers who, as Father Caffry had foreseen, were pleased to have a priest from their country ease them through the immigrant experience. This we know indirectly from the writings of the English missionary Robert Plunkett. After Caffry's departure for Ireland Plunkett noted that the city's Irish laborers had "either abandoned the sacraments or frequent them in the city of Georgetown."[5]

Unfortunately, Caffry did not long remain with the countrymen who so appreciated his services. Apparently always at odds with Carroll, he told the bishop of his hopes to free himself of "the chains of wretchedness in this territory" as early as the summer of 1800. In a letter that was alternately obsequious and accusatory, he told Carroll he knew there was "a tide of coalition of the clergy" conspiring against him, but he trusted the bishop would dispose of his accusers and the controversies they generated in an honorable and virtuous manner. Carroll owed him no less, he firmly believed. "Independent of your innate Justice I beg leave to make a claim, without cancelling the merit to your unbiased friendship," Caffry wrote in a postscript. "I exposed my life to save yours in the yellow fever time in Baltimore."[6]

Five years later Anthony Caffry was on his way home to Ireland. Before his departure the noted Boston convert John Thayer had cast envious eyes on St. Patrick's.[7] But Carroll chose instead a young priest named William Matthews, who appears to have been the right man at the right time to lay the foundations of a strong Catholic church in Washington City. A native of Port Tobacco, Matthews was a nephew of the Reverends Leonard, Charles, and Francis Neale. Like them, he was a descendant of one of the older Catholic families of southern Maryland and a near relation of the Boarmans, Brents, Youngs, and the Charles Carroll of Carrollton branch of the Carroll family. As one of the last young Americans to be sent abroad to the English Jesuit academy at Liège, he had returned in 1800 to be the first native-born priest to be ordained in the United States. His principal biographer has characterized him as a middling student whose "preference for practical action and for dealing with people may have inclined him to regard with a wary eye the heavy theological tomes of Georgetown and St. Mary's."

Matthews was, however, a true believer in the future of the capital city, a rare quality in 1804, the year he assumed his pastoral duties. This, along with a talent for making friends and getting things done quickly, put him in the company of such as William Thornton, a District Commissioner and first architect of the Capitol; Thomas Law, the British investor and husband of Martha Washington's granddaughter Elizabeth Custis; Samuel Harrison Smith and Joseph Gales, Jr., co-owners and editors of the *National Intelligencer*; and other leaders of Washington's emerging society, some of whom were to become close friends. In time, in fact, Matthew's great personal charm would enable him to have friendships with such opposites as Andrew Jackson and Henry Clay. Or to move easily among many different venues, from the President's House to the Irish laborers' camps.[8]

Like Trinity Pastor Francis Neale, William Matthews inherited a modest personal fortune, which he often tapped for the good of the church. Unlike Neale, however, he also had both a zest and a talent for business dealings. Soon after coming to St. Patrick's Matthews was quick to appreciate that the church's lots were located in a district that was fast becoming the prime urban cluster—the first real "downtown," we could as well say—in the City of Washington, where real estate values were sure to increase. He therefore did not hesitate to use his own funds to purchase eight more contiguous lots (the average lot was then approximately fifty by one hundred feet) to provide for the church's future growth. His confidence, events soon proved, was not misplaced.[9]

This done, William Matthews set about to gain something better than the "small and mean frame building" for his congregation. Within a relatively short time, even as Matthews had been pressed into temporary service as vice president and president of Georgetown College during the years 1808 and 1809, he achieved his goal. On June 30, 1809, the *National Intelligencer* announced that on the Sunday following the new Roman Catholic Church of St. Patrick's would be opened with a divine service by Bishop Leonard Neale, and a discourse by Archbishop Carroll. "At the conclusion of the discourse," the

Intelligencer notice added, "a collection will be made for defraying the expenses and completely finishing the new church." What eventually resulted was a not unhandsome brick building of simplified Gothic revival style facing on Tenth Street, enlarged and well finished by 1816.[10]

As far as we know the size of the second St. Patrick's—it measured 120 by 80 feet in its longest dimensions—was sufficient or more than enough for its swelling and varied congregation. Certainly the Catholics of the great manor houses and private chapels came to appreciate the convenience of a church which, while still distant to some, was much nearer than Georgetown's Trinity. By 1811, or the time of the church's earliest baptismal records, St. Patrick's congregation included members of the Brent, Carroll, Digges, Fenwick, Mudd, Queen, Semmes, Slye, and Young families. At this time also the first of a new aristocracy of Italian master craftsmen and artists engaged to make sculptures and frescoes for the Capitol— Giuseppe Franzoni, Giovanni Andrei, Pietro Bonanni, Carlo Franzoni—were beginning to add an exotic note to the St. Patrick's parish.[11]

But it would be wrong to assume that Father Matthews concentrated his attentions on his Maryland kinsmen or socialized only with the city's leaders. On the contrary he was a major force in improving the condition of the city's poor, both through charity and a variety of educational efforts. In all of these efforts, however, he was very much his own man, with a tendency to assume the commanding role in all projects that interested him. A good example can be found in the by-laws for the St. Vincent's Female Orphan Asylum, a model orphanage-school and the first of its kind in Washington City, which Matthews founded in 1825 with the help of Elizabeth Seton's Sisters of Charity.

Courtesy of St. Patrick's Church.

St. Patrick's Church, Washington, watercolor by J.H. Bockelman, circa 1830.

Among other provisions bearing Matthews's imprint was one that made it possible for him to serve as president of St. Vincent's board of trustees (a position he could hold for life) and another that declared that "the President will have total control of the admissions into the asylum and day school." It is unlikely, however, that Matthews' trustees objected to these provisions. There was first the fact that he had provided the sisters with a house he owned and $400 from his own pocket to found the orphanage. Then in 1832 Matthews rather remarkably succeeded in persuading Congress to include St. Vincent's in a federal appropriation of city land valued at $20,000, to be divided equally with the Washington City Orphan Asylum.[12]

William Matthews has also been portrayed as a man who occasionally gave way to blunt speech and harsh words, which he might later regret and seek to balance through kindness and extreme generosity. One such occasion, with spectacular result, occurred late in his life when his niece, Sister Juliana Matthews of the Sisters of the Visitation, came to ask immediate help in meeting a $3,000 mortgage payment due on a school building in which the sisters were trying to duplicate in Washington their highly successful Visitation Academy of Georgetown.

Matthews, who deplored lack of foresight or any other sign of unsound fiscal planning, was upset by his niece's request. He rudely told her and her companions to give up the enterprise and go back to their convent. He would have nothing further to do with their school project, the more especially since they had moved the school from a neighboring house on property belonging to him. But a few days later Matthews sent Sister Juliana a check for $10,000, or more than enough to cover all of the sisters' indebtedness. He reversed his decision, Matthews claimed, because the thought of the sisters' appeal would not leave his mind while he was celebrating a votive mass to the Blessed Virgin. "Thank the Blessed Virgin for it," he is said to have told the grateful sisters. "She made me do it."[13]

But for a man like Matthews, as some of his friends and fellow clerics would have been the first to allow, something besides the interventions of the Blessed Virgin was needed to achieve what he did in his lifetime. That something—a quality not shared by many priests of his time—was a remarkable ability to raise and administer money. Add to this his celebrated charm, whenever he chose to display it, and it is not difficult to understand how Matthews gained entrée into the capital's best drawing rooms and subsequent involvement in nearly all of the city's early civic projects.

In 1821 Matthews was elected president of the board of directors of the city's first permanent public library, whose members represented what might be called the beginning of a Washington establishment. Among them were the *National Intelligencer*'s founder Samuel Harrison Smith; William Seaton, a coeditor of the Intelligencer and later five-term mayor of Washington; Peter Force, the bibliophile publisher of the *National Journal* and, like Seaton, later mayor of Washington; and John Sessford, Washington's first demographer and the compiler of the *Sessford Annals*.[14]

*Georgetown University Library
Special Collections Division.*

*Rev. William Matthews, second
pastor of St. Patrick's Church,
G. Parker engraver.*

Earlier, or in the summer of 1813, Matthews had been elected to Washington's Board of Trustees of Public Schools, a position he held for thirty years, or longer than any other board member. In this role he was particularly successful in raising private subscriptions for the City's first Lancastrian school—it, like other "public" schools that followed, received both public and private funds—and in badgering the City Council to make good its pledges of municipal support.

Matthews has been described as one of the relatively few genuinely committed members of the School Board, which suffered frequent turnovers. He, along with such others as Samuel Harrison Smith, Robert Brent, Judge William Cranch, and the Presbyterian Reverend James Laurie, did much to push a sympathetic but impecunious City Council towards regular yearly appropriations for a true public school system. At one point, in fact, Matthews may have pushed too hard by having his St. Vincent's Orphan Asylum included in an amendment to a bill the council was considering in 1841 to establish a free school for girls on Capitol Hill. This caused the council, which evidently did not share the more tolerant attitudes of its Georgetown counterpart, to refuse consideration of the bill. In fact, one year later the city withdrew all aid to sectarian schools.[15]

Within the Catholic community, however, Matthews's most enduring contribution was one he neither planned nor foresaw. It began in 1815 when he gave the Georgetown Jesuits a plot of some of the St. Patrick's property he himself had purchased, with the intention of letting the Society build a house there for its own use. The thought was that quite possibly the house might serve as a small seminary where scholastics could be lodged far from the distractions of being mixed in with the students at Georgetown College. In return Father Matthews asked only the "loan" of a priest or priests to help him with his expanding parish. However, to raise money to complete the house and to launch the seminary on a firm foundation, the college decided to try a boys' school first—a private boys' school charging tuition, that is—under the noted convert Dr. George Ironsides, a former Episcopalian minister and schoolmaster who had recently come to Georgetown from New York.

Ironsides ran the trial school successfully for three years, from 1817 to 1820, after which the college politely asked him to move on to make way for ten seminarians, two faculty priests, and Anthony Kohlmann, who had been chosen to head the new seminary. Initially the college was highly pleased with this arrangement for what would be Washington's first and only Catholic seminary. So, too, was Father Matthews, who viewed his next-door neighbors as a splendid source of assistant pastors. Very soon, however, Kohlmann discovered that the support from the college and from charitable sources was not sufficient to maintain his seminary. He therefore quickly returned to the idea of a private school. The result was the inauguration in September 1821 of a prestigious college for boys somewhat inappropriately called the Washington Catholic Seminary. (It was neither exclusively for Catholics nor intended primarily as a seminary for priests.) It was an almost instant success. Offering courses from elementary through college levels, the Washington Catholic Seminary had a new building and some 170 students, or more than any of Washington's early public schools, within six years of its founding.

There was, however, one remaining problem. In the excitement attending the launching of the seminary, the original request for priests for St. Patrick's was all but forgotten. It did not take Father Matthews long to notice this, nor the fact that he had been effectively excluded from any direct role in the new institution. He therefore wrote a characteristically irate letter to Archbishop Maréchal. The Jesuits had broken their promise to him and were "trying to worm their way" into his parish. He in fact would have no more of them and wished them off his property.[16]

But before these differences could build up to a major confrontation, a new and greater threat to the seminary came from Rome. The father general of the Society of Jesus, Aloysius Fortis, objected to the practice of charging students, since the Society's rule clearly stated that all its schools should be free. Georgetown College had previously circumvented this provision by charging parents for their boys' board and lodging, not tuition. But this was a more difficult claim for the Washington Catholic Seminary to make, since none of its boys, apart from the few seminarians, were boarders. For a number of years Kohlmann tried to convince the father general of the school's special role and to gain from him a dispensation. He was soon supported by Father Matthews, whose personal pique was fast disappearing as he viewed the school's growing success. But, after almost seven years of debate and many different arguments, Fortis remained unconvinced. In September 1827 the Jesuits' father general handed down his decision. The Washington Catholic Seminary was to be closed forthwith.[17]

It was a severe blow to Matthews, who by then had been appointed the seminary's president by Kohlmann's successor. Only two years earlier Matthews had succeeded in persuading President John Quincy Adams to share the proscenium at the seminary's fourth commencement exercises. (Adams is reported to have listened with pleasure and not a little patience while some of the capital's best-educated young men received more than forty-two prizes for subjects ranging from Logic and Elocution to Latin, Greek, and Christian Doctrine.) His presence there was both a tribute to the school and a measure of the respect between Catholics and Protestants that had long prevailed in both Georgetown and the Federal City. Indeed, in attending the ceremonies President Adams may not have been unmindful that the sons of Daniel Webster, Commodore John Rodgers, Dr. Benjamin Rush, and Judge William Cranch, Protestants all, were among the school's students. For all of the seven years of its existence, the seminary was to Washington City in the 1820s what Georgetown College was to Georgetown in the 1790s. Both were respected institutions, open to students of all faiths, to which parents could entrust their sons for the best liberal education of the day.[18]

But some lasting good resulted in any case from the short-lived Washington Catholic Seminary. Like a number of Matthews' best works, it did not come into full evidence until after his death. Following what Matthews' biographer has called an underground period, the seminary's school building was reopened by the Jesuits in 1848 as Washington College, with the approbation of Archbishop Samuel Eccleston and the necessary dispensation to receive tuition payments; Washington College in its turn may be said to have inspired Gonzaga College, chartered by Congress in 1857, which soon became one of Washington's leading secondary schools. So it remains today, continuing to enjoy high academic standing. Another project that, thanks to his planning and munificence, was nearing completion when Matthews died in 1854, was the St. Joseph's Orphan Home for Boys. Intended as the male counterpart of St. Vincent's Female Orphan Asylum, it opened its doors in February 1855. Helping to secure its future was a $3,000 bequest from Matthews.[19]

Other good works aside, the vigorous growth of St. Patrick's was perhaps the greatest testament to William Matthews's enduring contributions to the spiritual welfare of the capital. During his term as pastor, the congregation grew very quickly, judging from relative numbers of baptisms. (Forty-five infants were baptized in 1812, the first year of complete records; whereas the number had risen to 258 ten years later, a rate of growth approximately five times that of the population of Washington for the same period.) As at Trinity the parish embraced a broad spectrum of society and had no one dominant ethnic-descent group or social class. On a typical Sunday a St. Patrick's

Gift of Jean McGinley Draper, © *National Gallery of Art, Washington.*

Mary Barry, by Gilbert Stuart, 1803-1805.

worshipper might find himself in the company of construction workers, government officials, foreign envoys, both free blacks and slaves, descendants of the Maryland gentry, and such public figures as Chief Justice Roger Brooke Taney or the French Minister Baron Hyde de Neuville.[20]

Still, one strong Catholic church was not enough for L'Enfant's "city of magnificent distances." St. Patrick's was more than two miles from the eastern- and southernmost reaches of the city, where the Washington Navy Yard and Greenleaf Point were the centers of growing communities. Thus "Roman

Gift of Jean McGinley Draper, © National Gallery of Art, Washington.
Ann Barry, by Gilbert Stuart, 1803-1805.

Catholics on or near the Eastern Branch [the Anacostia River] . . . experiencing great inconvenience for want of a place of worship" banded together probably as early as 1801 to start a subscription to build a church somewhere in their part of town. Daniel Carroll of Duddington donated an entire square of his property to the purpose; prominent contributors included Notley Young, Mayor Robert Brent, Daniel Carroll Brent, Henry Hill Carroll, James Hoban, the widowed Mrs. George Fenwick, James Barry, and Captain Thomas Tingey, first commandant of the Navy Yard.[21]

But progress was slow. Well before the above campaign, James Barry, a wealthy shipping merchant and one of Bishop Carroll's closest friends, had decided to build what was meant to be a small family chapel and burial place close to the Eastern Branch and not far from Greenleaf Point. However, recognizing the need for more places of public worship, Barry directed that the chapel, to be called St. Mary's, and to be designed by James Hoban, be opened to all and that no pew rents or "payments under any shape be ever demanded of any persons for attending at divine services."[22] But Barry, a kind and generous man who would invest too much of his energies and fortune in the early development of Washington, was destined to live a life almost constantly scarred by tragedy.

Barely had the cornerstone of St. Mary's been laid in 1806 when the oldest of his two beautiful daughters—both were painted by Gilbert Stuart—was fatally stricken with tuberculosis. Two years later James Barry himself died of consumption, as tuberculosis was then commonly called. Meanwhile his wife Joanna had taken the younger daughter who was similarly stricken to the Madeira Islands in the hope that the climate there might bring her back to health. But neither mother nor daughter was to be spared. Within a year the body of the daughter was shipped home for burial at St. Mary's alongside her father and her older sister. Two years later, or in 1811, it was the turn of her mother, who had been sojourning in Ireland. She, too, was interred in the family crypt at St. Mary's. A brave and pious woman, Joanna Barry had found strength and support from the attentions of Bishop Carroll and her long friendship with William and Elizabeth Seton of New York.[23]

Occasional services for neighborhood Catholics were held at St. Mary's until approximately 1819, or some eleven years after Mrs. Barry's death. Unaware of her husband's business losses she left many generous bequests that could not be honored, including a thousand-dollar sinking fund for weekly masses to be said for the repose of herself and her family. But even before she died, St. Mary's was already showing signs of neglect. This we know from an anonymous traveler writing for the *Norfolk Herald* in 1810:

> Passing through the city of Washington a few weeks ago, I was forcibly impressed by the melancholy appearance of a small and interesting building, with a cross on the top, nearly incompassed by tall and waving poplars, and which presented to my mind the idea of a little village church. I was informed that it was a chapel built by a Mr. James Barry, late of the place, on one of his own lots for the accommodation of those of his Catholic brethren whose residence was remote from a Parish Church; my informer added, with a sigh that seemed to come from the heart, that Mr. Barry and his amiable daughters were all dead, and buried in the vault beneath the chapel. I was surprised to find no memorial of the founder, nor any inscription by which the traveller might learn the names of those interred there.[24]

Short as his years in Washington were, James Barry was a major figure in the development of the capital, welcomed everywhere from Mount Vernon to the halls of Congress for his kindness and civility. But all that remains of his church is its cornerstone, removed by his nephew James D. Barry at a time when the chapel yard was overgrown with weeds and the building itself in ruin. The younger Barry also removed the bodies of his family for reinterment in the St. Patrick's Cemetery. But in 1863 St. Patrick's sold its cemetery to make way for its present church building. What happened after that, or where James Barry, his wife, his two daughters were finally buried, is unclear. The site of St. Mary's is now a low-income housing area.[25]

With the demise of St. Mary's, the Catholics in the eastern sector of Washington City were even more "experiencing great inconvenience for want of a place of worship." Thus in 1820 a number of the original petitioners of 1804, fortified now by Father William Matthews, began another campaign. This time their efforts met with success, although not precisely for "Catholics on or near the Eastern Branch." Since the always generous Daniel Carroll of Duddington had donated some prime property on C Street on Capitol Hill, their efforts were redirected there. Within a year, or by September 1821, St. Peter's Church, Washington City's second oldest Catholic parish, had opened its doors.

All too quickly, it is perhaps fair to add. St. Peter's first pastor, James Lucas, found that he had inherited some substantial debts incurred by his zealous building committee, including more than $1,300 due the building contractors, and this in the wake of a national depression. Lucas reported to Archbishop Maréchal in 1823 that most of his parishioners were mechanics and laborers, "the majority . . . so poor that more than one third of the pew rents have not been paid for the past two years."[26]

The stalemate that followed and the arguments concerning various possible solutions were in fact late reflections of some of the American Catholic church's most pressing early problems. Father Lucas did not want to go back to his well-to-do building committee lest too much lay financing encourage too much control of St. Peter's, or a revival of the trusteeism that had so bedeviled Bishop Carroll. His fears were not without reason, since four years later Archbishop Ambrose Maréchal was considering a transfer of Lucas because he had permitted "a system of administration adopted by the Building committee, which is subversive of ecclesiastical governance."[27]

Father William Matthews suggested that the church be turned over to the Jesuits. (Mainly, some said, to get them out of his own backyard.) But this in turn brought up the long-simmering debate over whether or not Jesuits should serve as regularly appointed parish priests. To be sure, they had in effect done so on their country estates. But should they now as members of a religious order traditionally engaged in education and missionary work take on parishes in the cities? None of these questions was soon resolved. But St. Peter's struggled on, with only the security of some land held in trust donated by Notley Young's son Nicholas, as it continued to reach out and serve its expanding congregation.[28]

St. Peter's was followed by four more churches within the next two decades. First came St. Matthews', a handsome Greek revival church near Lafayette Park completed in 1838. (It was sacrificed in 1910 to the demands of downtown real estate, however, and replaced by the neo-Byzantine mass of the present St. Matthews' Cathedral on Rhode Island Avenue.) Next was St. Mary Mater Dei on Fifth Street, Northwest, described in 1846 as "a new church intended for the use of German Catholics" on land graciously donated in the last year of his life by the popular General John Peter Van Ness, who was not a Catholic. St. Mary Mater Dei was followed by St. Dominic's south of the Mall in 1852 and, finally, St. Aloysius, next to Gonzaga College on North Capitol Street in 1859. St. Aloysius was permitted Jesuit management because it was being built in association with a school and "at a reasonable distance from the existing churches."[29]

In this way, here and there and little by little, Catholic churches were dotting the urban landscape of the emergent capital. They at least kept pace with the city's growth and they at least accommodated the larger part of "the Catholics who pour in upon us," as Carroll had first described the immigrant influx. This, as he had predicted, continued unabated.

Meanwhile, much the same could be said of Georgetown. Trinity Church was about to experience a period of accelerated growth under what the church's first historian called the equivalent of a second founding. Nor was Trinity any longer Georgetown's only Catholic church. In addition to the Georgetown College chapel in Old North, a new church not three blocks away was opened for public worship by 1821. This was the Chapel of the Sacred Heart, built by the Sisters of the Visitation. Its origins traced back to 1798, when three French nuns of the order known as Poor Clares started a small school called the Georgetown Academy for Young Ladies. After various ups and downs and the departure of the Poor Clares, the school became the responsibility of a newly formed community of the Visitation Sisters.

Visitation Academy, as it soon became known, was founded on the liberal principle of "widen[ing] the sphere of female tuition, and duly proportion[ing] it to the actual demands of society" at a time when most women's education was still directed to their role in homemaking. An important addition to Georgetown's cultural assets and open to students of all faiths, the academy immediately attracted the daughters of Catholics and Protestants from far and wide in the capital area. Among the latter were Britannia Peter, a granddaughter of Martha Washington and Robert Peter, Georgetown's first mayor; Mary and Jane Threlkeld, daughters of the John Threlkeld who gave the lot for Trinity Church to John Carroll; and the daughters of John Cox, longtime mayor of Georgetown and the proprietor of the handsome town houses bearing his name built by Joseph Brooks. Among Catholics the familiar names of Brent, Boarman, Carbery, Carroll, Digges, Fenwick, Mudd, Matthews, Queen, Neale, and Semmes—in short, many of the descendants of Maryland's first families—appear with frequency on early student lists.

To the convent and academy were added a free day school for poor students in 1819. (One of the convent sisters, apparently forgetting the academy's expanding view of female education, reported that in its first year "about a hundred little girls of poorer classes are taught all that is suitable for their condition.") Then, feeling the need for a more commodious place of worship, the sisters asked their chaplain, Father Joseph de Clorivière, a French nobleman and self-taught architect, to design a new chapel. The result was a white stucco church that has been charitably described as "an unusual but not unpleasant combination of Ionic and Tudor styles," consecrated as the Chapel of the Sacred Heart in November of 1821.[30]

Standing between the academy and the convent—as it does now with their successor buildings on 35th (then Fayette) Street—the chapel soon attracted many townspeople for Sunday services. (It must have been around this time, one imagines, that the concentration of Catholic institutions in the western heights of Georgetown caused the area to be dubbed "Holy Hill," a nickname still used today by its older residents.) Even before it was finished, in fact, the Visitation Chapel had caused some Trinity pew holders to hold back on renewing their pew rents in anticipation of renting in the new church. The then-pastor of Trinity, Theodore De Theux, claimed that Visitation had no pews allotted for "the poor whites and coloured persons"; he therefore saw it as attracting an elite congregation, while Trinity would be left with the poor and the black. His fears proved groundless, however. In reality what De Theux failed to see was that there would be more than enough worshippers to go around for both churches. In 1837, or sixteen years after Visitation Church was built, Trinity parishioner Julia Compton wrote to a friend of hearing mass at Visitation at seven o'clock in the morning and then returning "at ten o'clock . . . to Trinity Church where as usual an immense concourse had assembled."[31]

The person most responsible for building up Trinity to the point where immense numbers were accepted as a matter of course came from the church's own ranks. This was John McElroy, the young Irish immigrant who joined Father Francis Neale's first novitiate in 1806 as a temporal coadjutor, or brother. Before he died in 1877 at the age of ninety-five, McElroy had left a deep spiritual imprint on a number of parishes, served as an Army chaplain in the Mexican-American War, and founded Boston College. Of his contribution to Trinity, Father Aloysius Roccofort, who knew him in his old age, has written: "The Priest who had produced the deepest and more lasting impression on the population of Georgetown is the venerable John McElroy; . . . he is still considered by the oldest inhabitants almost as the founder of Trinity Church." A contemporary historian, Reverend Robert Emmett Curran, S.J., has summed up McElroy's lifetime contribution more succinctly. "No American Jesuit in the first half of the nineteenth century," Curran writes, "left a greater mark on the religious landscape."[32]

McElroy's first assignment to Trinity in 1817 was as a young assistant, not a pastor, shortly after Francis Neale suffered a debilitating stroke and was sent to St. Thomas Manor in his native Charles County to recover. Benedict Fenwick, the second of George and Margaret Fenwick's four sons and also a product of Neale's first novitiate, was hastily summoned from New York to be

114   Neale's replacement and Trinity's second pastor. It was a prideful moment for the aging Neale, who was as eager as Carroll to see the emergence of a native clergy. But, sadly, Archbishop Carroll was not to share it; the architect of the American church had died eighteen months earlier at the age of eighty. Nor was the church's dependence on foreign-born priests at an end. Within a year the talented Benedict Fenwick was sent to Charleston to take over a faction-ridden congregation torn between a French pastor and an Irish assistant. Although some sixty appointments to Trinity were made between Fenwick's departure and the Civil War period (pastors remained for an average of two years; assistant pastors, one), only one pastor and six assistants among the sixty were American born.[33]

During his brief term, Fenwick established a free school for boys that took more than 100 students within a few months of its opening. An intensely spiritual man, Fenwick also organized one of the earliest attempts at a Catholic revival meeting in the United States. Whether this was entirely his own inspiration is difficult to say. Like other priests of his time he may have had an eye on the successes of the evangelical Protestants in this field. Or, he may have been reviving the older tradition of Catholic evangelical missions popular in Europe since the Counter-Reformation and first tried in the United States by Jean-Baptiste David and Anthony Kohlmann near the beginning of the century. Whatever the answer, Fenwick's meeting, held in the form of a one-day spiritual retreat, attracted only a few female parishioners. Before he could organize another, Fenwick was off to Charleston and other way stations of his career. These would eventually lead to Boston and a bishop's crozier.[34]

John McElroy, as an assistant to Theodore De Theux, Trinity's third pastor, would soon attempt further revivals. But there were other needs that demanded as much or more attention. In his report to Rome on the Catholic religion in the United States in 1818, the Reverend John Grassi spoke of Trinity as a church so crowded that it was "unfortunately not large enough to contain more than a third of the people who flock to it." This was surely no exaggeration, and in the next year De Theux and McElroy set about to follow up on Francis Neale's initiatives for temporary enlargements to the church. Accordingly, at a mass on July 3, 1819, McElroy gave a ringing appeal "to show the necessity of enlarging our church by a temporary addition" and asked for a monthly subscription from every member of the congregation scaled from twelve-and-a-half cents to twelve-and-a-half dollars.

The next day McElroy set out on a house-to-house canvass with parishioners Ignatius King, Jr., and the architect Joseph Brooks. He must have found most members of the congregation at home or conveniently attending Georgetown's all-day Fourth of July celebrations, for his diary tells of obtaining $2000 in pledges that day and an additional $400 the next. These quick results, which even present-day parish clergy might envy, were quite enough. McElroy immediately engaged Brooks and another parish member, the brick mason and sometime street superintendent George Mahorney, to knock out two arches in Trinity's west wall and add the two wooden lateral-wing chapels that Aloysius

Roccofort and many others found so ugly yet so necessary. It was probably at this time also that makeshift stairways were built outside the east wall for the black congregation to ascend directly to their gallery seats. On October 3, 1819, or only three months later, "the largest congregation ever known in this town of Catholics assembled in our Church," as McElroy put it, gathered to celebrate the completion of the new additions.[35]

Earlier in that busy year, or during the Lenten season of 1819, De Theux and McElroy launched Trinity's second attempt at a revival retreat. This time their efforts were an unqualified success. This may have been because the two priests had more time and more assistants, borrowed from the college, to plan the various events. Or perhaps McElroy's eloquence as a preacher, already well known, and some of his experimental methods were the great attraction. Among the latter McElroy hit upon the idea of taking on different roles as he conducted the retreatants through the Ignatian examen of conscience. "I made [the examen] twice each day in a loud voice, placing myself in the person of a Parent, [then] at another time, of a Child, or Servant," he wrote in his diary. "This I found by experience to be very profitable."[36]

The first retreat held on March 22 lasted one long day, or from eight in the morning until six in the evening, and included meditation, selected readings, confession, mass, instruction, reflection periods, and a final benediction. To their surprise De Theux, McElroy, and two college priests found they had to spell each other in the confessional for most of the day. Many who presented themselves, McElroy found, had not received the sacrament in five or more years. Spurred by this success De Theux and McElroy planned a second mission two weeks later that was to last three days. More than five hundred attended, including the remarkable presence of eighty-four men. As was often the case, McElroy's sermons excited the curiosity of a number of Protestants. Before the three days were out, ten Protestants had been converted and a great many lapsed Catholics had re-entered the church.[37]

Other changes were coming to Trinity. For the first time the church had a pastor and an assistant whose primary and undistracted concern was their parish. And, with the appointment of a resident pastor at St. Mary's in Alexandria in 1818, Trinity was relieved of responsibility for the last and most burdensome of its outlying missions, which was soon thereafter to be wracked by a serious outbreak of independent trusteeism.[38] The result was a period of more and better planned liturgical celebrations and a heightened spirituality for both clergy and congregation. Whereas under Neale's pastorate Trinity could provide little more than a Sunday service and a reliable source of sacraments, De Theux and McElroy offered at least two masses on Sunday and three or more on major feast days. The principal Sunday mass and all feast day services included organ music, choir, and lengthy sermons. On Christmas morning of his second year, for example, McElroy started the day with a pre-dawn mass lighted by one hundred candles; he gave communion to approximately two hundred in what was the first of three masses celebrated that day. "The morning was fine and the church tolerably full," he noted simply in his diary.[39]

Father McElroy also organized the first formally celebrated First Communion for children of the congregation in 1819. At this event forty boys and girls "communicated apparently with great devotion" before some two hundred parents and friends, with music provided by the Georgetown College choir and Father Enoch Fenwick at the organ. In 1822 Theodore De Theux organized the Confraternity of the Living Rosary, one of the first such societies in the United States. Its goals were to strengthen its members' personal piety and have them effect conversions, or as De Theux more carefully phrased it, "to enable them by the influence of virtuous example to be instrumental in the propagation of their faith among our dissenting Brethren." It was quickly followed by the Confraternity of the Holy Scapular that same year and, in 1840, the popular Bona Mors Society. The latter sought to "help our Neighbors to live piously and justly in this Life that they may at last Die the Death of the Just."[40]

Sermons as well became increasingly important in the revival period of Trinity. Surprisingly, a congregation whose parents and older members had been brought up to worship in private with what might be called the home-study sermons of prayer manuals and devotional guides took to communal worship and lengthy preaching with what seems to have been considerable relish. If so, the credit must largely rest with a new generation of preachers, as exemplified by McElroy. In Neale's day it was quite common for priests to borrow from each other's sermons or from printed sermons of European origin. But the new generation prepared their own material and, what was more important, practiced and gained proficiency in *ex tempore* speaking. ("I wish I had the talent of doing it *ex tempore*," the British-born Robert Molyneux, second president of Georgetown College, wistfully noted of their efforts. "To preach with a paper does not suit this place so well; and now, from want of time and habit, I should find it difficult to speak without.")

Sermons were most often given at the end of the principal Sunday mass and seldom lasted less than an hour; instructions were in order for most other services. Then as now the congregation praised good preachers and criticized poor ones. Both Benedict Fenwick and John McElroy were among the former, whereas the Dutch priest Peter Kroes appears to have alienated some among the parishioners by delivering sermons and instructions "at the utmost pitch of his lungs."[41]

After McElroy such priests as James Ryder, who preached often at Trinity when he was president at the college in the 1840s, and Joseph Aschwanden, pastor of Trinity a decade later, were highly regarded for different reasons. Miss Julia Compton, the school teacher and parishioner whose letters are a rich source of parish life, commended Ryder's lecture series on Catholic doctrine at Trinity during which "the church is always filled and some [non-Catholics] are convinced of the truth and beauty of Catholicity." By contrast Father Aschwanden, a jovial Swiss-German with a heavy accent who would carry loads of wood to poor parishioners or walk miles with blistered feet to visit the sick, simply overwhelmed the congregation with his charitable acts and the zeal and enthusiasm of his preaching. "His manner of preaching was unique [and] so full of straightforward piety, logic and usefull counsell," his contemporary Aloysius Roccofort said of him, "that the most refined people, forgetting the incorrectness and often the oddity of his expressions . . . derived a real benefit."[42]

In 1830 Jonathan Elliott's *Historical Sketches of the Ten Miles Square Forming the District of Columbia*, one of many directories of the period designed to promote the capital city, listed Trinity Church as having a congregation of five thousand, with St. Patrick's not far behind with four thousand. The congenital boosterism of Elliott and other Washington pamphleteers undoubtedly inspired this inflated figure. Still, it is entirely possible that by the 1830s and '40s Trinity's extended congregation, meaning occasional as well as regular communicants, went well over one thousand. On any given Sunday in those years men gathered at the entrance to Trinity in such numbers before and during services that they became "a cause of annoyance to the ladies . . . who, naturally, do not like to see themselves exposed to the gaze of such a crowd." Or, on Christmas, the church was inevitably jammed at all masses with worshippers "some of whom conducted themselves with proper decorum" while "others [were] thinking of eggnog and fun." Always, too, on any given Sunday there was the cheerful distraction of small children freed from Sunday school playing in the churchyard.[43]

Trinity and the other early Catholic churches were growing. They were growing, moreover, in ways far more important than numbers. We must consider what all the above-mentioned innovations—multiple masses, improved liturgies, spiritual retreats, engaging sermons, confraternities and sodalities—meant to Catholics brought up in a tradition of individual piety. What it all meant to those whose forebears had received most of their faith at home by the fireside was a new and welcome sense of congregation, a sense of belonging. This sense of congregation in turn created parish communities that shared both religious and lay interests. The church was in fact central to the lives of its members, uniting them more than we know today and augmenting their existing ties of family, friends, and business associations.

In this context parish priests could and did set moral standards, within limits, and serve their congregations as counselors, arbitrators, and confidants. When, for example, Pastor Stephen Dubuisson, De Theux's successor, thought a young lady in the congregation was being corrupted by the "permiscuous effects of theaters," he quietly and effectively prevented her marriage to "the player Scott, a man of dubious morals." In many other cases pastors spoke out about the loss to religion whenever a parishioner married outside the church. They refrained, however, from giving the names of those participating in such mixed marriages, which most of the congregation knew in any case. When one priest tore away the veil of anonymity and forced a mixed-marriage couple to kneel before the altar throughout the Sunday high mass, the congregation was outraged and the Catholic spouse vowed never to set foot in the church again.[44]

Another unifying force, always strongly urged by the clergy, was parish concern for the education of the poor. At Trinity this concern began with

Francis Neale, who intended the house he bought across the street for the Jesuit novitiate in 1806 to be made into a school.[45] But Neale apparently never found the time to apply his considerable organizational talents to this purpose, and it remained for Benedict Fenwick to establish Trinity's first Free School for Boys in 1818.

Much the hardest task at the time was to find qualified schoolmasters. This problem Fenwick solved by taking a talented convert, Joseph Brigden, originally a Connecticut shoemaker and at the time a handyman-carpenter at Georgetown College, and making him into an accomplished teacher. The Free School counted more than one hundred poor boys within months of its founding, receiving some support from parents who paid what little they could. It ran successfully until 1829, when Brigden returned to his native Connecticut to found a similar school and write a memoir, *Connecticut Convert*.[46]

In 1819 John McElroy launched the previously mentioned Sunday school for black children. Classes, taught by volunteer white members of the congregation, were held once a week in the evening. The Sunday school priorities, frankly stated by McElroy were "1st to prevent Catholic Negroes from schools kept on Sundays by Methodists, etc. [and] 2nd to teach them their prayers and Catechism at the same time they learn to spell and read." In 1824 a bolder attempt to meet the needs of the black congregation came in the person of Maria Becraft, the daughter of a prominent free black family, who established a female black academy in Georgetown only to have it close a few years later when she entered the black Oblate Sisters of Providence in Baltimore. While it lasted, however, Miss Becraft's academy so inspired the then-pastor of Trinity, John Van Lommel, that he gave it what support he could and started a companion school for boys nearby. In 1831 Father Benedict Fenwick, by now bishop of Boston, was shocked upon visiting Georgetown to find that his Free School had ceased with Brigden's departure. "In vain will you expect to share in the lights of heaven," he pleaded from the Trinity pulpit, "while your children, by your neglect, are wandering stars, given over and buried in darkness. Up with the school, up with it!"[47]

Bishop Fenwick's exhortations had their intended effect. Both the Trinity congregation and the Maryland Province of the Society of Jesus lent sufficient support to re-establish the school. Parents who could pay some small amounts continued to do so. At this time, too, as mentioned in an earlier chapter, the municipality of Georgetown voted to provide the school with an annual subsidy. As Pastor Stephen Dubuisson quite correctly observed, this was "a remarkable event, that the Board of the Common Council had a majority in our favor on such a subject." Both Visitation Academy and St. Patrick's, as we have seen, also started schools for the poor and orphanages soon after their founding.[48]

The churches of the District were growing. Problems, to be sure, remained. The debate over rural versus urban concentration of effort continued. But here the rapid growth of the church was itself providing a de facto answer. In the summer of 1835 the Jesuit delegates to the first congregation of the

Maryland Province might still argue over a recommendation to reduce rural Maryland and Pennsylvania missions in order to concentrate more forces on the cities. In fact, however, the sweep of events, meaning the burgeoning of the cities everywhere and the church's efforts to serve them, were rapidly rendering such debate academic.

It would be some years before the church would take a position on slavery. But here, too, local and individual actions would speak louder than what the church at large said or, better, left unsaid. In liberal Georgetown the ratio of slaves to the free black population declined as more and more heads of households freed their servants and more slaves purchased their own freedom. (Slaves numbered 1,521 and free blacks 894 in the 1820 Georgetown census; by 1830 there were 1,115 slaves and 1,204 free blacks.)[49] In 1827 Father Peter De Vos withheld the sacraments from a parishioner who had separated a woman slave from her husband, refusing various local offers to reunite the couple; area Catholics backed De Vos, calling the refusal the "astonishment and crying shame of the congregation." In the same vein, when in 1836 the Jesuit Superior General in Rome made a heartless decision to sell all the slaves of the Maryland manors, priests at St. Inigoes and Whitemarsh helped their slaves to hide when it was known that the latter would be shipped to New Orleans to be sold indiscriminately.[50]

On other fronts more American-born priests were emerging from seminaries to take up ministries in local churches. And the experiences of the Visitation sisters and men like Fathers Fenwick, McElroy, and Matthews in starting free schools, halting and intermittent though they may have been, were laying the groundwork for one of the Catholic church's greater achievements of the century—the establishment of a national parochial school system.

For the nation it was a time of manifest destiny. For Catholics it was a time of confidence, a time to assert their right to share in this destiny. Although the darkest forces of bigotry were yet to come, most Maryland Catholics emphatically agreed with Father Stephen Dubuisson when in 1841 he reported to his European colleagues: "The principles and the law of the country are with [us]; it is probable that they will finally prevail."[51]

The next year, as a measure of this confidence, Georgetown College, the Calvert Beneficial Society of Baltimore, and various organizations from southern Maryland staged a commemoration of the landing of the *Ark* and the *Dove* in 1634, the two-hundreth anniversary of which had passed uncelebrated eight years earlier. Thus, on a spring day in May 1842, two steamers from Baltimore and one from Georgetown transported a host of "new pilgrims," including most of the Georgetown College faculty and student body, to the ancient capital of St. Mary's. President John Tyler, citing other public duties, graciously declined an invitation to attend. But such luminaries as John Pendleton Kennedy, a United States congressman and Maryland's leading man of letters; William Seaton, mayor of Washington and co-owner of the *National Intelligencer*; George Washington Parke Custis, General Washington's step-grandson and sometime poet, playwright and artist; William G. Reade, both a noted scholar and one of Baltimore's leading lawyers; and Emily Harper, Baltimore's reigning lady of fashion and a granddaughter of Charles Carroll of Carrollton, lent their presence to what by all accounts was an impressive and well-planned, three-day event.

Representing the Church hierarchy were Archbishop Samuel Eccleston of Baltimore; Bishop Benedict Fenwick of Boston (who seems never to have missed an opportunity to revisit his native land); and James Ryder, the president of Georgetown College. Upon reaching "the now obliterated city of St. Mary's," the *Baltimore Sun* reported, the dignitaries and the pilgrims found over two thousand people from St. Mary's and neighboring counties awaiting them. Ferried ashore by an armada of small craft, they marched with flying banners through a landscape of great natural beauty to a large mulberry tree, believed to have been planted by the first settlers. Here one after another of the principal speakers invoked the original colonists' spirit of tolerance, or the Toleration Act passed by the Maryland Assembly in 1649. Bishop Fenwick urged Catholic listeners to imitate the universal toleration shown by their forefathers and make it the chief element in the practice of their religion. Father Ryder hailed the colonists of St. Mary's as the victors of "liberality against bigotry, religion against superstition" and the first Americans to put forward the concept of civil and religious liberty for all. "Let then no man dare," he concluded, "to reprove their enthusiasm on this glorious day."

Perhaps more mindful of the many Protestants in the audience and on the speaker's stand, the principal orator George Reade was reported to have "depicted the matchless virtues of Maryland's founders, and, though avoiding with scrupulous care every word that could offend the most sensitive, proved that the Catholic colony of old St. Mary's had no competitors for the glory of founding universal freedom, civil and religious." The aging George Washington Parke Custis loudly sang a Pindaric ode he had composed for the occasion, dedicated to Archbishop Eccleston and the Catholics of Maryland. "That Mary's fair land be the land of the free" was its epodic refrain.

The ceremonies concluded, the pilgrims re-embarked while a German band played "Hail Columbia" and the Georgetown Choir chanted the litany of the Virgin. After leaving "this elysium almost too beautiful for man to inhabit," the *Intelligencer* reported, the various steamers reached their destinations without incident the next morning. Thus ended what all concerned praised as a never-to-be-forgotten commemoration unmarred "by the slightest departure from propriety or politeness, either in word or act."[52]

Kind words and sincere praises aside, the Catholics of Maryland were sending an unspoken message to their Protestant friends. We were here at the beginning, the message as much as said, hoping always to live in peace and comity with all. Our history proves we have done so. This we should not forget.

PART III

The Nation's Capital

7

To Force a City

The year 1800 will soon be upon us. The necessity therefore of hurrying on the public buildings ... [is] too obvious to be dwelt upon.

-PRESIDENT GEORGE WASHINGTON
to Commissioner Alexander White, May 17, 1795

In the first week of January 1800, Dr. William Thornton, one of the three Commissioners of the District of Columbia, received what must have been an unsettling New Year's message. His good friend Secretary of the Navy Benjamin Stoddert had written to say that the lease on the house President John Adams was occupying in Philadelphia was about to expire and that the President therefore looked forward to shipping his furniture to Washington in June.[1]

Could this mean that Adams, previously so little interested in the President's House, meant to move in soon thereafter? Thornton could at least console himself with the fact that the House was much farther along—its exterior was essentially completed—than any other of the public buildings of his responsibility. But as for the President moving into a finished and completely livable house in June, that was another matter. After all, had not the 1790 act of Congress that created the District required that suitable buildings for the accommodation of the President, the Congress, and the executive branch be ready by the first Monday in December 1800? That was almost a year away, not six months or less.

A few days later Anna Maria Thornton, the commissioner's wife, wrote in her diary that her friend Sarah Forrest had returned from a shopping and social visit to Georgetown "where she heard a great deal of the impossibility of accommodating the Congress in the vicinity of the Capitol." This, she suspected, was merely the wishful thinking of still-jealous Georgetown proprietors. "We hope differently," she stoutly concluded.[2]

Later in the same month a more ominous warning came to Daniel Carroll of Duddington, on whose land the Capitol was being built. Richard Henry Lee, a member of the Virginia delegation to the sixth United States Congress, had written in confidence from Philadelphia to warn Carroll that "Congress will remove to the city [Washington] as by law agreed & will remove back again, after the first session if not well accommodated." He emphasized the need for proper lodgings near the Capitol, as well as the Capitol building itself. "This

124 you may rely on," Lee added, cautioning Carroll to disregard any contrary opinions.[3]

Even Benjamin Latrobe had his doubts. During his early years in Washington as surveyor of public buildings, Latrobe in his darker moods thought it a folly "to remove the seat of Government from a large and convenient town to an anomalous kind of settlement, neither village, town nor city." In fact, the more he thought about it the more it seemed equally foolish to think that any government could "force a city" on a place that had no real advantages and a number of well-established rivals not too far away.[4]

The Thorntons, Carroll, and Latrobe, not to mention many others concerned with the capital's future, shared two concurrent fears. The first was immediate: if the public buildings required by the act of 1790 were not ready by the first Monday of December 1800, Congress or even the administration itself might choose to remain in Philadelphia. To be sure, the act contained no precise language to this effect—to be ready by the deadline or else, that is—but there was little doubt it could be so interpreted.

President Washington understood this from the beginning. As early as 1792, writing from Philadelphia, he judged the temper of Congress and the executive departments on moving the seat of government as so equivocal "that a feather will turn the scale either way." To make sure the three District Commissioners understood the urgency of speeding up their efforts, he wrote privately to one of them, David Stuart, his step-son-in-law and a personal friend. "If inactivity and contractedness should mark the steps of the commissioners," the President warned Stuart, "whilst action on the part of this state [Pennsylvania] is displayed in providing commodious buildings for Congress, etc., the government will remain where it is now." This was no idle threat. Even as Washington wrote, Philadelphians were busy remodeling the Philadelphia County Courthouse to serve as "Congress Hall" and the City Council had rented the home of financier Robert Morris for the President's residence.[5]

The second fear, more long term in nature, concerned the basic viability of what Latrobe called a forced city. As the most skilled engineer and architect of his time, he understood perfectly well that the first public buildings could be rushed to completion on time, helter-skelter and come what may. But more than any of his contemporaries, he foresaw the greatest problems in the economic survival of a city that had no provisions for industry, little potential for commerce, and, notwithstanding President Washington's obsession with the Potomac, an inferior and difficult-to-reach port that was already falling far behind Baltimore in maritime activity.[6] The sole business of Washington would be the business of government. Was such business enough to support a city and attract outside investors? That was the real question.

But precisely because of these difficulties, precisely because Washington was a planned city unencumbered by any history, traditions, or ruling class, its invisible gates were open to all comers. Investment capital would at first have to be sought from the very few local residents of substance. Builders, craftsmen, and laborers would have to be recruited from far and wide, wherever, in fact, they could be obtained. And where political leadership at the municipal level would come from no one at first knew or, it would seem, much cared.

Catholics responded well in all three categories. It would be an understatement, in fact, to characterize their collective role in the early municipal history of Washington as anything less than prominence. Some may have been moved by expectations of great personal gain, soon to be dashed. Others hurried to what they thought was Washington's booming job market. Still others, notably the descendants of Maryland's Catholic gentry, heeded John Carroll's call to civic action and volunteered or were persuaded to run for the capital city's first public offices. Whatever their motives, Catholics were prominent among those who invested heavily in Washington's future, literally built its first great buildings, and began its long campaign for self-rule. The nature of their contributions and how they shaped the perception of Catholicism in the capital area are the principal subjects of this and the next two chapters.

First to be called for professional help in building the city, Major Pierre L'Enfant excepted, was the previously mentioned Leonard Harbaugh, who came at the request of the commissioners in March 1792.[7] Described as a pious man who "in consequence of some misunderstandings withdrew himself from the [German Reformed] church," Harbaugh gave rise to families prominent in Trinity and St. Patrick's parish records. He himself, if not a convert, maintained close professional ties with the local Catholic community. He was, we will remember, the builder of Trinity Church. And, as noted before, there remains the possibility that Leonard Harbaugh may also have been the builder of "Old North," which stands today as Georgetown University's oldest building.[8]

After the alleged failure of his Rock Creek bridge in 1793, Harbaugh received no major government commissions for some five years. But the commissioners had never wanted to let a man of his professional repute completely out of their grasp, nor could they have been unaware of Harbaugh's success in finishing the Little Falls locks for the Potomac Company in 1795. Thus it was that they occasionally gave him such interim jobs as "measur[ing] the painting done at the President's House," meaning inspecting it and verifying costs, or determining the cause of its leaking roof.[9]

Then, in the spring of 1798, Harbaugh had his big chance. The commissioners, who had been concentrating their efforts on the President's House and the Capitol, were all too well aware that buildings for the executive departments were also required by the Act of 1790 before the federal government could move from Philadelphia. Accordingly, they announced they would receive bids for what was first called the Executive Office, to be located immediately east of the President's House. Harbaugh, even though he was then beginning the monumental task of constructing the Potomac Company's locks on the Virginia side of the Great Falls, submitted the winning bid in what was apparently an open and honest competition, albeit with the usual complaints and charges of complicity from the losers. On June 23, 1798, Leonard Harbaugh was awarded a contract to build the Executive Office for a total of

126     $39,511. It was to be ready for occupancy on or before July 1, 1800, or within a little more than two years.[10]

The design of the Treasury Building, as the Executive Office soon became known, was the work of a talented young Catholic architect who among others would eventually leave a significant imprint on the capital city. This was George Hadfield, who had come from England in 1795. Born in Florence where his parents ran a fashionable boarding house for British travellers, Hadfield and his older sister Maria made their way back to England while they were both relatively young after enduring the shocking trauma of the murder of four brothers and sisters by a lunatic nurse and the death of their father shortly thereafter. Maria, who had almost entered a convent in Italy upon their father's death, eventually married Richard Cosway, an art dealer and miniature painter, and soon became a favorite of London and Paris society. Although a talented artist herself, she remains best known for her great beauty, her close friendship with Thomas Jefferson, and her generosity in founding Catholic girls' schools and convents.

Meanwhile, her brother George had entered the Royal Academy as a student. There he won top honors in drawing and architecture, including a scholarship to Rome. By 1794 his growing reputation attracted the attention of the American painters Benjamin West, then president of the academy, and John Trumbull, who recommended him to President Washington for the vacant position of supervisor of construction of the Capitol. It was in this role—obviously miscast, as it would prove—that George Hadfield sailed for America in the spring of 1795.[11]

Hadfield drew the Treasury Building plans in 1797, or almost a year before construction began, offering them without fee to the government. By that time, however, he had gotten himself deep into a major confrontation with Commissioner Thornton, which eventually resulted in his dismissal as supervisor of the Capitol. (Soon after his arrival Hadfield had given an honest if highly impolitic report to President Washington to the effect that Thornton's plan for the Capitol building was an aesthetic and structural disaster.) Much as he wanted to remain in charge of building the Treasury, the commissioners, led by Thornton, would have nothing more to do with George Hadfield. The young Britisher's fortunes would eventually take a better turn, we will see, enabling him to make substantial contributions to both the construction and the government of the capital city. Meanwhile the time lost had to be made up by the "generally usefull" and "modest and well-tempered Mr. Harbaugh," as the commissioners often spoke of him.[12]

Hadfield's original design for the Treasury called for a two-story brick building fronted by an elaborate portico with four Ionic columns that would nevertheless retain the character of what has been called the Federal plain style. (Harbaugh subsequently added a half-story of dormer windows and may have modified the portico.)[13] It thus offered an agreeable contrast to what critics sometimes derided as the imperial grandeur of the President's House. In fact, the design so pleased both the President and the commissioners that they agreed it should be repeated in a twin building to be known as the War Office. Both buildings were to be built of "the best stock-brick, and slightly ornamented with free-stone to make them correspond with the President's House, to which they will appear as wings." Not so pleased were some members of Congress and the Capitol Hill proprietors, including Daniel Carroll of Duddington, who complained that the executive department buildings should be close to them or at least in the eastern half of the city. "As the business of the Executive Officers will be chiefly, if not altogether with the President," President Washington told them, "Sites for their Offices ought to be convenient to his residence." And so the matter was decided. So, too, was the capital's first area of urban concentration, since the decision was a major factor in what historians have called the westward march of the city.[14]

Harbaugh kept to the rigorous schedule for the Treasury Building in spite of numerous distractions and work stoppages. First there was a fire at a construction site workshop. Next came delays in the delivery of materials, a common enough problem with all of Washington's public buildings. Then in the summer of 1799 the District Commissioners and other interested parties evidently used Harbaugh as their front for buying large tracts of prime city property, probably as a holding action to forestall speculation at a time when the commissioners might have believed prices would soon rise in anticipation of the transfer of government from Philadelphia the next year. (The auctions and sales of government lots, beginning in 1791, had been disastrously low; by 1799 the commissioners may well have thought the impending transfer would give their property sales a much-needed boost.) In any event Leonard Harbaugh is recorded as the buyer of more than 200 lots at a total price of $23,312, nearly all in the last two weeks of August 1799. In that same month, what is more, the commissioners gave Harbaugh the contract for the twin War Office building, also for the sum of $39,511, but this time with a requirement that he finish in fourteen months. In the spring of 1800, as the completion date for the first building drew very close, there were further requests from the commissioners to inspect leaking roofs, this time at both the President's House and the Capitol.[15]

Yet in spite of these additional duties and responsibilities, Leonard Harbaugh finished the government's first office building ahead of time. On May 15, 1800, the Treasury Building was ready to receive the vanguard of the federal bureaucracy. In the weeks that followed some seventy members of the Treasury Department plus some nine men who then constituted the entire State Department moved into the Hadfield-Harbaugh building with reasonable comfort. It was a politically important moment. The White House was not yet ready to receive the President and Mrs. Adams. The Capitol was far from being finished, although one wing was judged sufficiently advanced to be able to accommodate the Congress when it convened in November. But the Treasury Building, alone, was finished some six months before the due date set by Congress. It is said that anxious Washingtonians trooped down to Lear's Wharf on the Potomac during the first week in June to cheer the arrival of the first sloops from

Philadelphia bearing the archives and furniture of the Treasury, State, and War Departments. Little wonder. Here was the first visible evidence. It was true, after all. The government was moving from Philadelphia.[16]

Harbaugh's success in finishing a major construction project ahead of time was a rare event in the early history of official Washington. As might be expected, he was subsequently in more demand than ever. The Potomac Company, after suffering a temporary standstill for want of funds, importuned him to return to the awesome task of surmounting the Great Falls. Ironically, in October 1800, the commissioners asked their once-failed bridgemaker to inspect the city's bridges over the James and Tiber (formerly Goose) Creeks and make recommendations on any needed repairs. In the same month Harbaugh was chosen chairman of the City of Washington's committee to prepare welcoming ceremonies for the arrival of Congress. Then, by April 1801, perhaps aware that their most able assistant was being pulled in too many directions, the commissioners asked that he give his "immediate and uninterrupted attention" to completion of the War Office. This he apparently did before the end of the year and then quickly turned his full energies to the engineering problems of the Great Falls lock system.[17]

In August 1802 the Potomac Company proudly announced that Harbaugh had succeeded where others had failed. The canal and lock system at the Falls had been operating successfully on a trial basis since February, boats were now passing through, and the Potomac River was navigable from Georgetown to Cumberland "during a considerable part of the year." Not only that, the

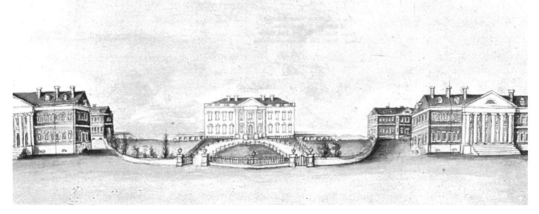

I.N. Phelps Stokes Collection
Miriam & Ira D. Wallach Division of Art, Prints & Photographs
The New York Public Library Astor, Lenox and Tilden Foundations.

"Washington City 1821 (sketched in June 1820)," the President's House flanked by the identical Treasury, War, State, and Navy Department Buildings designed by George Hadfield, modified by Leonard Harbaugh, and restored by James Hoban; watercolor by Baroness Hyde de Neuville, 1820.

State Department, last of the Hadfield-Harbaugh-Hoban executive department build-ings to be demolished, making way for the north wing of the present Treasury Building, 1866.

press and international visitors were hailing the system as one of the engineer-ing wonders of the world.

The press did not exaggerate. Locks with the extreme vertical drop of those at Great Falls—seventy-six feet overall, with the last three of five locks descending like a staircase through forty-seven feet of solid rock—did not exist in Europe. Nor is it likely that any engineering projects of the day suffered as many difficulties and hardships as those faced by Harbaugh and his mainly Catholic labor force. The company's daily journals, quite different from its opti-mistic annual reports, give terse accounts of the accidents and deaths, espe-cially among river-bed workers and "the Blowers," as the gunpowder blasters were known. ("We had our Blowers, one Run off and the other Blown up," reads one bi-weekly report.) They also detail experiments with both German and Irish laborers, instructions for preventing disturbances between black and white work crews, and the practice of shaving the heads and eyebrows of Irish indentured servants to discourage runaways.

To its credit the company understood and appreciated the full range of Harbaugh's services. In the Christmas season of 1803, the board of directors resolved to present a suitably inscribed silver cup to Harbaugh at its next meeting for his role "in opening the interior navigation of the Potomac River as superintendent of the works generally, and more particularly on account of the useful improvement made in the lockgates by him."[18]

Today Harbaugh is little known, even to Washington historians, and few of his works remain with us. The Treasury and War Office buildings, both rebuilt after being gutted during the British invasion of 1814, were demolished in 1866 and 1879 respectively. The canal system and workers' houses at Great Falls have all but disappeared under encroaching vegetation, so much so that were it not for the National Park Service's restoration efforts, passersby might wonder what was there. Before he died in 1822 Harbaugh gave most of his later years to the Potomac Company in what proved to be a losing battle against the seasonal ravages of the river, failing funds, and the constant need for repairs. But in his lifetime the Great Falls locks operated virtually without flaw. As a proof of what could be done to overcome nature's greatest obstacles, they at least kept alive the hopes of Georgetown and Washington for a great commerce with the West, reborn in the form of the Chesapeake and Ohio Canal Company in 1828.[19]

Leonard Harbaugh's grave is marked by a badly weathered tombstone in Washington's Congressional Cemetery. But there remain two monuments to his achievements that are perhaps more fitting memorials than any tombstone. One is a dizzying cleft, a deep gash in the sheer rock wall of a wooded gorge, down which curious hikers sometimes descend; it is all that is left to mark the route of the staircase locks that conquered Great Falls. The other is Trinity Church, standing all the tests of time.

Next to come among the early builders of Washington was a young Irishman from County Kilkenny who would prove to be the single most effective force in meeting the capital city's deadlines. This was James Hoban, known today mainly as the architect of the White House. Hoban had come to America in 1785 at the age of twenty-seven, following studies at the Royal Dublin Academy and apprenticeship to Thomas Ivory, one of Ireland's master architects. He settled briefly in Philadelphia, where he advertised himself as a builder of "elegant style . . . who can execute the Joining and Carpenter's business in the modern taste." Perhaps because of the competition in the new republic's largest and busiest city, Hoban soon moved to Charleston, South Carolina. There he established a successful practice with Pierce Purcell, an Irishman and a Catholic who like himself was not long out of County Kilkenny.[20]

Hoban's arrival in Washington was the result of what might be called President Washington's selective memory for what pleased him most in the way of public buildings. No sooner had Jefferson convinced the President in the spring of 1792 to hold a nationwide contest for the best designs for both the President's House and the Capitol than Washington kept mentioning some fine buildings he had seen in Charleston a year before. They were the work of a young architect who certainly ought to be considered, the President thought. He remembered the buildings very clearly and the fact that the man who designed them was highly recommended by his good friend Colonel Henry Laurens and other leading citizens of Charleston. The only thing the President could not remember was the architect's name.[21]

Inquiries were made, James Hoban got wind of them, and the national contest quickly took on a less-than-open character. As soon as Hoban heard of Washington's interest, he boldly wrote the President and suggested a meeting. The President received him in Philadelphia, liked what he saw and heard of Hoban's ideas, and promptly wrote the commissioners a letter about him. The letter, the President insisted, was to be viewed "merely as a line of introduction." The commissioners, we may be sure, took it as a strong recommendation, which is undoubtedly what the President intended, all protestations of impartiality aside. Even so the commissioners could scarcely have expected the President's next move. Early in July 1792, with the deadline for entries already at hand, the President informed the commissioners he thought he should journey to Washington to join them in judging the competitions for both buildings. Accordingly, on the sixteenth of July the President and the three commissioners met in Georgetown to review the entries. After a day of deliberation they shelved the numerous designs for the Capitol, without selecting a winner. But the award for the President's House, it should surprise no one, went to James Hoban.[22]

The award made Hoban's career. But it also brought on a small firestorm of criticism and false accusations from his rivals. Fueling the fire was the fact that Hoban had so obviously enjoyed what today we would call an inside track in the competition. Much more damaging, however, were some rumors that he was untrained in architecture and that his design for the President's House was a slavish copy of the Duke of Leinster's palace outside Dublin. The latter may well have originated with Sir Augustus Foster, the British minister, who claimed in his memoirs that Hoban was "an Irish mason who gave as his own the plan of the Duke of Leinster's house in Dublin, which being shown to General Washington was approved by him, and the Irishman who had been but a journeyman under the real architect and designer of the plan, was appointed to superintend the building." Quite possibly such false accusations were nourished by the constantly underlying but seldom spoken prejudices of the day against Irish Catholics, whatever their station in life. In any case they soon gained the widest currency. Even such an acute observer as Benjamin Latrobe joined the chorus, calling Hoban's plan "not even original, but a mutilated copy of a badly designed building near Dublin."[23]

The charges that Hoban used purloined plans clung to him well into this century, denying him his proper place in Washington's history. Not until the

132   present have they been accurately dispelled by the diligent research of William Seale. Seale's recent history of the White House is the first to give an authoritative account of Hoban's training in Ireland, his work in Charleston, and the difficult evolution of his design for the President's House, difficult because he had constantly to accommodate the sometimes conflicting advices of President Washington and the commissioners. In working the design, moreover, Hoban undoubtedly followed the usual practice of all architects of his time, who borrowed freely from each other's work or copied standard structural and ornamental elements from European pattern books. Thus the results of his efforts may well have been influenced by the Leinster House and other models. But they were far from unoriginal.[24]

Not only, then, was James Hoban a trained architect. He was also an experienced builder who unlike many of his contemporaries seemed to relish building supervision as much as or more than designing. These qualifications, along with a good business head, made him the commissioners' prime asset. Sensing his worth from the beginning, they offered Hoban the position of superintendent of construction of the President's House the day after the award, at the relatively high starting salary of three hundred guineas a year. In his contract the commissioners also stipulated that although his main concern was to be the building he had designed, his services might also be "extended to other objects they [the commissioners] may chuse." They wanted to be sure, in other words, that Hoban would be their general factotum, bound by contract to undertake anything that came within their purview.[25]

The commissioners need not have worried. From the beginning Hoban took on tasks and responsibilities that should have been the concern of others.

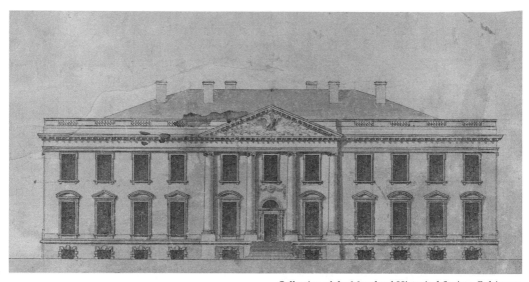

Collection of the Maryland Historical Society, Baltimore.

James Hoban's north elevation of the President's House, as modified, 1793.

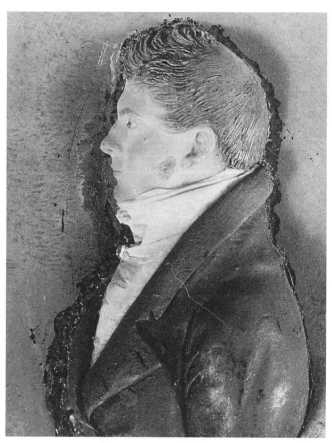

White House Historical Association.

James Hoban, colored wax bas relief on glass, attributed to John Christian Rauschner, circa 1800.

In his first year of employment, for example, he anticipated a shortage of building stones and launched a successful search for more quarry sites. (The fact that he found one lying within the President's lands near Mount Vernon may have been more than a coincidence.) Timber and dressed lumber were also a problem. In the summer and fall of 1793, Hoban made separate trips to Norfolk to inspect a captured Spanish ship loaded with mahogany, to the White Oak swamp below Mount Vernon to prospect for pine and oak, and to Stratford Hall farther down the Potomac to contract for dressed lumber.[26]

All such early preparations were necessary. Even though James Hoban had some eight years in which to carry out his design, he understood there was no time for delay or reflection. The organization essential to bringing together men and materials for the President's House was of a previously unknown magnitude. That this was so was mainly due to the President himself. From the beginning, or at the time of the design competition, Washington had insisted that the President's House "ought to be on a scale far superior to any thing in *this* Country." Thereafter, he stoutly resisted all efforts by Congress or the commissioners to reduce it.[27]

The necessary organization required Hoban and the commissioners to deal with a wide array of the area's Catholics. There were, first of all, the Brents. The building stone for the President's House and later the Capitol came mainly from the quarries of first cousins George Brent of Woodstock and Daniel Carroll Brent of Richland. As early as November 1791, Pierre L'Enfant had negotiated a ten-year lease with George Brent for a ten-acre quarry on an island near Aquia in the Potomac. Two of Brent's younger brothers—Robert, a future mayor of Washington, and William, at the time clerk to the commissioners—served as intermediaries for this and other government-leased quarries. But a sufficient supply of building stone of good quality, let alone its prompt delivery, was a constant preoccupation of the commissioners. They therefore subsequently turned to Daniel Carroll Brent, Jefferson's defender and a future marshal of the District of Columbia, and his partner, Colonel John Cooke. The Cooke and Brent quarries of Aquia Creek, as they were known, soon became the principal source of supply, especially for the Capitol.[28]

When early expectations that thousands of laborers and artisans would flock to Washington proved completely unfounded, the commissioners undertook such extreme measures as asking James Fenwick, American consul at Bordeaux, to promote their request for skilled French stonecutters. ("Our Country is young in the Arts," the commissioners wrote the mayor of Bordeaux, "from whence may we better expect assistance than from the only nation who think and act as American . . . ?") Other Fenwicks did well for themselves in the major task of making detailed surveys of the Federal City. Chief among the surveying Fenwicks was George Fenwick of Georgetown, the author of *Fenwick's Arithmetical Essays*, who was a first cousin to James and the father of the previously mentioned Bishops Benedict and Enoch. In the summer of 1792, when the long-awaited plan of the city by L'Enfant's successor Major Andrew Ellicott had not yet been published, the commissioners engaged George Fenwick at a good salary and gave him detailed instructions to fix "a [numbered] stone at every corner of each square in the City."[29]

Since there were more than one thousand squares and the stones were to be fixed and marked with great care—they might be referred to in certificates affecting property sales—the commissioners took the unusual step of allowing Fenwick as many hands as he could employ to advantage. This may account for the appointment of Bennett Fenwick, another cousin, who served briefly as an assistant surveyor in 1793 when he was not busy making bricks for Harbaugh and Hoban or not yet occupied in building what would later become Rhodes Tavern, one of the city's first hostelries. Indeed, George Fenwick himself may have owed his appointment in part to another cousin, Captain Ignatius Fenwick, the former ship owner and Trinity Church's first fund-raiser, who preceded him as an assistant surveyor in 1791.[30]

In the event George Fenwick did well in his arduous task. In 1793 he temporarily replaced Ellicott, whom the commissioners had discharged, even though he was a careful and competent surveyor, after many quarrels and complaints from proprietors that he was proceeding too slowly. The commissioners also accused Ellicott of insubordination because he objected to the services of a hard-drinking assistant they had assigned to him. This was James R. Dermott, an Irish Catholic and former mathematics teacher who "now and then drank to excess and when inebriated . . . [became] unruly and quarrelsome," as the commissioners themselves admitted. They nevertheless defended him because he worked for a very low wage and they doubted his drinking bouts impaired his performance. Dermott was subsequently asked to resurvey all the "reservations," or the grounds reserved for public buildings, avenues, and parks.

Meanwhile, or in March 1794, Fenwick received orders to re-survey some of the city's major boundaries starting with "a large stone lettered 'The Beginning of the Territory'" and also to survey anew "the north and south lines in the part of the City yet to be surveyed . . . so that errors in their direction if any may be rectified." The urgency of all this work, from basic boundary lines to square markers, was all too evident to the commissioners. The city's early property auctions had gone very badly. The government was having troubles enough with prospective buyers, that is to say, without the added confusion of faulty plats or squares and lots that no one could find.[31]

As the work on the President's House and the Capitol progressed, more of Maryland's old Catholic families became involved. Thomas Carbery of Georgetown, a member of one of the earliest Irish families to settle in Maryland, contracted with the commissioners to provide timber for the President's House from his holdings in St. Mary's County, although seldom in quantities to free the commissioners from all worry. George and Adam King, trustees of Georgetown's Trinity Church, agreed to back Carbery with security bonds.[32] George Brent, in addition to being a chief supplier of building stone, undertook to construct the rows of workers' cottages and workshops that soon became a small village in the "President's Square" in front of the President's House, in what is now Lafayette Park. Even Daniel Carroll of Duddington, greatest of the District's landowners, provided wood for firing up the brick kilns at the President's House at fourteen shillings six pence a cord. The main cost, he apologized, was "the waggonage from my place [that] comes so very high."[33]

Hoban undoubtedly had some role in involving these members of Maryland's Catholic gentry, since he could recommend contractors for the commissioners' approval. With the construction crews of buildings under his charge, however, he had a more direct responsibility for hiring and firing. It is within these ranks that Hoban appears to have made a conscious effort to favor his co-religionists and countrymen, whether members of Maryland families or recently arrived immigrants. Bennett Jarboe, whose forebears came to Maryland in 1646, supplied meat to the workers' quarters in the President's Square. Bennett Mudd, a Trinity parishioner and fifth generation descendant of Thomas Mudd of "Mudd's Rest" in Charles County, was one of the chief carpenters at the President's House. Nicholas Callan, a friend of Hoban's from County Kilkenny, was overseer of laborers. In addition, for skilled and semi-skilled labor Hoban willingly tapped the swelling tide of newly arrived Irish immigrants that so concerned Bishop Carroll. Casey, Flaherty, Flynn, Kelly, McCormick, McMahon, O'Neale—these are among the predominant surnames of the men who answered Hoban's daily roll call and shape-up. So much so, in fact, that some of Hoban's detractors accused him of preferring "Irish vagabonds" over trained workmen.[34]

In the private sphere Hoban could also bring his Catholic friends into the development of the city, often to the mutual advantage of both. With his eye for real estate and his early knowledge of the city's growth areas, Hoban was in an excellent position to do so. A good example is Pierce Purcell, who had been Hoban's partner in Charleston and moved with him to Washington. As early as 1792, when Hoban had won the design competition and was sure Washington would go ahead with the President's House very close to where L'Enfant had placed it, we find Purcell and Hoban purchasing choice lots in Square 200, immediately north of the President's Square (today's Lafayette Park), and Square 224, near the projected corner of F and 15th streets. The latter location could hardly have been closer to the eastern end of the grounds reserved for the President's House. Here they decided to build what became known as the Little Hotel, one of the District's earliest hostelries, which later became part of the better-known Rhodes Tavern.

Then, in the summer of 1797, after President Washington silenced all arguments by declaring that the government's executive departments should be next to or near the President's House rather than the Capitol, Bennett Fenwick quickly stepped into the picture. He bought the corner lot next to Hoban and Purcell's on 15th and F, which, as matters turned out, would be almost across the street from the projected Hadfield-Harbaugh Treasury Building. Here Fenwick built what was advertised as "a large and convenient three-story brick house." Two years later William Rhodes purchased the Little Hotel from Hoban and Purcell and then bought or rented Fenwick's adjoining brick house in 1801 to make up what was known as the Rhodes Hotel (later Tavern). Three or four years later Rhodes, who was soon to marry Sally Semmes at St. Patrick's, leased the hotel to Joseph Semmes of Georgetown's City Tavern while he went on to buy Lovell's Hotel north of the President's Square, originally another Hoban and Purcell property. Initially, all involved did very well. In the "city of magnificent distances," in the city whose streets, squares and lots existed mainly on Ellicott's map, they had chosen the right place. Rhodes Tavern quickly became early Washington's unofficial city hall. And F Street east of the President's House, as Hoban had foreseen, proved to be the center of the city's first and most fashionable "downtown" cluster.[35]

The James Hoban of these times was by any standards a remarkable entrepreneur and an incredibly busy man. In 1793, even as he profited from the transactions described above, Hoban received a commission to design Washington's largest hotel building for Samuel Blodget, a wealthy and generous Bostonian who offered the hotel as first prize in a lottery scheme that he hoped would help boost the city's flagging property sales. Known as the Great Hotel

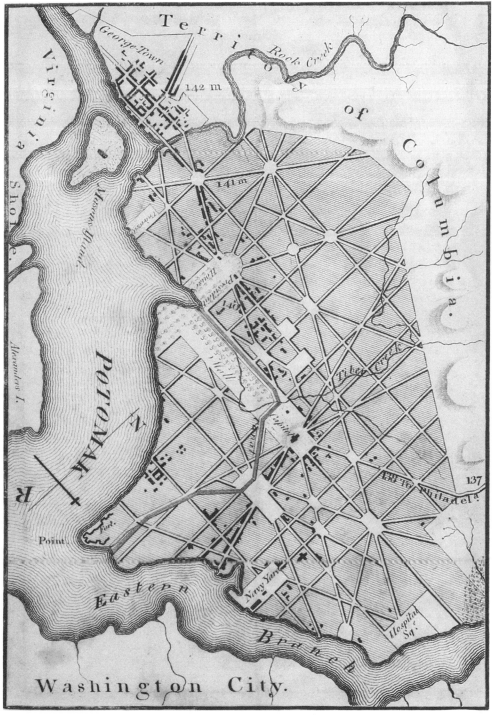

Map of the City of Washington showing the first centers of population on Pennsylvania Avenue, F Street east of the President's House, Capitol Hill, and the Navy Yard, from Moore and Jones' Travelers Directory, *1804.*

it was not finished until the summer of 1800, when it opened with great excitement, not as a hotel, but as Washington's first theater. (One of the earliest performances, however, a play by one Mrs. Moreton called "Cure for the Heartache" was in the words of Mrs. Thornton "rather dull.") By that time, unfortunately, Blodget was already in serious financial difficulty and well on his way to debtor's prison.[36]

But Hoban's work on the President's House never suffered. By 1795 the massive stone walls upon which the President had insisted reached the prescribed height. By that time too the number of laborers and craftsmen crowded into the cottage village on the President's Square had peaked. Hoban drove his work crews hard, although he was not without some concern for their general welfare. In one case he is on record for discharging a worker simply for being too old. In another a Thomas Sandiford complained that his wages were docked because he was unwilling to drill in the militia artillery company organized by Hoban. In all cases malcontents who complained too much or threatened their foremen were forcibly removed from the village by constables and if necessary run out of town.

The commissioners were no less severe and far more pinchpenny. As the work at the President's house began to shift from exterior to interior they reasoned that the wages of some nine stonecutters could be greatly reduced, even though it was known they might soon be needed for other public buildings. When the Stonecutters Lodge, an early labor association based in the President's Square village, protested on behalf of the nine, the commissioners responded by promptly dismissing all of them.[37]

Among the few amenities that Hoban and the commissioners provided were a daily free breakfast consisting of unlimited corn bread and one pound of meat or fish for each worker, a field hospital with a doctor on call, and small amounts of whiskey that could be consumed on the job in what seems to have been the equivalent of a modern-day coffee break. Hoban, who knew how to get the most out of his Irish workers, was probably responsible for the latter. Later on, during the construction of the Capitol, he asked "that each Carpenter engaged on the Roof of the Capitol shall be allowed half a pint of spirit (whiskey) per diem during the hot season." The commissioners readily agreed. If any of the Capitol's roofers ever fell off as a result of Hoban's proprietary for withstanding summer's heat, we do not know of it.[38]

And so the work proceeded. In March 1797, following President Adams's inauguration, George Washington stopped by on his long journey from Philadelphia to Mount Vernon for what would prove to be a last look at the building to which he had devoted so much attention. Happily, there was some progress to show—the roof was already framed—and a large crowd had assembled to give the former President their tearful good wishes. On hand also was Captain James Hoban and his Washington Artillery, one of Washington's earliest volunteer militia companies, who lent the occasion due ceremony with a sixteen-gun salute.[39]

The work at the Capitol presented another picture, however. There Redmond Purcell, foreman of carpenters, had been feuding with Superintendent George Hadfield, Hadfield with Thornton, and Thornton, whose original drawing had been much altered, with nearly everyone else involved with the building. All of this had resulted in serious delays. Small wonder, in fact, that Washington, who was well informed of these quarrels, characterized the Capitol as of "anybody's or nobody's design."[40]

Predictably the commissioners turned to the one man they might trust to surmount such troubles and get the job done. On May 28, 1798, George Hadfield was dismissed and Hoban named superintendent of the Capitol, even as he was to continue in the same role at the President's House. For this added responsibility the commissioners offered Hoban a short-term bonus of "the full Salary as Superintendants of both buildings untill after the 9th of June next." But true to their tightfisted ways, they would thereafter reduce his President's House salary, originally set at three hundred guineas, to one hundred guineas a year "untill the slating of the Roof . . . be completed."[41]

Hoban agreed to these terms and immediately took up his double duties. He left his trusted chief carpenter Bennett Mudd, a Trinity parishioner and one of three Mudd master craftsmen then living in Georgetown, to oversee the interior work at the President's House, while he himself devoted as much time as possible to the Capitol. Like Hadfield, he wisely decided to leave the great hole in the ground where a previous Capitol superintendent, Stephen Hallet, had begun to lay the foundations for the large central-dome section of the building. Instead he would redouble the effort to complete the north wing so that if necessary it could be used as a building in itself for the temporary reception of the Congress.[42]

The decision to put Hoban in charge of both buildings was eminently practical. At the time there were few if any other professionals with his ability in supervising construction. (Leonard Harbaugh, we will remember, was fully occupied between the Potomac Company and the Treasury Building; Benjamin Latrobe, who was a skilled engineer as well as a distinguished architect, had not yet arrived on the Washington scene.) Even so the commissioners must have worried about placing so much responsibility in the hands of one person.

Hoban now had thirty months in which to complete two major building projects. In one case there was interior woodworking, plastering, papering, and miscellaneous furnishing and ornamentation of such style and grandeur as the country had not known. In the other, most of the building still remained on paper, or more exactly on the confused palimpsest of alterations to Dr. Thornton's drawings. Moreover, neither of the two buildings—neither the President's House nor the north wing of the Capitol—could be pushed at the expense of the other. Even President Washington, for all the attention and care he gave to the former, understood this. A year before he had warned the commissioners that work on the President's House should never advance "at the expense or retardment of the Capitol" and that if necessary all work on the

140 President's House be suspended in order that "all the force be employed on the Capitol."[43]

The problem, Washington knew, would be the Congress, which would not move from Philadelphia without the suitable accommodations mandated by the Act of 1790. But to the commissioners the problem was two-fold. If Hoban should fail to have the Capitol ready on time, there was no doubt that Congress could elect to remain in Philadelphia *sine die* and thus keep postponing the transfer of government until—the thought was too distressing even to mention—until the will to move might fade away forever. If on the other hand the President's House were not comfortably finished, President Adams might be so displeased that he could easily persuade Congress to the same purpose. After all, as Washington had once said, the balance of opinion in the latter body could be tipped by a feather.

The degree to which the commissioners had come to depend on James Hoban is well illustrated by two small events (although very important ones for Hoban) that took place soon after his double appointment. In the summer of 1798 he informed the commissioners he planned to marry and therefore wanted a good kitchen added to the house they had promised him. The commissioners cannot have been much pleased by this request, although there is no record of their immediate reaction. Three months earlier, or at the same time they had named Hoban superintendent of both buildings, they had offered him the house of the unfortunate George Hadfield, which was close to the Capitol. If there were any problems or delays in moving Hadfield out, the commissioners assured Hoban, they would be glad to pay the rent of any temporary lodging he might choose. Now Hoban was asking more of them. But the commissioners, so accustomed to hard bargaining, backed down. On August 21 they agreed to have a suitable kitchen added to Hadfield's house. It would, however, have to be built "of the commonest materials and in the cheapest manner."[44]

Six months later, or on January 13, 1799, Hoban married Susanna Sewall of Georgetown and moved into his new house, with kitchen. At the wedding, held at Trinity Church, Clement Sewall is recorded as "the Father Sponsor" and Edward and Joseph Neale as witnesses. Clement Sewall, the reader may remember, was the energetic proprietor of Georgetown's City Tavern. Edward and Joseph Neale were the nephews of his wife, Eleanor Carbery Sewall.[45] Thus did James Hoban, born in a tenant's cottage in the hills of Kilkenny, become part of a Catholic family that had come to Maryland over a century earlier by invitation of the third Lord Baltimore.

But Hoban's worries were not over. In the spring of the same year, as had happened before to Hoban and other building supervisors, a group of disgruntled craftsmen and laborers lodged a string of complaints against him. But this time Joseph Middleton, a well-known cabinetmaker, accused Hoban of disregarding the commissioner's order to supply him with the wood and other materials necessary for making window shutters for the Capitol. Others put forward charges of improper accounting of materials and workers' hours at the

President's House. Hoban answered most of these charges with full and mea-sured responses. But he could not resist calling Middleton ignorant and unfit for the work assigned him, as the commissioners could readily ascertain by ex-amining the cheap knotty pine Middleton had tried to use in the Capitol's door frames, which had occasioned a loss of public funds. The commissioners, ap-parently taking umbrage at such a frank report, threatened a formal inquiry, and reprimanded Hoban for "very indecent and even insolent language . . . such as they are by no means disposed to suffer from you or any other person." But almost in the same breath the commissioners, who certainly had no desire to risk losing their most able assistant, swallowed their pride and ended their letter with a soothing word of praise. They sincerely hoped Hoban would be able "to clear up every doubt, and to prove your conduct has been as economi-cal and careful, as we believe it to have been honest and skilful." There was no subsequent inquiry.[46]

None of these events seems to have kept Hoban from fulfilling his ap-pointed tasks. The final years were especially difficult. In the summer of 1798 he had been given a supervisory role over the Executive Office or, more specif-ically, inspections "from time to time [of] the materials and workmanship" and the reporting of any defects for the commissioners' immediate attention. Thus, Hoban was in effect in charge of what were at the time the three major public work projects of Washington. As the date for the transfer of government from Philadelphia grew closer, there was a simultaneous push to finish all three, or the Capitol, the President's House, and the Executive Office. As a result build-ing materials were often insufficient or, as usual, delayed in delivery. Master craftsmen were also in short supply, making necessary constant borrowing or shifting of manpower. In February 1800 Hoban had the added distraction of being named a member of the Washington City committee to welcome the Congress. Other members included Leonard Harbaugh, who served as chair; Dr. Richard Thornton, the commissioner; Robert Brent, the future mayor and nephew of Bishop Carroll; Captain Clotworthy Stephenson, an attorney and, like Hoban, an organizer of the Washington Artillery; William Lovering, a building contractor; John Kearney, a doctor and friend of Hoban's; Richard For-rest, a nephew of Georgetown's Colonel Uriah Forrest; Thomas Munroe, clerk to the commissioners; and Daniel Carroll of Duddington, the proprietor. Simi-lar committees were formed to represent Georgetown and Alexandria, which resulted in time-consuming arguments over order of precedence and other pro-tocolary problems.[47]

But Hoban succeeded. Both the President's House and the Capitol were at least usable—finished is not the word—a month before the due date set by Congress. On Saturday, November 1, 1800, shortly after noon, Anna Maria Thornton happened to look out the shop window of the city's first silversmith and saw "the President with his Secretary, Mr. Shaw, pass bye in his Chariot and four, no retinue only one servant on horseback." The commissioners and the various reception committees had thought the President could not possibly complete his long journey from Massachusetts before the following Monday.

142 Thus it happened that without ceremony President Adams . . . "went immediately to the house intended for him," as Mrs. Thornton succinctly recorded the non-event.

What Adams found inside was a building with approximately half its thirty-six rooms plastered. Far fewer had wallpaper. In between were empty and cavernous hallways where little or no interior work was yet done. Unlike his wife, who joined him two months later and expressed herself freely on the building, we do not really know what Adams thought of this state of affairs. It is on record, however, that Adams went right to work, receiving his first callers

Library of Congress.

North wing of the capitol as completed by the time Congress moved from Philadelphia in 1800, watercolor by William Birch.

that afternoon. In the evening he climbed a narrow servants' staircase—no others were finished—to the rooms of the second floor. There he passed his first night alone and without complaint.[48]

A similarly uneventful beginning marked the arrival of the Congress. The opening session, originally scheduled for the seventeenth of November, was twice postponed for lack of a quorum, first by the House and then by the Senate. But on the twenty-second, a cold day with early snow on the ground, quorums in both houses gathered to hear the President's message. Somehow, whether because of the postponement, the inclement weather, or, most probably, bickerings over protocol, the various reception committees, including Harbaugh's Washington City committee, failed to carry out their long-planned marches and speeches of welcome.

Nevertheless, inside the north wing, although it stood starkly alone atop Capitol Hill, there was more than enough of both ceremony and warmth. "It [the opening session] was made in the Chamber, and the whole appearance was solemn and conducted with Order," Mrs. Thornton, the dutiful diarist, wrote of the occasion, although the galleries were so packed that many of "the Ladies sat and stood below, on the same floor as the Senate." But Hoban's wing was essentially finished; only one brick wall, later to be replaced by stone from the Brent quarries, and some pillars covered with lathing and plaster bespoke its temporary role. A contemporary newspaper spoke of it as "being handsomely painted and furnished, [presenting] a very magnificent appearance."[49]

Some members did not agree. Although the overall appearance may have suggested a touch of magnificence, the roof leaked and space was cramped. But to Washingtonians, not to say the commissioners, these were small matters. What was important was that the transfer of government was complete. The President, the Congress, and the better part of the executive departments were seated in the City of Washington in the District of Columbia. Had not President Adams boldly told the Congress "I congratulate you, Gentlemen, on the prospect of a residence not to be changed"? What better proof could there be that the threat of Philadelphia was no more. That was cause enough to be confident and to celebrate, not to dwell on temporary inadequacies.[50]

So it seemed, at least, to Washington's early inhabitants in the heady moments of November 1800.

8

A Residence Not to Be Changed

Upon the whole, the city "looks up" considerably. It must necessarily become one day or another a great place.

-Benjamin Henry Latrobe,
February 5, 1810

The inadequacies of the new capital, it soon became apparent, were more than temporary. Problems remained in greater number and for far longer a time than the city fathers even remotely anticipated. Such, of course, is the history of nearly all created capitals, all forced cities, as Latrobe might call them. But few if any have received more ridicule or came closer to failure than Washington. The New Rome, as its most ardent boosters often called it, was to the Irish poet Thomas Moore in 1804 a place

> *Where tribunes rule, where dusky Davi bow*
> *And what was Goose Creek once is Tiber now:*
> *This embryo capital, where Fancy sees*
> *Squares in morasses, obelisks in trees. . . .*[1]

Similarly, William Dunlap, one of the first portrait painters to come to Washington, gazed from his top-floor room in Semmes Tavern in Georgetown in 1806 and saw "the Capitol at two miles distance, towering like some antique Ruin." Everywhere he looked, in fact, Dunlap saw great unfinished works. He sadly concluded the city might fail since people cannot long "live much less grow rich upon prospects." A British writer who complained that to travel the early streets and avenues was "to threaten your limbs with dislocation," dismissed the entire capital enterprise as a disgrace to the new republic. His view was widely shared. In truth there was scarcely a traveler who came to observe the new capital or a public servant who came to live in it whose journals or diaries are not filled with references to coaches mired in mud, lodgings at overcrowded and overpriced boarding houses, losing one's way in the woods between Capitol Hill and Georgetown, and many other similar misfortunes. Perhaps the most charitable of all such commentary came from New York's Gouverneur Morris. "We only need here houses, cellars, kitchens, scholarly men, amiable women, and a few other such trifles to possess a perfect city," Morris wrote to a friend in France. "In a word, this is the best city in the world to live in—in the future."[2]

Yet what Morris said half in jest was the earnest conviction of other Washingtonians. These other Washingtonians may not have harbored any illusions about creating the world's most perfect metropolis, but they were firm in their determination to see the city succeed. From their diaries and correspondence there emerges a far different picture of the embryo capital.

"Tuesday was a delightful day, and Mr. S. and myself sallied forth," Margaret Bayard Smith, wife of Samuel Harrison Smith, the founding editor and co-owner of the *National Intelligencer*, wrote in early November 1800, not long after the Smiths had arrived from Philadelphia. She had thought she was venturing out "into a land of strangers," but before the day was done she and her husband walked more than four miles and made first calls at the homes of Captain Thomas Tingey, commandant of the Navy Yard, and Thomas and Elizabeth Custis Law, the latter being Martha Washington's granddaughter and the reigning belle of early Washington. At the Tingeys they sat for morning tea and at the Laws's, a roast-turkey dinner during which four or five gentlemen, including Robert Peter, the first mayor of Georgetown, happened to drop by. "Vivacity and good humor prevailed and our party was fifty times more agreeable than if we had all met by previous invitation," Mrs. Smith wrote of the latter event.[3]

For many who like Margaret Smith wanted the city to succeed, Washington offered an endlessly fascinating panorama. They, too, might suffer carriages mired or broken down in the mud, but they had the high-spirited energy to hike up their skirts or trousers and slog on to their destinations, confident in the knowledge that a warming fire and borrowed footwear might somehow be provided. The banks of the Potomac and Tiber Creek—the "wilderness" where Congressmen got lost and cursed—were for them as "distinguished by romantic scenery as any rivers in our country." For them the distances within the city of which almost everyone else complained were both a challenge and a social boon because friends and new acquaintances often visited "without form of ceremony" to see if they could be of mutual help.[4]

Social distractions were many. Foremost among them were the subscription dances known as the Washington Assembly, organized within a month of the transfer of government. There was "no want of handsome ladies for the balls," British envoy Augustus John Foster wrote of them, "indeed, I never saw prettier girls anywhere." There were also shopping trips to Georgetown, which were nearly always mixed with social visits, horse races featuring the nation's finest thoroughbreds from the breed stocks of Maryland and Virginia, and well-attended interdenominational Sunday services in the House of Representatives with sermons by distinguished visiting clergymen. "Some opposition was made both to a Roman Catholic [chaplain] and Unitarian," Mrs. Smith has carefully noted, "but did not succeed."[5]

Even the arrival of the post—the "northern mail," it was sometimes called—was an eagerly awaited daily event for the citizens of what historians have been too prone to call a city in isolation. So, too, were copies of the *National Intelligencer*, which gave its readers the Congressional debates *in extenso* and as many reliable notices from traveler-correspondents at home and abroad as space would permit. Under the leadership of Samuel Harrison Smith and the British-born Joseph Gales, Jr., whose family Thomas Atwood Digges helped escape from England during the Revolution, the *Intelligencer* became one of the better newspapers of its day. It came closer than most, at least, to its stated objective of "diffus[ing] correct information through the whole of this nation."[6]

But nothing commanded more interest than the constant flow of new government officials, ministers from abroad, wealthy investors, and notable travelers who had to be met, entertained, and known. Margaret Smith has best described the process and its significance:

> Washington possesses a peculiar interest and to an active, reflective, and ambitious mind, has more attractions than any other place in America. This interest is daily increasing, and with the importance and expansion of our nation, this is the theater on which its most interesting interests are discuss'd, by its ablest sons, in which its greatest characters are called to act; it is every year, more and more the resort of strangers from every part of the union, and all foreigners of distinction who visit these states, likewise visit this city. There are here peculiar facilities for forming acquaintances, for a stranger cannot be long here, before it is known.[7]

The drama that the ablest sons were playing out, as Mrs. Smith so clearly understood, was nothing less than the creation of a great nation state. The stage, moreover, was as much in the drawing rooms of newly arrived officials and some of the older Maryland families as it was in the President's House or the halls of Congress. The most influential of these stages, graced by a constant stream of statesmen, authors, politicians, and diplomats, was at the home of the Smiths.

Urged by Jefferson to come to Washington in 1800, Samuel Harrison Smith was an ardent but open-minded Jeffersonian Republican whose sound judgment and conciliatory talents both as publisher of the *Intelligencer* and president of the Washington branch of the Bank of the United States earned him the nickname of "Silky-Milky" Smith. His wife Margaret Bayard, born of a prominent Federalist family from Pennsylvania and Delaware, was by all accounts early Washington's most accomplished hostess. The Smith home has been described as a meeting ground for "statesmen, philosophers, poets, diplomats . . . [and] men of opposite political faith [who] associated there on friendly terms." Much the same could be said of Richard Thornton and his wife Anna Marie Brodeau, the principal difference being that they more frequently hosted or visited potential investors and the government officials most concerned with the city, as befitted Dr. Thornton's position as a commissioner. Always, in these exchanges, an infectious optimism for the future of the capital city prevailed.[8]

Roman Catholics were part of the process. Although Protestants might be expected to bridle at a Catholic chaplain for Congress, no obstacles whatsoever stood in the way of the Maryland Catholic gentry who wished to join the mainstream of Washington society. If anything, traditional social positions were reversed. In her first year in Washington, Margaret Smith was both pleased and flattered when Anne Brent Carroll of Duddington Manor visited with her twice within a week and subsequently sent "salad and asparagus, and what I still more highly value, large bunches of fine roses and magnolias" from the Duddington gardens.[9]

Nearly everyone from foreign envoys to cabinet officers valued the rare invitation to the great riverfront home of Notley Young. Even more was this the case with Daniel Carroll of Duddington, who entertained very little. The Thorntons were honored to exchange visits with the venerable Mr. George Digges, the patriarch of Warburton. The James Barrys frequently entertained the Thorntons, Bishop Carroll, and Thomas and Elizabeth Custis Law. The Laws in turn entertained the Barrys and often made calls at the Thorntons. So, too did Bishop Carroll, who liked to discuss ideas or look over architectural drawings for his cathedral in Baltimore with Dr. Thornton.[10]

Of all the older Maryland Catholic families, however, none were more active than the Brents. Three of the sons of Robert and Anne Carroll Brent of Woodstock—Robert, the future mayor; Daniel of the State Department; and William, later councilman and court clerk—were on nearly everyone's invitation list. The Brents reciprocated, thanks mainly to Robert, who first lived in the city house of his father-in-law, Notley Young, and then much later at "Brentwood," the country seat designed for him by Benjamin Latrobe near what is now the campus of Gallaudet College. The list could go on; very few, if any, of the fifth- or sixth-generation Maryland Catholic families, so closely interrelated, would be absent from it.[11]

Historically, the Catholic presence in this process was important for two reasons. The first was the creation of an atmosphere of understanding and respect between the many Protestants who were beginning to know American Catholics for the first time. For such Protestants the result of this experience was often close to a revelation. Father John Grassi, the "second founder" of Georgetown College, has best described it. After talking of Catholics and Catholicism with many of his Protestant friends, Grassi found they might often "exclaim with amazement: 'Is that the teaching of the Catholic Church? Is that upright gentleman a Catholic? How different from the idea I had formed of it!'"[12]

The critic Anne Royall, we will remember, underwent just such a change of feeling when she first visited Georgetown College and Visitation Academy and found herself "never . . . amongst people more liberal, more affable, . . . or courteous." Among her acquaintances William Thomas Carroll of Belle Vue, long-time clerk of the Supreme Court, was "one of the best men in the city," nor could she forget that William Brent furnished her with a room in the boarding house of the old Brick Capitol when she was virtually destitute. Benjamin Henry Latrobe unabashedly called Bishop Carroll *"one of the best men in the world,"* underlined, in his journal. Later he would execute the plans for

148   Carroll's Baltimore Cathedral without fee. Following the precedent of General
Washington, James Madison was pleased to visit Georgetown College. So, too,
were various delegations from Congress. For so many who came to Washington—cabinet officers and other officials, journalists, legislators from each state
in the union, financiers, builders, merchants—the first face of Catholicism was
not what they had been led to expect. Here were no abject servants of a foreign
power or ignorant victims of superstition and prejudice. Here were loyal and
informed Americans, not so very much different from themselves.[13]

Second, the Catholic presence was important to the extent that many of
the leading Catholics would become active in the political life of the capital
city. As activists, if we may so call them, they needed allies. They found them in
the person of Samuel Harrison Smith, whose *National Intelligencer* consistently
defended Catholics against every manifestation of bigotry. They found them in
his wife's drawing room, where by Mrs. Smith's own weary admission "of an
evening some one or more of the gentlemen of congress are always here." Once
they were there, moreover, Mrs. Smith, as the doyenne of government society,
would enforce harmony between Federalist and Jeffersonian and demand due
respect for even the most rustic of legislators. ("Do not think now these good
men are fools, far from it," she once wrote to her sister, "They are very sensible
men and useful citizens, but they have lived in the backwoods, that's all.")
They found them also at Mrs. Thornton's, who claimed that more and more
callers dropped by every day, since "we are just about half way from the Capitol to George Town." In these and similar settings the overture to the capital's
battle for survival was played out with the utmost civility.[14]

Other Catholics, however, took part in this process under different circumstances. "Mr. Hoban called to speak about the plaistering in the President's
House," Mrs. Thornton recorded in her diary for 11 June 1800. Or, equally
tersely, that "Dr. T. sent by Mr. Munroe an order on Adam King George Town
for the amount of the bill sold by Mr. Wells $1044/10 to be paid in ten days."[15]
Whereas the Brents and the Barrys might come to dinner, others such as Hoban
and Trinity trustee Adam King came to the Thorntons' strictly for business. Social stratification, in other words, was not unknown, both among Catholics and
in Catholic-Protestant relationships.

At the upper levels, the leading Catholic families were not only all related
to each other, but also in many cases to the leading Protestant families. This occurred, as previously noted, because of mixed marriages. The marriages between Catholics and Protestants that had begun in colonial times continued to
be commonplace, seldom causing enduring friction among participating families. Catholic Lees married Episcopalian Ringgolds; Quaker Clouds married
Catholic Carberys; Protestant Ann Key, sister of Francis Scott, married Catholic
Roger Brooke Taney; and, in what Bishop Carroll came to call "the cause of
most poignant sorrow," both his own and the Charles Carroll of Carrollton
branch of the Carroll family engaged in more interfaith marriages than all the
rest. (Ever the realist, however, Carroll recognized that these marriages were

inevitable because "Here our Catholics are so mixed with Protestants in all the intercourse of civil Society, and business public and private.") But for other Catholics social acceptance was to be harder gained, by professional achievement or civic function, only.[16]

Fortunately, there were two institutions in early Washington where class distinctions among or against Catholics were blurred or entirely absent. One was St. Patrick's Church, which served as a force in binding the Catholic community together. This was especially true after the installation of Pastor William Matthews in 1805 and the opening of the new church in 1809. To the brick church on F and 10th streets came members of all the prominent Catholic families mentioned above, as well as such other old Maryland families as the Queens, Boones, Mattinglys, Spaldings, and Fenwicks. There were also what we have previously called the new aristocracy of builders and artists—Hobans and Harbaughs, Franzonis and Bonanis, Dermotts and Callans—engaged in creating the capital. Occasional communicants are said to have included Chief Justice Roger Brooke Taney, the naval hero Commodore Stephen Cassin, the consul general of France, the minister from Mexico, and the family of James Ord, the reputed son of King George IV and Maria Fitzherbert. But, as before, many in the congregation probably continued to be "the poor people of the eastern sections," as they were sometimes called. Yet in a report to his Archbishop, Father Matthews characterized his congregation as "[in] all things proceeding in perfect harmony and fraternal charity." He did not exaggerate. Matthews was himself the principal philanthropist of St. Patrick's and, as noted before, a relative of the Carrolls, Youngs, and Brents. When he mounted the pulpit to ask more fraternal charity of his kinsmen, he usually got it.[17]

Outside of the Catholic community the crowded and smoky public rooms of Rhodes Tavern offered the other meeting place where class or sectarian differences were of little significance. It was there, for example, that the *National Intelligencer* of April 3, 1801, reported "a meeting of the Freeholders and Inhabitants of F Street North . . . [at which] it was unanimously agreed that, agreeable to Advertisement, Capt. James Hoban, Mr. John Kearney, and Capt. Clotworthy Stephenson be appointed a committee to provide subscriptions for carrying into execution the improvement of said street."

Undoubtedly, this meeting was held because neither Congress nor the commissioners had provided sufficient funds for street paving. At the time Congress had already appropriated approximately $40,000 for furnishings for the President's House and the Capitol.[18] But nothing had yet been spent on F Street, the one street in Washington that had begun to take on the aspect of a city. Citizen action was therefore beginning. At its head, in spite of his continuing construction commitments, was the indefatigable James Hoban.

We do not know what improvements, if any, came from Hoban's committee. In all probability his friends and neighbors of F Street were still too preoccupied with the subject matter of a meeting held a little more than a week before. The *National Intelligencer* for March 25 so announced it:

Notice. F Street North. A meeting of the Inhabitants of F Street, in the City of Washington, is particularly requested at Mr. Rhode's Little Hotel on Thursday evening next 6 o'clock P.M. on business of Importance to the Inhabitants and Proprietors.[19]

The reason for this meeting and the relatively urgent tone of the notice are easy to determine. The same issue of the *Intelligencer* carried a lengthy report on the debate in Congress "on the bill for the government of the District of Columbia." The debate, which at first commanded far more attention in the press than in the halls of Congress, centered around Article I, Section 6 of the Constitution requiring the Congress "to exercise exclusive legislation in all Cases whatsoever . . ." over the ten-mile square of the District of Columbia. This was the provision, so applauded in theory, whereby the national government would have its permanent home in a place free from the influence, special interests, or pre-existing legal structures of any one state. The language, to be sure, was clear enough. How to translate it into a practical form of government for the District was another matter. Did the Constitution really intend the citizens of Washington to be stateless wards of the federal government, with neither voice nor vote in its affairs? Yes, some said, that was exactly what the exclusive right vested in Congress meant. There was no doubt about it; the District's inhabitants should be pleased and honored to place their trust in the national government. They could rest assured that it would never be abused. Not at all, replied Samuel Harrison Smith and a chorus of voices in the *National Intelligencer*. Such an assumption was nothing less than a despotic denial of a natural right of all citizens.[20]

These and other aspects of the District's government, we may be sure, were what first brought the inhabitants of F Street to a series of urgent meetings. Citizen action, in the form of a lengthy campaign for what later came to be called District home rule, was having its small beginnings. At the time Rhodes' Little Hotel served not only as an unofficial city hall, but also the District sales office for government-owned land and the meeting place for such diverse groups as militia companies, volunteer fire brigades, and the patrician organizers of the Washington Assembly.[21]

Those who gathered at Rhodes' to determine Washington's future government were Catholic and Protestant alike, both from the older families and the newly arriveds, without social distinction. No record of their meetings survives, but we may reconstruct the participants first from those who were previously active at Rhodes Tavern in organizing militia companies, volunteer fire companies, and the committees to welcome Congress or improve the city's services and, secondly, from those who emerged as appointed or elected officials when a limited form of municipal government was soon gained by their collective efforts. In the first group would be Hoban, his friend and F Street neighbor Dr. John Kearney, attorney Clotworthy Stephenson, Richard Forrest, Commissioner Thornton, and Leonard Harbaugh. The second includes, among others, the Catholics Daniel Carroll of Duddington, the brothers Robert and William

Brent, James Barry, and George Hadfield, and the Protestants Benjamin Moore, William Prout, Nicholas King, and John P. Van Ness.[22]

What most concerned such citizen groups in the spring of 1801 was that the first Congress to convene in Washington had not, after all, much concerned itself with the District. An act passed on February 27, four days before the expiration of President Adams's term, sidestepped the suffrage issue except to say that the right to vote might be limited to freehold property owners. For the rest it said not a word about a corporate form of municipal government for Washington City, such as the Georgetown and Alexandria portions of the District of Columbia already enjoyed.[23] As the year wore on, neither the new administration of President Jefferson nor the new Congress that convened in November brought about any significant changes. The latter, like many to follow, continued to grumble about the primitive state of the capital. Some members in fact, might even be heard to say that they favored a return to Philadelphia.

Such talk only spurred the city's activists to greater efforts. Earlier in the year the commissioners had asked Hoban to erect a temporary brick building for the House of Representatives to relieve overcrowding in the Capitol's north wing; it was ready when the seventh Congress convened in November, complete with a covered passageway between the two buildings. At this time also the first oil-fired street lights, centered mostly around the Capitol, began to appear. Nor were private efforts lacking. In December a proper market was opened, thanks in part to a citizen committee that included Hoban, Commissioners Thornton, William Brent, and Clotworthy Stephenson. More hotels and boarding houses were springing up, especially around Capitol Hill, drawn by the example of Daniel Carroll of Duddington, who had invested heavily in the well-known Carroll Row apartment building and other of his nearby properties. Not far from these stood the neo-Georgian dwelling of Robert and Mary Brent Sewall, newly re-modeled and enlarged. It was then and stands today as one of Capitol Hill's finest.[24]

If these efforts failed to impress Congress, two forces now came into play which at least focussed its attention. First, in March 1802, a group of the city's activists decided the time had come to present a formal "Address to Congress." Heading the list of the committee chosen to do so were Robert Brent, who was made chairman; Notley Young, by now the patriarch of the local Catholic community; and, as might be expected, Daniel Carroll of Duddington. Their greatest wish, the drafters solemnly declared, was for Congress to consider "the situation in which the inhabitants of the City of Washington are now placed by the assumption of the jurisdiction of the United States, praying Congress to give them a corporation."[25]

At about the same time sectional differences were springing up between Georgetown, Washington, and Alexandria concerning bridges, canal, or roadway proposals that might benefit one community at the expense of the others. The most ambitious of these proposals, the Eastern Branch Bridge Company, headed mainly by William Brent, and the Washington Canal Company, whose early organizers included Daniel Carroll of Duddington and Daniel Carroll

Brent, required such substantial sums that their backers knew private subscriptions alone would never suffice and therefore went to Congress requesting substantial federal aid. As a result, Congress found itself immersed in lengthy and controversial debates on what were essentially local matters, to the neglect of its national mandate. So much was this the case, in fact, that one congressman complained that "There are as many interfering interests in this ten-mile square as in the whole of the United States." The combined effect of the petitioners of the Address to Congress and the partisans of sectional interests was too much. The citizens of the District, members now began to say, should take care of their own affairs.[26]

Results were not long in coming. On 3 May 1802, Congress cautiously passed "an Act to incorporate the inhabitants of the city of Washington" which gave Washington corporate government for a trial period of two years. The new corporation consisted of a mayor appointed by the President and a twelve-member city council to be elected annually "by the free white male inhabitants of full age who have resided in the city and paid taxes therein the year preceding." Once again nothing was said of the right of citizens to vote for the President or to be represented in Congress, but the trial period act of 3 May 1802 did give the corporation fairly broad powers. These included the authority to enact ordinances for the regulation of many municipal functions, from the establishment of markets and the licensing of theaters or other places of amusement to the patrols of watchmen and "the size of bricks that are to be made and used in the city." Of much more importance to residents, we may be sure, was a provision authorizing the corporation "to lay and collect taxes." (This was not the complete taxing authority Washingtonians wanted, however; it gave the City Council the power to set or "levy" tax rates, but left the assessment of real and personal property against which the rates were applied to the District Court, whose officials were federally appointed.) Finally, Congress showed no hesitation about the timing of this experiment in self-rule. The election of council members, the act specified, was to be held within a month.[27]

It was enough. More, perhaps, than the activists at Rhodes Tavern had reason to expect. But now that a doorway to citizen participation was suddenly opened, who would rush through on such short notice to put their names before the public, or for that matter, accept Presidential appointment? The political horizons offered few rewarding prospects. The city lacked anything resembling a street system, except on paper, and even the most rudimentary sanitation. It was deeply in debt and looking to an indifferent Congress for help. Talk of failure, meaning a return to Philadelphia, had not ceased.

For Maryland Catholics raised in a strong tradition of public service, Washington's first municipal government posed a formidable test. Granted that Catholic landowners and building contractors had a vested interest—some much more than others—in seeing the city succeed. But a strong sense of commitment was also required to represent without pay a fledgling and problem-plagued city that was fast becoming the butt of national ridicule, a city that in fact might officially expire from one day to the next.[28]

Catholics responded well, both in accepting appointments and in standing for elections. Among the candidates for the councils of 1802 and 1803 were James Barry, William Brent, Daniel Carroll of Duddington, Griffith Coombe, George Hadfield, Thomas Herty, James Hoban, and John Kearney.[29] The first election, held on June 9, 1802, witnessed the unusual spectacle of the candidates themselves forming a significant portion of the electorate. The federal census of 1800 for Washington City estimated four to five hundred "heads of households" out of a total population of 3,120, but two years later those who met the residency and property qualifications for the first election and who were interested enough to vote numbered only 233. By contrast some twenty-three candidates vied for the twelve council seats. Thus one-tenth of the voters were themselves candidates. Taking the most active role in what was a hurried and highly informal process for the first election (candidates could be nominated simply by putting notice in the press, normally without any party affiliation), James Hoban organized a ticket for the western part of the city, and Robert Brent, himself not a candidate, for the eastern. The Catholics elected were Hoban, William Brent, James Barry, George Hadfield (1803 only), and Daniel Carroll of Duddington, with Carroll receiving the highest number of votes and Brent and Barry not far behind.[30]

In accord with the act of incorporation, the twelve members then voted Carroll and Hoban as aldermen, or members of the five-man "second chamber." In addition, James Barry was voted president of the "first chamber," later called the Common Council, as was Daniel Carroll of Duddington of the "second chamber," later the Board of Aldermen. Although not elected, Thomas Herty, a parishioner of Trinity and later St. Patrick's, was made secretary to the first chamber and register (read registrar) of the city. In the latter position Herty was in effect the city's principal administrator, since the register was responsible for such essential tasks as budget preparation, tax assessments, keeping records of all the mayor's official appointments, and granting business licenses in the latter's absence. He was succeeded after eight years by William Hewitt, who may also have been a parishioner of St. Patrick's. About the only prominent Catholic who had no role in Washington's first municipal government was Notley Young. But for this he can scarcely be blamed. The patriarch of Duddington Pasture had died on 23 March 1802, a day after signing the manifesto to Congress in behalf of a corporate government.[31]

Catholics did equally well in presidential appointments. On March 3, 1801, or the last day of his term, President John Adams named British-born William Kilty chief judge of the newly established "circuit court," which at the time was the District's highest judiciary post. Both William and his older brother John were among the last students to attend the English Jesuit colleges at St. Omers and Bruges before their closure. Brought to America before the outbreak of the Revolution, John Kilty captained ships in Maryland's infant navy. William Kilty studied medicine, served as a surgeon's mate to the 4th Maryland Regiment, was captured in the battle of Camden, and probably began the study of law while on parole. In 1798 he was commissioned by the

154 Maryland Assembly to compile the laws of the state, an assignment that eventually bore fruit as *The Laws of Maryland* in six volumes. An ardent bibliophile, Kilty was almost as well known for his poetry and translations of the classics as for his respected legal opinions. His two associate justices, both holdovers from the Adams administration, were William Cranch and James Marshall, whose brother John was at the time just beginning his term as chief justice of the United States. After serving the circuit court for five years Kilty resigned to become chancellor of Maryland, or the state's highest legal officer. There he served until his death in 1821.[32]

Answering the call to serve in Kilty's first grand jury was a remarkable assemblage of the District's leadership, both Protestant and Catholic, from Georgetown as well as Washington. Among the Protestants were Colonel Francis Deakins, the landholder who sold John Carroll the acre and a half of Georgetown College's original campus; Thomas Corcoran, the shoemaker to the college who became Georgetown's mayor and a successful merchant and realtor; John Plater, son of Governor George Plater and a member of one of Maryland's foremost political families; Clotworthy Stephenson, the Washington attorney; and Thomas Peter, the son of Mayor Robert Peter and husband of Martha Parke Custis, one of the granddaughters of Martha Washington. Working with them were such well-known Catholics as James Barry, Robert Brent, Daniel Carroll of Duddington, and Marsham Waring, private banker to Bishop Carroll.[33]

To round out the circuit court, President Thomas Jefferson appointed Daniel Carroll Brent of the Richland Brents as marshal of the District of Columbia. Often confused with his exact namesake and first cousin who was chief clerk at the State Department and later consul at Paris, Daniel Carroll Brent of Richland was a long-time member of the Virginia House of Delegates from Stafford County. Jefferson had good reason to reward Brent. It was he, the reader may remember, who as the Republican elector for northern Virginia so ably defended Jefferson from a Federalist vilification campaign in the election of 1796. At the time of Brent's appointment, the marshal of the District and his deputies were solely responsible for the administration of the court system, from issuing subpoenas and bringing in prisoners to jury empanelment and the management of court costs. In addition the District marshal served as master of public ceremonies—he was, in effect, the government's chief of protocol—and the compiler of the District's census.[34]

Among Jefferson's other early appointments was Robert Brent, great-great-grandson of Captain George Brent of Woodstock, son-in-law of Notley Young, and nephew of Bishop John Carroll, whom Jefferson chose as the first mayor of the City of Washington in June 1802. It was a good choice. Brent was a relatively young man of thirty-eight, but he had been active in capital city affairs and the campaign for a municipal government for more than a decade. Although possessed of some wealth, he was not a major District landowner of the stature of Notley Young or the Carrolls and had little direct interest in Washington property sales. More important, he moved easily in early Washington's government and society, from St. Patrick's Church to the President's House.[35]

Robert Brent, first mayor of Washington (1802-1812), attributed to William Cranch.

Still another Brent, William—"Billy," as the youngest of the eight children of Robert and Ann Carroll Brent of Woodstock was known to his family—did more for the city and the District in general than anyone else in the extended family, with the possible exception of his older brother Robert, the mayor. As popular at the polls as he was in the drawing rooms of Mrs. Smith and Mrs. Thornton, William Brent received the highest number of votes in the election for the second city council in 1803, on which he initially served three terms. In January 1804 President Jefferson asked him to serve as his private secretary, apparently for the second time, with the President assuring him that he would make "every accommodation which may reconcile the new duties it will superadd to the prosecution of your present pursuits." We do not have Brent's reply, but he evidently begged off to finish his term on the city council. The next year, however, he did accept the President's appointment to serve as clerk to Judge Kilty's circuit court, replacing Colonel Uriah Forrest of Georgetown, who had died in July 1805. There William Brent remained for twenty-three years, making improvements in court administration and putting together the first

William Brent, younger brother of Mayor Robert Brent, clerk of the District Circuit Court, City Council member; engraving after an original crayon portrait by Julien Fevret de Saint-Mémin.

Georgetown University Library
Special Collections Division.

comprehensive report on the government's troubled property sales. This done, in 1828 he returned to the city council, where he was elected for thirteen more terms, or a period of service equalled only by James Hoban. During all these years it is difficult to find any of the capital's social, cultural, or commercial institutions of which he was not a part. The Washington Dancing Assembly, the Eastern Branch Bridge Company, the Bank of the United States, the Washington Theater Company, Washington's first School Board—all these and more bear the name of "Billy" Brent as an active participant.[36]

Mayor, chief judge, president of the Board of Aldermen, president of the Common Council, five of twelve council members, marshal of the District, clerk of the court, city administrator—all these were the posts occupied by Catholics in the first two years of Washington's municipal government. The older among them had been young men in the time when Catholics were barred from all public office and refused the right of public worship. Now they were in a position of leadership in the nation's infant capital. Although prejudice would always remain, there is no record of any public outcry, much less official opposition, to the Catholic prominence in Washington's first government. Rather, Catholics and Protestants appear to have worked mainly in harmony in the difficult task of steering the capital through its most vulnerable years. To be sure, there was more than a grain of truth in the often-repeated joke that Washington's first mayor and council members presided over a city of great streets with no houses, whereas their counterparts in Georgetown managed a city of great houses with no streets. But precisely because early Washington was a city of intention, a city of promise more than reality, a correspondingly greater commitment to the common good was required of all who had the will to serve it. That so many Catholics did is much to their credit.

Their task was never easy. The process of transforming intention into reality was in the case of Washington attended by constant discouragements and a special risk. That special risk, it cannot be stated too often, was the threat that the process could be aborted at any moment by the whim of Congress. Thus, for example in 1803, Congressman John Bacon of Massachusetts introduced a resolution that, although couched in the language of having the District "retrocede" its land to the states of Maryland and Virginia, was widely understood to be the first step in having the capital moved to another city.[37]

We can but little imagine the effect this must have had on Washington's builders and investors. The Bacon resolution, as it was known, came at a time when the city's activists were making a concerted effort to improve the capital's growth and governance. In the year 1803 James Hoban, although heavily engaged with private commissions and real estate transactions, was called upon to make some major changes in the President's House ordered by its second occupant. George Hadfield, rescued from his misfortunes through his sister's enduring friendship with President Jefferson, had built the city's first jail on what is now Judiciary Square, which he now followed with the much-admired Marine Barracks near the Navy Yard and the Washington Arsenal at Greenleaf Point.[38] For its part the city council worked with unusual dispatch. In its first two years it passed a spate of bills and ordinances on market regulations, licensing of taverns and theaters, and fire and crime prevention. In addition, after Congress turned down the city's first request for federal aid, the council members painfully dipped into their own meager municipal funds, derived mostly from license fees, to begin road improvements and street paving.[39]

In the private sphere more hotels, taverns, and boarding houses were everywhere apparent. By 1804 the Capitol Hill area could boast of at least four commodious hotels or boarding houses and a host of smaller lodgings. Others were springing up to the west along Pennsylvania Avenue, all the way to Georgetown's Union Hotel, the District's largest "with forty to fifty lodging rooms judiciously arranged, and eight to ten private parlors, with bedrooms adjoining." Although some officials claimed that they lived in rooming houses "like scholars in a college or monks in a monastery," as Treasury Secretary Albert Gallatin once complained, others found the upper stories of Daniel Carroll of Duddington's Carroll Row apartments offered an inspiring view, while downstairs in the drawing rooms the after-dinner pianoforte and song recitals by the landlord's daughter were "truly delightful after we have been fatigued with the harangues in the Hall all day." Stagecoach routes and ferry services were expanding rapidly, thanks in part to lucrative government mail contracts. In 1804 the *National Intelligencer* and several other newspapers carried announcements for both the newly established Eastern Market and the Centre

Market, which had been organized by the now-familiar trio of James Hoban, William Brent, and Clotworthy Stephenson. There were also announcements for such varied amenities as McCormick and Cochran's men's furnishings on Capitol Hill, John Gardner's City Repository and Auction Room, Robert Ware Peacock's lecture courses on the law, and "Mr. Xaupi's Dancing School, three doors above Mr. Rhodes Tavern." By that time, too, artists Gilbert Stuart and Charles Saint Memin were both in residence, exercising their talents in portraiture. The United States Theater in Blodget's Hotel, which Mrs. Thornton described in 1800, was joined in 1804 by the Washington Theater built by George Hadfield and organized mainly by Robert Brent, Daniel Carroll of Duddington, and Thomas Herty. (One of its first offerings was a drama titled "Honest Thieves, or the Faithful Irishman," of which it may be just as well we know nothing more.)

But the most popular of all public events—one of which Congress never complained—was the thoroughbred racing staged by the Washington Jockey Club. The Jockey Club's three-day race meets attracted the city's gentlemen and ladies of fashion in their best equipages and "between 3,000 and 4,000 people—black and white, from President of the United States to the beggar in his rags, of all ages and both sexes." To which add the Congress of the United States, who, as one senator observed, so relished "the sport that there was a serious wish of a number of members to adjourn." As in fact they often did, always conveniently declaring that there was "no business in due state in preparation to be acted upon" on the days of the meet.[40]

The sum total of all these efforts, however, did not fully persuade Congress. As the new Congress met in 1804 there were further debates and resolutions about moving the capital. The next year Congressman Andrew Gregs of Pennsylvania introduced a resolution calling for the retrocession of all lands within the District "as are outside the City of Washington" to Maryland and Virginia. But opponents saw through his resolution as another stratagem ultimately aimed at moving the capital. It was finally defeated after four days of continuous debate. To Washington's activists the unkindest cut of all came from Senator Robert Wright, a Jeffersonian and Marylander who by every standard should have been a Washington booster. Wright introduced a bill that not only called for retrocession of the District's lands to Maryland and Virginia, but also removal of the seat of government to Baltimore. When it met with an indifferent reception in the Senate, Wright quickly and apologetically explained that it was not his intention that the bill should be passed, "but that it should operate as a stimulus to the inhabitants of the city to exert themselves in providing more convenient accommodations for the members of Congress." Washingtonians may have derived some slight satisfactions from the Senate's rebuff, but they scarcely needed the gratuitous prodding of Senator Wright.[41]

But problems remained, as every citizen concerned with the capital well knew. Beyond the race meets or the drawing rooms of the city's leaders was another Washington. Viewing it with the first government officials to arrive in June of 1800, Treasury Secretary Wolcott called it a scattered collection "of miserable huts, which present an awful contrast to the public buildings." Its inhabitants were very poor, he added, "and as far as I can judge, they live like fishes, by eating each other." He scarcely exaggerated. The shifting population of laborers, the homeless artisans who had flocked to the New Rome to find neither the promised grandeur nor the opportunity to create it—these were by all contemporary accounts a highly visible and significant element in Washington's early population.[42]

Granted that Catholics had a leading civic and social role in early Washington, we may logically ask at this point what, if anything, was particularly Catholic about their contribution to the founding of the capital. Help to the city's poor and homeless provides one answer, if not a uniquely Catholic one. So, too, does the extraordinary commitment to public service in general, which in the case of some Washington Catholics continued to pass from one generation to the next.

The first city council, for example, which had the highest Catholic representation of any, incurred a deficit by voting almost half of its meager resources to poor relief. Pathetic and inadequate as its budget may have been—it totalled $1,715, derived mainly from municipal property taxes and tavern licensing fees—the sum of $720, or forty-two percent, was disbursed for "support of the poor." (By contrast street repair, so often demanded and so seldom provided by Congress, received but $250). The councils of 1803 and 1804 voted slight increments, but it was soon apparent that much bolder measures were needed.[43]

The next year, therefore, Mayor Robert Brent appointed a three-man board called Trustees of the Poor, who first assigned themselves the difficult task of determining who most deserved help on an individual or case-by-case basis. They did this in part because transient paupers were becoming such a problem that, as the council put it, "we cannot comfortably or economically provide for our own numerous poor." Among the transients were not only laborers, but also increasing numbers of pension claimants, job seekers, and what the council called "straggling vagabond beggars" who descended on Washington with the opening of each new Congress. Supporting the councils' attitude toward transients was the tradition long held both in England and America that itinerant paupers should be sent back to their place of origin, since communities were responsible only for their own poor. Accordingly, the trustees appointed screening committees who announced they would "sit every morning at half after nine, and every afternoon at half after four at Mr. Rhodes Tavern, where, as well as at their respective homes, application may be made to them."[44]

In this manner, unusually accommodating for its time, the Trustees of the Poor attempted to determine not only the neediest, but also who among them were resident and who were not. For those qualifying as residents the trustees authorized clothing and room and board for single persons either by contract with private households or in a small wooden poorhouse on Judiciary Square. Also provided were the services of a public physician and a two-dollar weekly

160 allowance for "resident families." But the problem only grew, in spite of such efforts. The council therefore asked Congress for a lease if not a gift of some of the vast unsold acreage of federal land near the northern limits of the city. The Congress refused. Thereupon, or in October 1806, the council voted $2,000 to purchase a square of land and build a more adequate poorhouse, officially known as the Washington Infirmary. (It was to serve the city until 1861, when it burned to the ground shortly after being taken over by the government as an Army hospital.) The cost of the Infirmary, moreover, was over and above an increased appropriation for poor relief in general of $1,750, all from a budget of approximately $10,000.

These council actions, small as they may seem in terms of dollars and cents, at least had a stimulating and more lasting effect on private relief efforts. In the years that followed the Washington Humane Society, the Washington Benevolent Society, the Female Benevolent Society of Georgetown, the Thespian Benevolent Society and many others, not the least of which was Father William Matthews's Female Orphan Asylum, did much to share the burden first assumed by the city government.[45]

Much the same is true of public education. In 1804, at a time when free schools were virtually unknown outside of New England, the council took an ambitious first step. In December the council members passed an act "to establish and endow a permanent institution for the education of youth" with an annual appropriation of $1,500, to be managed by a board of trustees that initially included, among others, Mayor Robert Brent, his youngest brother William, and James Barry. In this case however, the response by the private sector was much quicker and greater than with aid to the poor. Within six months the school board raised an additional $3,782 by private subscription; the list of subscribers, headed by President Jefferson, included almost everyone who had some role in the founding of the city. Even so, the "permanent institution," which was originally intended to be a combination grade school, college, and university, had to settle for something less.

By January 1806 the school board had obtained private and public support sufficient only to open two grammar schools, known as the Washington Academies, which offered instruction in reading, writing, mathematics, Latin, and geography to both free and tuition students. (The tuition was $15 per quarter for those parents who could afford it; the board directed that the names of the non-paying students, or "those educated as poor children," be divulged only to the principal, who was to keep this knowledge in strict confidence.) The council continued to support the two academies at the original level—$1,500 annually, or fifteen percent of its budget—until by 1812 the city's fiscal woes and complaints from taxpayers temporarily halted the appropriations. The two Washington Academies were thereupon closed and replaced by a single school of the Lancastrian system, much cheaper to operate, in which older students instructing the younger did most of the teaching.

Here again St. Patrick's William Matthews played a role. As chairman of the school board's Lancastrian subcommittee, Father Matthews importuned his parishioner, Mayor Robert Brent, and otherwise directed his considerable talent and energies to fund raising for the Lancaster School, which at one point had less than fifty dollars in operating expenses and two teachers unpaid for over six months. Matthews was successful both in raising the necessary private support and in convincing the council to restore a modicum of municipal funds. By this time, however, private schools were springing up all over the District and public schools would soon see better days. But for a few years the Lancaster Schools alone represented the slender continuum of public education in the City of Washington.[46]

It would be interesting to know the exact part played by the Catholic members of the council in the initiatives for both public education and relief of the poor—their views that is, on the humanitarian issues. Unfortunately, the journals and proceedings of the early councils, which were available to historians early in this century, have since been lost. But we do know that a number of Catholic members remained as community leaders throughout their lives, whether serving the municipal government or not. A representative list would once again include the familiar names of Hoban, Hadfield, Carroll, the Brent brothers, and James Barry. Of these James Hoban and William Brent established records for length of service on the council. Brent ran successfully for six one-year terms on the Common Council and for five two-year terms on the Board of Aldermen. His service spanned the years 1802 through 1840, with one long break, as previously noted, during which he held the position of clerk to the circuit court.[47]

James Hoban followed much the same pattern, winning seats on the Common Councils of 1802, 1806, and 1808 through 1813, and on the Board of Aldermen from 1820 through 1826. His longest interruption came after the War of 1812 when, as we will see, he was heavily engaged in what might be called the rebuilding of the capital. And, just as William Brent continued to serve the city through many public and private efforts to improve its commerce, so also did Hoban in building both public and private projects. Of particular interest to this study were his work for the church and his participation in civic organizations. Much as we would like to learn more of these and, indeed, more of the life of James Hoban in general, all the papers and letterbooks of the man who did most to make ready the national capital have unfortunately been lost to fire. We do know, however, that Hoban drew the plans and "attended the building" of James Barry's St. Mary's Chapel in 1806, for the sum of $70, which was below scale for a man of his reputation. In 1815 he offered and was apparently chosen to plan the novitiate on the plot next to St. Patrick's given by Father Matthews to the Georgetown Jesuits. (This was the building, referred to in a previous chapter, first used as the home of the short-lived Washington Catholic Seminary; there is no record of Hoban's fee, if any.) And there remains the possibility, as yet undocumented, that Hoban was also the architect and supervisor of the St. Patrick's brick church which opened in 1809. In lay organizations Hoban was a member of one of the committees formed at Mayor Brent's urging to establish volunteer fire companies, beginning in 1804. As a next-door neighbor to Rhodes Tavern he was also presumably a member of the Society of the Sons of Erin, which began meeting there around 1810. In 1828, along with Brent and many others, James Hoban was a signatory to a memorial asking Congress to outlaw the slave trade in Washington.[48]

By contrast George Hadfield, by all accounts a modest and sensitive man, served but one term on the Common Council of 1803, preferring thereafter to devote himself entirely to his chosen profession. The road back, after his contretemps with Commissioner Thornton and his dismissal from the Capitol, had not been easy for Hadfield. At one point he found himself in such reduced circumstances that he pawned the gold medal for design awarded him by London's Royal Academy. (Benjamin Latrobe, hearing of it, bought the medal and sent it back to him.) It was at this point, or in the spring of 1801, that Hadfield at last swallowed his pride and wrote President Jefferson, whose love for Hadfield's sister, Maria Cosway had never diminished. His sister Maria soon followed suit, urging the President to do what he could for her brother, and while he was at it, the condition of all Catholics in the United States.[49] Jefferson thereupon recommended Hadfield for the previously mentioned City Jail, and, as nearly as can be determined, the Marine barracks, arsenal and commandant's house in southeast Washington.

Thereafter Hadfield enjoyed a highly successful career—in critical acclaim, that is, if not always in material gain—during which he made significant contributions to the growth of the city. Both private and public commissions now came his way. In the private sphere his works included the Washington Theater on 11th and C streets in 1804, Commodore David Porter's Meridian Hill residence in 1819, and the Second Bank of the United States (later the Riggs Bank) on Pennsylvania Avenue in 1824. Hadfield is also believed to have designed the Benjamin Ogle Tayloe row houses, later converted into the Willard Hotel, and the Way row houses, which were opened in 1806 by the printers Andrew and George Way.

In addition, when the Washington Theater burned down in 1820, Hadfield was engaged by Gaetano and Lewis Carusi, two stranded Italian musicians who had originally been invited to the United States by President Jefferson to improve the Marine Band, to design a combination theater, ballroom, and convention hall on the same site. The building, later known as the Washington Assembly Rooms or more familiarly Carusi's Saloon, became a Washington institution, serving for many years as the site of presidential inaugural balls and the city's best theater. So, too, did the enterprising Carusis, whose descendants remain prominent today in Washington's Catholic community.[50]

But there remain two masterworks, one private and the other public, which have secured Hadfield's place in architectural history. The first of these, described with some accuracy as "the most conspicuous residence in America," is Arlington House, completed in 1818. It stands today high on a hilltop overlooking the Arlington National Cemetery, commanding the most spectacular approach to monumental Washington. Better known as the Custis-Lee man-

sion, it has often been characterized as appearing noble and impressive from a 163
distance, but solemn, heavy, or too massive for residential purposes when
viewed close at hand. But such was the express intention of Hadfield's client,
George Washington Parke Custis, the eccentric grandson of Martha Washington whom president Washington adopted as a son.

Custis, who worked with Hadfield on the design, dedicated most of his
adult life to honoring his foster father. More than a home, therefore, he wanted
a museum for his vast collection of Washingtoniana and the battle scenes that
he himself painted to exalt General Washington's military triumphs. (His
paintings were not always well received; one, a thirteen-by-eleven canvas of
the Battle of Trenton, was so savaged by critics that Custis ordered it thrown
into the Potomac River.) Consciously or not, Custis also wanted the exterior of
Arlington House to be a theatrical backdrop, a proscenium against which he
could stage elaborate outdoor pageants, often with free refreshments, open to
the public. (Although born to the Virginia planter society Custis was a coura-
geous defender of the poor and the oppressed; he regularly marched with Irish
laborers on St. Patrick's Day, spoke out on every possible occasion against
religious intolerance, and attacked slavery as an institution that debased both

Library of Congress.

Arlington House, also known as the Custis Lee Mansion, George Hadfield, architect.

164   slave owner and slave.) Given his patron's requirements, therefore, Hadfield achieved the intended dramatic effects by various stratagems, most notably a grandiose portico with Doric columns five feet thick at their base. The building was at first dismissed as "Custis' folly" by some critics. But today architectural historians tend more to admire Arlington House for what it was intended to be. A temple to George Washington, one of them has called it, with Custis as its resident sacristan.[51]

Hadfield's other masterwork was entirely his own, done without undue interference or any major accommodations to a client's wishes. In 1814 the city council, which had met in such borrowed quarters as the Capitol, Lovell's Hotel, and a Masonic Hall, decided the time was at hand to have a home of its own and authorized a $10,000 lottery to build "a Town House or City Hall." Four years later, with the lottery still not a success, Hadfield submitted a design for a combined municipal government and court building, which the council initially rejected as too costly. After further delays, mainly because of the necessity to give priority to the repair and reconstruction of the buildings

Library of Congress.

Front entrance of the former Washington City Hall, George Hadfield, architect. The building is now part of the District Superior Court complex on Judiciary Square.

damaged or destroyed by the British in 1814, the Council of 1820 adopted Hadfield's slightly revised plan and named a commission to choose the site and supervise the construction of the City Hall. In August of that year, William
Hewitt, the long-time Register of the City, laid the cornerstone of the City Hall
near Judiciary Square, amid ceremonies enlivened by the Marine Band and
salvos from Navy Yard guns. But the city's chronic financial problems caused
long delays in construction, and the City Hall, now the District Superior Court,
was not completely finished until 1849, or twenty-three years after Hadfield's
death at the age of sixty-two.[52]

His design, however, which featured wings that separately contained the
courts and the city government, and a handsome portico with well-propor-
tioned Ionic columns, was essentially followed in the completed work, which
endures as a fitting memorial to "the architects' architect," or the one professional from early Washington who has been most universally admired by his
fellow architects. Today Hadfield's modest structure is all but overwhelmed by
a concentration of nearby District Court and federal office buildings. But the
passerby who approaches slowly from the Mall, pausing to consider scale and
proportion, will understand its particular appeal.[53]

Progress, although slow and painful, was coming to Washington. In 1810
Benjamin Henry Latrobe, once a severe critic of the capital's site, was confident
enough to declare that "the city 'looks up' considerably and must necessarily
become one day or another a great place."[54] Many of the major public buildings were built or nearing completion. Housing and services were improving.
The two-year trial period for Washington's municipal government had been
long extended by Congress. For the moment all talk of moving the capital had
ceased. "The prospect of a residence not to be changed," as President Adams
had said to Congress in 1800, now seemed a reality.

But one great shadow still hung over the growing city. It first showed itself well before the city was born, or in October 1791, when the first auction of
what was later surveyed to be ten thousand government-held lots valued at
$800,000 resulted in a sale of only thirty, for a total of approximately $7,650.[55] It
continued to cast a pall over all the subsequent property auctions that the federal government had looked to as the principal source of funds for constructing
the capital. The shadow, in short, was the city's questionable economic viability. Ironically, it was Latrobe at an earlier time who had first considered it.
Could the "forced city," he had asked himself as he looked over his shoulder to
fast-growing Baltimore and Philadelphia, prosper or even continue to exist
without any of the advantages of its rivals? Putting the problem another way,
could the seat of government draw to itself people and money if that were its
only attraction? If, that is, the sole business was the business of government.
That was the question.

9

Daniel Carroll of Duddington

Towards the close of his life, the example which he furnished of cheerfulness, submission to the visitations of Providence, the loss of property, and the infirmities of age, and all the Christian virtues, was not only consoling, but beautiful.

-GEORGE WATTERSTON,
Librarian of Congress, 1849

During Washington's first decade the answer to the question of whether or not the city could survive solely on the business of government was a clear no, although the city's perennial activists were slow to hear it and to recognize that efforts to promote commerce were failing. The final and hardest test for the capital, it soon proved, would be the struggle for some measure of financial stability. To this effort the area's Catholics applied themselves to a notable degree, equalling or even surpassing their participation in local government. Some of their initiatives were outright failures, even though they might represent moves in the right direction. Others were at least partially successful.

Prominent among the failures were the extensive wharves and warehousing facilities built on the Eastern Branch of the Potomac by James Barry and Thomas Law, who had been associated in the East India trade in New York and Philadelphia before either moved to Washington. Urged on by the ebullient Law, whose optimism for the Federal City knew no bounds, Barry built a large wharf on Greenleaf Point near the foot of New Jersey Avenue, Southwest, not far from his residence, as early as 1795.[1] There he waited for the ships of the world to sail up to the major port President Washington and other capital city visionaries had long anticipated. Within a year the inactivity at the wharf convinced Law and Barry that commerce might be stimulated if Washington had some manufactories. Accordingly, with Law taking the lead and with considerable help from Daniel Carroll of Duddington, they commissioned a huge brick warehouse—at eight stories high, it was said to be the biggest building in the District—for their use initially as a sugar refinery. Operations began early in 1798, but the venture failed very quickly. By January 1801 the building and the wharf, popularly known as "Castle Thunder" and Barry's Wharf, were described by future Treasury Secretary Albert Gallatin as "a very large but perfectly empty warehouse, and a wharf graced by not a single vessel." Shortly thereafter, Dr. Cornelius Coningham, an Englishman who owned a small brewery and whiskey distillery, leased Castle Thunder to enlarge his business. But by 1811 this enterprise had moved to lesser quarters.[2]

If Barry, Daniel Carroll of Duddington, or any other of the city's leading Catholics were concerned about these early portents, their subsequent actions showed no sign of it. In 1808 Mayor Robert Brent directly confronted the problem of commercial viability by convening a committee to consider "the expediency of organizing a plan for the incouragement of DOMESTIC MANU-FACTURE." Patriotically citing Jefferson's recent Embargo Act and the consequent need to make the United States free of dependency on European manufactures, the committee passed a resolution that clung to the long-held belief that the city was "the nearest navigable port to the Western Country" and therefore eminently suited to develop as an important manufacturing center.

At least two business ventures resulted from the Mayor's initiative. One was the Commercial Company of Washington, which set up shop at Barry's Wharf with $10,000 in capital and a board of directors which included James D. Barry, Barry's nephew whom he adopted as a son, and James Cassin, a ship owner and a member of a large and prominent Catholic family of both Georgetown and Washington. The Commercial Company served more or less successfully for three years as a market where farmers could sell or exchange their produce for clothing and other staples. It was succeeded by the Columbian Manufacturing Company, which accepted the proposal of one John Gardiner, who claimed to have had "the superintendence of a Cotton Manufactory for some years in Ireland," to manufacture cloth of cotton, wool, hemp, and flax. (At one point the Common Council recommended that all its members make their annual Fourth of July visit to the President dressed in the Company's homespun.) But the mills of the Columbian Manufacturing Company ground to a halt within four years.[3]

There were different reasons for the failure of these two companies—the Columbian was never sufficiently capitalized, for one—but the most important was common to both. This was simply the fact that Washington and its neighboring areas offered too small a market for anything but small-scale manufacturing for regional consumption. Much less could its difficult-to-reach port facilities ever serve as a center for world trade, although the dream of a great harbor dotted with sails at the foot of Capitol Hill died very hard.

The one exception, the one apparent center of industry in early Washington, was the Navy Yard, which by 1806 had a busy shipbuilding program complete with dry docks and a work force of over two hundred. But strictly speaking it, too, was "the business of government," since it had been favored by almost double the amount spent by the federal government on any other navy yard in the United States, not to mention a contract to build fifty gunboats. There was no escaping the reality. In the private sector the normal business of Washington was to attract more people to the seat of government, sell them property, build them houses, and stimulate small-scale commerce in the process.[4]

But, as we have seen, prospective home owners were slow to flock to the New Rome on the Potomac. Although the population of Washington was increasing, the sales of property were not showing a proportionate growth. In fact, neither the governmental nor private-owner sales improved much after the disastrous first auction of 1791. By the turn of the century less than one thousand of the government's ten thousand lots had been sold, and the pace of competitive private sales was no better.[5] The flow of investment capital from outside sources was even slower, held back primarily by the grumblings of Congress and the consequent uncertainty over the capital's political future. As a result the economy of Washington in its early years rested on a phantasmagoric structure of debt financing that included domestic and foreign loans, easy terms for speculators, unsecured bank notes that passed as currency, and occasional pump priming by the federal government and the District's wealthiest citizens.

Catholics served the city's troubled economy in many ways, most often to their personal disadvantage. A prime example is James Barry who, unknown to his family, kept investing in the future of the city to such a degree that he was insolvent by the time of his sudden death in 1808. Notley Young, Robert Sewall, Marsham Waring, Adam King, James D. Barry, Robert and William Brent, Griffith Coombe, and Daniel Carroll of Duddington were either founders or directors of Georgetown's and Washington's first banks.[6] But one man stands alone, above all others in his degree of commitment to save the capital. The reader will already know him as the name that appears on almost every committee or board of directors concerned with the city's general welfare. That one man was Daniel Carroll of Duddington II, grandson of Daniel Carroll of Duddington I, son of Charles Carroll of Duddington and Carrollsburg, and a relative by blood or marriage to most of the old-line Maryland Catholics mentioned in this work.

Surprisingly little is known of the person of Daniel Carroll of Duddington. He has not attracted much attention from Washington historians, and his voluminous papers, now at the Library of Congress, shed light principally on his business affairs. What rare personal glimpses they do afford, especially of his early life, suggest a serious young man who was perhaps awkward in bearing—he was known within the family as "Cousin Long Legs"—and heavily burdened both by his own strong sense of duty and an extended family that looked to him to perpetuate its fortune. Indeed, Carroll's father had died when Daniel was but nine years old, and Charles Carroll of Carrollton, Daniel's first cousin once removed and scion of "the rich Carrolls," soon took an interest in his younger cousin when it became apparent that his one and only son, Charles Carroll of Homewood, had little interest in the family fortune other than spending it on the beautiful home that still bears his name and is now a house-museum on the main campus of Johns Hopkins University.[7]

Charles Carroll of Carrollton by Thomas Sully, 1834.

170   It was at the urging of Charles Carroll of Carrollton, therefore, that Daniel of Duddington was sent to Europe in 1785 at the age of twenty-one to be "bound over," or apprenticed, to commercial agents in France and England. In the words of his elder cousin, he was "to perfect himself in the knowledge of the mercantile business." He was also to improve himself not only by studying the language of the French, "but also by the acquirement of some of the polish of their manners."[8] But Daniel had barely arrived in London when he was already worrying about spending his time in Europe to best advantage. "I wish not to throw away these few years," he wrote to Captain Ignatius Fenwick, his stepfather and closest counselor. "I mean to derive as much benefit as possible."[9]

The young Carroll had reason enough for his concern. Upon arrival in London he found that his younger brother Charles (later Charles Carroll of Belle Vue, Georgetown) with whom he intended to stay on the continent had left the Jesuit academy at Liège, where Charles was expected to begin studies for the bar. The circumstances of his departure, he told Fenwick, were enough to cause "my mother to make herself miserable should she hear of it."[10] Then came a letter from Charles Carroll of Carrollton saying that his daughter Mary, whom Daniel hoped to marry, was engaged to an English gentleman by the name of Richard Caton. "Time will wear away the impression which an early attachment may have made on your heart," the elder Carroll counselled.[11]

The bad news from home did not stop. There were troubles at the Hockley Mills, one of the iron-ore works outside of Baltimore on which the Carroll wealth was first founded. ("I believe you may employ your money to greater advantage in the city of Washington than in the Hockley concerns," Charles of Carrollton later wrote to Daniel in what may have been the eminent financier's worst single piece of advice.) Then came some problems with Notley Young over the boundary line between Young's "Duddington Pasture" and Daniel's contiguous "Duddington Manor" estates. These might entail re-surveys and examinations of the validity of titles going back two or three generations, matters not easily settled by trans-Atlantic correspondence. Finally, or by April 1789, Daniel's stepfather and most faithful counselor could hold back no longer. Four years of education and gentlemanly living in France and England were more than enough, Ignatius Fenwick thought, for anyone with his stepson's talents and prospects. "I again repeat my desire of your returning," he wrote to him. "Be assured no one is so proper to look after the business as a proper owner."[12]

Back home by 1790, Carroll faced a series of misfortunes that might have broken the spirit of anyone less imbued with the Maryland Catholic tradition of civic duty and noblesse oblige. First and foremost was a serious confrontation with the French engineer and city planner, Major Pierre L'Enfant.

In August 1791 L'Enfant claimed that a large house Carroll had been building on the southeast slope of Jenkins Hill protruded by some seven feet onto the diagonal line for New Jersey Avenue as newly proposed in L'Enfant's master plan for the city. Although Carroll had begun building his house before the Federal City was created and the proprietors' agreement with the President concluded, L'Enfant considered it to be on government property and gave it as his opinion that it should be torn down. After voicing objections Carroll was twice assured by Major Andrew Ellicott, L'Enfant's principal assistant, that the avenue width would be reduced or other accommodations "might be made without the least injury to the plan and that he [Ellicott] would be answerable that D.C. of Dudd. would be safe," according to the commissioners' investigation. Nevertheless, by the following November, when L'Enfant was away in Philadelphia and the two-story house had reached the flooring stage, workmen began to carry out L'Enfant's orders to destroy it. Carroll thereupon wrote a letter of protest to President Washington and hastened to Annapolis to secure a court injunction. But when he returned it was too late. L'Enfant's crew had finished their work. The one great house on Jenkins Hill—alone in a landscape of farmlands and forest—was destroyed down to its foundations.

President Washington was at first inclined to support L'Enfant as much as possible in public and in his letters to Carroll, arguing the legal technicalities of the case and suggesting some proposals for partial compensation.[13] (This was more than could be said for Mayor Robert Peter, Uriah Forrest, and others of the still-jealous Georgetown proprietors, who quickly distinguished themselves by urging the District Commissioners to deny Carroll any compensation whatsoever and praising L'Enfant "for his zeal, activity, and good judgement in the affairs of the city.") But privately the President was shocked, unable to understand how his trusted planner could have taken such a step without a prior word to him or the commissioners. "A similar case cannot happen again," Washington had first written L'Enfant. Later, after receiving more information on the incident, the President sternly enjoined him "to touch no man's property without his consent, or the previous order of the commissioners." L'Enfant should understand, Washington added, that "In this [matter] you have laid yourself open to the Laws."[14]

To the commissioners, also, the President expressed his indignation, telling them to make sure L'Enfant knew "that there will be no interference from me on his behalf" should the matter come before the courts. But the imperious Frenchman continued in his ways. His long awaited street map of the city on which Washington and the commissioners were depending to improve the flagging sales of government lots was not yet ready. He would not be hurried. Moreover, he continued to insist that he should in no way be subject to the authority of the commissioners.[15] Then, three weeks after Washington's stern rebuke, L'Enfant penned a letter to the commissioners to inform them that the great house of Notley Young overlooking the Potomac was at the end of another projected avenue and thus might be considered "a nuisance to the City." There was as yet no need for its immediate removal, he conceded. Rather, the major simply wanted the commissioners to be informed of the matter, as he had already informed Mr. Young, so that they could "adjust matters with Mr. Notley Young so as to ensure the house may be removed when necessary." A little less than two months later Pierre L'Enfant, not the Young mansion, was removed from the Washington scene.[16]

In due course, or by June 1792, Attorney General Edmond Randolph ruled in favor of a compensation of £1,697, or approximately $4,500, and Carroll doggedly began building his Duddington Manor anew, set back this time from the proposed building line of New Jersey Avenue, with the help of Benjamin Latrobe.[17] Then in 1793 there began the great real estate promotion known at first as the Greenleaf or Dutch loan and ultimately as the Greenleaf, Duncanson, Morris, Nicholson, and Law syndicate. At its heart was an elaborate scheme whereby the government sold the syndicate thousands of city lots at reduced prices (later, for no down payments at all) in return for constructing ten buildings a year for seven years and lending the government $2,200 a month until the buildings' completion.

The plan was at first widely hailed as the answer to the city's woes. Among the syndicate's members were Robert Morris, "the financier of the Revolution" and one of the United States' wealthiest citizens, and Tobias Lear, President Washington's private secretary, who served as its chief publicist. But with little thought of how they might be overreaching themselves, the members also bought a considerable acreage of private land, including 220 lots from Daniel Carroll of Duddington and 429 from Notley Young.[18]

In a separate agreement by which he hoped to spur the development of fine houses near the Capitol, Carroll gave Greenleaf, "free of any charge," twenty lots along South Capitol Street. Carroll's sole condition was that Greenleaf build a two-story house of good quality on each of the lots within three years. Failure to do so would mean forfeiture of the lots and "the sum of one hundred pounds for each lot so unimproved." Subsequently, or in May 1796, when there was but one year left to the agreement and the lots remained untouched, Greenleaf reassigned the agreement to the redoubtable Robert Morris and his Philadelphia associate John Nicholson. Morris thereupon made his first real inspection of the future capital and pronounced himself highly pleased with its prospects. Without exaggerating he wrote his son-in-law that lots were going for double and triple his first estimates, thanks largely to the prestige of the syndicate. "I am delighted with the place," he further wrote. "Nature has done for it all that could be desired, and I see that *man* will soon do the rest." On such assurances from a man of Morris's stature, Daniel Carroll and all of Washington rested their hopes.[19]

But not for long. After Morris learned more about the syndicate's affairs he quickly asked Carroll to extend the agreement. Carroll, already owed large sums by both private individuals and the federal government, refused. Morris and Nicholson thereupon determined to build the buildings, come what may. On September 26, 1796, three years to the day after the signing of the original agreement, Morris and Nicholson entertained some two hundred laborers, craftsmen, architects, and eminent citizens, including Carroll, at a barbecue featuring roasted oxen to celebrate the completion of the "Twenty Buildings." But in fact the buildings were far from ready for occupancy. Nicholson had just managed to "cover," or roof over, some of his buildings earlier that day. Morris had done the same with some of his three days before. Neither was able to do more. Within less than a year their capital was depleted, and the notes by which they paid private landowners could not be redeemed. The buildings remained as they were, gaunt and windowless monuments to the speculative orgy of early Washington real estate. Twenty-eight years later, a visiting journalist so described them:

> On a knowl south of Capitol Hill stands an object of peculiar dreariness: it is a row of twenty brick buildings. . . . There they stand, with roofs sunk in and grass growing in the windows, looking as if they had been bombarded by the British. One of them has a family in it, but the inmates look like Arabs among the ruins of Balbec.[20]

By that time the incident of the Twenty Buildings had run its long and troubled course, which included seizure of the unfinished buildings by Carroll and a suit by Morris and Nicholson disputing Carroll's right of possession. So, too, had the syndicate, which broke apart in 1797. In its aftermath two of the partners fought an abortive duel; Thomas Law lost much of his fortune; and Greenleaf, Morris and Nicholson all found themselves in debtors' prison in the closing years of their lives. "No man in this world . . . has suffered as much as I have by placing confidence," Morris had written Governor Thomas Sim Lee, three years before the breakup.[21]

And not surprising, Daniel Carroll remained unpaid. Greenleaf had not even settled accounts for the bricks Carroll supplied—Carroll owned the city's largest brick kilns—for the first buildings, including Greenleaf's home on the point of land that now bears his name. "It is reasonable as my bricks are in your houses," Carroll wrote him in October 1795, "that I should after waiting eighteen months receive my money." But in truth this was a trifling matter, a mere jot in the ledger books of Daniel Carroll of Duddington in the years following his return from Europe in 1790.

By 1792 his bachelor brother-in-law Richard Brent, then launching his political career in Virginia, had involved him in loans to the Fitzhughs and Josiah Watson of Alexandria that sometimes exceeded £1,000. By that time, too, Carroll had £6,050, or $16,214, outstanding in Baltimore Company bonds on which interest was due. (The Baltimore Iron Works—Hockley Forge, Baltimore Furnace, and other holdings—were collectively known as the Baltimore Company; "bonds" as then used meant promissory notes on money lent.) From time to time William Hammond, his Baltimore Company agent, reported vigorous applications "to your Debtors for the interest due on your Bonds, but none of them has paid as yet."[22] Then, too, it would be many years before the District Commissioners paid Carroll the £25, or approximately $66, per acre of ground appropriated for government buildings and "reservations." Investments in the Potomac Company were returning nothing. Nor is it likely that Carroll was ever remunerated for his 220 lots sold to the syndicate in the wake of its denouement in 1796. There was also the expense of building the new "Duddington Manor." And relatives, including his wayward brother Charles, constantly asking for money.[23]

By October 1797 Daniel Carroll of Duddington, once the richest man in the District of Columbia, had very little money in hand. He therefore asked his cousin Charles Carroll of Carrollton, considered by many the richest man in the nation, for a loan of $2,000. As he had done before and would do again, Charles Carroll of Carrollton refused.[24]

In view of these and other reverses, we might expect Carroll to have turned his back on the capital scene and gone into retirement, at least until the recovery of some of his losses. But this was scarcely the case. Rather, he continued to invest in the District and participate even more in its public affairs. In 1799, as the deadline for the transfer of the government from Philadelphia drew near, Carroll purchased $3,860 worth of lots. Some were to fill in gaps in his extensive holdings around or near Capitol Square; others extended them westward along the south side of L'Enfant's projected Mall.

Why Carroll invested further presents an interesting question. The uncertainty of Washington's future and the disaster of the syndicate were as well understood by him as anyone. Nor were the lots yet going for knock-down or bargain prices. The choicest of them were priced at $400 and $500, or at the upper range of what was so optimistically offered by the commissioners at their first auctions in 1791 and 1792. Certainly the possibility of long-term appreciation prompted his actions to some degree. But it is also possible that Carroll's civic spirit—more specifically his realization of the urgent need to boost fiscal confidence in Washington's future—played a much larger role. By 1799 Carroll was fully aware of Congress's misgivings about moving from Philadelphia. Nor could he forget Congressman Richard Henry Lee of Virginia's warning that Congress would make the move mainly to comply with presidential directives, remain for a year, and then return to Philadelphia if suitable accommodations were not available for them, especially around the Capitol.

Another Catholic who fully shared Carroll's concerns for the city's immediate future was his friend James Barry. In 1795 Barry had already spent over $6,000 to buy up a large tract of waterfront property immediately east of Greenleaf Point, property that was ideally situated for commerce if the vision of a great Washington Harbor was ever realized. But he, too, continued to invest in 1799, buying some thirty lots around Capitol Hill and along both the Potomac and the Eastern Branch waterfronts for the sum of $3,566. Barry, who had previously been a successful businessman and merchant shipper in New York, was not inexperienced or unaware by then of the pitfalls of Washington realty. Rather, we must bear in mind that the most trusted and revered figure in the nation, President George Washington, then in his last year of life, was in effect asking Barry and others like him to keep faith. The New Rome, the President kept insisting, must someday rise on the banks of the Potomac.[25]

Carroll and Barry are typical of all who were infected with this faith. In one way or another they were determined to see Washington survive its most critical moment. In the case of Barry and Carroll, they would save the city, if possible, by what might best be called emergency re-investment. Others, Catholic and Protestant alike, did the same to equal or lesser degree. (Among

The Art Museum, Princeton University. Bequest of Aileen Osborn Webb (Mrs. Vanderbilt Webb).
James Barry, by Gilbert Stuart, 1803-1805.

Protestants one thinks immediately of Thomas Law and Samuel Blodget, both of whom lost nearly all they had in the process.) Indeed, the cost was high to all.

But in a certain sense the faithful, each in their own way, succeeded. The embryo capital did not fail. As we have seen, James Hoban quickly built a temporary addition to the Capitol's north wing after Congress complained of overcrowding; Leonard Harbaugh pushed forward the completion of the executive buildings on either side of the President's House, and Daniel Carroll of Duddington owned or bought back from the government many of the lots on

176   Capitol Square and its immediate vicinity for development as hotels or boarding houses. City Register Thomas Herty's Washington Building Company made a modest start in housing along the middle section of Pennsylvania Avenue. And, in the everyday task of finding accommodations for Congress and government officials, Catholics Bennett Fenwick, Joseph Semmes, and Nicholas Queen opened taverns and boarding houses, which in early Washington were always a high-risk enterprise marked by frequent turnovers.[26]

Cumulatively, these efforts succeeded at least as stopgaps, or measures that from one year to the next were important in defusing Congressional criticism and forestalling the dreaded return to Philadelphia. Then, too, there was on the one hand Mayor Robert Brent and the council taking on more responsibility for municipal affairs and thus relieving congressional anxieties over getting bogged down in District minutiae. On the other hand there were the reinvestments of the Barrys and the Carrolls, which at least gave the appearance of fiscal confidence in the capital's future. Thus did the City of Washington budge slowly forward, always in debt and barely escaping one crisis after another.

Daniel Carroll of Duddington stayed with this painfully slow process, although constantly troubled by hostile commissioners and litigation arising from the Twenty Buildings fiasco. Eventually, by July 1814, Judge William Cranch, who had replaced William Kilty as chief judge of the District's circuit court and was both the brother-in-law of James Greenleaf and originally the agent of his estate, ruled in favor of the Greenleaf plaintiffs and fined Carroll $39,847 for illegal seizure of the Twenty Buildings.[27] Not surprisingly, therefore, Carroll soon began to show some small signs of discouragement. One of the first was disengagement from elective office. After serving as president of the city council's "second chamber," later the Board of Aldermen, for its first two years, he chose not to run for another term in 1804.

But Carroll continued to take on other civic posts, both public and private, to a degree that was unequalled in the city's early history. Even before the turn of the century he had become a major investor in George Washington's Potomac Company. As a consequence he joined Thomas Tingey, Thomas Law, and District Marshal Daniel Carroll Brent in 1802 as one of the original directors of the Washington Canal Company, a major engineering project, born in part of the Potomac Company, to which we will return. In the next two years he served as treasurer of the Washington Assembly and chairman of the subscription committee for the Washington Theater.

By 1805 Carroll was involved in the Washington Bridge Company, which was then petitioning Congress for authority to build a bridge-causeway across the Potomac for faster and more convenient travel between Washington and Alexandria. After strenuous opposition from Georgetowners, who correctly predicted the bridge would aggravate the silting of Georgetown's up-river ship channel, Congress finally granted the company a charter in 1808. Carroll was then elected its president. Under his direction the Washington Bridge Company was a resounding success, at least by comparison with all other District engineering projects of the time. The company's initial stock offering of $200,000 sold out in four days, and the bridge, known familiarly as the Long Bridge, was open for use in eleven months.[28]

Perhaps encouraged by this achievement Carroll continued with efforts to improve the District's communications as well as its fiscal institutions. In September 1809 he was elected first president of the board of the Bank of Washington, in which he was a major shareholder. This was the capital city's first locally organized and capitalized bank; it also served as a government depository when Congress refused to renew the charter of the Philadelphia-based Bank of the United States in 1811 and forced a temporary closing of its Washington branch. Carroll continued as the Bank of Washington's president for ten years, through various reelections.[29]

In 1810 he was chosen president of the Columbia Turnpikes Company, which held charters to build paved access roads from Washington north and east to the Bladensburg-Baltimore post road, southwest from the Long Bridge causeway to Virginia's Little River Turnpike, and north and west to Frederick, via Rockville. After intensive surveys under the direction of Benjamin Latrobe, the company began turnpike construction in earnest in 1812, at least on the Baltimore and Little River links. Carroll's role was to raise money, settle right-of-way landowner claims, and compose differences of opinion over the survey routes. In these tasks he succeeded, although it took the company more than ten years to realize most of its objectives. Helping him, as was so often the case, were Catholics Robert and William Brent, James D. Barry, and Griffith Coombe, who were directors of both the Washington Bridge and Columbia Turnpikes Companies.[30]

But beginning in 1810 Carroll also accepted positions with the restructured Washington Canal Company, first as a commissioner and later as a director. This appears to have been a turning point in his civic career, since the Canal Company was a major engineering project that in its own way would prove to be as much of a failure as the Greenleaf syndicate. At the heart of the project was a canal, originally envisioned in L'Enfant's plan, which was to run from the Potomac River south of Georgetown across the breadth of the city passing close to Capitol Hill and then down through locks to the Eastern Branch, or today's Anacostia River. Once completed, its directors promised, the Washington Canal would permit the small barges that came down from the upper Potomac via the Potomac Company's locks at Little and Great Falls to meet and transfer cargos to the larger sailing vessels at the Canal's terminal on the Eastern Branch. In addition to linking the Eastern Branch with the upper Potomac, the canal would also be a boon to the deep-draft vessels capable of trans-Atlantic passage that were having increasing difficulty negotiating the shoal and narrow ship channel to Georgetown.

Echoing as it did George Washington's vision of a great commerce with the interior, the canal was highly acclaimed. Benjamin Stoddert, Georgetown's leading merchant, declared that once peace came to Europe the canal would make Georgetown a center of trade the equal of Baltimore, Boston, Philadelphia, or New York. The ever-sanguine Thomas Law, who would invest what

178   remained of his fortune, had no trouble in predicting that "should this canal be finished, Washington need not envy London its Thames, nor New York its North River." In fact, he planned to run a line of cross-town packet boats on the canal from Capitol Hill to the President's House for "a conveyance which may be rendered more economical and comfortable than the Hackney-Coach." Even the astute Latrobe, who was engaged as the project's chief engineer, thought it might be the answer to the city's lagging commerce.[31]

But the company's backers chose to overlook two all-important factors. One was the Potomac Company's early difficulties and the low volume of goods being transported on its narrow-beam barges and crude rafts. The other

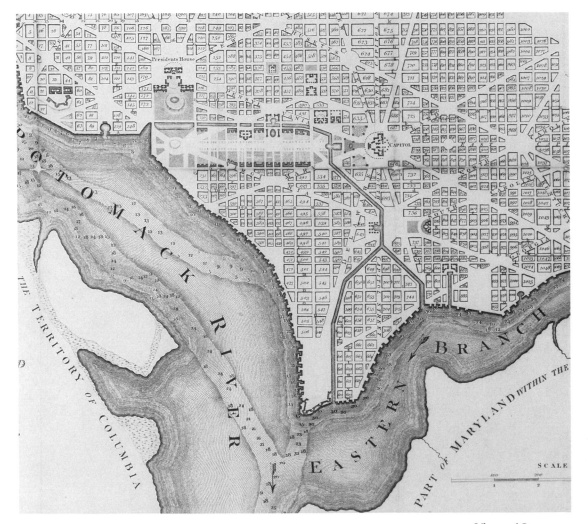

Plan of the City of Washington, showing the proposed route of the Washington Canal, from American Atlas, *J. Russell, London, 1795..*

was the fact that only a few more ships were making their way up the Potomac than ten years earlier when Barry and Law built their "very large but perfectly empty warehouse and a wharf graced by not a single vessel," as Treasury Secretary Gallatin had described them. Meanwhile, in spite of the Napoleonic wars and other disruptions, Baltimore continued to experience its phenomenal growth as a port of entry. To this must be added the Canal Company's miscalculations, cost-cutting, and consequent scaling down of the canal's dimensions. As a result, some ten years after the opening ceremonies in 1815, Washington merchants complained that unless the canal were widened and deepened to its original specifications it was creating "an insurmountable impediment to the commercial prosperity of the City of Washington" that should be removed. To these objections were added those of city health officials, especially after the outbreak of cholera in 1832. By then the Washington Canal was in effect an open sewer. A stagnant open sewer, in fact, in sections that were periodically closed off for repairs.[32]

In the aftermath Thomas Law was ruined, Benjamin Stoddert saw part of his properties sold for debts, and Daniel Carroll of Duddington was beginning to suffer what he later described as the most disastrous consequences. Especially damaging was an act of Congress of May 4, 1812, which permitted not only the taxation of unimproved property, which had previously been authorized in the city charter of 1802, but also the seizure and public sale of such property if owners did not pay the taxes thereon within two years. Always searching for every possible source of revenue, the city government had urged this measure on the Congress for two reasons. First, although long authorized, the unimproved property tax had been unenforced and therefore unpaid by anyone; second, quite obvious to any citizen in 1814, Washington still had a vast acreage of "unimproved" woodlands, fields, and swamp. The most tempting targets, of course, were such large landholders as Carroll and Notley Young. Carroll long fought the measure with every means at his disposal, including appeals to Congress and reelection to the Board of Aldermen after a lapse of seventeen years. In the end, however, he lost. By the 1820s, by his own account, Carroll's lots and squares were being sold at public auction at one-tenth and one-twentieth of their original price "and in some instances $2, 3, and 4 a lot."[33]

Carroll would take on one more great civic role, as we will see, at another critical moment in the city's history. But from approximately 1815 onwards he gradually withdrew from active participation in Washington's fiscal institutions and public works. Not only the Canal Company and property taxes, but also the general country-wide depression of 1819 and Carroll's problems in recovering generous loans to his extended family further impelled him in this direction. In June of that year his friend John Mason, speaking for Georgetown's Columbia Bank, urged Carroll to refloat a note of $6,000 for Carroll's young brother Charles. Failure to do so, Mason added, would force him to take legal steps, although, as he said, "nothing would give me more pain." Later in the same year a loan Carroll was requesting for Charles, who was by then engaging in upstate New York and western land speculation, was refused by the board of the Bank of the United States, even though Carroll offered Washington real estate as collateral.

Shortly thereafter, the Bank dunned Carroll for a $2,000 promissory note he had signed in favor of his nephew Henry, a year before. At this time also a paper mill Daniel had purchased on Rock Creek with his brother Charles and one Elie Williams was experiencing heavy losses. "I really feel for your brother's and your situation," Charles Carroll of Carrollton wrote in January 1820, even as he refused Daniel's offer of his Washington and Baltimore county properties as security for a loan to help recover the mill and other investments. Eventually, before the troubles with his brother Charles were over, Carroll was threatened with a $30,000 attachment suit by the very Bank of Washington he had served as founding president for nine years.[34]

In 1829 Carroll agreed to grant land and right-of-way for a railroad and settlement scheme to Richard Caton, the Englishman who married Daniel's first love Mary Carroll. Caton thereupon cut so much timber for his projected railroad that Carroll complained of the "utter destruction of the value of the lands adjoining" and refused Caton's request for more land as "ungenerous and illiberal." That same year Carroll sat down to draft an advertisement for the Washington newspapers. The first sentence read: "For Sale: The Hotel on Capitol Hill, at present occupied by Nicholas L. Queen, this property is well known and does not require a particular description." Then, in what seems a half-hearted postscript, he added, "I would also sell one-third, or one-fourth of my interest in the City of Washington on accommodating terms. Persons wishing to become largely interested, will please to call on me, when every information will be given."[35]

Five years later, when the government proposed to tax the original proprietors for paving the streets and avenues on the land they had freely given the government, Daniel Carroll of Duddington could not help but reflect on the sorry consequences for all who like himself had agreed with the government's "half and half" plan almost fifty years earlier. In answering a letter from a cousin on the subject, he wrote:

> I nevertheless perfectly remember that the general opinion was that so great was the gift that the citizens would never be subject to taxation for the improvement of the streets—having relinquished every alternate lot to the governemnt. Indeed, some were so wild as to suppose the donation was so great the government might pave the streets with ingots of gold or silver. After nearly half a century the result is now fully known; the unfortunate proprietors are generally brought to ruin, and some with scarcely enough to buy daily food for their families. This subject is so truly frightful to me that I hate to think of it, much less to write of it.[36]

Daniel Carroll of Duddington in his later years, silhouette by Auguste Edouart, 1841.

In the succeeding years Carroll found satisfaction mainly in Duddington Manor, "one of the finest houses ever reared within the bounds of the District," as one historian of architecture has called it. Here Carroll grew old in the company of his one son and six daughters, four of whom remained unmarried. Here, too, he assembled what was probably the city's most notable collection of portraits, English and American furniture, silver, and Oriental porcelain. But even in retirement Carroll continued to serve the city as a committee member for such events as presidential inaugurals or the welcoming ceremonies for distinguished visitors. An occasional parishioner at St. Patrick's, where some of his younger daughters were baptized, he also made generous contributions of land, money, or both to all of the other early Catholic churches in Washington. Over the years these included "Cathedral Square" on South Capitol Street in 1801, so named because Washington Catholics hoped the capital city would later merit a diocese (it is now the site of the Church of St. Vincent De Paul); another "entire square of ground" plus what was probably a major share of the cost of James Barry's St. Mary's chapel in 1804-1806, and as mentioned in a previous chapter still another prime property on Capitol Hill for St. Peter's Church in 1820.[37]

Considered aloof and stern in manner by some, Daniel Carroll of Duddington was "very genial and hospitable " to those who knew him best. For Benjamin Latrobe, the architect of the rebuilt Duddington Manor, he was an ideal client and a man of great integrity and "uniform kindness." Carroll's life had a remarkable span. As a boy of twelve he witnessed the outbreak of the Revolution. As a man of eighty-five he lived to see the Mexican-American War, the age of manifest destiny, and the storm clouds gathering over the issue of slavery. In his last public act Carroll served as an honorary member of the inaugural committee for President Zachary Taylor in 1849. He attended the ceremonies in a wheel chair, two months before his death.[38] His young friend, George Watterston, a novelist, newspaper editor, and the first librarian of congress, wrote of him:

> When the city was laid out Mr. Carroll was about twenty-five years of age, and possessed an estate of considerable magnitude. The mansion stood on a beautiful eminence, which commanded a view of the Anacostia and Potomac as far as Alexandria, and the magnificent sweep of hills which belt the city like a natural amphitheatre. From his residence to the river the land was laid off into fields of grain and meadows. And to a considerable distance to the north, east and west it was covered with a thick growth of forest trees. The site of the Capitol was in the midst of this forest, and I have often heard while a boy the sound of the woodman's axe amid the deep silence of that almost primeval forest. More than one-half of his fine estate was given to the Government by its proprietor, from the expectation that the remainder would much more than compensate the gratuitous transfer of the other part. He looked through the long vista of the future, and the prospect which presented itself to his imagination was in no ordinary degree brilliant and radiant with golden hues. But, alas! those golden dreams were never realized. He commenced life in comparative affluence, and without any vices, without extravagance, with the mere indulgence of his hospitable and charitable feelings of his nature; he left the world, at the advanced age of eight-five years, in poverty, and with scarcely a part of the large tract of land he owned when this city was laid off. To the growth and advancement of that city he contributed with all his means and energies—it might be, too rapidly at first for his own in-

terest. The improvements he made were perhaps too extensive for his means, and not suited to the condition of our infant city. This and a weighty and oppressive tax by the corporation on unimproved property, involved him in difficulties, to which he was forced to yield, and which he was never able to surmount. But he bore up under them, not with the stern philosophy of the stoic, but with the calmness and humility of the Christian. Towards the close of his life, the example which he furnished of cheerfulness, submission to the visitations of Providence, the loss of property, and the infirmities of age, and all the Christian virtues, was not only consoling, but beautiful.[39]

To this the *National Intelligencer*'s obituary added a more prosaic note on Carroll's role as the city's principal developer and landlord:

He made every exertion for the accommodation of the first Congress in Washington by the erection of numerous buildings. He was an indulgent landlord, and always generously favoured the widow and other needy tenants, yielding thousands of dollars rather than distress them for his rents. He was a friend to the poor and dispensed much private charity from his own abundant stores; but alas, the mutability of fortune deprived him of late years of the means of giving to the poor.[40]

But well before the mutability of fortune curtailed Carroll's public services and philanthropies, there occurred a great event that would test his commitment—indeed, the commitment of nearly all Washingtonians—to the preservation of their capital city.

Early in the morning of August 16, 1814, Navy lookouts at Cape Henry, Virginia, spotted a large British fleet entering the Chesapeake Bay. Three days later the main body of the fleet, which ominously included several large troop transports as well as the usual ships of the line, sailed up Maryland's Patuxent River, between the Potomac and the Severn. The War of 1812, the war of European entanglements that three presidents had tried to avoid, was at the capital's doorstep.[41]

As they did during the Revolution, Maryland's Catholics played their part in the nation's defense. The most distinguished of them, undoubtedly, was Captain Stephen Cassin, a young naval officer whose handsome appearance so affected the young ladies of Trinity Church that Pastor John Lucas barred him from singing in the choir. In the closing months of the War, Cassin handled the schooner *Ticonderoga* with such skill and bravery in Commodore McDonough's victory over the British fleet on Lake Champlain that Congress awarded him a gold medal.[42] Less distinguished, perhaps, but no better or worse than the poorly organized and ill-equipped militia that provided the bulk of American forces throughout the War were the Catholics serving in the District militia and the more elite volunteer militia companies. Those known to have served as of-

184 ficers between 1803 and the close of hostilities in 1814 include District Marshal Daniel Carroll Brent, William Brent, Benjamin Burch, James Hoban, John Kearney, Adam King, and Joseph Cassin. In addition, Colonel Henry Carbery, who commanded the 36th U.S. Infantry Regiment, was a member of the regular army and a veteran of the Revolution. Serving as a first lieutenant in Carbery's regiment was Charles Jerningham Queen.[43]

Those who saw the most action were Dr. William Queen, who served as field surgeon for Commodore Joshua Barney's spirited detachment of marines and Navy Yard sailors, and the Washington Artillery Company commanded by Benjamin Burch. Made up largely of Irish-descent volunteers, Burch's Artillery showed great mobility and held well, first at the battle of Bladensburg and then when guarding the bridge over the Eastern Branch that led to the Navy Yard. Barney's marines and sailors put up the stiffest resistance of all at Bladensburg, even refusing orders to retreat and momentarily checking the British advance. Queen, charged with attending the battlefield wounded, counted eighty Americans and two hundred and forty-nine British dead.[44]

But nothing that the Artillery Company, Commodore Barney, and other staunch defenders could do had an effect on the outcome of the key battle for Washington. In what the newspapers later took to calling "the Bladensburg Races," a brigade of Baltimore militia backed by District and Maryland state units totalling seven thousand men, all handicapped by an incredible confusion of command, broke lines and ran in a pell-mell retreat before slightly less than two thousand crack British regulars, some of whom were veterans of Wellington's Peninsular campaign.

By nightfall of August 24, British troops entered a virtually deserted city, free to carry out the destruction of government buildings without opposition. In Georgetown Father John McElroy wrote that the flames from the Capitol, soon followed by more from the President's House and the Treasury Building, "were so great that a person could read at the College." Throughout the night more and more frightened citizens who had neither the means nor the physical stamina to escape the city crowded into St. Patrick's Church for protection and prayer. When someone suggested to Pastor William Matthews he would do well to flee, he is said to have answered, "Why should I? I have more business here now than ever before."[45]

Three days after the British forces left, President Madison re-entered the city for his first tour of inspection. The Washington he found had lost all its major public buildings. Both the President's House and the Capitol were little more than skeletal structures, with gutted interiors and cracked and blackened walls. Many private houses had also been fired, either by the British or high winds. In military terms what remained of the city was totally defenseless. The militia companies were in disarray, and Fort Warburton (later Fort Washington) on the Digges estate on the Potomac had been blown up by its American commander, thus rendering useless the city's most strategically placed military outpost. "I do not suppose Government will ever return to Washington," Margaret Bayard Smith, summing it all up, wrote to her sister.[46]

For once, however, the astute Mrs. Smith would be proven wrong. Well before the end of hostilities, City Superintendent Thomas Monroe asked George Hadfield to conduct a survey of the damage done to government buildings. Hadfield was also asked to determine if the buildings should be repaired where they stood or rebuilt anew, possibly in new locations. To many, especially members of Congress, this posed the larger question of whether the capital city should remain where it was or make a fresh start at a new site. Hadfield submitted his report on October 13, 1814, which, as matters turned out, was none too soon.[47] Three weeks earlier Congressman Jonathan Fisk of New York had introduced a resolution asking that a committee be appointed "to study the possibility of moving the capital . . . to a place of greater security and less inconvenience than the City of Washington." The resolution, which came to the floor on October 3, passed by one vote, 72 to 71. Predictably, Congress soon thereafter received petitions from Philadelphia and many other localities offering themselves as alternative sites. First to do so, however, was Georgetown, whose proprietors were quick to see one more chance of pulling the capital back to the "salubrious heights" west of Washington. On September 28, or two days after Congressman Fisk's initial resolution, Mayor Thomas Corcoran and the city council rushed to offer Georgetown College to the Congress, explaining that the spaciousness of the college's buildings would "admit of every comfort and convenience, both to Halls and committee Rooms." They did this, moreover, without first gaining the approval of the college's trustees.[48]

The debate over the future of Washington now reached new heights of intensity and passion, largely along sectional north-south lines and with undertones of the possible dissolution of the union. It also spread quickly to the national press. "The fate of Washington appears to be decided," a *Philadelphia True American* correspondent crowed. "A most powerful party in Congress are determined to abandon it, and will never be at rest among its ruins." But even as some diplomats began to move their offices to Philadelphia, a succession of events both large and small swelled the tide of opinion in Washington's favor. The repulse of the British at Baltimore, followed quickly by the brilliant victories at Lake Champlain and Plattsburgh, ushered in a new wave of national euphoria and confidence. With it came a feeling that the national capital need not, after all, run and seek cover in places with more security. Hadfield's report recommended the virtual rebuilding of the walls of the President's House, which suffered the most damage, and the repair of those of the Capitol, the Treasury, and the War Office Buildings, which were all found to be structurally sound. Although it may have been in Hadfield's interest to make such recommendations, his report was nevertheless professional and convincing, giving building-by-building detail.[49]

On October 15, or the same day Hadfield formally submitted his report, the select committee reported to the House at large a bill calling for the temporary removal of the capital. Two days later, after much debate and various parliamentary maneuvers, a motion by Congressman John Rhea of Tennessee to reject the bill failed 79 votes against 76. After some attempts to amend it by

186   inserting Philadelphia and Georgetown as "the places of removal," the bill was presented for a third reading. This time, with a handful of switched votes and two more members in attendance, the bill was defeated by nine votes, 83 to 74. The greatest threat to the city's future was, for the moment, forestalled.[50]

By February 3 of the new year, the Senate took action and passed its version of a House appropriations bill "for repairing or rebuilding the public buildings within the City of Washington" by a comfortable margin, or a vote of 20 to 13, in spite of some vigorous last-ditch stands by the removal forces. The next day, a Saturday, an amendment setting the amount of appropriations at $50,000, with authorization to borrow from banks or private individuals at six percent interest, was added. Later in the same day, President Madison and all of Washington heard the exciting news of General Andrew Jackson's masterful victory at New Orleans. Five days later, or on February 9, after two days of renewed debate, the House ironed out its differences with the Senate and staved off attempts to reduce the possible appropriation and an amendment to have the Treasury and War Office Buildings reconstructed on Capitol Hill. There was no further question. The government would remain within the City of Washington and its public buildings repaired or rebuilt where they stood.[51]

But more joyous news for both Washington and the nation at large was still to come. On the night of February 11, or two days after the House's final action, young Henry Carroll of Belle Vue, Daniel of Duddington's nephew and Commissioner Henry Clay's private secretary at Ghent, arrived in New York with the peace treaty concluded with Great Britain. Three days later, as mentioned in Chapter 4, he reached Washington and delivered a signed copy to Secretary of State James Monroe and President Madison.

Confidence returned to Washington. In short order the president appointed three commissioners to supervise the reconstruction effort; the commissioners then promptly engaged James Hoban to rebuild the President's House and the two adjoining executive buildings. Aided by his old friend Nicholas Callan, who again served as foreman of laborers, Hoban was hard at work in March with final approval over all work, materials, and employees. At about the same time Benjamin Latrobe began the much more formidable task of repairing and completing the Capitol, which was far from finished at the time of the British attack.[52]

Meanwhile, government had been functioning in temporary quarters. The District Court met in one of the better Carroll houses on Capitol Hill, while most of the executive departments rented space in private buildings close to the President's House. The business of government, apparently, was going forward without undue hindrance or complaints. There was, however, one glaring and serious exception. Congress had been moved into what was once Blodget's Hotel, in cramped space shared with the Patent Office and the city post office. Representative Richard Stockton of New Jersey, a leader of the removal forces in the House, so described its plight: "here we are in the Patent Office; in a room not large enough to furnish a seat for each member when all are present, although every spot, up to the fire-places and windows, is occupied." He wondered what would happen when "winter comes and fires must be lighted" and predicted that if a summer session were called, the members' health would be endangered by overcrowding. Many, in both the Senate and the House, shared his views. Talk of removal was once again heard in the crowded passageways.[53]

In response spirited private citizens joined ranks to address this last and greatest of problems. Aware that the Capitol construction would take some years and that Congress' complaints about the limited space in the Patent Office were entirely justified, a group of activists formed a stock company to provide a more substantial building for the Congress' interim home. Shares were quickly sold and the cornerstone for a substantial building was laid with appropriate fanfare on the 4th of July, 1815, on a site where the Supreme Court Building now stands. Dubbed the Brick Capitol, it was three stories high and offered both the Senate and the House more chamber space with better lighting than either body had ever known. Rushed to completion, it was ready to receive Congress the following December. Here Congress remained, relatively content, for four years. Here too James Monroe was sworn in as the fifth president of the United States, following a brief dispute between the House of Representatives and the Senate over use of their respective chambers for the ceremony. Ever the diplomat, Monroe settled the dispute by taking his oath outdoors in front of the Brick Capitol before a large crowd. So began the traditional outdoor ceremony followed to this day.[54]

To build the Brick Capitol the citizen group sold $17,362 in stock at $100 per share. One-third of the stockholders were Catholics. They purchased thirty-six percent of the stock. Among them were former Mayor Robert Brent, Clerk of the Court William Brent, Griffith Coombe, William Dudley Digges, Charles Carroll of Belle Vue, Daniel Brent of the State Department, James D. Barry, Nicholas L. Queen and Benjamin Burch. But heading the list and leading the initiative, from the first approaches to the District Commissioners and President Madison to the completion of the building, was Daniel Carroll of Duddington.[55]

Four years later, as Congress prepared to move into the reopened Capitol, Representative William Darlington of Pennsylvania introduced a resolution calling for the retrocession of the District's lands to Maryland and Virginia. This was the by-now familiar stratagem to cloak the resolution's real purpose, which was the removal of the capital. The House refused to consider the resolution. So ended the last serious attempt at moving the seat of government.[56]

President Adams's prospect of a residence not to be changed was, at last, a fact.

PART IV
The Passing Storm

10

Time of Wonder, Time of Trial

They say we do not love thee, flag of my native land.

-REV. CHARLES CONSTANTINE PISE, S.J., 1833

One knows that the spirit of opposition to Catholicism among the sectaries, sometimes results in hostile acts. . . . In our Province we are pleased to have made the majority among our separated brethren have a more favorable spirit.

-REV. STEPHEN DUBUISSON, S.J.
"Commentary on the Maryland Province," 1841

In August 1834, or approximately two years after the Georgetown City Council voted municipal funds for Trinity Church's Free School, Benedict Joseph Fenwick, who had been the school's founder and was now the bishop of Boston, reported a frightening event. A great howling mob had come by night to the convent he had founded for the Ursuline sisters in Charlestown, set it completely on fire, and forced the nuns to flee for their lives. More than the anti-Catholic tirades of the Reverend Lyman Beecher and the New England Tract Society were at work here, Fenwick thought. Like the Georgetown College he knew so well, the convent school had been open to students of all faiths. "After some months the daughters of the most respectable and best families in Boston and its neighborhood, both Catholic and Protestant, filled its classes," Fenwick later wrote of the event. The school's very success, he reasoned, was at the root of its downfall.[1]

In May 1844, or approximately two years after Protestants and Catholics had together celebrated the two-hundredth anniversary of the founding of Maryland at St. Mary's, the anti-Catholic riots in Philadelphia reached their peak. The principal issue that inflamed the mob was the Philadelphia school board's approval of a Catholic request to allow Catholic children to be excused from the Protestant bible reading and religious instruction then mandatory in the city's public schools. Mass meetings to protest what the American Protestant Reform Society called "the banishment of the Bible" soon got out of hand. Before the riots were over, whole city blocks in the Irish working-class suburb of Kensington were set aflame, men were killed in the streets, and the church and seminary of St. Michaels was burned to the ground. "I have no confidence in the calm," Father James Ryder, president of Georgetown College wrote after order had been restored. "I should not be surprised to see demonstrations similar to those of Kensington and Philadelphia proper, made in any of our large cities, Baltimore alone excepted. . . . "[2]

For American Catholics the first half of the nineteenth century was a time of mixed emotions, of both growing confidence and disquieting uncertainties. As the foregoing events illustrate, there was on the one hand the growth of the church, its successes in education, and its stronger voice in government, especially at the municipal level. On the other, however, was the dark cloud of nativism. Before the half-century was over, it would spread a long shadow across much of the nation. Marking its passage was the gradual erosion of tolerance from the era of good feelings of the late Federalist period to the unbridled bigotry and violence inspired by the Know Nothing Party in the decade before the Civil War.

The national capital was scarcely immune from these contrasting phenomena. As mentioned earlier, the rapid growth of the Catholic Church in the Washington area virtually kept pace with that of the nation at large, which saw some 1,600,000 Catholics become the country's single largest denomination by mid-century. To be sure, Washington could not match the largest immigrant populations, still largely Irish and German, that began to arrive in unprecedented numbers in other cities in the 1830s. (Washington's greatest influx would come later, when the foreign-born population of the District jumped by sixty percent in the 1860s.)[3] But what the capital lacked in the number of newly arriving Catholics was to some degree offset by conversions of Protestants—spectacular conversions of public and religious figures, that is—that attracted considerable notice and had far more effect than their mere number might suggest. So much was this the case that in 1818, Belgian-born Father Charles Van Quickenborne told his colleagues abroad that they might rejoice in the fact that many non-Catholics in the Washington area held a favorable attitude towards conversion. "Consequently we may look to gathering fruit in plenty," Van Quickenborne promised, "for the harvest is abundant and ripe to fullness."[4]

Van Quickenborne's enthusiasm was not misguided. The year before, Georgetown had marveled at the arrival of a second "Yankee priest" who like John Thayer had journeyed south from New England. This was the Reverend Virgil Horace Barber of Claremont, New Hampshire, accompanied by his wife Jerusha. Both were recent converts to Catholicism and both had expressed strong desires to enter monastic life. Accordingly, Archbishop Leonard Neale formally pronounced their separation—then, as now, separation was required of both husband and wife before entering religious communities—in a ceremony at the Georgetown College chapel on June 12, 1817. Two days later Virgil Barber began his studies as a Jesuit novice with a trip to Italy accompanied by Father John Grassi. Shortly thereafter, Jerusha received the veil as a Visitation postulant from Archbishop Ambrose Maréchal. With her into the cloistered convent went four daughters, while a fifth child, a son, was lodged in a private home.

In February 1820, or approximately two-and-a-half years later, all of the 193
Barbers were once again reunited in the Visitation Chapel, where Virgil and
Jerusha, now Sister Mary Augustine, took their respective vows before church
dignitaries, friends, and their five children. By that time, moreover, Virgil's father Daniel, who had also been an Episcopalian minister in New Hampshire,
and his sister Abigail Barber Tyler and her immediate family had also converted to Catholicism. And this was not all. In time the five Barber children all
entered religious communities, the son as a Jesuit and the daughters as Ursuline and Visitandine sisters.[5]

Unlike the flamboyant and better-known John Thayer, who had a falling
out with Archbishop Carroll and thereafter went very much his own way, the
Barber family made enduring contributions to the church both in New England
and Maryland. Jerusha Barber, who was an experienced teacher, is largely credited with raising the standards of the Young Ladies (later Visitation) Academy.
Virgil Barber, when not serving on the faculty of Georgetown College or as a
missionary to Indian communities in Maine, devoted himself to his native
Claremont, where he established the first Catholic church and the first sizeable
Catholic community in New Hampshire.[6] ("I wish I had twenty more like him

*Georgetown University Library
Special Collections Division.*

*Benedict J. Fenwick, S.J., second
pastor of Trinity Church, president of Georgetown College,
bishop of Boston, founder of
Holy Cross College.*

194   in my diocese," Bishop Benedict Fenwick of Boston, who had played a major role in Barber's conversion, said of his New England efforts.) Helping Barber at Claremont was his father Daniel, who is best known as the author of two books of popular apologetics, *Worship and Piety Explained* and *The History of My Times*. In the next generation Barber's son Samuel would grow up to become the master of novices at the Jesuit seminary in Frederick, Maryland, and later the principal of Washington's Gonzaga College, while his nephew William Tyler would be selected the first Catholic bishop of Hartford, Connecticut.[7]

Few of the converts of this period could match the Barbers in their far-reaching effects. Rather, priests at Trinity, St. Patrick's, and the college were reporting widespread conversions among people in every walk of life. Father John McElroy, for example, marvelled at "the conversion from a bad life" of a young woman "publickly known as a dishonest person" who renounced her way of living and embraced the Catholic faith. Trinity Pastor Stephen Dubuisson was proud of the previously mentioned Joseph Brigden, the New England carpenter and handyman who taught at Trinity's Free School for Boys and later wrote an interesting narrative of his conversion. At the college Father James Ward converted "a Presbyterian boatman . . . [who] had come from Virginia along our canal and was stopped for some time at his daughter's house near the College." In the year 1818 Archbishop Maréchal, who liked to make periodic tours of his diocese and issue terse reports, noted that he had "confirmed in Trinity Church 213 persons. Number of commts. [communicants] last Easter about 800. Converts 60 at least."[8]

So it went. But in 1824 there occurred a sensational event—a miraculous event, quite literally, in the eyes of many—that both gave a great spur to conversions and made a significant rift within the Catholic community. At four o'clock in the morning of March tenth of that year, Father Stephen Dubuisson, then assistant pastor of St. Patrick's, brought communion to Ann Carbery Mattingly at the home of her brother Thomas Carbery, Jr., a former mayor of Washington. A forty-year-old widow, Mrs. Mattingly had suffered for seven years from a breast tumor, high fever, aches, chills, and long fits of coughing and vomiting blood. Dubuisson had come to her chambers in Mayor Carbery's house because for the previous six months she had been bed-ridden with pain and exhaustion from loss of blood. Indeed, she could no longer sit up in bed without help, and her doctor thought "that her case was hopeless, and simply advised the use of palliatives."[9]

Dubuisson's visit in the small hours of the morning had been planned to coincide, or be in union, as the expression then had it, with the end of a novena to the Holy Name of Jesus being conducted in Bamberg, Bavaria, by Prince Alexander Hohenlohe, a priest to whom various miraculous cures had been attributed in many parts of Europe. By the time of Mrs. Mattingly's illness the cult of the prince-priest had spread beyond the continent, and Hohenlohe himself had set aside the tenth of each month to pray for all believers outside Europe who might want his help. Presiding over the novena and scheduling it to end in union with Bamberg was Pastor William Matthews of St. Patrick's.

Matthews was an open-minded supporter of the event. Dubuisson had inspired it.[10]

At the culminating moment of the early morning communion, Father Dubuisson and five other witnesses watched in distress as Mrs. Mattingly struggled for five minutes before she could swallow the host. Then, in the words of her friend Anna Maria Fitzgerald, who was one of the witnesses, "I saw her raise herself in the bed with her hands clasped, and heard her exclaim in an audible voice 'Lord Jesus! What have I done to deserve so great a favor?'" She then declared herself free from pain, put on a pair of stockings, got out of bed without assistance, and knelt for fifteen minutes before an improvised altar Father Dubuisson had prepared. Later Dubuisson and all five witnesses would make sworn statements before different justices testifying to the same sequence of events. Reinforcing these statements were the depositions of Mayor Thomas Carbery (sworn before Chief Justice John Marshall), James Hoban, various physicians, and many friends and members of the family who had observed Mrs. Mattingly before and after the event.[11]

In the days immediately following, Ann Mattingly by her own account received "many hundreds of persons" who came to call as news of her cure spread rapidly through the city. Almost as quickly the church found itself in a deep and divisive crisis. On the one hand there were those who like the nuns at the Visitation Convent and most of the faculty of Georgetown College wanted the miraculous recovery to be reported immediately and as widely as possible. On the other were those who either flatly denied any miraculous element in the cure or, what was much more common, urged caution and patience prior to publication, lest insufficient documentation and exaggerated word of mouth accounts bring ridicule to the church. Among the latter was Pastor William Matthews. He was especially annoyed by Father Anthony Kohlmann, the former president of Georgetown College and at the time superior of the Jesuit community at Whitemarsh, since Kohlmann was treating the event as an established miracle and according to Matthews had even gone to Annapolis to spread the news and claim many converts. Backing Matthews and urging even greater caution was Archbishop Ambrose Maréchal, who was particularly concerned by the fact that members of Congress had expressed interest in the event. He therefore wanted to delay any publication pending a complete and full report. Mrs. Mattingly's brother, Mayor Carbery, understood. "We shall not make public this affair," he promised the archbishop, "till we hear from you, which I trust for the honor and glory of the Catholic cause will be soon."[12]

It was a promise the Mayor could not possibly keep. Ten days after Mrs. Mattingly's recovery a letter in which Father Kohlmann told a friend of her "miraculous restoration like unto, and equal to . . . Lazarus from the grave" surfaced in the Baltimore *Federal Gazette*. The rush was on. An attack on the event by a Georgetown faculty member published by the *National Intelligencer* caused a clamorous front-page press debate between miracle supporters and detractors. ("We hope [this] . . . will be the last word on the subject," the ever-tolerant *Intelligencer* confessed after a week of it.) Thereafter the news spread rapidly, first nationally and then in religious journals in France and England. Archbishop Maréchal's circumspect report—compiled by Father Matthews, it never once used the words miracle or miraculous—was not issued until early May. But later in the same month Father Kohlmann was summoned to Rome. There Pope Leo XIII listened patiently and with great interest to Kohlmann's description of the cure and Father Matthews's report. Impressed, the Pope ordered the report to be translated immediately into Italian and printed by his own printer. Thus the Mattingly miracle was published, or given a degree of Vatican recognition. What the Visitation sisters and the Georgetown Jesuits had so devoutly desired had come to pass.[13]

Viewed in retrospect, it could scarcely have been otherwise. Ann Carbery Mattingly represented the union of two large and prominent southern Maryland Catholic families. Both included members who had held or were holding high office in the church or city government. Seldom, therefore, has the recipient of a miraculous cure been seen by so many well-known friends and relatives, both before and after the event. Seldom, too, have the straightforward, matter-of-fact statements of attending and consulting physicians, sworn before a justice of the peace, been more convincing. To those reading about it today the conclusion that something beyond the limits of conventional medicine occurred in the case of Mrs. Mattingly seems inescapable. That it attracted so much attention is not surprising. The Mattingly miracle had nothing in common with young peasant girls struck by celestial visions on lonely country roads. Rather, as the *Orthodox Journal* of London told its readers, it was a case where "God has manifested his power in the midst of a shrewd and sensible people." In the midst of sensible public officials, we may add, in the capital city of a free and growing nation. And that Mrs. Mattingly lived thirty-one more years in good health, reaching the age of seventy-one.[14]

The effects of the Mattingly miracle were many. The fact that Kohlmann and other of the European-born Jesuits were soon trying the Hohenlohe novenas once every month was distressing to many who saw this as an attempt to routinize an event which by its very definition could never be routine. By what was surely more than coincidence, fifteen more persons, nearly all women and most of them members of religious orders, claimed miraculous cures over the next twelve years. (Six of these took place in Visitation Convent; the best known was that of Sister Mary Apolonia Digges, whom Father Dubuisson tested against the advice of the convent physician by having her lift two fourteen-pound clock weights with her little finger one day after her recovery from pulmonary consumption, as tuberculosis was then known.) These did nothing to reinforce the authenticity of the Mattingly miracle. Rather, as might be expected, they only served to stir up public reaction to what opponents called the miracle hysteria. The debate thus continued and gradually took on a broader ecclesial character. On the one part were those who felt the enlightened American church had no need to rely on cults, special devotions, or the expectation of more miraculous cures to prove its dynamic character. On the other were those who saw the Mattingly and subsequent cures as a miraculous phenomenon visited upon America which gave the church new strength and esteem in Rome.[15]

On balance the Mattingly miracle was probably a plus for the church, especially in terms of both Catholic and Protestant public reactions. For Catholics it ushered in a new era of piety. With it came the increasing practice of special devotions, especially to Mary and the Sacred Heart of Jesus, which had not previously been a prominent part of the Maryland Catholic tradition. Among Protestants there is little doubt that the Mattingly miracle caused a new wave of conversions. Here again most of the converts were women.[16]

Among these the most dramatic example was provided by Wilhelmina Jones of Georgetown, the beautiful daughter of Commodore Jacob Jones, a naval officer who had won renown in the War of 1812 and with Stephen Decatur's Mediterranean squadron. Wilhelmina's first knowledge of Catholicism came from a French boarding school she attended in New York, where she also met Father Benedict Fenwick, then pastor of St. Peter's Church. In 1822 her father, a recent widower, was appointed naval commissioner and established his residence in Georgetown. Here Wilhelmina again met Father Fenwick, who was by then serving his second term as president of Georgetown College. According to her principal biographer, Wilhelmina now wanted to convert Fenwick to the Episcopalian church. This may have been an unconscious reaction to the strong influence of her family, who were shocked to hear of her attraction to Catholicism. In any case all her conversion attempts failed. After various meetings with Fenwick, in fact, they took an entirely opposite turn.

In March 1825, after her father threatened to throw her out of the house and never see her again should she become a Catholic, Wilhelmina Jones at the age of twenty-four entered the Visitation Convent as a novice, later taking the religious name of Sister Stanislaus. Georgetowners reacted with astonishment, and rejected suitors both in New York and Georgetown could scarcely believe the news. Rumors soon spread that a ghostlike figure, said to be the wraith of Wilhelmina's dead mother, was to be seen pacing outside the convent walls. This was all that was needed to draw large crowds. What happened then has been well described by Rose Hawthorne Lathrop, Nathaniel Hawthorne's youngest daughter, who with her scholar husband George Parsons Lathrop was co-author of a detailed history of the Visitation Convent and Academy based on the convent archives:

> The children of the academy . . . gazed out of the upper windows timorously, wondering about the unwonted crowd and disturbance. Carriages and buggies came, full of ladies, and drew up all around, the whole assembly waiting intently for the ghost to promenade, or for anything else that might kindly please to happen for their entertainment. . . . Then they would all cry in chorus, under the window: "Wilhelmina Jones, come out! Wilhelmina Jones, come out. *Come* . . . OUT! COME . . . OUT!"[17]

Collection of Mr. and Mrs. William Machold, Georgetown University Library/Special Collections Division.
Susan Decatur, attributed to Gilbert Stuart.

Three years later President John Quincy Adams, after speaking at the Academy commencement, noted in his diary: "At the side of the piano in the sable weeds of the order, was the young and beautiful daughter of Commodore Jones, who not long ago took the veil." Wilhelmina Jones was not to come out. For the fifty-three remaining years of her life she remained in the convent as a brilliant teacher of languages and music. "She is highly endowed both by nature and grace, and has had the benefit of receiving a liberal education," a convent contemporary wrote of her. "She was one of the most accomplished young ladies I ever saw. Her name is in religion Sister Stanislaus."[18]

Later in the same year Susan Decatur, the young widow of Commodore Stephen Decatur, made her first communion at Trinity Church. Her conversion to Catholicism attracted far more public notice than Wilhelmina Jones's or the Mattingly miracle, not only because her husband had become a national hero before his fateful duel with Commodore Barron, but also because she herself was widely praised as Washington's most attractive and accomplished hostess. What is less known and what her correspondence concerning her conversion best reveals is that she was an intelligent and thoughtful woman. After her baptism in 1828 she renounced the social life of Washington and devoted herself to charities for the poor and support of the church. Taking a small house near the college, she became a strong presence in the community and had many of the faculty as friends, especially Fathers John Beschter and Benedict Fenwick.[19]

Many more conversions during this period occurred through the continuing practice of mixed Protestant-Catholic marriages. William Carroll, grandson of District Commissioner Daniel Carroll II of Upper Marlboro, married Henrietta Williamson, the daughter of a Scot Presbyterian ship owner of Baltimore. Henrietta not only accepted Catholicism, but also converted her father in the process. Catholic Offutts married Protestant Clagetts, whose forebears included the first Episcopal bishop of Maryland. The Protestant daughter of Dr. Charles Worthington, Georgetown's leading physician, married William Gaston, the young Catholic from North Carolina who was Georgetown College's first student.[20] Eliza Loughborough, one of thirteen children of the wealthy landowner and Treasury Department official Nathan Loughborough, converted to Catholicism and convinced a number of her siblings to follow suit, at least one of whom gave origin to a line of Catholic Loughboroughs that exists to this day. Before her death in 1831 Eliza Loughborough may have succeeded in converting her husband, Dr. Benjamin S. Bohrer, a Georgetown physician who had studied under Dr. Worthington.[21] In any case Dr. Bohrer next married Maria Forrest, a daughter of the staunchly Anglican Colonel Uriah Forrest, who had herself converted to Catholicism. Another of Forrest's daughters, Ann, became a strong Catholic after marrying John Green, a Catholic naval officer, evidently much to the displeasure of her family. Then in the next generation Ann's daughter Alice Green married Prince Angel de Iturbide, the son of Anna Maria Huarte, the widow of the short-lived Emperor Agustin de Iturbide of Mexico, in a match that evidently displeased both families. Judging from her correspondence, the empress, whose arrival in Georgetown in 1826 caused considerable excitement, would seem to have preferred a daughter-in-law with more noble antecedents.[22]

But the record for conversions through mixed marriages must go to Thomas, Lewis, and James Carbery, the three youngest of the ten children of Thomas Carbery, Sr. All three married Protestants. Thomas Jr., the mayor, converted his wife and his mother-in-law. Lewis did not at first succeed with his Quaker wife Artemesia Cloud until three years after their marriage, at which time Artemesia also brought three of her sisters with her into the church. In

200   1820 James Carbery married Emza, still another sister of Artemesia Cloud. How many mixed marriages these unions in turn may have produced—at least one is known—is difficult to determine. But there were probably many more, given the Carbery tradition of large families.[23]

Examples of conversions among men during this period are not lacking, although they appear to have been considerably fewer in number than among women. For some twelve years Trinity Church and St. Mary's of Alexandria benefited from the services of Reverend John F. Aiken, born an Episcopalian in Tennessee, who converted while a student at Georgetown, persuaded his family to follow suit, and was ordained a priest in 1844.[24]

Bladen Forrest, a grandnephew of Colonel Uriah Forrest and owner of Forrest Hall, Georgetown's largest public meeting and theater building, became a Catholic along with his wife in the late 1840s. Preceding him was Francis Lowndes, formerly a vestryman at St. John's Episcopal Church in Georgetown, who was converted by Father Peter Kroes and other Trinity priests in 1843. Lowndes was a direct descendant of one of the founding families of Bladensburg that was closely related to the politically prominent Taskers, Lloyds, Bladens, and Stodderts. Most notably, he was a nephew of Benjamin Stoddert, a former partner of Colonel Uriah Forrest who was appointed the first secretary of the navy by President John Adams in 1798.[25]

Although never himself a convert, Stoddert made some unusual gifts to the church. In 1804, or two years after the death of his wife Rebecca Lowndes, Benjamin Stoddert offered Bishop Carroll a deed of gift of five thousand acres of land in Kentucky not far from the pioneer Catholic settlements in Bardstown "for the benefit of the Roman Catholic Church." Later in his life, when Washington property speculation had considerably diminished his fortune, Stoddert gave a large marble clock formerly used in the Charleston, South Carolina, slave market to Visitation Academy, although none of his daughters attended there. Two recent discoveries suggest a possible motive. First, an analysis of the well-known Charles Willson Peale portrait of three Stoddert children has revealed that what may have been a necklace with a medallion or crucifix on the neck of the oldest daughter Elizabeth, later the wife of Dr. Thomas Ewell, was apparently cut out and painted over some time after Peale finished the portrait in 1789. Second, cellar excavations connected with the current reconstruction of the Stoddert residence in Georgetown have turned up records showing six rosaries, three crucifixes, and one black cross inventoried among the belongings of Elizabeth Stoddert Ewell. The possibility that Stoddert at first repressed his wife's or his daughter's Catholic inclinations and later regretted his actions certainly suggests itself. If indeed either Mrs. Stoddert or Mrs. Ewell were hindered from becoming Catholics, the same is not true of the next generation. On January 18, 1843, the Trinity baptismal registers record the adult baptism of Mary Rebecca Ewell, "daughter of the late Thomas Ewell and Elizabeth Stoddert." Five months later her first cousin once removed, Francis Lowndes, mentioned above, followed her.[26]

The Benjamin Stoddert children by Charles William Peale, 1789. Elizabeth "Becky" Stoddert, later Mrs. Thomas Ewell, is on the left.

The year 1832 produced yet another spurt of conversions, but for reasons far removed from miracles or examples of saintly religious life. Ironically, it came at a time when Washington was at last coming into its own as a capital city; war-damaged public buildings had been repaired or rebuilt, property sales were booming, Congress no longer thought of moving elsewhere, and the city's financial structure, although still weak, had at least weathered a severe national depression. But in the summer of 1832 the dread Asiatic cholera, spreading southward from New York and Philadelphia, reached Washington. Before it was over many citizens fled the city, cart drivers periodically made their rounds shouting "bring out your dead," and the District's churches were filled. "God makes the disease an instrument of much good in bringing many to their duties," the visiting Irish Jesuit Peter Kenney sternly noted. During the one month of September 1832, when the cholera epidemic was at its height, Trinity parish recorded thirty-seven conversions, a figure that exceeded most previous yearly totals. And, sadly, some one hundred and twelve burials, from August through December of the same year, which represented a 250 percent increase from the full year before.[27]

Washingtonians did their best to check the disease's spread. A few, especially doctors and volunteer nursing aides, became seriously ill or died of their efforts to halt it. But the epidemic also brought out a darker side in some of the citizenry. The Board of Health, after having noted that the highest incidence of the disease was among canal workers and those laboring on the city's water mains and streets, roundly attributed the cholera's first infestation to "the large number of foreign emigrants . . . from Germany and Ireland, men who neither understood our language or were accustomed to our climate, habits, and mode of living." From there it was but a short step for some to blame "foreigners" for the many ills—social, political, and otherwise—the city might suffer. Or to hang a stereotype effigy of Paddy, as Irish immigrants were beginning to be called, on the Georgetown College campus. "The figure of an Irishman was hung from one of our windows," a college official quietly noted in his diary for the year of the cholera.[28]

What the epidemic was bringing to the surface was an undercurrent of prejudice and bigotry towards the foreign born that had existed almost as long as the republic. In Washington its earliest public manifestation came in the city's second year, when James McGuirk, the first man to be hanged in Washington, was brought to trial for the murder of his wife in April 1802. The *Washington Federalist* used the occasion to editorialize on how it was "a matter of astonishment to those, who are accustomed to attend our Courts of Justice, to observe how few native Americans are found charged with the different crimes, which stain our records." It was the foreign born, the *Federalist* insisted, who "hasten the strides of vice, [and] disturb the peace and security of our country."[29]

Two years after the cholera, or in January 1834, what was first described as armed rioting between rival Irish labor gangs broke out on the Chesapeake and Ohio Canal near Williamsport, Maryland. The rioting was in fact a strike over layoffs and lowered wages, exacerbated by the jealousies of loosely associated "Corkonians" from southern Ireland and "Longfordians" from the north. As might be expected the news of the riots caused much concern in Washington, where the C and O Canal was viewed as the answer to the Potomac Company's failure and the new hope for trade with the west. The disturbances also made national headlines because President Andrew Jackson, friend of labor and the common man, answered the request of a nervous Maryland governor for troops. (They arrived after most of the violence was over.) Jackson thus became the first American president to call federal troops to quell a strike. What all this added to popular perceptions of the Irish—and not incidentally to the church, which by then had at least one resident priest on the canal—is easily imagined.[30]

By the next year, or in the summer of 1835, the *Washington Metropolitan* found that some of its readers held such strong anti-Irish and anti-Catholic sentiments that the paper's tolerant stand had caused them to cancel their subscriptions. "We are not ourselves Catholic; yet we have expressed, and repeat it, a sincere respect for that denomination of Christianity," the *Metropolitan* replied. Then, in what showed obvious awareness of the Maryland Catholic tradition, its editors took pains to make an important distinction. "We know well that Catholicism is a different thing, in spirit and in fact, in this age and this country from what it has been in others," they continued. "We know well that those tenets, which, under other circumstances have made it politically dangerous, are, here and now, mere nullities of which even the empty forms are fast fading away."[31]

In a commencement address at Georgetown College that same summer, George Washington Parke Custis, President Washington's adopted son and the doyen of Arlington House, found it necessary to mention "the mists of intolerance and error which now darken our prospects." He hoped Protestants and Catholics would work together as brothers to dispel them as they had before. "What matters it to me whether the Catholic citizen, erects his altar for the worship of the ever living God, in a church or a chapel?" he asked his audience. "If he is honest, if he is faithful to the Constitution, he is my brother and under the protection of the laws."[32]

But neither the rhetorical flourishes for which Custis was famous nor the tolerant attitude of the *Metropolitan* and other newspapers could completely curb the growing hostility toward the foreign born that was taking form across the nation as the American nativist movement. That this phenomenon did not strike as deep roots nor have as dire consequences in Washington as in other cities such as Boston and Philadelphia was in large part the result of the Maryland Catholics' long history of ecumenism and commitment to public service. In the latter sphere, it is important to note, the tradition did not die with the older generation who were among the founders of the capital. To be sure, some members of this older generation continued to hold public office after the War of 1812 and well on into the 1830s. Among the founding families the popular William Brent, youngest brother of Mayor Robert Brent, had set the tone. When he died in 1848 at the age of seventy-three, Brent had served the city for more than fifty years in his various roles as court clerk, council member, and bank director.

Other Catholics from the older Maryland families who served on the city council in the first thirty years of the new century included Nicholas L. Queen, the hotel and property owner; Griffith Coombe, builder and realtor; James D. Barry, James Barry's nephew and adopted son; and Joseph Cassin, the younger brother of naval hero Commodore Stephen Cassin.[33] In 1822 the previously mentioned Thomas Carbery, Jr., achieved the distinction of becoming Washington's second Catholic mayor and the first to be popularly elected. Sometimes known as "the poor man's mayor" because he attempted to abolish property qualifications for voter eligibility, Carbery was defeated in a close election after serving only one term. Nevertheless, he remained a popular and important figure on the Washington scene, serving on numerous building committees, bank boards, and commissions while he held court at his home on 17th Street, widely known as the "Miracle House" after his sister's cure. Described as "genial . . . [and] not above speaking to anyone" Carbery was also extremely

Georgetown University Library/Special Collections Division.

Thomas Carbery, Jr., mayor of Washington, 1822-1824.

generous to the church. So generous, in fact, that upon his death in 1863 his two surviving sisters were astonished to find that he had given the largest part of his estate, valued at approximately two hundred thousand dollars, to the St. Vincent's Orphan Asylum that he and Father Matthews had founded. Carbery's sisters in fact contested his will; St. Vincent's eventually accepted $15,000 in a compromise settlement.[34]

More typical of a rising middle class were the Catholics Gustavus Higdon, who operated a dry goods store; George Sweeney, chief clerk of the city post office; John Dobbyn, a ship owner who became a successful tavern keeper and tobacco dealer; and Benjamin Burch, doorkeeper of the House of Representatives. All were elected to the Common Council, the Board of Aldermen, or both. Sweeney, who ran unsuccessfully for mayor in 1830, served as president of the Common Council for three terms and as an alderman for two.[35]

By the 1830s and '40s, moreover, other area Catholics were achieving national prominence. On the national scene Roger Brooke Taney became the first Catholic to achieve cabinet rank when President Andrew Jackson named him attorney general in 1831, thus launching him on a long government career during which Taney would rise to chief justice of the Supreme Court. Others were overcoming the traditional obstacle of state-wide elections to gain seats in the United States Congress. Among them were Dr. Benedict Joseph Semmes of Piscataway, mentioned in a previous chapter, and William Duhurst Merrick of Port Tobacco and Georgetown, who was a brother-in-law of St. Patrick's Pastor William Matthews. Semmes was elected for the first of two terms as an anti-Jacksonian Democrat to the House of Representatives in 1829, while Merrick, who prepared at Georgetown College and ran as a Whig, served one term in the Senate beginning in 1838.[36]

But for most Catholics, entry to the government, whether elected or appointed, remained at the municipal level. To be sure, as Washington's population surged from 19,000 to 40,000 during the 1830s and '40s, Catholics were no longer nearly so prominent on the enlarged Common Council and Board of Aldermen as they had been in the city's earliest years. But those who continued to seek public office, it is gratifying to note, were often the sons or the younger relatives of the founding generation. Joseph Harbaugh, a son of Leonard and a parishioner of the Trinity Church his father had built, was elected to the Common Council for five terms and to the Board of Aldermen for two during the years 1830-36. James Hoban's elder son James was a prominent lawyer who served on the Common Council, ran for mayor in the municipal elections of 1840, and thereafter served as U.S. attorney for the District of Columbia. Greater still were the contributions of Lewis and James Carbery, the youngest of Mayor Carbery's nine siblings. Lewis, who lived in Georgetown, was a District surveyor, justice of the peace, and president of the Washington County Levy Court. His brother, the naval architect James, was a mainstay of the City Council who won ten elections to the Common Council, including four as its president, and two to the Board of Aldermen during the period 1826 through 1842, when he often found himself working with the now-aging William Brent. Similarly, Ignatius Mudd, a nephew of the Bennett Mudd who was overseer of carpentry at the President's House, was elected to five terms on the Common Council and two on the Board of Aldermen from the years 1833 to 1849. Thereafter Mudd served as commissioner of public buildings, the single position that replaced the earlier three-man Board of Commissioners. Serving lesser terms were Nicholas Callan, Jr., son of another of James Hoban's overseers at the President's House, who was a Common Council member for seven years, including two as its president, and John R. Queen, a nephew of Nicholas L. Queen, a member of the same body from 1844 to 1849.[37]

Thus it was that in the two decades before mid-century Catholics in the District of Columbia might regard with some pride their continuing participation in local government and their place in society at large. But at about this same time they undoubtedly also harbored anxious feelings about the new brand of anti-Catholicism, more virulent than ever, that was beginning to sweep the nation. For this was the time of Maria Monk's *Awful Disclosures of the Hotel Dieu Nunnery in Montreal* and many other wildly fabricated "revelations" supposedly written by nuns who had escaped convents that had become dens of iniquity. It was a time when scores of nativist newspapers, magazines, and lurid pamphlets regularly attacked the American Catholic church as the advance guard of a Papal conspiracy bent on subverting republican government and displacing American-born workers with masses of cheap immigrant labor. It was also the time, we have seen, of the Philadelphia riots and the torching of the Ursuline convent in Boston.[38]

On the face of it, these events seemed to be having little or no effect on the Catholic presence in the capital area. Georgetown College continued to enjoy its place in the community as never before. In the space of three years in the early 1830s, for example, the college received its first federal grant from the Congress, received President Andrew Jackson's son as a student, and saw its talented poet and professor of literature, Charles Constantine Pise, elected chaplain of the United States Senate.[39] Trinity Church's thoughtful correspondent and private-school teacher Julia Compton noted that the lecture series on Catholic doctrine by Georgetown College President James Ryder was so successful in persuading Protestants "of the truth and beauty of Catholicism" that Reverend C.M. Butler of St. John's Episcopal Church felt compelled "to put a stop to the growing evil" by starting a series of his own, not to mention establishing new schools and, as Miss Compton was led to believe, trying to win over some of her students. In Washington the popular Pastor William Matthews of St. Patrick's was spreading good will and making his influence felt in every level of society. Although Stephen Dubuisson in a report to France on the Maryland Province of the Society of Jesus worried over the nationwide "spirit of opposition to Catholicism among the sectaries, [which] sometimes results in hostile acts," he at least noted with pride that "in our province we are pleased to have made the majority among our separated brethren have a more favorable spirit."[40]

Nevertheless, in July 1837, the local press reported the first meeting of an organization whose principal goal was the repeal of the naturalization laws that allowed citizenship to foreign born whites who had lived in the United States for five years or more. The organization was known as the Washington Native American Association; it was one of the earliest of many similar groups that were taking shape across the nation. The first meeting, held on July 11, was variously described by the press as "very large and respectable" and "composed of Native Americans of all parties." Within a month the association had launched its own newspaper, the *Native American*, with Henry J. Brent as editor. The repeal of the naturalization laws, Brent told his readers in the first issue, was essential "to save our institutions from the corruption of foreign countries, and ourselves from the loss of our birthrights." The association, he pledged,

*Georgetown University Library
Special Collections Division.*

*John Carroll Brent, journalist and lit-
terateur.*

would never cease its campaign to bring the issue to a favorable resolve in the
halls of Congress.

Joining him in the effort was young John Carroll Brent, later to become a
leading literary figure of Waashington who regularly contributed to the *Southern Literary Messenger*, the New York *Knickerbocker*, and many other periodicals.
Both were Catholics and in fact the sons of William "Billy" Brent, the youngest
of the four brothers of former Mayor Robert Brent. Other early members of the
association who were Catholics include Edward Simms, William Clements,
and the previously mentioned chief clerk of the city Post Office, George
Sweeney. To these we may probably add Daniel Carroll of Duddington, who if
not a member at least provided his Duddington estate grounds for the association's Fourth of July celebrations. Among the non-Catholic officers of the association in its first year were Joseph H. Bradley, director of the Franklin
Insurance Company; Henry A. Morfit, an attorney; Benjamin K. Morsell, a local
magistrate; and John N. Moulder, a government clerk.[41]

That Washington Catholics would initially join such a group is not as surprising as it might seem. Catholics were repeatedly assured by the association
that it was "not actuated by a spirit of hostility against the Roman Catholic Religion." Indeed, so it appeared, at least in the association's official pronouncements and on the front page of its newspaper. Washington Catholics, moreover,
could make as strong a claim to native birthrights as anyone. Many of them
who were descendants of Maryland's older Catholic families were by now
sixth- and seventh-generation Americans; in Washington they were more
firmly entrenched in the mainstream of society than anywhere else. Should not

they, too, be concerned with the new wave of famine immigrants that was rapidly boosting the nation's foreign born population, now close to one million counting the Irish alone?[42]

As early as 1790 when the wave was but a trickle by comparison, John Carroll worried about the problem. Now, 50 years later, Washingtonians faced the specter of mass unemployment. As the *Native American* pointed out in one of its more accurate social observations, immigrant labor in the capital had up to that time been mainly spared from actual pauperism by "the great extent of internal improvements, in 'Roads and Canals,' made through borrowed means." But once these public projects stopped, as some already had, the editors knew what would happen. "This tide of foreign laborers will fall back upon us," they warned, "and thus form a body politic of paupers, or, like the spirits of Macbeth, rise to push us from our stools."[43]

It was true. Washington not only had a high percentage of foreign born relative to its small population (sixteen percent of the white popultaion in 1850), there was also a large proportion of indigents among the immigrant laborers and artisans, as Latrobe had been the first to observe. The Washington city council's long efforts to relieve the poor also readily attest to the city's precarious economy. The prospect of more and the warnings of job displacement therefore played to real fears. With themes that echo down to the present, the Washington Native American Association not only promised to save America for Americans, but also "to restore the spirit of 1776" by reducing the excesses of government, promoting temperance and industrious work habits, and fighting favoritism in municipal and federal government appointments. All things considered, its appeal was not limited.[44]

But whether nativism could survive in Washington presents a far more interesting question than how it first planted fragile roots in the capital area. For Catholics and Protestants alike, the early pronouncements of nativism held many incongruities. These surfaced very quickly. In the first days of its existence the association was attacked for not welcoming naturalized citizens, who, according to the press, had been "studiously excluded from all participation." The association replied that it had no intention of waging a campaign against the rights of already naturalized citizens. Rather, it simply wished to draw the line at naturalizing any more. The line, moreover, was to be firmly drawn "between the present and the future, broad, deep, and forever impassible." This was necessary, the *Native American* told its readers, because "it is for this generation—it is for us to achieve a great moral revolution. Already the American Eagle lies bleeding on the ground!"[45]

The association's stance provoked one of the more lively debates in Washington's nineteenth-century press. Fortunately for readers, it was not without some rare bits of humor and mordant satire. In a country forged by recent immigrants, in a country where many citizens were but one or two generations removed from foreign born parents, as numerous letters to editors pointed out, the claim that no good would come from further immigration was tantamount to saying "our fathers are bad; . . . to say those who have nurtured and raised us are bad; to say that brothers, uncles, and cousins are bad!" This reaction soon brought the debate to the *pons asinorum* of how native a native American had to be. A writer styling himself "An American Pat-Riot" thought he had the answer:

> In the first place it is manifest that we, the native Americans, have been in possession of the water, fire, earth, and air, of these United States from time immemorial. Our remote fathers, not long after Noah's flood, crossed over in flat boats from Southern Asia, and after having stopped at the Sandwich Islands to take in water, finally reached this continent, and took possession of it, exclusively for themselves and us, their beloved descendants, *in eternum et ultra*. It is in this way that Pocahantas was uncle to our great-grandfathers and that our dear brethren are the Cherokees and Winnebagoes.[46]

But to George Sweeney and other members of the association of Irish descent the question was more serious. To have their forebears castigated, as the association tended more and more to do, surely racked their consciences. It was perhaps for this reason that Sweeney asked the association's indulgence at its second general meeting "to relate an incident in the life of a foreigner, an Irishman, whose memory is dear to me." The Irishman, who from the context of Sweeney's speech was undoubtedly his father, had refused to take part in a local election in Baltimore because although long entitled to naturalization and the right of suffrage "he had abstained from its exercise because he doubted the strict propriety of any interference by foreigners in the election of the country, content that his children, all of whom were natives, should have a *natural* right to all the privileges of American citizens."[47]

This was a perfect paradigm of nativist thought on the subject, and Sweeney, later elected the association's president, must have been loudly applauded. More curiously, however, he also asked the association not to present a memorial to Congress for the total repeal of the naturalization laws, but perhaps only their modification. In any case, the good judgment of the Congress, composed as it was almost entirely of native citizens, could be depended upon to take care of the problem, Sweeney thought. He did not wish to press the matter, however, if any fellow members disagreed. They did, as he must have expected, since a congressional memorial was their often-stated primary objective. One can only conclude that Sweeney, who was in a good position to exercise patronage as the chief clerk of the city post office, had friends to look after in the Irish community here and abroad. Buying time before the gates might close, in other words, may have been his motivation. Or, as we say today, simply speaking for the record.[48]

Other troubles soon plagued the Washington Native American Association. In the general meeting of October 12, 1837, John Carroll Brent made a passionate appeal to keep alive "the engine of our creed and opinions" by negotiating with a willing and experienced publisher who could be counted on to print and distribute the *Native American* regularly. At a meeting a week earlier Edward Simms and three other members, presumably Catholics, resigned from the organization because they had noted "strong feelings of proscription in the minds of many of its members as well as in respect to politics as to a certain denomination of religion." Simms and his friends were the first manifestation, we will see, of a problem that would not disappear. Virtually the only trouble-free issue that the association first put forward was its claim that the foreign born were occupying too many positions in the federal government, which they saw as fast becoming swollen in the extravagant manner of its European counterparts. One member claimed to have examined "the Blue Book of 1835-36" and found employed "*sixty-one salaried officers*, natives of foreign countries: and I believe that twenty or thirty more have been added since the reorganization of the General Post Office and the General Land Office."[49]

On matters of religious belief the Native American Association showed every sign of trying to avoid sectarian differences and, more especially, not giving offense to Washington's Catholics. "We will not, in any manner whatever, connect ourselves, or be connected with any religious sect or denomination, leaving every creed to its own strength," the fifth article of the association's constitution held. Initially, the association's officers tried to live up to its vow of religious disinterest. To their credit they ruled speakers who attempted to introduce sectarian themes out of order, at least at their earlier meetings, and refused a request from a nativist association in New York to join a petition to Congress to pass a law specifically prohibiting foreign Catholics from further entry into the United States, a goal often voiced by other nativist groups. "This is outrageous," the *Native American* protested. "We will not hold with these bigoted sectaries for one moment in their particularizing patriotism." In fact, the more the editors thought about it, the more they became convinced the petition was the work of the opposition "intending by this *ultra* movement, to bring them into disrepute."[50]

But the association could scarcely restrain the attacks on the character or the industry of the new order of immigrants, since the difference between them and the earlier generations of "true Americans" who had created the republic was one of the nativists' principal arguments for halting further immigration. And, of course, the new order of immigrants appeared to be Irish, Irish, and still more Irish. (The Germans, by now also arriving in considerable number, received little attention by comparison; Washington nativists criticized them mainly for not speaking English or not learning it quickly enough.)

In its first year the association exercised some caution—hesitancy is perhaps the better word—in its criticism of the Irish. The *Native American*, in fact, preferred to dwell on conditions in Ireland, rather than directly attack the Irish here. ("Ireland—Its Situation—Its People Unfit to Govern Americans" was a typical headline of this period.) But by January 1838, after the first troubles broke out among the labor gangs on the C and O Canal, the tone of the *Native American* and the association's meetings grew both more specific and more strident. The Irish on public payrolls were now so numerous, the *Native American* claimed, that from the government buildings at the west end of the city to the Irish labor camp at the base of Capitol Hill one could not avoid "the flourish of shillelahs" or "the flavour of whiskey." Everywhere you looked there were grog shops and "an Irishman . . . ever perambulating in all 'the insolence of office.'"[51]

The tone continued. Letters to the editors began to criticize Irish-descent office holders by name. The St. Patrick's day celebrations were a base attempt at cloaking "a political parade . . . under the honored name of a saint"; George Washington Parke Custis was attacked for joining the celebrants and listening to "the hiccuped toast, the stale jest, the maudlin hypocrisy of the Irish." The same issue of the *Native American* that stoutly proclaimed the association waged no war of opinion against foreigners (but only the law that allowed them equal political footing with the natives) might also carry a dire warning for its readers:

> The Irish battle for supremacy whenever and wherever they can muster a band together, and plenty of whiskey. The Germans—a cold, calculating people—do not often lose sight of their characteristic caution, even under the ordinary liberal indulgence of gin; they will remain passive for a few years longer, till the circumstances are ripe for them to assert their political superiority, and back that assertion by an array of numbers.[52]

And it was not long before the same issue of the *Native American* that might repeat the association's policy of excluding the subject of religion from all its deliberations would also print stale anti-Catholic jokes.[53]

It is difficult to gauge how much of an effect the increasingly anti-Catholic stance of the *Native American* had on the association's decline. There is no question, however, that these two developments were coterminous. The general meeting of the Washington Native American Association of February 22, 1838, was attended by two hundred persons, the association announced, in contrast to the several hundreds of its first year. In October of 1838 Henry S. Brent resigned as editor of the *Native American*. Soon thereafter his brother John Carroll Brent went to Paris, where he became United States Consul *ad interim* upon the death of his uncle Daniel Brent and finished the latter's *Biographical Sketch of the Most Rev. John Carroll*. In the summer of 1839 the second editor of the *Native American* resigned, apologizing for occasionally having "hurried into expressions, which, on reflection, my judgement would have condemned" and thereby having alienated naturalized citizens. By that time the association's memorial with some one thousand signatures for the repeal of the naturalization act had been tabled in

212   Congress for more than a year. By that time, too, or in the same summer of 1839, a member complained of going to a previously announced meeting of the association at which there was not sufficient attendance to conduct a meeting. In November 1840, after three-and-a-half years, the *Native American* ceased publication.[54]

    Washington, in short, had weathered the first ill winds of the nativist movement. But a greater storm was yet to come.

11

A Final Test

[The] principles and purposes of the Roman Catholic Church in the United States . . . constitute aggressions of such a character that, if not now resisted, will lead, at no distant day, to the overthrow of the American Consitution and the complete establishment of despotism.

RESOLUTION, WASHINGTON KNOW NOTHING PARTY
Carusi's Saloon, September 14, 1854

As they had earlier, the signs of the times remained mixed and confusing for the District's Catholics during the next two decades. In the 1840s many nativist societies went underground or into momentary eclipse, much like Washington's, as they pondered their failure to achieve their goals through the legislative process. This did not, however, bring any surcease in the violent anti-Catholicism of the era. Quite the opposite, the summer of 1844 brought the dreadful days of the Philadelphia riots. In New York, where nativist Mayor James Harper and his family-owned *Harper's Weekly* did much to excite anti-Irish and anti-Catholic prejudices, a similar tragedy was averted only when Catholic Bishop John Hughes coolly informed Mayor Harper that Catholics could take care of themselves and that if one Catholic church was burned, New York would resemble Moscow as Napoleon had seen it. Other disturbances, some of them admittedly precipitated by Irish or German laborers, broke out in Cincinnati, Louisville, and St. Louis.[1]

At the same time, however, the outbreak of the Mexican-American War in 1846 saw Catholic officers distinguish themselves on the battlefield. Similarly, Trinity Church Pastors John McElroy and Anthony Rey, who were personally appointed by President Polk to serve as chaplains with the expeditionary forces, bravely carried out their mission to cross enemy lines in an effort to counteract Mexican rumors that the United States Army was made up of heretics out to destroy their churches. Father Rey died of his efforts, cruelly tortured by guerrillas, and McElroy served with distinction. The achievements of all—chaplains, officers and troops—won wide respect and did much to dispel the nativists' age-old accusations that Catholics owed primary allegiance to the Pope and were therefore not to be trusted in wars against Catholic nations.[2]

Thus it was that as bigotry and its accompanying violence spread across the nation, the city where Catholics raised in the tradition of living at peace with their neighbors remained relatively calm and free of any public disorders. Washington, by all outward appearances, might be spared from further manifestations of the nativist phenomenon. But by June 1853 a sharp-eyed observer of the city's normally placid and apolitical municipal elections, signing himself "Washingtonian," wrote to the *Intelligencer*:

> It is with deep regret, indeed mortification, that we perceive an effort on the part of some of our citizens to introduce politics into our approaching municipal elections; thus making it a political test, at the expense of local benefits and sectional views. Has not every well-inclined citizen, for years past, irrespective of party bias, sustained by his voice the best and not politically eligible candidate? . . . Why arouse in our quiet community the rancor of party influence? . . . In the late election for Mayor the line of demarcation was not drawn, (though our city is proverbially Whig). Whigs and Democrats then, as of old, met at the polls and voted, not blindly or politically, but for the common interest and common good.[3]

Three days earlier a letter to the editor of the *Daily Evening Star* complained that a candidate for canal commissioner had been defeated for no other apparent reason than Irish birth. "There is but too much of this *anti-republican* and *anti-social* virus of a pseudo-American party in active operation in this community," the writer concluded.[4]

Stated simply, what these two observers were witnessing was the birth of a political arm of the nativist movement. A decade earlier most nativist associations, certainly Washington's among them, insisted that they "look[ed] not at the mansion of our President" or any other political office, but sought only repeal of the naturalization laws through memorials to Congress.[5] Now, having failed, they would achieve the same goal through political organization and candidates of their own. The party they formed was a descendant of various secret fraternal societies such as the Order of United Americans, founded in 1844, or, more directly, the Order of the Star Spangled Banner, established in 1850. It was to be formally known as the American Party. But because its members held secret meetings and repeatedly said "I know nothing," or the equivalent of today's "no comment," to questions about the party's existence or which candidates it might be supporting, it was soon much better known as the Know Nothing party. One of its first objectives was Washington.[6]

Keeping their identity secret, the Know Nothings' initial Washington effort came in the municipal elections in the spring of 1853. As the *National Intelligencer* had tried to emphasize, these elections were rarely political and normally free of any semblance of campaigning. Candidates for mayor and the Common Council were usually chosen by a circle of friends; their candidacy was then announced through advertisements in the press without reference to party. But, in spite of the advantages of an organized effort, the Know Nothings' debut was marked by mixed results at best. A completely accurate count of their gains in council seats is difficult if not impossible, since Washington newspapers had a long tradition of not publishing the political affiliations of any candidates, nor of course did the Know Nothings themselves. Nevertheless, of the seven aldermen winning election (the Board of Aldermen now had fourteen members serving two-year terms, half of whom were elected annually), it is possible to identify two of the winners and four of the holdovers from the previous election as Know Nothings. But the Common Council, now enlarged to twenty-one members elected annually, saw only two new members and three repeaters who can be identified as Know Nothings.[7]

As always the elections were held in the first week of June. On the last day of the same month there occurred an event that had it occurred earlier might well have improved the Know Nothings' chances. On June 30, 1853, a ship arrived in New York bearing Archbishop Gaetano Bedini, a papal diplomat ostensibly en route to Brazil where he would serve as nuncio to the court of Dom Pedro II, Emperor of Brazil. Among other tasks Bedini's real mission was to sound out the possibilities for diplomatic relations between the United States and the Holy See. At the time Rome had hopes of establishing a nunciature in the United States, but it was not until 1893 that a papal delegate was received in Washington and then only after considerable opposition from American bishops.

Bedini's visit could not have been more inopportune. Catholic efforts to have some measure of their own religious instruction or Bible readings in public schools and the Jesuits' successes in establishing missions in the far West, all grossly distorted by the anti-Catholic press and tract societies, were beginning to convince a significant number of Americans that the Roman Catholic Church was indeed plotting the conquest of the United States. When Archbishop Bedini's diplomatic mission became known for what it was, the nativist forces across the nation united in full chorus to take advantage of the opportunity the church had given them. Disturbances greeted Bedini in Pittsburgh and near-riots in Cincinnati and Wheeling, West Virginia. Unable to complete his tour, the Archbishop was finally smuggled aboard a ship in New York sailing for Rome. American church leaders called it "a blunder from every point of view."[8]

But by early spring of the next year it was the nativists' turn to commit a blunder—the first of two that earned them lasting condemnation. In the pre-dawn hours of March 6, 1854, a gang of men overwhelmed the night watchman at the construction site of the Washington Monument, removed a stone donated by Pope Pius IX from the Temple of Concordia in Rome (one of a number of stones given by states and societies), broke off pieces for souvenirs and dumped the stone into the Potomac. Although the Pope's stone incident, as it came to be known, was not directly attributed to the still-secret Know Nothings, it was presumed to be their work and widely denounced in the metropolitan press. When the New York *Crusader* published an editorial praising the perpetrators as true patriots, the Washington *Daily Evening Star* answered that it "did not think that a paper published in this country, could be found so lost

216 to a sense of everything that is decent and right." Most Washingtonians agreed. But, as we will see, this was not the end of nativist attempts on the Monument.[9]

Later that spring, on the twenty-fifth of May, a writer signing himself "Old Citizen" warned the citizenry that "a *secret society*, denominated KNOW NOTHINGS, has recently sprung up in our midst, . . . and has its own candidate for the Mayoralty and boasts of its ability to elect him, through the secret and invisible influences that it controls." His warning was essentially correct and apposite, except that it came at the eleventh hour. The Know Nothing party had been working for over a year, most often without identifying itself or its candidates, and did indeed have a qualified candidate for mayor. On the second of June, or three days before the elections, the *Evening Star* published a letter from one "Civis" who claimed that John T. Towers was the Know Nothing candidate for mayor, based on the fact that none of Towers' close friends would deny it. In the days that followed there were charges that gangs were coming from Baltimore on election day to disrupt the voting, that large sums of money had been transmitted from the executive boards of the Baltimore, Philadelphia, and New York Know Nothings to secure Towers' election. These in turn provoked countercharges that the forthright Archbishop Hughes of New York was coming to Washington to influence the elections.[10]

On June 6, 1854, Washingtonians woke up to read in their morning newspapers that the American Party, better known as the Know Nothings, had gained control of their municipal government through victory at the polls. John T. Towers, president of the Board of Aldermen, owner of one of the city's leading print shops, and a former publisher of a Whig party newspaper who had been appointed the first superintendent of public printing by Congress, had been elected mayor by a substantial majority over the incumbent John W. Maury. What is more, the Common Council showed a remarkable turnover, with the presidency and at least ten seats going to candidates who can be identified as Know Nothings. Similarly, the party elected the president and six members of the Board of Aldermen, which meant Know Nothing majorities in both chambers.[11] At a moonlight victory celebration Towers, adopting a populist tone, told his cheering supporters: "This has been a peculiar election, for the people had to go to the workshop for a candidate and there they found one." Sharing the platform was a certain Mr. J.T. Wilmot of Baltimore, who told the cheering crowd that it gave him "great pleasure to inform you that the Mayor elect has given assurances that none but Native Americans will be placed as sentinels on the outposts."[12]

It was the first plum for the Know Nothings, with Baltimore next, with its city elections set for the autumn of 1854. That same year, as the break-up of the Whigs signaled the end of the traditional opposition to the Democrats, the Know Nothings rapidly became a national force. By the end of 1855, the party had won more than seventy congressional seats. State strongholds where the Know Nothings won governorships or pluralities in legislatures included Connecticut, Delaware, Kentucky, Maryland, Massachusetts, New Hampshire, Pennsylvania, and Rhode Island.[13]

The Know Nothings' startling successes both in Washington and on the national front were due largely to fears of the ever-accelerating flow of immigrants and the consequent desire to halt it or at least slow it down through the naturalization process. There could be no doubt that the rate of immigrant entry had not fallen off from the peaks reached as a result of the Irish potato blight of 1846-47. Indeed, the nation's foreign-born population rose from 1,240,000 in 1850 to 2,192,230 in 1860, while the District's swelled at one and a half times the national average, or from 4,913 to 12,465 during the same decade.[14]

Almost as important was a general voter dissatisfaction with the established two-party political system. The Whigs, the party of privilege, had at first been the nativists' most receptive political host. But it had finally failed them in their quest for naturalization reform and was now on its way to extinction, the victim of its own incompetence and internal schism over the issue of extension of slavery to the territories. The Democrats by contrast were perceived as contributing to the immigration problem through their catering to what was called the foreign vote. This perception was not without some foundation since from 1851 onwards naturalized citizens tended to vote as a bloc for the Democrats. Furthermore, corrupt party bosses in the gateway cities of New York, Philadelphia, and Baltimore sometimes flouted the naturalization laws by recruiting newly arrived immigrants, providing them with fraudulent citizenship papers, and taking them to the polls to vote Democratic. The Know Nothings thus might proclaim that they alone were looking after the interests of the native-born, working- and middle-class Americans. They alone, they claimed, were ready to replace the corrupt and hack politicians with new and younger men free of political ties. And many Americans listened, flocking to their secret lodges.[15]

To all this was added the anti-Catholicism of the day, which by 1854 had reached what contemporary observers and present-day historians have called its maximum influence. It is in this area, however, that certain differences of degree existed between the approaches of the Washington Know Nothings and their national counterparts. While Know Nothings everywhere exercised some caution in their official pronouncements on Catholicism in order not to alienate too many Catholic voters, the Washington Know Nothings and their colleagues in Baltimore and Maryland in general were especially cautious in their initial efforts, in obvious recognition of the church's history and standing in both the District and the state.[16] Thus while Know Nothing party organs in many cities might indiscriminately attack what they called the tyrannical and subversive followers of Romanism here and abroad, the Washington party took pains to recognize what had so often been noted by the local press and independent observers since the earliest days of the republic; namely, that American Catholicism was different from the church abroad. At a mass meeting in September 1854, for example, the Washington Know Nothings resolved "that every Protestant denomination in the United States maintains the constitutional principles of a separation of Church and State—in which principle many American

218   Catholics sincerely concur, while on the other hand, the Papal Church abroad openly, and always, and everywhere maintains the doctrine of obedience of the civil to the ecclesiastical authority."[17]

Similarly, whereas the party in other cities showed no hesitancy in promoting prohibition of public office-holding by naturalized citizens and Catholics, the Washington Know Nothings agonized over the propriety of such an affront to the Declaration of Independence and the Bill of Rights. Telling street crowds that "none but Native Americans" would be appointed to public office, as the mysterious Mr. Wilmot did at Mayor Towers' victory celebration, was one thing. To come up with some kind of acceptable public policy statement on proscription was another and far more difficult. The most that the Washington party's newspaper, the *Daily American Organ*, would attempt, in fact, were borrowed words in the form of a reprint from the *New York Christian Advocate*. The *Advocate* acknowledged that it might be a Know Nothing objective "to counteract the political influence of Romanism, by resisting the political elevation of foreigners." This did not mean excluding Catholics from office as such, the *Advocate* went on to explain, "yet as the great body of Romanists in this country are emigrants from Europe it cannot be denied that the exclusion of foreigners will necessarily affect the Roman Catholic Church more than other churches . . . [which] may be necessary to the conservation and perpetuation of civil and religious liberties." No such niceties were observed at the ward level, we may be sure.[18]

Another factor influencing the Washington Know Nothing victory of 1854 was secrecy. Secrecy, or better said dissimulation, was a commonplace of Know Nothing political strategy, practiced to some degree on all fronts during the party's first years. In Washington, however, the local press tradition of political anonymity for city government candidates could not have been more helpful to this purpose. To the party's reticence about whether or not it was putting up its own candidate for a given post or if a given candidate who told voters he was of the "people's party" was in fact a Know Nothing was added the difficulty that newspapers were no help. True, letters to the editor might sound warnings, and there is no doubt that at the ward level the man on the street understood the anti-foreign rhetoric of the party's tub-thumping candidates. But there is some doubt that many Washingtonians fully understood the nature of the organization that was backing a well-known figure like John Towers. Neither Towers' prior record as a city council member nor his writings as the founding editor and publisher of the *Whig Standard* gave voters much indication of strong nativist and anti-Catholic inclinations, if indeed Towers had any.[19] Certainly most qualified voters in the spring of 1854 knew something about the man, but very little about the party behind him.

Thus the Know Nothings swept into office. Again, as with the Native American Association seventeen years earlier, the question of whether or not the party could survive is as interesting as how it came into power. Phrased another way, one might question whether the roots of the Maryland tradition—the centuries-old tradition of ecumenism that worked to the benefit of

Protestant and Catholic alike—were strong enough to hold up against a seemingly popular and increasingly hostile political force.

Based on the press debate during the campaign of 1854, the prognosis for the Know Nothings' future growth was not promising. Letters to the editors in the principal metropolitan dailies ran almost four to one against it. Those who opposed the Know Nothings or tried to warn fellow voters of the party's concealed agenda directed their principal criticism to its intolerance and secrecy. "I would ask those who have been beguiled into the brotherhood of these mysterious 'Know Nothings,'" a writer signing himself "Common Sense" asked, "if they do not feel abased holding membership with a fraternity they are ashamed to own, of having pledged themselves to objects and schemes that they are afraid to avow, and seeking in silence and concealment the covenants of a dangerous association."[20]

Others took the opportunity to reemphasize the particular nature of American Catholicism or to remind readers of how any attempt to proscribe Catholics was totally contrary to the spirit and letter of the Constitution. "What American citizen, native or naturalized, would not drop his head in shame," asked "A Native Protestant," "if the Constitution were amended so as to prohibit naturalization and extinguish religious freedom?"[21]

In the same vein another non-Catholic writer known as "Civis" reminded readers that King George III, as the Declaration of Independence clearly stated, had tried to keep the population of the American colonies down by "obstructing the Laws for Naturalization of Foreigners" and otherwise discouraging migration. "What think you, Mr. Towers, . . . of this little piece of history?" "Civis" asked.[22]

"The history of Catholicism in this country furnishes no excuse for this attempt at proscription," another writer signing himself only as "A" maintained. "They [American Catholics] neither concede nor are asked to concede to any mortal power, civil or ecclesiastical, an allegiance inconsistent with that which they owe their country."[23]

To all of this, Know Nothing supporters mainly replied by citing the good civic record of their mayoral candidate or, in some few cases, answering the secrecy charges by maintaining that "the Masonic fraternity, the Odd Fellows' Association, the fraternity of Jesuits, and numerous others carry out their designs and transact their business in secret session." Even the United States Senate on occasion, they added.[24]

But the most insistent theme of those who opposed the Know Nothings was historical recognition of all that the foreign born and Catholics had done in the forging of both the nation and its capital. The Irish-American and French troops during the Revolution, Lafayette, DeKalb, Kosciusko, Charles Carroll of Carrollton—all were recognized in one letter or another. As for specific contributions to Washington, "A Native Protestant" seemed to have the last word:

Of all places this city should be the very last to entertain narrow-minded and proscriptive prejudice against Catholic and naturalized citizens. . . .

220   Among the original proprietors of the soil were Notley Young and Daniel Carroll, two gentlemen of the Roman Catholic faith, who patriotically gave to the Government one half of their land. The very ground upon which the Capitol stands belonged to one of those gentlemen. Pierre C. L'Enfant, a Frenchman, under the direction of Gen. Washington, planned the city. Dr. William Thornton, the author of the plan of the Capitol, was born a British subject, and so were George Hadfield, the first architect of that building, and James Hoban, the architect of the President's house. Washington and his compatriots had no unworthy prejudices against a man because of his religion or nativity. In making appointments to office they looked exclusively to qualifications and character. . . . 25

But after the last Towers vote had been counted Washingtonians quietly went about their business. The alarms that had been sounded during the campaign seemed largely forgotten. Postmortem election coverage was notably absent from the metropolitan dailies, whose pages were now filled with the threatening events surrounding the abrogation of the Missouri Compromise and the possible extension of slavery into the Nebraska and Kansas territories. The *National Intelligencer*, by now losing its place as the capital's leading newspaper, blissfully ran only a short editorial expressing gratification that the election was "remarkable for the admirable order, quiet, and forbearance that prevailed in every Ward," though the results "were distasteful to many." The *Daily Evening Star* echoed the same opinion and dismissed as ridiculous rumors of possible Know Nothing violence against Catholics.26

The Know Nothing government also quietly went about its business. First on the agenda was placing its own people—"the sentinels on the outposts," as promised—in nearly all of the city's appointive offices, including most of the school board members. This done, the party next used its majority on the city council to transfer the contract for printing the records of the council's proceedings and ordinances from the *Intelligencer*, which had enjoyed this subsidy since 1802, to its own newspaper, the aforementioned *Daily American Organ*.27 Launched on November 13, 1854, the *Organ*'s first issue, after giving the customary lip service to the free exercise of all religions, declared itself solidly opposed to "foreign domination over American citizens . . . in ecclesiastical as well as political matters." Then, much as the *Native American* had done over a decade earlier, the *Organ*'s editors chose to use numerous reprints from other party-line papers for stronger fare. From the *Lancaster Gazette* readers were told, "The Roman crusade in America . . . is a political crusade to raise the red flag of Pius IX on American soil." From the *New York Christian Advocate* came warnings that a convention of bishops in Rome had declared that when American Catholics had attained "a sufficient numerical majority there would be an end to civil and religious liberty." Or, lest there be any doubt, that "the Roman Catholic church is a secret society directed by its hierarchy, [and] absolutely controlled by its priesthood." So it went, monotonously, issue after issue.28

Thus to the disinterested observer the national capital in the mid-1850s presented a great paradox. Here was a city under the control of a fast-growing national political party whose ultimate aim, one way or another, was to prevent Catholics from holding public office. Yet at the same time the Catholic presence in both Washington and the District had never been stronger. In Georgetown, where the party saw little success, Trinity Church (by now officially known as Holy Trinity) had moved into an elegant and far more commodious church building on 36th Street, where it stands today. At the dedication ceremonies James Ryder, president of Georgetown College, preached to a large gathering "of all classes and denominations, among them many non-Catholics who wished to witness the imposing ritual and ceremonies of the church." Among the first Americans to receive holy orders there, it is pleasing to note, was the Reverend Henry Hoban, one of the ten children of James and Susana Sewall Hoban.[29]

Downtown, or in Washington City proper, overcrowding at St. Patrick's had spurred the construction of St. Matthew's Church five blocks to the west. A handsome Greek Revival building, St. Matthew's would witness the marriage of Senator Stephen A. Douglas to Adele Cutts, the grand-niece of Dolley Madison, and later have as its pastor Thomas Sim Lee, the namesake and youngest of eight grandchildren of Maryland Governor Thomas Sim and Mary Digges Lee.[30] On May 3, 1854, or scant weeks before the Know Nothing victory, the funeral procession of St. Patrick's long-lived Pastor William Matthews drew enormous crowds, as bells from Catholic and Protestant churches alike tolled throughout the city and all five of the metropolitan newspapers vied to pay tribute to Matthews' extraordinary civic career. "The Right Rev. William Matthews came among this community on the first settlement of Washington as a town, grew with its growth, strengthened with its strength, and ripened with its age," the *Daily Evening Star* was quick to note. "He was known personally to almost every young man, woman, and child living here for fifty years. . . . It is a remarkable fact, that . . . no one was ever known to say aught against him, even when sectarian jealousies ran highest. . . . Washington will hardly look upon his like again."[31]

Georgetown College, too, was experiencing a period of phenomenal growth. The revolutionary convulsions that began in Europe in 1848 had sent scores of Italian, German, and Swiss Jesuits to America, where many of them provided needed additions to the College faculty. By the 1850s the College could boast forty-six faculty members, sixteen of whom were laymen; a student body of more than 200 now ranging in age from eight to twenty-eight; a much enlarged curriculum; one of the country's largest libraries; and an astronomical observatory of national prominence.[32]

Visitation Academy continued to attract many Protestant students. Its commencement exercises, always a premier social occasion for all of Georgetown, had previously been attended by Presidents John Quincy Adams, Tyler, Polk, and Taylor. The 1850s would see President Buchanan continue the tradition, the more so because his niece and talented White House hostess, Harriet Lane, was a Visitation graduate. And, as the intolerance of the Know Nothings became more and more evident, alumni rallied in opposition. Among them was the venerable George Peter, a son of Georgetown's first mayor and a former congressman who had been one of Georgetown College's first Protestant students. Described as a man of stentorian voice and rugged physique, Peter effectively denounced the Know Nothing party through the Buchanan campaign of 1857. By then seventy-eight and bedridden, he nevertheless held political meetings "on the lawn in front of his house; having his bed brought out on the porch, [where] he addressed his fellow citizens and neighbors."[33]

Against this backdrop the Know Nothings made their second and more serious Washington Monument blunder. This time control of the Washington Monument Society, not destruction of the stones, was the objective. In February 1855 party members placed a fraudulent notice in the press announcing a general meeting of the Monument Society at City Hall on Washington's Birthday. Since the society had launched a national fund-raising campaign that offered membership certificates and the right to vote for the society's officers at only one dollar, many Know Nothings showed up with certificates to pack the City Hall meeting and vote out all of the officers and board of managers. They then replaced them with their own candidates and eventually seized the society's books. Thus did the party capture control of the city's prime expression of civic pride.[34]

Outrage over the seizure was instant and far stronger than over the Pope's stone incident the year before. Reasons are not hard to find. First was the fact that the Monument Society board was Washington's most prestigious. Founded in 1833 under the leadership of Librarian of Congress George Watterston and chartered by Congress to erect the national monument to General Washington, the society had long attracted the capital's leaders. Chief Justice Marshall was its first president, followed by former President James Madison. Among its board members and officers at the time of the takeover were Thomas Carbery, Peter Force, William Seaton, General Winfield Scott, Benjamin Ogle Tayloe, William Wilson Corcoran, and an older and wiser John Carroll Brent, who now served as the society's secretary. To see them replaced by a band of unknowns was an affront to the Washington establishment. To this was added the subterfuge and questionable tactics employed by the Know Nothings, which caused equal indignation.[35]

But the Know Nothing takeover had at least one salutary effect. It quickly stirred Washington voters to the realization that their municipal elections could no longer be an informal and apolitical matter. Organization was necessary if the disciplined and often devious forces of the Know Nothings were to be defeated. In the early autumn following Towers's election, opponents had twice held a mass meeting at Carusi's Saloon to denounce Know Nothing principles and tactics. But by the spring of 1855 Washingtonians put aside political differences to rally behind a loose local coalition of Democrats, former Whigs, Republicans, and Free Soilers known as the Anti-Know Nothing Party. Unfortunately, however, there was very little time to organize and take full advantage of the Know Nothing blunder before the next city elections. Less than one week remained, in fact, between the first full reports of the Know Nothings' forcible removal of the Monument Society's superintendent and the seizure of its books and the off-year municipal elections of June 4, 1855.

As a result the Know Nothings managed to keep five of the seven Board of Aldermen seats up for election and retained a fifteen to six majority in the Common Council in an election with some very close contests, disputed returns, and a generally substantiated charge that election commissioners in most wards had refused the vote to recently naturalized citizens. The Anti-Know Nothing Party had lost its first round. But a lesson was learned. And the Washington press, at last, clearly identified the party affiliation of all candidates.[36]

As the mayoral and council elections of 1856 approached, the Towers administration had little to show in the way of municipal progress. Apart from Towers's personal encouragement of free schools, his term was notable mainly for a brief "dry" spell—temperance was long a nativist cause—through a city-wide prohibition ordinance which the circuit court promptly annulled two months after its passage.[37] For the rest, the Washington Know Nothing Party seemed without any discernible platform or policies other than the traditional nativist hostility to immigration, the foreign born, and the Catholic church. From contemporary accounts its energies seemed to be concentrated mainly on remaining in office, which was proving far more difficult than gaining it had been. To this end, in fact, the local party went to unusual lengths for the 1856 elections. Nationally, the party was reaching its zenith, having had its first national platform meeting and presidential nominating convention in Philadelphia on February 22 of that year. But while the national party exuded confidence and for the first time in its short history had a presidential candidate of its own in the person of ex-President Millard Fillmore, the Washington Know Nothings were apparently worried enough to appeal to the national organization for help.[38]

In May 1856 local party leaders used the Know Nothings' new strength in Congress to steer through a bill innocuously titled "An Act to Provide for at least two Election Precincts in each Ward in the City of Washington, and for other Purposes." In this case, however, one of the other purposes was in reality the act's main objective. This was to deny the vote in the forthcoming municipal elections in June to foreign born citizens of Washington who had been naturalized after the first of January of the election year. The act's rationale, which took advantage of a local election ordinance, was rooted in vintage nativism. "Whereas native-born citizens, resident of the city of Washington who arrive at the age of twenty-one years between the 30th day of December [previous] . . . and the day of the election are not allowed to vote," the act's introductory language proclaimed, there was no reason not to mete out the same treatment to the recently naturalized as well.[39]

After twenty years of memorials and petitions to Congress, the nativist forces had won a small victory. Very small, in fact, since it denied the vote to what was probably no more than a few hundred foreign born. And only in the city of Washington.

If anything, the act had the unintended effect of further galvanizing the opposition. This time the Anti-Know Nothing Party was better prepared and put forward an able and popular candidate, Dr. William B. Magruder, a physician who had studied under Dr. Benjamin S. Bohrer and had performed heroically during the cholera epidemic of 1832. Magruder was also a descendant of one of the area's oldest families that, like many others, had some Catholic branches. What was equally significant, he took the unusual step of public campaigning, even carrying his message to the most solid opposition wards.

The Know Nothings by contrast found they could no longer persuade John Towers, who for reasons that are not entirely clear declined to run for a second term. In his place the party nominated Silas H. Hill, an attorney and president of the Washington Gas Light Company who had served for some eight years on the Common Council and the Board of Aldermen.[40] Aware that they now had a real contest, the Know Nothings brought into the campaign the notorious John S. Orr, a fire-breathing nativist street preacher who had incited riots in New York, Boston, and throughout much of New England. Better known as "the Angel Gabriel" because he habitually wore a white robe and called his followers together with a brass horn, Orr called Magruder a perjurer, threatened to crop his ears, and predicted violence, in which he was more than ready to take part.[41]

To nearly everyone's great relief, none of the Angel Gabriel's threats or prophesies came true. In a mainly peaceful but hotly contested election, Dr. Magruder defeated Silas Hill by 52 votes out of 5,840 cast. In addition the Anti-Know Nothing party won eight council seats in the First and Second Wards, as it had in 1855, and also gained four more in the Fourth. Although the Know Nothings managed to keep a reduced majority in the City Council, the Anti-Know Nothing forces celebrated what they considered a significant victory. "Leave publicly if you will," they challenged the Know Nothings, "leave privately if you will; leave loudly or silently, but leave!"[42]

The Anti-Know Nothings' exultant mood was not without foundation. Close as they were, the 1856 municipal elections marked a distinct turning point. From then onwards, in fact, the Washington Know Nothing Party went into a swift and continuous decline. Speeding the decline was the intervention of one of Baltimore's infamous political clubs in the next year's elections. These clubs, originally established as competing firehouse companies, had been unofficially adopted by both the Know Nothings and the Democrats in Baltimore as their front-line militia at election time. Bearing such names as the Rip Raps, Butt Enders, Rough Skins, and Blood Tubs, their members used intimidation, beatings, and other roughhouse tactics to such an extent that Baltimore came to be called Mobtown by the press. The Know Nothings claimed extreme measures were necessary to keep illegal voters from the polls. The Democrats claimed they were acting in self-defense and safeguarding American democ-

Collection of the Maryland Historical Society, Baltimore.

"A Sketch from the New Tragic Farce of 'Americans Shall Rule America,'" political cartoon of electioneering by the Know-Nothing mayor of Baltimore.

racy in the process. Over the years the violence escalated, as one excess engendered another.[43]

On June 1, 1857, Mobtown came to Washington. Early that morning approximately thirty members of a club known as the Plug Uglies arrived by train from Baltimore carrying guns, knives, and clubs. They marched directly to the first precinct of the Fourth Ward—a swing ward that had gone to the Anti-Know Nothings the year before—and there began attacking anyone in the line waiting to vote who looked foreign to them. The ward's election commissioner, a justice of the peace, the chief of police, and several voters were badly wounded. This done, the Plug Uglies set off in the direction of the Second Ward, an Anti-Know Nothing stronghold, shooting their pistols along the way.

Meanwhile, however, an alert Mayor Magruder, well aware of Washington's pathetically small police force, sent an urgent message to President James Buchanan requesting federal troops. Buchanan referred the matter to the secretary of the navy, who promptly detached a contingent of 100 United States Marines under the command of Major H.B. Tyler. As word of the marines'

226   engagement spread, a growing band of local rowdies, no doubt encouraged by the Plug Uglies, dragged a six-pound swivel gun up Pennsylvania Avenue to the Northern Liberties Market, next to the Fourth Ward polling stations where the morning's troubles had begun. What happened next was brief and tragic. Mayor Magruder, never one to shirk responsibility, marched to the now-closed polling station and demanded that it be reopened. His request was rudely rebuffed. He next addressed what the *National Intelligencer* described as a crowd of "about twelve to fifteen hundred people in a state of maddened excitement," appealing for restraint and order. At about the same time two of the gang controlling the cannon approached Major Tyler and told him they would fire on the Marines if they did not immediately withdraw. Tyler responded by leading the marines in a fixed-bayonet advance.

Shots were fired. One marine fell, seriously wounded. His comrades thereupon returned the fire directly into the crowd. When the crowd scattered, six persons lay dead and many more were wounded. Among the wounded was one tentatively identified by the *Intelligencer* as "a young man, a 'Plug Ugly' from Baltimore, name not known." His colleagues had left him behind, hurriedly jumping an evening train for Baltimore from which, according to the press, "they expended the contents of their revolvers, originally intended for the persons of the citizens of Washington, upon the bodies of the cows and horses that were grazing in the fields along the road."[44]

The next day the accounts of what came to be known as the Liberties Market Riot shared headlines with another surprising and more heartening event. The Anti-Know Nothing party had won majorities in both the Board of Aldermen and the Common Council, not to mention the three elective offices of collector of taxes, register, and surveyor. What is more, these victories were posted in spite of irregularities and intimidation, which the press claimed kept many naturalized citizens and other potential supporters from voting. Know Nothing control of the Washington city government was coming to an end.[45]

In the mayoral elections of 1858 the remnants of the party gave their endorsement to an able candidate who did not wish to acknowledge their support and took pains to deny any Know Nothing associations. Even with these precautions and the safeguards of an orderly election, he did not win. His so-called Independent Party running mates, whose ranks included a number of former Know Nothings, carried but one of the city's seven wards.[46]

In 1859 a coalition of Democratic Union and Anti-Know Nothing candidates gained all but one of the twenty-eight Board of Aldermen and Common Council seats up for election. In a number of wards they ran unopposed. The American Party of Washington, also known as the Know Nothings, was no more.[47]

The decline and fall of the Know Nothings in Washington seems the more remarkable in view of the fact that it occurred precisely as the party was gaining its maximum strength in neighboring Maryland and the nation at large. In

Historical Society of Washington.

*Northern Liberties Market Riot,
June 1, 1857.*

October 1854, just as in Washington the previous June, Baltimore elected a Know Nothing mayor, with the party revealing support of his candidacy only weeks before the election. But there all parallels stop. The next year not only Baltimore but all of Maryland was coming under Know Nothing control as the party elected four of the state's six United States congressmen, fifty-four of the seventy-four members of the state's House of Delegates, and six of the state Senate's eleven contested seats. That year also, as we have seen, the party was gaining its national high-water mark of more than seventy seats in Congress. By 1856, the year the Anti-Know Nothings recaptured the mayoralty of Washington, the Know Nothing party in Maryland commanded from forty to sixty percent of the vote in every county except St. Mary's, gave the party's presidential candidate Millard Fillmore his only electoral votes, and elected Thomas H. Hicks, a farmer and sheriff from the Eastern Shore, as governor. Know Nothing control of the state was now complete. It would remain so, moreover, until the end of the decade, well after the party had been banished from the Washington scene.[48]

There are many reasons for this divergence. First was the fact that the party in Maryland, once firmly in power, realized that its old battle cries were not the best way to win re-election in a state with significant populations of Catholics and the foreign born. When for example its more hotheaded delegates in the state legislature called for a bill to prolong the naturalization period and outlaw Catholic convents, the party leadership considered them an embarrassment and refused to consider their petitions. As the most recent studies of the Know Nothing phenomenon in Maryland have shown, the higher echelons of the party clearly understood that maintaining control in the state meant a softening if not total abandonment of its traditional nativist attacks on the Catholic church and the flow of immigrants. An interesting result

FRANK LESLIE'S ILLUSTRATED NEWSPAPER.

Historical Society of Washington.

Northern Liberties Market Riot, June 1, 1857.

was the fact that the party's newspapers, usually the most vocal instruments of bigotry, began to moderate their rhetoric. Nothing of the kind, however, occurred during the party's briefer moment of power in Washington. By contrast the Washington Know Nothings, like the party's "Angel Gabriel," grew ever more strident and used more threatening tactics as their power waned. Even the local party paper, the *Daily American Organ*, did not continue to exercise its initial restraint. Quite the opposite, by 1856 the *Organ's* editors were retailing rumors that Catholic priests in the West were boasting that "the time would come when Catholics would make Protestants wade knee deep in the blood of the Mississippi Valley."[49]

Another factor, undoubtedly, was the difference in the ethno-cultural backgrounds of Washington and such gateway cities as Baltimore, New York, and Philadelphia. To the Protestant establishment of the latter cities, Catholics were mainly members of what historians of a later generation have called the "immigrant church," a church that was at the least vaguely menacing because of the rapid growth of its foreign born members. In Washington Catholics were very much part of the establishment. Immigrants there were, too, but the most visible element of the church was what we have called the first face of American Catholicism. It was the benign face of a Bishop Carroll, a Robert Brent, or a Thomas Carbery. It menaced no one.

Equally important were the many mistakes of the Washington nativists. Some may seem relatively insignificant, like the increasing anti-Catholic rhetoric of their party organs. Others like the Pope's stone incident or the proscriptive legislation against District citizens naturalized six months or less before elections seem almost risible or ineffectual gestures. Still others like the high-handed capture of the Monument Society or the vicious Plug Ugly riot provoked deep and universal outrage.

The cumulative effect was too much. In the heat of the municipal campaign of 1854, the reader may recall, the writer who signed himself "A Native Protestant" reminded fellow citizens that a city that had benefited from such public-spirited figures as Notley Young, Pierre L'Enfant, James Hoban, Daniel Carroll of Duddington, and George Hadfield "should be the very last to entertain narrow-minded and proscriptive prejudice against Catholic and naturalized citizens."[50]

It is true, of course, that in the elections in question the party that entertained just such a prejudice scored its first victory. But if "Native Protestant" had qualified his statement to the effect that such prejudices when recognized for what they were should never be tolerated, his challenge to his fellow Washingtonians would have taken on the character of prophesy. Indeed, if Washington was the first city to elect a Know Nothing mayor and government, it was also the first to reject them when the party's true nature was revealed.

Ultimately, then, the roots of the Maryland tradition in the national capital were both too deep and too strong to tolerate a political movement that attempted to undermine the tradition's basic precepts. Protestants and Catholics who had learned over two centuries that the second Lord Baltimore's injunction to treat each other "with as much mildness and favor as Justice permits" was indeed to their mutual advantage would not in the end embrace a party that provoked sectarian differences. The citizens of a capital city largely planned and built by foreign hands, the citizens of a capital city who delighted in the procession of ministers plenipotentiary and "all foreigners of distinction who visit these states" could not long endure blanket condemnations of the foreign born. Citizens of all faiths could not long be expected to look the other way while the Catholics among them with whom they had socialized, worked, and intermarried for generations were more and more castigated as un-American and the subjects of a foreign power conspiring to conquer the United States. Not, we must re-emphasize, in the City of Washington, which Catholics had done much to build and save.

The fiery rounds that bombarded Fort Sumter in April 1861 signalled the onset of a national crisis that overshadowed all other issues. Among these was nativism, blown away as quickly and surely as if it had been the target of General Beauregard's salvos. With it went the most extreme period of religious bigotry the United States has ever experienced. Subsurface prejudices would of course remain. But never again would the Catholic church be the victim of a major political movement that sought its temporal destruction.

The roots, in short, had held. In this the citizens of the District, both Catholic and Protestant, might take some pride.

Acknowledgments

Anyone who has read this work in all its parts will know that it could not have been done without the assistance of a great many persons and organizations. First in point of origin is Father James Connor, S.J., currently director of the Woodstock Theological Center at Georgetown University. It was he who first asked me to consider a bicentennial history of the Trinity Church of Georgetown, D.C., where he formerly served as pastor. This request set me off on an inviting journey towards a much larger goal. If at times the journey seemed overly long and difficult (to the point of misgivings about taking it on, I must confess), I had only myself to blame. For his part Father Connor was always at hand as a constant source of encouragement, advice, and good cheer.

For both the beginning and the ending of this larger enterprise, I would like to thank Sally Engelhard Pingree and Sophie Engelhard Craighead of the Engelhard Foundation and the late Edward Bennett Williams and his wife Agnes for their generous support. Their contributions have made possible the help of two research assistants, indispensable in launching this book, and the portraits, maps, illustrations, and other production factors, indispensable to its finished form.

Along the way no one has been more helpful than Margaret H. McAleer. Her first-hand knowledge of archival sources, her patient searching, and her ability to grasp principle from particulars, always the mark of a good historian, have combined to make her an ideal research assistant. I wish therefore to thank her for so helping me with all the gratitude I can muster. In the same vein I would also like to thank Anna Watkins, who did patient work for me both at the Library of Congress and the National Archives.

A large measure of gratitude is also due my brother, Professor Charles K. Warner, who has always lent a critical and sympathetic ear to all my previous works. His help with this book has been especially valuable, since it more nearly coincides with his lifelong professional interests.

Fathers James Hennesey, S.J., and Gerald Fogarty, S.J., gave good advice at the beginning of my labors. Emmett Curran, S.J., did the same throughout. His research interests while preparing his exemplary history of Georgetown University often intersected with mine, and I only hope our mutual exchanges were as helpful to him as they were to me. Many others within the Woodstock Theological Center, where I was graced with an office, and the Jesuit Community of Georgetown, with whom I was a lunch-time boarder, deserve mention. They are too numerous to list, so let me thank them all collectively for their warm spirit of collegiality and good counsel.

Philip W. Ogilvie, District of Columbia Public Records Administrator, has been a fountainhead of knowledge on Washington history. The city is fortunate to have such an informed and dedicated archivist; the chronology of District

232   history he is currently preparing will be a boon to future generations of scholars. Much the same in the field of Maryland genealogy can be said of my faithful correspondent, Frances X. Flaherty-Knox, now residing in Branson, Missouri. As on prior occasions, Director Edward G. Papenfuse and his talented staff at the Maryland State Archives have been most helpful in solving problems of their state's early history. Marty Barringer, Jon Reynolds, Nicholas Scheetz, and all of the staff of the Special Collections Division of the Georgetown University Library have played the same role for Georgetown College and the early years of the Maryland Province of the Society of Jesus.

Many other persons and institutions have rendered valuable assistance. Among them are Mark Sherry, William Seale, Father John Langan, S.J., Priscilla McNeil, Robin Darling, Don Hawkins, Judy Frank, Sister Mada-anne Gell, V.H.M., Phoebe Jacobsen, Nora O'Callaghan, Robert Lyle, and Father Eugene Rooney, S.J. Institutions not previously mentioned include the Archives of the Archdiocese of Baltimore, the Maryland Historical Society, the Archives of Visitation Convent of Georgetown, D.C., and the Historical Society of Washington, D.C.

The support and cooperation of John Samples, director of the Georgetown University Press, has been most gratifying. Jane Freundel Levey has proved a highly knowledgeable and keen-eyed editor with whom it has been a pleasure to work.

To anyone chary of computer-age word processing, competent and thoughtful typists are very important persons. Three such who toiled over my manuscript are Elizabeth Nobbe, Jelita McLeod, and Jude Howard. I thank them all for their good work and friendship.

WILLIAM W. WARNER
Washington, D.C.
January 20, 1994

Abbreviations

AAB	Archives of the Archdiocese of Baltimore
BDML	*A Biographical Dictionary of the Maryland Legislature, 1635-1789*
BDUSC	*Biographical Directory of the United States Congress 1774-1989*
CHS	*Records of the Columbia Historical Society*
DAB	*Dictionary of American Biography*
DCD	Daniel Carroll of Duddington
DCD Papers	Daniel Carroll of Duddington Papers
GUA	Georgetown University Archives, Special Collections Division, Georgetown University Library
HLC Papers	Horsey, Lee, Carroll Papers, Maryland Historical Society, Baltimore
HTA	Archives of Holy Trinity Church, Georgetown, D.C., Special Collections Division, Georgetown University Library
LC	Library of Congress
MHM	*Maryland Historical Magazine*
MPA	Archives of the Maryland Province of the Society of Jesus, Special Collections Division, Georgetown University Library
MSA	Hall of Records, Maryland State Archives, Annapolis
NA	National Archives
NCE	*New Catholic Encyclopedia*
RDCC	Records of the District of Columbia Commissioners and of the Offices Concerned with Public Buildings, 1791-1867, Record Group 42, National Archives
WL	*Woodstock Letters*

Notes

NOTES TO CHAPTER 1

1. *Impartial Observer and Washington Advertiser*, 31 July, 1795; Rev. Aloysius J. Roccofort, S.J., "An Essai on the History of Trinity Church in Georgetown D.C.," 325 N 4, Archives of the Maryland Province of the Society of Jesus, Special Collections Division, Georgetown University Library [hereafter MPA]. Father Roccofort was a priest at Trinity from 1861 to 1863 and again in 1875–76. Although his "Essai" is most informative on the Civil War period, he also took pains to collect "the oral traditions of some of the oldest inhabitants" of the parish and found they agreed about "a small but neat graveyard, the resting place of the first Catholic settlers," which pre-existed the selection site for the area's first Catholic chapel. See also n. 2 below.

2. Montgomery County Court (Land Records) C 1126–3, 1–13–6–7, Hall of Records, Maryland State Archives, Annapolis [hereafter MSA]. The fact that the deed describes the lot as "a parcel of ground with all the appertinances" probably refers to the pre-existing cemetery.

3. Unless otherwise specified, these and other sums are in Maryland currency, which had a value of 7s 6d to $1.00. The use of "pounds Maryland" and "pounds sterling" was discontinued by the turn of the century.

4. *Georgetown Architecture—Northwest*, Historic American Buildings Survey Selection Number 6 (Washington: Commission of Fine Arts, 1970), 17–20; Rev. Thomas Bloomer Balch, *Reminiscences of Georgetown* (Washington: Henry Polkinhorn, 1859), 8.

5. Augustus John Foster, *Jeffersonian America: Notes on the United States of America Collected in the Years 1805–6–7 and 11–12* (San Marino, CA: Huntington Library, 1954), 108.

6. James Thomas Flexner, *Washington: The Indispensable Man* (Boston: Little, Brown, 1974), 196–99. For more on the Potomac Company and its problems and eventual failure, see n. 19, Chapter 7.

7. "Scheme of a Lottery for raising the sum of One Thousand Five Hundred and Nine Dollars, for the purpose of finishing the Church, between Georgetown and Bladensburg, called Rock Creek Church," *The Times and Patowmack Packet*, 25 November 1789 and various issues thereafter; *Proposals for Establishing an Academy at George-Town, Patowmack River, Maryland* (Baltimore: 1787), 56 R 1, MPA. There are also various references to a log structure built as a church for Lutherans near today's Wisconsin Avenue and Volta Place as early as 1770, but there are no records to indicate it was used as such.

8. The Junior League of Washington, *The City of Washington: An Illustrated History* (New York: Alfred A. Knopf, 1981), 38; *Inventory of the Diocese of Washington Archives: Vol. I: The Protestant Episcopal Church* (Washington: Historical Records Survey, Works Progress Administration, 1940), 161. Robert Madison Beatty, the grandson of Colonel Charles, married a Catholic, raised his children as such, and was buried in the Trinity Church yard. Such prominent Catholics as Adam and George King, Clement Sewall, and Marsham Waring, Bishop Carroll's private banker, contributed to the building fund for St. John's Episcopal Church. John Threlkeld, as previously noted, gave the land for Trinity Church, and Thomas Corcoran, a vestryman at St. John's, contributed to the Trinity and Holyrood Catholic cemeteries. Marriage Register 1805–1875, Deaths Register 1818–1867, Archives of Holy Trinity Church, Special Collections Division, Georgetown University Library [hereafter HTA]; "A List of Subscribers to the Protestant Church in Georgetown," 1803/4, Record Group 1-A, Archives of St. John's Episcopal Church, Georgetown.

9. See especially John Gilmary Shea, *Memorial of the First Centenary of George-town College, D.C., Comprising a History of Georgetown University* (New York: P.F. Collier, 1891), 9; Rev. Laurence J. Kelly, S.J., *History of Holy Trinity Parish* (Baltimore: John D. Lucas, n.d.), 9; Shea assumes some involvement by suggesting Carroll may have been influenced in his choice of a site for Georgetown College, first considered in January 1787, by the prior construction of Trinity Church. ("The choice of the locality finally adopted by Dr. Carroll is said to have been prompted to some extent by Mr. Alexander Doyle, a surveyor and architect, who was then erecting old Trinity Church on a knoll in Georgetown.") However, this statement places too early a date on the plans for Trinity, let alone its construction, as the text of this chapter and the next will show.

10. And only one from the trustees of Trinity Church to Carroll, 20 May 1797, 11 A 1, Archives of the Archdiocese of Baltimore [hereafer AAB]. The same source contains considerable correspondence between Carroll and Trinity's first pastor, Francis Neale, but only on Neale's assignments and his administrative duties for Georgetown College and the Corporation of the Roman Catholic Clergy.

11. *Proposals for Establishing an Academy at George-Town*, 56 R 1, MPA; John Carroll, *The John Carroll Papers*, ed. Thomas O'Brien Hanley, S.J., 3 vols. (Notre Dame: University of Notre Dame Press, 1976), 1: 198, 275.

12. Carroll, *Papers*, 46.

13. Ibid., 192.

14. Ibid., 68, 407–08. For a concise, readable account of Carroll's early years in the United States, see James Hennesey, S.J., *American Catholics: A History of the Roman Catholic Community in the United States* (New York: Oxford University Press, 1983), 69–74.

15. Ibid., 83, 93.

16. *The Metropolitan Catholic Almanac and Laity's Directory for the Year 1844* (Baltimore: F. Lucas, Jr., 1844), 64, and for 1845, 61; Hennesey, *American Catholics*, 93. Although privately printed, the Almanac was the only directory of its kind and may be considered quasi-official. Trinity Church appeared simply as "the chapel in Georgetown" in correspondence and in college accounts in its first few years. The earliest written reference to the name Trinity Church found by the author occurs in a letter from Pastor Francis Neale to Felix Kirk, 7 January 1796, concerning payment to George Fenwick (Fenwick Papers, Georgetown University Archives [hereafter GUA], Special Collections Division, Georgetown University Library). There is a singular absence of records and no known explanation for the name change to Holy Trinity. One possibility is that the trustee problems at Holy Trinity Church of Philadelphia, which eventually caused Bishop Carroll to declare it in schism, were coming to a head in 1792–93 as the Georgetown chapel was being built. Thus the Georgetown church's founders might well have wished to avoid any possible confusion with Philadelphia. The use of the name Trinity Church continued *passim* in documents and correspondence for approximately ten years after the *Almanac's* change to Holy Trinity.

17. Frederick R. Goff, "Early Printing in Georgetown (Potomak), 1789–1800, and the Engraving of L'Enfant's Plan of Washington, 1792," *Records of the Columbia Historical Society* [hereafter CHS] 50–51 (1950–51): 109–10; A.P.C. Griffin, "Issues of the District of Columbia Press in 1800–'01–'02," *CHS* 4 (1901): 36; Joseph P. Chinnici, "Organization of the Spiritual Life: American Catholic Devotional Works 1791–1866," *Theological Studies* 40 (June 1979): 236–37. The assessed value of Alexander Doyle's lots and houses in Georgetown reached £2,000 in 1793, a figure approached only by such wealthy residents as John Threlkeld and Benjamin Stoddert, assessed that year at £1,125 and £1,500 respectively. Montgomery County Commissioners of the Tax (Assessment Records) 1793–1797, C 1110–1, 1–18–14–17, MSA.

18. Last Will of Alexander Doyle, 7 March 1787; Thomas G. Slye to Rev. Mr. Van Borne, 19 February 1829; the Heirs of Alexander Doyle to Rev. Mr. Feiner, 19 February 1829; Rev. Francis Neale to Rev. Mr. Beschter, 5 March 1829; Property Files, GUA. Georgetown College Ledger 1793–1796 and "Old College Entry Book," GUA. Doyle died in November 1794. Three of his sons attended the college for various periods between 1792 and 1798. In 1796 Doyle's widow claimed that the equivalent of four years and three months of free education were still due her, and the college paid her £25 to resolve the matter. But this did not end the Doyle claims. Mrs. Doyle and other of Alexander Doyle's heirs continued to seek recompense from the college for what they alleged were Doyle's considerable expenses in building the church. In June 1798 Mrs. Doyle successfully petitioned College President William DuBourg for $100 "for all claims on Trinity Church." But after the turn of the century Thomas Slye, Doyle's son-in-law, and other heirs were continuing to seek compensation by claiming that Doyle had "purchased the lot on which the Catholic Church of Georgetown stands, built the church out of his own pocket, and in 1791 sold it to the Georgetown College for a certain sum to be taken out in Board and Schooling for his Sons." The claim that Doyle purchased the lot and paid for all the building is contradicted by both the terms of the deed to the church lot and the strength of Pastor Neale's rebuttal.

19. *Impartial Observer and Washington Advertiser*, 31 July 1795. There is considerable evidence that the need for more ground was an early concern. (The average Georgetown lot measured only 60 by 120 feet.) On August 7, 1788, Alexander Doyle went back to John Threlkeld for another five-shilling gift of a lot that lay catty-corner to the original Lot 72. This "purchase" was made and recorded on the same day, an extremely rare event in Maryland land records. It may be that Doyle was acting so quickly to forestall criticism that the project as a whole was impractical or that there would be insufficient property for both the church and the pre-existing cemetery. This possibility is born out by the fact that Trinity's first pastor later found it necessary to use his own money to purchase contiguous lots on either side of the original lot soon after the church was completed. Threlkeld to Doyle, Montgomery County Court (Land Records) C 1126–4, MSA.

20. Wilhelmus Bogart Bryan, *A History of the National Capital*, 2 vols. (New York: Macmillan, 1914), 1:36–39.

21. Kenneth R. Bowling, *The Creation of Washington, D.C.: The Idea and Location of the American Capital* (Fairfax, VA: George Mason University Press, 1991), 209–10.

22. *Gazette of the United States*, 12 September 1789.

23. Bryan, *History*, 1:136–39, 149. For a more detailed account of the opposing Georgetown and "Carrollsburg" or Eastern Branch landholders and how President Washington secured their agreement, see "The Location of the District," in Bryan, *History*, 105–58. See also Kenneth R. Bowling, "The Other G.W.: George Walker and the Creation of the National Capital," *Washington History* 3, no. 2 (Fall-Winter 1991–92): 5–21, for new evidence on the role of one of the land owners.

24. "L'Enfant's Reports to President Washington," *CHS* 2 (1899): 35. The original City of Washington was bounded by Rock Creek from its mouth up to the present P Street, Northwest, from there along Boundary Street, now Florida Avenue, over to Fifteenth Street, Northeast, from there south along Fifteenth to C Street, Southeast, and from there east on C to the Eastern Branch (Anacostia River). The Potomac River and the Eastern Branch formed the city's natural limits to the south. Georgetown, to the west of Rock Creek, and Alexandria, across the Potomac to the southwest, were both separate municipalities lying within the original District which, like Washington, had their own municipal governments. The area north of Boundary Street, the District's largest, was designated as Washington County. See map, p. 64.

25. Carroll, *Papers*, 1:454.

NOTES TO CHAPTER 2

1. Oliver W. Holmes, "The City Tavern: A Century of Georgetown History, 1796–1898," *CHS* 50 (1980): 11, 17; Georgetown College Catalogue 1791–1792—1803–1804, College Ledger 1789–1793, GUA.

2. Carroll, *Papers*, 1:158.

3. College Ledger 1789–1793, GUA.

4. William Hand Browne, ed., *Archives of Maryland, Proceedings of the General Assembly of Maryland, Proceedings of the Provincial Court of Maryland*, 72 vols. (Baltimore: Maryland Historical Society, 1883–1972), 46:593.

5. Carroll, *Papers*, 1:193.

6. College Ledger, 1789–1793; *Proposals for Establishing an Academy at George-Town, Patowmack River, Maryland*, 1787, 56 R1, MPA; "Proceedings of the Board of Directors of the college at Geo-Town held at said College," 20 December 1797, in College Catalogue 1791–1792—1803–1804, 53, 58–59. In addition to such practical courses as navigation and geography, the college also offered instruction in music, drawing, and dancing at a surcharge of one guinea a month for music and nine dollars for three months of both drawing and dancing.

7. The President and Professors of George Town College, to Geo. Washington, 15 March 1797, George Washington Papers, Manuscript Division, Library of Congress [hereafter LC].

8. Minutes of the Meeting of Consultants of the Maryland Province of the Society of Jesus, Province Consultors Minutes, 18 December 1845, Maryland Province Archives at Roland Park, Baltimore.

9. Carroll, *Papers*, 1:192, 311.

10. Ibid., 332.

11. Ibid., 419–20; Rev. Francis Neale to Rev. Doct. J. Carroll, 5 April 1797; 5 O 1, AAB.

12. Browne, *Archives of Maryland*, 4:233, 250–52, 258; Christopher Johnston, "Neale Family of Charles County," *Maryland Historical Magazine* [hereafter *MHM*] 7 (June 1912): 201–18; Thomas Hughes, S.J., *History of the Society of Jesus in North America: Colonial and Federal*, Part II Documents (New York: Longmans, Greene, and Co., 1908), 721 n.; Newman, Harry Wright, *The Maryland Semmes and Kindred Families* (Baltimore: Maryland Historical Society, 1956), 209–10, 246–47, 288–90, 310.

13. Carroll, *Papers*, 1:460.

14. Ibid., 429–30.

15. College Ledger 1789–1793, GUA.

16. Francis Neale to Capt. Ignatius Fenwick, Georgetown, 11 August 1792, HTA. Captain Fenwick is sometimes confused with his cousin and namesake Colonel Ignatius Fenwick of "Wallingford," St. Mary's County, who died in 1784 and is not known to have resided in the Washington area.

17. "Mr. Fr. Neale to Harbaugh and Wehrly on a/c of Chappel for Materials and Work," 12 March 1794, HTA.

18. Browne, *Archives of Maryland*, 16:492–93, 511; 21:227; 48:404–05. Charles E. Fenwick, "The Fenwick Family of Southern Maryland," unpub. ms. donated to St. Mary's City Commission, St. Mary's, Md., n.d.; *Guide to Microfilm Edition of Charles Carroll of Carrollton Papers*, Ronald Hoffman and Eleanor Darcy, eds., (Annapolis: Maryland State Archives, 1992), Genealogical Chart VII; College Ledger 1789–1793, GUA; Rev. Robert Molyneux, S.J., to Ignatius Fenwick, 6 July 1793, 56 V 0, MPA.

19. *Inventory of the Diocese of Washington Archives: Vol. I: The Protestant Episcopal Church* (Washington: Historical Records Survey, Works Progress Administration, 1940),

161; Mary Mitchell, *A Short History of St. John's Church, Georgetown from 1796 to 1968* (Washington: privately printed, 1968), 1–4.

20. Receipt signed by Francis Neale, 15 December 1794, HTA.

21. Deed of sale, John Threlkeld to Rev. Francis Neale, 15 June 1794, HTA; deed of sale, John Threlkeld to Francis Neale, 24 March 1810, Montgomery County Court (Land Records), Md HR WK 320–22, MSA; "Diary of Archbishop Maréchal, 1818–1825," *Records of the American Catholic Historical Society of Philadelphia*, 11 (1900): 418. Neale paid $500 for the 1810 purchase, which secured all of the lot immediately west of the church.

22. "Mr. Francis Neale to Harbaugh and Wehrly on a/c of Chappel for Materials and Work," 12 March 1794, HTA. The erroneous assumption that Doyle was the builder of Trinity probably traces back to a diagram sketched by Archbishop Ambrose Maréchal in his diary, cited in the note immediately above, after a tour of his see in 1818. Maréchal labeled the original church lot as "Bt. by Mr. Doyle who left it in trust to Abp. Carroll." This caused John Gilmary Shea and others to read the "Bt." as built, bought, or both (Shea, *Memorial of First Century of Georgetown College*, 9). But the original deed of the lot to Carroll leaves no doubt that it was a gift in perpetuity, not to be sold. Similarly, the billing by Leonard Harbaugh and related materials leave no doubt that Harbaugh was the actual builder. Finally, in all the extant references to Alexander Doyle, the author has found none to suggest that he was an architect or builder, but rather a property owner, general merchant, granary operator, and, with his brother, printer and publisher.

23. Corabelle Harbaugh Cooprider, *Harbaugh Family History* (Evansville, IN: privately printed, 1947), 260. Cooprider states that one of Harbaugh's sons described his father as once active in the German Reformed Church, but "in consequence of some misunderstandings, occasioned by a heavy draft on his time and means, he withdrew himself from the church and congregation." As mentioned in a later chapter, at least two of his sons were parishioners at Trinity and later St. Patrick's. Two others attended Georgetown College. For more on Harbaugh's forebears, see C.E. Schildknecht, ed., *Monocacy and Catoctin: Some Early Settlers at Frederick and Carroll Counties, Maryland and Adams County, Pennsylvania, and Descendants*, (Shippensburg, PA: Beidel Printing House, 1985). On Harbaugh, see especially 184–89.

24. J. Thomas Scharf, *The Chronicle of Baltimore; Being a Complete History of "Baltimore Town" and Baltimore County from the Earliest Period to the Present Time* (Baltimore: Turnbull Brothers, 1874), 62–63; District Commissioners to Thomas Jefferson, 30 March 1792, Letters Sent, Records of the District of Columbia Commissioners and of the Offices Concerned with Public Buildings, 1791–1867 [hereafter RDCC], Record Group 42, National Archives [hereafter NA].

25. Leonard Harbaugh to Commissioners, 3 July 1792, Letters Received; Commissioners to President Washington, 23 June 1793; Commissioners to Jefferson, 14 April 1792, Letters Sent, RDCC; Commissioners to Thomas Jefferson, 5 January 1793, Letters Sent. In all the ensuing correspondence on the "ticklish state" of the bridge, there is no report of the bridge actually falling down. It was probably dismantled, in view of the fact that building stone was always in short supply at the time. As late as 1801 Harbaugh himself was asking the commissioners' permission to remove free stone from the pile "at the lower bridge on Rock Creek." Harbaugh and partners to Commissioners, 3 October 1801, Letters Received, RDCC.

26. College Ledgers 1798–1793, 1793–1796, GUA; John M. Daley, S.J., *Georgetown University: Origin and Early Years* (Washington: Georgetown University Press, 1957), 77; Carroll, *Papers*, 2:158. In the absence of complete documentation, the identity of "Old North's" builder must remain unknown. But a close examination of the timing of events surrounding its construction, as well as the amount of payments to Harbaugh, suggests that he is a likely candidate. The billing for Trinity Church leaves no doubt that its construction was completed by March 1794, if not earlier, by which time the Corporation of the Roman Catholic Clergy had already set aside funds for a second college building.

Construction undoubtedly began in 1794 and continued through most of 1795, with Carroll writing to Robert Plowden in November of that year that "the new building of the college is nearly completed, and a noble one it is." Cash payments totalling $600, the college's largest for the year, were made to Harbaugh by President Robert Molyneux "on Mr. Neale's order" through Marsham Waring, the college's private banker, in three installments dated November 29, December 3, and December 8, 1794. Another payment of $200 was made in what appears to have been May 1795. Within this time frame it must be remembered that Francis Neale was simultaneously a member of the corporation, the unofficial treasurer of the college, and pastor of Trinity. Having experienced many difficulties with the builder of the college's first building ("Old South"), Neale was thus more than likely to have recommended the switch to Harbaugh for the second. It is also worth noting that from 1794 onwards, Harbaugh appears to have made a conscious effort to cultivate good relations with the college. In January 1794 he entered two of his sons as English students, paying their tuition in advance, and on the 4th of July of the same year he led a procession to the college in his capacity as president of the Georgetown Architects' and Carpenters' Society to address a flowery tribute to President Molyneux and the faculty. Harbaugh first took on an additional contract to finish the locks at Little Falls for the Potomac Company in the spring and summer of 1795, thereafter moving to the larger task at the Great Falls. "Reverend Robert Molyneux In Account with Marsham Waring," Catholic Historical MSS Collection, 6.9, GUA; *Columbian Chronicle*, 15 July 1794; Records of the Potomac Co., Proceedings of the President and the Board of Directors, Meetings of the Board of Directors, 27 December 1794, 6 August 1795, Record Group 79, NA.

27. James Kent's manuscript observations, written in fly leaves of his copy of Tobias Lear's *Observations on the River Potomack, the Country Adjacent and the City of Washington* (New York: 1793), Rare Book Room, LC; Roccofort, "Essai." Kent was at the time a member of the New York Assembly and Columbia College's first professor of law. A noted lawyer who subsequently became chief justice of the New York Supreme Court, Kent kept detailed journals of all his considerable travels. St. Paul's Episcopal Church on Rock Creek Church Road in Northwest Washington began as a wooden frame chapel in the 1720s, replaced by a brick church in 1775. The 1775 church was redesigned in 1868, however, and then suffered a disastrous fire in 1921, which left standing only parts of the original walls. The author is indebted to Gerrit Craig Cone, archivist and historian, for this information.

28. Francis Neale to Archbishop Carroll, 21 January 1809, 5 O 3, AAB.

29. Baptismal and Marriage Register, Trinity Church, 1795–1805, HTA. This is the oldest church register of its kind in the Washington area. It is complete except for a gap in the last half of 1795.

30. Rev. Robert Molyneux to Francis Neale, 24 January 1806, 203 S 1, MPA; Roccofort, "Essai"; *Woodstock Letters* 98 vols. (Woodstock, MD: Woodstock College Press, 1872–1969), [hereafter WL] 33 (1904): 319. The design for a temporary lateral structure, to be used as a sacristy, was approved in 1806, but it is not clear if the outside stairways were built then or in 1819.

31. "John McElroy Papers, Diaries, 1813–21, 1834–36," entries for 5 April 1818 and 25 December 1819, GUA.

32. See Chapter 6.

33. Francis Neale to Bishop Carroll, 5 April 1797, 5 O 1, AAB; Minutes of the Corporation, 29 March 1797, 90 M 0, MPA. The property in question was a Jesuit mission in Pipe Creek, Pennsylvania, first attended from Frederick, Maryland, and later Conewago, Pennsylvania.

34. Neale to Carroll, 26 April 1797, AAB 5 O 2.

35. Trustees of Trinity Church to Bishop Carroll, 20 May 1797, 11 A 1, AAB. This letter is the only known document giving the names of Trinity's first trustees.

36. Carroll, *Papers*, 1:198–205, 216–17; Hennesey, *American Catholics*, 77–79, 83, 93.

37. Minutes of the Board of Directors, Georgetown College, 1797, College Catalogue 1791–92—1803–04. Daley, *Georgetown University*, 86.

38. Hennesey, *American Catholics*, 82, 91; *New Catholic Encyclopedia* 15 vols. (New York: McGraw Hill, 1967) [hereafter *NCE*], 4:1081, 5:956–57, 9:197–98; Baptism and Marriage Register 1795–1805, Marriage Register 1805–1875, Baptismal Register 1805–1834, HTA.

39. Ibid.; *NCE* 5:844, 845, 8:245; McElroy Diaries, 19, 31 May 1818, 3 December 1820.

40. Charles W. Turley to Alexander Turley, 10 July 1833, Commencement Files, GUA. The above letter is from a student telling his father that the graduation exhibition "was in the Church last year, but it is to be at the College this year." *Centinel of Liberty and Georgetown Advertiser*, 25 February 1800.

41. Printed handbill prospectus, *Georgetown College, District of Columbia*, 1 May 1814; "A Collection of Chronological Notes for a History of Georgetown College," 28 July 1831, GUA.

42. College Catalogues 1791–1792—1803–1804, 1804–1805—1814–1815, GUA.

43. Daley, S.J., *Georgetown University*, 73, 110–13, 169 ff.; Carroll, Papers, 2:383.

44. Prospectus printed in *Centinel of Liberty and Georgetown Advertiser*, 27 November 1797. The widow was probably Mrs. George Fenwick, whom the College Ledgers show as taking in occasional students. But, as the prospectus makes clear, the college would only maintain a separate house for the non-Catholic boarders if sufficient parents requested the same.

45. Handbill prospectus, *Georgetown College, District of Columbia*, 1 May 1814, GUA. The complete sentence reads: "The object of this institution is principally for the education of those who possess the Catholic religion, which is the religion uniformly practiced by the boarders; the schools are however open to students of every denomination and the same attention is paid to them in their literary improvement as to those who reside in the house."

46. John E. Semmes, *John H. B. Latrobe and His Times 1803–1891* (Baltimore: Norman Remington Co., 1917), 55;

47. Handbill prospectus *Georgetown College, District of Columbia, 1820, Rev. Enoch Fenwick, President*, GUA.

48. Other Presidents who visited the college include James Madison, John Quincy Adams, John Tyler, James Polk, Zachary Taylor, Franklin Pierce, James Buchanan, Abraham Lincoln, Andrew Johnson, Ulysses Grant, Rutherford Hayes, Grover Cleveland, William McKinley, and Calvin Coolidge. The author is grateful to Rev. Emmett Curran, S.J., for this listing.

49. *Georgetown Times and Patowmack Packet*, 3 April 1789, 21 April 1790, 6 April 1791; *Georgetown Weekly Ledger*, 26 June 1790, 25 July 1791. For James Kent, see n. 27 above.

50. Hennesey, *American Catholics*, 76–100. Hennesey offers a convenient account of the problems in New York, Boston, Philadelphia, Charleston, and Norfolk. The controversy surrounding St. Peter's of Baltimore is best followed in Carroll, *Papers*, 2:363–67, 396, 432, 439.

51. Issues of 10 July and 11 December 1790.

NOTES TO CHAPTER 3

1. Bruce E. Steiner, "The Catholic Brents of Colonial Virginia," *Virginia Magazine of History and Biography* 70 (October 1962): 392–93; Edward C. Papenfuse et al., eds., *A Biographical Dictionary of the Maryland Legislature, 1635–1789*, 2 vols. (Baltimore: Johns

Hopkins University Press, 1979–1985) [hereafter *BDML*], 1:161–62. Professor Steiner's article is one of a kind and the source, unless otherwise indicated, for much of what follows on the Brent family in Virginia. In the original conditions of plantation, gentlemen investors were granted 2,000 acres for every five men transported to Maryland, or 400 acres per man. If an investor brought fewer than five men he received 100 acres per man, plus 100 for himself and 100 for his wife. As more settlers arrived and less prime land was available, these conditions were reduced. See also n. 50 below. Browne, *Archives of Maryland*, 3:47.

2. Browne, *Archives of Maryland*, 4:301.

3. *Calvert Papers* (Baltimore: Maryland Historical Society Fund Publications No. 28, 1889), vol. 1:138; Edwin W. Beitzell, *The Jesuit Missions of St. Mary's County, Maryland*, 2nd ed. (St. Mary's: privately printed, 1976), 8. Beitzell makes a good case for the chapel being attached to or part of the Jesuit residence.

4. Browne, *Archives of Maryland*, 4:266, 292–93, 301; Beitzell, *Jesuit Missions*, 9–11.

5. *History of the Colonization of the United States*, 10 vols. (Boston: Charles C. Little, 1840–74), vol. 1:244.

6. For more on the disputes between the Calverts and the Jesuits, see Beitzell, *Jesuit Missions*, 8–11; and Russell R. Menard, "Maryland's 'Time of Troubles': Sources of Political Discord in Early St. Mary's," *MHM*, 76 (June 1981): 124–27.

7. *Calvert Papers*, 1:172. Cornwallis was an ancestor of the Lord Cornwallis who was defeated by the Franco-American forces at Yorktown in 1781.

8. Ibid., 132. For Lord Baltimore's experiences in Newfoundland, see Thomas M. Coakley, "George Calvert and Newfoundland: 'The Sad Face of Winter,'" *MHM* 71 (Spring 1976): 9–17.

9. Lois Green Carr, "The First Expedition to Maryland," in *A Relation of The Successfull beginnings of the Lord Baltemore's Plantation in Mary-land* (Annapolis: Maryland State Archives, 1984), xxv–xxviii; Menard, "Maryland's 'Time of Troubles,'" 126. Hennesey, in *American Catholics*, 42, gives the proportion of Catholics as no higher than one-tenth by 1708. See also Michael Graham, "Meeting House and Chapel: Religion and Community in Seventeenth Century Maryland," 247, and Menard, "British Migrations in the Chesapeake Colonies in the Seventeenth Century," 100–02, both in *Colonial Chesapeake Society*, Lois Green Carr et al., eds., (Chapel Hill: University of North Carolina Press, 1988). Graham believes Catholics constituted about seven percent of Maryland's estimated population of 46,000 by 1700. Menard gives details for estimating the colony's total population.

10. Hughes, *History of the Society of Jesus*, vol. 1:336; Beitzell, *Jesuit Missions*, 8–9; Hennesey, *American Catholics*, 43–44.

11. David W. Jordan, "Maryland's Privy Council," in *Law, Society and Politics in Early Maryland*, Aubrey C. Land et al., eds. (Baltimore: Johns Hopkins University Press, 1977), 67.

12. Chester Horton Brent, *The Descendants of Coll⁹ Giles Brent, Capt George Brent and Robert Brent Gent* (Rutland, VT: privately printed, 1946), 50; W.B. Chilton, "The Brent Family," *Virginia Magazine of History and Biography*, vols. 16–21 (1908–13). Unless otherwise indicated all genealogical information on the Brents is based on these two works. Chester Horton Brent's genealogy, although based in part on Chilton's earlier work, is presented in a much more convenient form.

13. Henry F. Thompson, "Richard Ingle in Maryland," *MHM* 1 (1906): 125–36. Thompson's article, which includes depositions made in the chancery trial of Brent and Copley against Ingle, gives the best detail on the attempted arrest of Ingle and the latter's return to sack St. Mary's. Captain James Neale, the great-great-grandfather of the Revs. Francis, Leonard, and Charles, was among those charged with aiding Ingle's escape. Neale at first refused to appear in court. But after being held in contempt and dismissed from the Council, he changed his mind and succeeded in having his case dismissed for want of proof. Browne, *Archives of Maryland*, 4:223, 250–52, 258.

14. *BDML*, 1:18–19; 161–62; *Dictionary of American Biography* [hereafter *DAB*], 2:18. Brent returned from England in time to attend the Assembly of 1647–48. He apparently left Maryland by 1650. Steiner, "Catholic Brents of Colonial Virginia," 394n.

15. Steiner, "Catholic Brents of Colonial Virginia," 389–91; Francis X. Curran, *Catholics in Colonial Law* (Chicago: Loyola University Press, 1962), 16, 21–23, 70–73. Many of the penal statutes were relaxed during the brief reign of King James II. But the test oath, disenfranchisement, and the prohibition of priestly functions returned after the Glorious Revolution of 1689.

16. Steiner, "Catholic Brents of Colonial Virginia," 396–97.

17. Chester Horton Brent, *Descendants of Coll° Giles Brent*, 56–57. As Steiner points out, the governor and the Assembly's revocation of all Brent's public and military commissions should have included his militia captaincy ("Catholic Brents of Colonial Virginia," 395–96). But this was apparently not recognized on the frontier, where he continued to be called captain and lieutenant colonel. Captain George Mason (c. 1629–1686) was the first of the well-known Virginians to bear this name and the great-grandfather of George Mason the constitutionalist.

18. Ibid., 82, 86–87. Steiner computes the total acreage patented in Virginia by Brent and his sisters Margaret and Mary as between 1651 and 1666 at 10,752 acres ("Catholic Brents of Colonial Virginia," 394n.).

19. Steiner, "Catholic Brents of Colonial Virginia," 408n.; Brent, *Descendants of Coll° Giles Brent*, 123ff. As Steiner suggests, the first William Brent (1710–1742) may have been brought up an Anglican by his Protestant mother and stepfather, his true father having died young. It is more likely, however, that his son William Brent (1733–1782), whose baptism was recorded in an Anglican parish, reverted to Catholicism either before or as a result of his marriage to Bishop Carroll's sister Eleanor. If theirs had been an interfaith marriage with William remaining a Protestant, it is extremely unlikely that Bishop Carroll, who wrote so often about the distress mixed marriages caused him among cousins and more distant relatives, would not have made some mention of it. (See, for example, Carroll, *Papers*, 2:408, 509–10, 514). In addition, four of William and Eleanor's seven children can be identified as Catholics. Of these, three also married prominent Catholics (Eleanor Brent to Clement Hill, Anne Brent to Daniel Carroll of Duddington, Mary Brent to Robert Darnall Sewall) and a fourth, the bachelor Senator Richard Brent, is buried in the consecrated ground of the Brent family cemetery in Aquia, Virginia.

20. *BDML*, 1:148; 2:581; Newman, *The Maryland Semmes and Kindred Families*, 191. The author is grateful to Brice M. Claggett for providing information on the will and codicils of Col. Philemon Lloyd.

21. *BDML*, 1:170–71; Aubrey C. Land, "Provincial Maryland," in *Maryland: A History*, Richard Walsh and William Lloyd Fox, eds. (Annapolis: Maryland Historical Society, published for Hall of Records Commission, Maryland State Archives, 1983), 12.

22. Land, "Provincial Maryland," 12–13; *BDML*, 1:168, 171–72.

23. *BDML*, 171; James Hennesey, S.J., "Several Youth Sent from Here: Native-born Priests and Religious of English America, 1634–1776," in *Studies in Catholic History in Honor of John Tracy Ellis*, Nelson H. Minnich et al., eds. (Wilmington, DE: 1985), 5.

24. Christopher Johnston, "The Brooke Family," *MHM* 1 (1906): 186–87; *BDML*, 1:172; 2:529–30.

25. *BDML*, 1:271–72; Newman, *The Maryland Semmes and Kindred Families*, 289; *BDML*, 1:171; 2:798–99.

26. Browne, *Archives of Maryland*, 26:44–45; Three years later, or by June 1707, Thomas Brooke II was himself considered suspect and dismissed from the Council because he had "two owne Brothers Jesuits in the Province, and [was] himselfe but late a [Church of England] Convert." Although he was subsequently reinstated, Brooke in his old age sought unsuccessfully to sue the estate left in remainder to his Jesuit brother

Robert, who had died in 1714 and previously conveyed his share to the Jesuit mission. Hughes, *History of the Society of Jesus*, 526–27; Beitzell, *Jesuit Missions*, 56.

27. Browne, *Archives of Maryland*, 26:44. Charles Carroll the Settler (1660–1720), also known as the Attorney General, was the father of Charles Carroll of Annapolis and the grandfather of Charles Carroll of Carrollton. In taking this case he may have been purposely testing the applicability of an act passed six years earlier prohibiting Catholics to practice law "in any manner directly or indirectly . . . in public pleading or otherwise soliciting any Cause." (Ibid., 8:448). Catholic lawyers could, however, continue to serve the Prerogative and Chancery Courts on probate and other administrative cases which were conducted in writing and thus did not require "public pleading." Lois Green Carr to author, 1 October 1986.

28. Browne, *Archives of Maryland*, 26:44–46. The Catholic chapel in this case was the second to be built on the same site.

29. Ibid., 340–41.

30. Land, "Provincial Maryland," 12–13.

31. *BDML*, 1:187, 188; Jordan, "Maryland's Privy Council," 72–75; Land, "Provincial Maryland," 21–22.

32. *BDML*, 2:724; Jordan, "Maryland's Privy Council," 74. It was not unusual for council members to hold additional posts such as collector of revenues at the county level or probaters of estates.

33. Ibid., 75; Lois Green Carr and David W. Jordan, *Maryland's Revolution of Government, 1689–1692* (Ithaca, NY: Cornell University Press, 1974), 57–62.

34. Browne, *Archives of Maryland*, 26:341.

35. Ibid., 26:431–32, 591, 597, 630.

36. Curran, *Catholics and Colonial Law*, 92–95.

37. Ibid., 93, 94, 96, 97. Trials, tests, and examples of enforcement include those of Fathers Robert Brooke and William Hunter, which resulted in the closing of St. Mary's Chapel, and the Provincial Court's refusal to let Charles Carroll plead their case, as mentioned above. In addition, in 1756 Father James Beadnell was arrested for saying mass in a private home and trying to proselytize a Quaker, but both charges were dropped, the first because the law allowed it and the second for want of evidence. Very few examples of county sheriffs applying the test oath are known, but much further research is needed at this level.

38. Dolan, *The American Catholic Experience*, 87; Hennesey, *American Catholics*, 42.

39. T. Geoffrey Holt, "Americans at St. Omers, Bruges and Liège," *The Stonyhurst Magazine* 39 (Summer 1976): 241–47; Hennesey, "Several Youth Sent from Here," 3–5.

40. *BDML*, 2:724, 725; Hughes, *History of the Society of Jesus, Documents*, 1, pt. 2: 674, 784; Minutes of the Corporation of the Roman Catholic Clergy, 90 M O, MPA; Carroll, *Papers*, 1:435–36, 511; 2:353.

41. Hennesey, "Several Youth Sent from Here," 23. Both Charles and Nicholas Sewall were at St. Omers when the French government closed it in 1762. Thereafter, the principal Jesuit educational effort on the continent shifted to Bruges in the Austrian Netherlands and the principality of Liège in present-day Belgium. The Emancipation period in England saw English Jesuits returning to their native land and founding Stonyhurst College at Lulworth Castle, the estate of Thomas Weld in Lancashire where Bishop Carroll was consecrated.

42. Ibid., 4, "List of Sisters at Carmelite Monastery," 18 R3, MPA.

43. Browne, *Archives of Maryland*, 26:314–15, 340; Gerald P. Fogarty, S.J., "Property and Religious Liberty in Colonial Maryland Catholic Thought," *Catholic Historical Review* 72 (October 1986):593–95.

44. *BDML*, 1:59, Session List for 1758–1761 Assembly and appropriate biographical entries. Beitzell, *Jesuit Missions*, 54. Benjamin Tasker, president of the Upper House, had a Catholic grandmother. His wife, Ann Bladen was the daughter of Protestant

244   William Bladen and Catholic Ann Van Swearingen, who were married by Father John Hall, S.J., at St. Inigoes in St. Mary's County in 1695. Benjamin Tasker, Jr. was his son. Philip Thomas had distant Brooke and Sewall relations. William Goldsborough's second wife was a granddaughter of Henrietta Maria Neale, who married Philemon Lloyd. Richard Lee was the uncle of Maryland Governor Thomas Sim Lee, who converted to Catholicism prior to marrying Mary Digges. Edward Lloyd was a grandson of Henrietta Maria Neale Lloyd, and Benedict Calvert, whose grandfather Benedict Leonard Calvert conformed to the Anglican church, was a direct if illegitimate descendant of the Lords Baltimore. Benjamin Tasker and Daniel Dulany, Jr., were two of the five partners of the Baltimore Iron Works, the others being Charles Carrol the Immigrant, Charles Carroll of Annapolis, and Daniel Carroll of Duddington I.

45. Browne, *Archives of Maryland*, 1:97; Lorena S. Walsh "Servitude and Opportunity in Charles County, Maryland," in Land et al. *Law, Society, and Politics*, 113, 120–23. The latter reference provides interesting detail and some case histories.

46. Newman, *The Maryland Semmes and Kindred Families*, 2. Newman accords Marmaduke Semmes the status of Gentleman upon arrival, but the fact that Semmes proved his right to fifty acres in 1666, four years after coming to Maryland, suggests that he was either a free adult receiving a head right for his own person (see Notes 50 and 51 ahead) or an indentured servant receiving the customary fifty acres after completing his service, in his case as doorkeeper, for a period of four years, which was the most usual term of indenture. The status or pay of doorkeepers to the Maryland Assembly is not known, but in Virginia there is a record of persons of reduced circumstances applying for the position. William M. Palmer, et al., eds., *Virginia Calendar of State Papers and Other Manuscripts Preserved in the Capitol at Richmond* 11 vols. (Richmond: 1875–93), 1:58.

47. Newman, *The Maryland Semmes*, 43, 47; Hennesey, "Several Youth Sent from Here," 21.

48. *BDML*, 1:319; Browne, *Archives of Maryland*, 4:266, 292–93; Beitzell, *Jesuit Missions*, 8–10.

49. Newman, *Maryland Semmes*, 187–91; *BDML*, 1:148; Holt, "Americans at St. Omers, Bruges, and Liège," 245; Hennesey, "Several Youth Sent from Here," 22; College Ledger 1796–1799, GUA; *Georgetown College Journal* 16, no. 5 (February 1878): 52; "List of Sisters at Carmelite Monastery at Port Tobacco, 1791–1825," 18 R3, MPA; Rev. C.F. Thomas, *The Boarmans* (Washington: privately printed, 1934), 77, 79, 85. The priests were Rev. Sylvester Boarman, S.J. (1746–1811), a participant at the Whitemarsh meetings, and his cousin, Rev. John Boarman, S.J. (1743–1797). Sylvester's younger brother Charles also entered the Society, but left in the year of its suppression, married, and eventually became a professor at Georgetown in 1796. The three great-granddaughters were Matilda Boarman, professed as Sister Ignatia of the Immaculate Conception, 1796; Harriet Boarman, Sister Agnes of the Presentation, 1796; and Mary Bradford, Sister Austin of the Purification, 1802.

50. Richard D. Mudd, *The Mudd Family of the United States* (Ann Arbor, MI: Edwards Brothers, 1951), 29–34; *BDML*, 2:581. By 1649 the original conditions of plantation had changed to a uniform head right of fifty acres per adult entering the province. Thus Thomas Mudd's four hundred and fifty acres, or fifty acres for himself and fifty for each of the eight servants he brought into Maryland.

51. Dolan, *The American Catholic Experience*, 91.

52. Ibid., 87, 111.

53. *The Premier See: A History of the Archdiocese of Baltimore, 1789–1989* (Baltimore: Johns Hopkins University Press, 1989), 18.

54. Carroll, *Papers*, 1:53.

55. *Biographical Directory of the United States Congress 1774–1989*, Bicentennial Edition [hereafter *BDUSC*] (Washington: Government Printing Office, 1989), 40–44. Charles Carroll of Carrollton served from 1776 to 1778, and Daniel Carroll, the Bishop's brother,

from 1781 to 1783. Another Carroll who served, Charles Carroll the Barrister, was a Protestant and no relation. Other Catholics elected to the Continental Congress include Thomas Sim Lee (1783) of Maryland and Thomas Fitzsimmons (1782–83) of Pennsylvania.

56. Carroll, *Papers*, 2:305.

NOTES TO CHAPTER 4

1. Carroll, *Papers*, 2:53; *BDML*, 2:529–30. Lee's wife Mary, the only child of Ignatius Digges of Melwood and a relative of Carroll's, also was a strong factor in the conversion, as was her father.

2. John Carroll to Thomas Sim Lee, 5 March 1792, Horsey-Lee-Carroll Papers [hereafter HLC Papers], 2361/2364, 982–2010, MSA, at Maryland Historical Society, Baltimore.

3. Carroll to Charles Plowden, 1 June 1792, Carroll, *Papers*, 2:53.

4. Carroll to Lee, 4 November 1793, HLC Papers, 1016–730.

5. Curran, *Catholics in Colonial Law*, 112–120; Carroll, *Papers*, 1:432. Massachusetts, New Hampshire, Vermont, New Jersey, North Carolina, South Carolina, and Georgia all had restrictions of one form or another against Catholics holding public office, especially as members of state legislatures. Ironically, the constitutions of some of these states contained preambles extolling religious freedom.

6. Carroll to Daniel Brent, 23 January 1792, HLC Papers, 976–1278.

7. Edmond Randolph to Lee, 24 July 1794, J. Ellsworth to Lee, 26 November 1794, HLC Papers, 1025–739, 1037–763; *BDML*, 2:530.

8. Although heavily populated by German Catholics, the Church of St. John in Frederick Town and the entire Frederick Valley were without a resident priest from 1774 to 1796. It was to remedy this situation, at Lee's urging, that Carroll attempted to send Francis Neale there in 1790 (see Chapter 2). Governor Lee left $1,000 in his will to build a Catholic church "in the vicinity of my farm Needwood" and an additional $1,000 for its maintenance. The church stands today as St. Mary's of Petersville, Maryland. Thomas R. Bevan, *200 Years. . . A History of the Catholic Community of Frederick Valley* (Frederick, MD: 1977), 3; Carroll, *Papers*, 1:429–30; Sister M. Virginia Geiger, *Daniel Carroll: One Man and His Descendants, 1730–1978* (Baltimore: privately printed, 1979), 58, 276.

9. Mary Mitchell, "The Thomas Sim Lee Corner in Georgetown and Its Preservation," *CHS* 73–74 (1969–70): 511. Lee gained the Federalists' acclaim and a commendation from President Washington for his prompt actions in crushing a serious uprising of the Whiskey Rebellion in western Maryland in 1794. (Henry Knox to Lee, 8 December 1794, HLC Papers, 1083–525). Business schemes, real estate and foreign trade form the largest part of Lee's correspondence in the Horsey-Lee-Carroll papers. See, for example, Robert Morris to Lee, 18 April 1793, and "Dr. Thomas Sim Lee in Account with the Commissioners of the City of Washington 1791–1794," HLC Papers, 1006–44, 1024–223.

10. Baptism and Marriage Register 1795–1805, HTA; Marriage Register 1805–1875, HTA; Bryan, *History*, 2:34–35; Geiger, *One Man and His Descendants*, 267–69. Family sources describe Stephen Horsey, the first of the family to come to America, as a free thinker who was prominent in the Northampton County protests against tithing and taxation without representation in the Virginia Assembly. Matthew Page Andrews, *Virginia: The Old Dominion* (New York: Doubleday, 1937), 137; author's conversations with Helen Horsey, 12 October 1986, Georgetown, DC.

11. Geiger, *One Man and His Descendants*, 288; Student Files, GUA; *BDUSC*, 1357, 1212; Ann C. Devanter, ed., *"Anywhere So Long As There Be Freedom," Charles Carroll of Carrollton, His Family & His Maryland* (Baltimore: Baltimore Museum of Art, 1975),

254–55, and Genealogical Charts II and III; *DAB*, 2:528. Another Catholic elected to Congress in the 1820s was Raphael Neale, about whom not much is known. Apparently not a member of the prominent Neale family described in the previous chapter, Neale won a seat in the House in 1819, 1821, and 1823. He is described as "a Representative from Maryland born in St. Mary's County, Md., resided in Leonardtown, [who] received a limited education" in what is the shortest entry in the *Biographical Directory of the United States Congress*, 1379. Margaret K. Fresco, *Marriages and Deaths, St. Mary's County, Maryland, 1634–1900* (Leonardtown, MD: privately printed, 1984), 222–435.

12. Helen Estelle and Imogene Philbert, *Saint Matthews of Washington* (Baltimore: A. Hone, 1945), 68–69.

13. Brent, *Descendants of Coll⁰ Giles Brent*, 136; Geiger, *One Man and His Descendants*, 301. Eliza Walsh died three years after her marriage to Brent, after bearing two children, neither of whom survived. Baptismal Register, 1811–1816, St. Patrick's Church, Washington, D.C.

14. Student Files, GUA; *DAB*, 10:391–92; Carroll, *Papers* 3:86; Foster, *Jeffersonian America*, 264–65. *Southern Literary Messenger* 2, no. 6 (May 1836): 399. Walsh is probably not better known because of the accidental loss of all his papers shortly after his death. He was also much more the editor than writer.

15. "Statement of the Applications for Clerk Hire in the Department of State for the Years 1799, 1800, 1801," *Reports: State Department, 5th Congress 3rd Session—11th Congress 3rd Session*, 3:166–67, NA; *Officers Connected with the Department of State and Diplomatic Services of the Government October 25, 1774—December 31, 1882, List of Consular Officers, Dispatches from U.S. Consuls in Paris, 1790–1906*, Record Group 59, NA; Henry Clay to Daniel Brent, 3 March 1829, in Chester Horton Brent, *Descendants of Coll⁰ Giles Brent*, 137; Christian Feest, "Lukas Vischer in Washington," *CHS* 49 (1973–74): 101–03. For a contemporary description of the duties of the State Department's chief clerk, see Noble Cunningham, *The Process of Government Under Jefferson* (Princeton: Princeton University Press, 1978), 93–95. While consul in Paris, Brent began the first biography of his uncle, Archbishop John Carroll. Following his death in 1841, Brent's nephew John Carroll Brent finished the work, published as John Carroll Brent, ed., *Biographical Sketch of the Most Reverend John Carroll, First Archbishop of Baltimore* (Baltimore: John Murphy, 1843).

16. Dumas Malone, *Jefferson and the Ordeal of Liberty* (Boston: Little, Brown, 1962), 280–81. Daniel Carroll Brent always signed his name in full; Daniel of the State Department used only his first and family name. Manuscript sources showing Daniel Brent the consul invariably signing as such (that is, without using his middle name or initial) include Dispatches from U.S. Consuls in Paris, July 24, 1832—December 30, 1835, General Records of the Department of State, Record Group 59, NA. Daniel Carroll Brent the marshal is found in District Court records as Daniel C. Brent. See, for example, U.S. District Court Minutes 1803–1804, Record Group 21, NA.

17. *BDUSC*, 593–94; James Monroe, *The Writings of James Monroe* ed. Stanislaus Murray Hamilton, 5 vols. (New York: G. P. Putnam's Sons, 1893–1903), 5:108–20, 178–80.

18. Richard K. McMaster, "The Tobacco Trade with France: Letters of Joseph Fenwick, Consul at Bordeaux," *MHM* 60 (March 1965): 26–28.

19. Thomas Jefferson, *The Papers of Thomas Jefferson*, ed. Julian P. Boyd et al., 24 vols. (Princeton: Princeton University Press 1950–), 11:60; 16:232, 244–50; 20: 745n.; 17:493; 20:559. Jefferson recommended that all consuls be citizens of the United States (although vice consuls might be foreign born) and that more thorough searches be made for qualified candidates. He also agreed with Washington and Madison that the Senate might appropriately be consulted on appointments. Fenwick was on the first list of consuls thus sent to the Senate.

20. Henry Clay, *The Papers of Henry Clay*, ed. James F. Hopkins, 8 vols. (Lexington: University of Kentucky Press, 1959), 1:910; Bernard Mayo, *Henry Clay: Spokesman of the*

New West (Boston: Houghton Mifflin, 1937), 292; Bernard Mayo, "Bishop Flaget and Henry Clay," *Catholic Historical Review* 27 (July 1941): 210–13; Carroll, *Papers*, 3:257. Clay speaks of Charles Carroll as a "particular friend"; Carroll found Henry Carroll "a young gentleman of amiable manners, considerable acquirements in litterature & above all, commendable piety and regularity of life."

21. Clay, *Papers*, 1:1009, 1013; 2:4n.; Fred Engelman, *The Peace of Christmas Eve* (New York: Harcourt, Brace & Ward, 1960), 289–90; Robert F. McNamara, "John Carroll and Interfaith Marriages: The Case of the Belle Vue Carrolls," in *Studies in Catholic History in Honor of John Tracy Ellis*, ed. Nelson Minnich et al. (Wilmington, DE: M. Glazier, 1985), 43–44, 54. *Register of Officers and Agents, Civil, Military, and Naval in the Service of the United States* [hereafter *Official Register*] (Washington: Davis and Force, 1822). William Thomas Carroll remained clerk of the Supreme Court from 1827 to 1862; he was the Court's sole administrative officer until the 1840s, after which the position of deputy clerk was added to his office.

22. John Tracy Ellis, quoting Arthur M. Schlesinger, Sr., in *American Catholicism*, 2nd ed. rev. (Chicago: University of Chicago Press, 1969), 151; Jay P. Dolan, *The American Catholic Experience* (New York: Doubleday, 1985), 87, 111. Dolan and others estimate the Catholic population in the United States at the time of the first Federal census in 1790 at 35,000. At that time an estimated 22,000 Catholics lived in Maryland in a statewide population of 320,000. By 1810 the Maryland population had grown to 381,000, with Catholics probably in the same proportion, since this was well before the great immigrations of German and Irish Catholics of the 1830s and '40s.

23. *National Intelligencer and Washington Advertiser*, 26 August 1808. Fenwick apparently lost his temper on one occasion during the campaign as a result of taunting by his opponents. Theophilus claimed it was "the *first* quarrel he [Fenwick] ever had in his life."

24. Governor and Council (Election Returns), 3 October 1808, AL-WO U.S. Representatives, 40, 132–459/478, MSA, for Fenwick; 7 October 1822, 40, 132–832/839, and 4 October 1824, 132–859/877, for Lee; *Archives of Maryland, New Series: Historical List of Public Officials of Maryland* (Annapolis: Maryland State Archives, 1990), 422, 460; *BDUSC*, 666, 1357. For Raphael Neale, see n. 11 above. Fenwick subsequently served in the Maryland Senate for five years. John Lee lost by 860 votes, or 4,351 to 3,491, in his bid for re-election in 1824; his congressional district was made up of Allegany, Washington, and Frederick counties. William Leigh Brent, originally of Port Tobacco, was a nephew of Virginia Senator Richard Brent of the William and Eleanor Carroll Brents of Richland; he was elected to Congress for three terms, from 1823 to 1829, later affiliating himself with the nascent Whig Party.

25. Ellis, *American Catholicism*, 36; George Washington, *The Diaries of George Washington, 1748–1799*, ed. John C. Fitzpatrick, 4 vols. (Boston: Houghton Mifflin, 1925), 2:167, 3:219.

26. Daniel Carroll of Duddington II was the son of Charles Carroll of Duddington II and Carrollsburg and Mary Hill. His father died in 1773 at the age of forty-four, and Mary Hill Carroll subsequently married Fenwick. For readers disconcerted by the confusing array of Carrolls, the genealogical charts in *"Anywhere So Long As There Be Freedom": Charles Carroll of Carrollton, His Family and His Maryland*, ed. Anne C. Devanter, can be very helpful.

27. Priscilla McNeil, *Map Showing Tracts and Lands in Prince George's County, Maryland, Conveyed for the Federal City & Ownership of the Land on June 28 & 29, 1791, when the First Trust Deeds were signed*, cartography and design by Don Alexander Hawkins (Washington: privately printed, 1991), reproduced in *Washington History* 3, no. 1 (Spring-Summer 1991); Priscilla McNeil to author, 18 October 1987. The city of Washington within the District totalled approximately 6,000 acres; the holdings of Daniel Carroll of Duddington and Notley Young, approximately 2,000.

28. Constance McLaughlin Green, *Washington: A History of the Capital 1800–1950*, 2 vols., (Princeton: Princeton University Press, 1976), 1:16; Allen C. Clark, "Daniel Carroll of Duddington," *CHS* 39 (1938–39): 41. See also Chapter 9. Carroll is said to have priced his Capitol Hill area lots so high that buyers were forced to buy cheaper lots far to the west. A study of land sale records fails to show this, nor could anyone familiar with the process of government-versus-private sales in Washington's early years entertain such a charge. It should be understood that under the terms of the "half-and-half" agreement each proprietor's land was surveyed first into squares and then into lots of approximately 5,625 square feet. The lots within the squares were then divided in a checkerboard pattern so that both the government and the private owner might have approximately equal clusters of desirable property. Thus the government and private landholders were offering lots almost side by side in the same neighborhoods. As it happened, the government soon offered such easy terms of payment and low prices after the disastrous first auctions of 1791 and 1792 that it was very difficult for the proprietors to compete, much less profiteer.

29. Kenneth R. Bowling, *The Creation of Washington, D.C.* (Fairfax, VA: George Mason University Press, 1991), 222; The original text of the agreement may be found in William Tindall, *Origin and Government of the District of Columbia* (Washington: Government Printing Office, 1908), 91–94. The reservations for public buildings and improvements, as determined by President Washington and incorporated in Pierre L'Enfant's plan for the city, were first taken by the government, after which the half and half division was made.

30. Harold D. Eberlein and Cortlandt Van Dyke Hubbard, *Historic Houses of George-Town & Washington City* (Richmond, VA: The Dietz Press, 1958), 393, 399; Clark, "Daniel Carroll of Duddington," 44; Sir Augustus John Foster, *Jeffersonian America: Notes on the United States of America Collected in the Years 1805–6–7 and 11–12* (San Marino, CA: The Huntington Library, 1954), 16. At the time of Foster's observations, the Notley Young mansion had been given to Robert Brent, Young's son-in-law and the first mayor of Washington. Thus Foster refers to it as Mr. Brent's house.

31. Douglas Southall Freeman, *George Washington: A Biography*, 7 vols. (New York: Charles Scribner's Sons, 1948–1957), 4:413, 588–89; "Proceedings at the General Meetings of the Patowmack Company, May 17, 1785—August 1, 1796," Letter Book A, Record Group 79, NA; Washington, *Diaries*, 2:336, 3:10, 25, 27, 83.

32. Washington, *Diaries*, 3:312. Most of President Washington's contributions to churches are recorded in his private account books without naming the recipient churches. However, there is one "toward building a Dutch Roman Catholic Church in Baltimore," probably meaning the German-speaking parish of St. Peter's. Thus a contribution to the Alexandria church is not out of the question. Stephen Decatur, Jr., *Private Affairs of George Washington: From the Records and Accounts of Tobias Lear, Esquire, his Secretary* (Boston: Houghton, Mifflin, 1933), 252.

33. See Chapter 2.

34. *BDML*, 1:270–72.

35. Washington Irving, *Life of George Washington*, 2 vols. (New York: G. P. Putnam and Sons, 1876), 1:179. Washington, *Diaries*, 2:34, 90, 134, 181.

36. Washington, *Diaries*, 4:306; Carroll, *Papers*, 2:25–26; Robert H. Elias, "The First American Novel," *American Literature* 12 (January 1941): 419–31; Robert H. Elias and Michael N. Stanton, "Thomas Digges and 'Adventures of Alonso': Evidence from Robert Southey," *American Literature* 44 (March 1972): 118–22; Digges's novel was published in England and Germany. *The Power of Sympathy*, attributed to William Hill Brown and printed in Boston in 1789, is the first novel by an American published in the United States.

37. Allen C. Clark, "Joseph Gales, Jr.," *CHS* 23 (1920): 89.

38. Thomas Attwood Digges, *Letters of Thomas Atwood Digges* ed. Robert H. Elias and Eugene D. Finch (Columbia, SC: University of South Carolina Press, 1982), xxxviii–lv, lxvi–lxix; Sheldon S. Cohen, "Thomas Wren: Ministering Angel of Forton Prison," *Princeton Alumni Weekly* (October 5, 1983): 43–44; George Washington, *The Writings of George Washington from the Original Manuscript Sources* ed. John C. Fitzpatrick, 39 vols. (Washington: Government Printing Office, 1931–1944), 33:340–41. Elias and Finch's pioneer work offers a comprehensive introduction to a little known figure in the history of Revolutionary espionage. Various historians, most notably Francis Wharton and Julian Boyd, have accepted Franklin's harsh accusations uncritically (see, for example, Jefferson, *Papers*, 20:316–17), whereas Elias and Finch offer a more accurate and balanced account. Their overall conclusion concerning Digges's role as an intelligence agent for the American cause is worth quoting in full:

> It had been maintained under difficult and dangerous circumstances by a man well aware of the value of intelligence and propaganda, an American with connections with shippers, Spanish, Portuguese, French, and Dutch, with English manufacturers, with the London press, and, most importantly with members of the British opposition. He had been able to write of Benedict Arnold's treachery before the *Courant* reported it. He had been able to provide Adams with accounts of Laurens for the munitions to America. There were not many like him in England with the desire, the opportunity, the daring, and the ability to serve. His faults may have been many, but his services great.

Digges sought President Washington's assistance in reclaiming Warburton mainly through Colonel John Fitzgerald, who was his brother-in-law. Washington, *Writings*, 33:340–41.

39. Digges, *Letters*, lxx, lxxi, lxxvi, lxxvii, 588, 558, 580, 614, 618; *DAB*, 6:169; Washington, *Diaries*, 4:297, 304, 306, 311. Monroe made L'Enfant director of reconstruction at Fort Warburton in September of 1814, but L'Enfant, offended by some War Department criticism of his plans, was dismissed a year later after he refused to submit any reports of his progress. Digges, himself suffering ill health, was extraordinarily patient and helpful with L'Enfant, who stayed at Warburton until well after Digges's death. L'Enfant subsequently moved to William Dudley Digges's "Green Hill," where he spent the last year of his life.

40. William Tindall, "The Executive and Voters of Georgetown, District of Columbia," *CHS* 11 (1908): 98–99, 106–109. Common Council members were elected yearly by free whites of 21 years or more with one year's residence and property, valued at £30 or more. The six members of the Board of Aldermen, who served for two years, were initially appointed in 1789, but thereafter chosen by the Common Council from within its ranks. The mayor, elected annually, initially had to be chosen from among the aldermen and elected by joint ballot of the incumbent mayor, the Common Council, and the Board of Aldermen. After 1805 the mayor need not have been selected from among the aldermen, and the aldermen were elected popularly. After 1830 the mayor was also elected popularly, but for a two-year term.

41. Peter Casanave of Georgetown and Washington has often been confused with the Cazenoves of Virginia. (See, for example, Talbot Hamlin, *Benjamin Henry Latrobe* [New York: Oxford University Press, 1955], 463n.) Anthony Charles Cazenove, a cousin of the well-known Theophile Cazenove of the Holland Land Company, was a wealthy French-Swiss of Huguenot descent who came to the United States in the company of Albert Gallatin and settled briefly in Pennsylvania before taking up residence in Alexandria in 1797, where he was a successful merchant and banker. Although he married Catholic Ann Hogan of Alexandria in Georgetown's Trinity

Church that same year, their many children, one of whom married into the Lee family of Virginia, were prominent Episcopalians. By contrast Peter Casanave, by his own account, had two cousins (not identified in his extant correspondence) and a deceased uncle, Juan de Miralles, when he came to Georgetown in 1785. De Miralles served as the Spanish envoy or "agent" in Philadelphia from 1778 until his death two years later. A requiem mass for him, attended by his French counterpart and some members of Congress, was held in Philadelphia's historic St. Mary's Church on May 8, 1780. John Askling, ed. "Autobiographical Sketch of Anthony Charles Cazenove: Political Refugee, Merchant, and Banker, 1775–1852," *Virginia Magazine of History and Biography* 78 (July 1970): 295–96, 301, 302n., 303–307; Marriage and Baptismal Register, 1795–1805, HTA.

42. Advertisements, *Georgetown Times and Patowmack Packet*, 25 November 1789, 21 April 1790; *George-Town Weekly Ledger*, 15 May 1790, 5 March 1791, 9, 23 April 1791; Deering Davis et al., eds., *Georgetown Houses of the Federal Period* (New York: Bonanza Books, 1964), 102; Hugh T. Taggert, "Old Georgetown," *CHS* 11 (1908): 159; Peter Casanave to Notley Young, ? June 1791, partially quoted in Junior League, *Illustrated History*, 61; Peter Casanave to Notley Young, ? June 1791, privately owned letter in possession of descendants.

43. *George-Town Weekly Ledger*, 1 October 1791; Allen C. Clark, "The Old Mills," *CHS* 31–32 (1930): 83–84; College Ledger 1789–1793, GUA; Tindall, "Executive and Voters of Georgetown," 98. Casanave himself attended Georgetown College for English tutoring in 1792; his widow entered their son Peter in 1811. Student Files, GUA.

44. Oliver W. Holmes, "The City Tavern: A Century of Georgetown History, 1796–1898," *CHS* 50 (1980): 1–29; Holmes, "Suter's Tavern: Birthplace of the Federal City," *CHS* 49 (1973–74): 20, 21. Unless otherwise indicated, Holmes's excellent study is the source for what follows concerning the Tavern during Sewell's and Semmes' tenancies. As Holmes makes clear, Semmes' tenancy was intermittent from 1801 to 1805, 1809 to 1812, and 1822 until his death in 1832. During the intervals Semmes leased the Rhodes Tavern and other properties in Washington. W. B. Bryan "Hotels of Washington Prior to 1814," *CHS* 7 (1904): 81.

45. See also Oliver W. Holmes, "Stage Coach Days in the District of Columbia," *CHS* 50 (1948–50): 16–19. The Bank of Columbia was chartered December 28, 1793.

46. Constance McLaughlin Green, *The Secret City: A History of Race Relations in the Nation's Capital* (Princeton: Princeton University Press, 1967), 19–20. Slave auctions were unknown in Georgetown at the time, and sales of slaves in any large numbers were rare. An 1810 newspaper, however, carried one notice from an unsigned advertiser wishing "to purchase 15 or 20 young negroes from 15 to 25 years of age," advising any suppliers to inquire at Semmes Tavern.

47. For the King brothers and all others who follow in the text as aldermen, council members, or appointed officials of the Georgetown municipal government, the author has correlated the lists of elected and appointed officials as they appear in "Proceedings of the Georgetown Corporation: Appointments by the Corporation of Georgetown" Georgetown, DC, Corporation Records 1751–1851, Manuscript Division, LC, and *Ordinances of the Corporation of Georgetown* (Georgetown, DC: James C. Dunn, 1821) and *Ordinances and Resolutions of the Georgetown Corporation from the Year 1751 to 1858* (Georgetown, DC: E. Hughes, 1858) with the Holy Trinity Baptismal and Marriage Registers, HTA, for appropriate years. The sample thus obtained probably errs on the low side, since it will not show Catholics who were not married or did not have children baptized during the period under review.

48. Montgomery County Land Records, Commissioners of the Tax (Assessment Records), 1793–1797, C 1110–1, 1–18–14–17, MSA.

49. "Memorandum Book of Family Expenses and Other Accounts of Geo. Fenwick," 110 S 11, 110.5 C 1, MPA; Richard K. McMaster, "Benedict Fenwick, Bishop of Boston, American Apprenticeship (1782–1817)," *United States Catholic Historical Society Records and Studies* 47 (1959): 78–79, 81–82. Fenwick's *Arithmetical Essays* was first printed by John W. Butler of Annapolis in 1809 and reprinted by Cotton and Stewart of Alexandria in 1810. Francis Fenwick was first assistant surveyor in 1817–18 and then surveyor from 1820 to 1823. The only concurrent appointments that the Corporation allowed council members were to non-salaried boards, such as the Board of [School] Visitors or the Poor Board.

50. *Georgetown College Journal* 6, no. 5 (February 1878): 52; Frances Flaherty-Knox, genealogist and Boone family descendant, to author, 28 January 1988; *Ordinances of the Georgetown Corporation*, resolution of 4 November 1826; Baptismal and Marriage Register 1795–1805, Baptismal Register 1805–1834, HTA; *Georgetown Directory* 1830; Deering Davis et al., *Georgetown Houses of the Federal Period*, 58–59. The Cox's Row houses, completed in 1817, were named after Colonel John Cox, a prosperous merchant and realtor, who was mayor of Georgetown from 1823 to 1845. A biographical entry in the nineteenth-century *Georgetown College Journal* identifies Joseph Brooks as the "carpenter who built the row of brick dwellings known as 'Cox's Row' on First Street east of Frederick." In the practice of the day the builder was more often than not also the designer, and the terms carpenter and architect were still used interchangeably. Brooks was a well-established builder in Georgetown by the time Cox's Row was finished.

51. *Georgetown Directories, 1830, 1834*; Newman, *The Maryland Semmes*, 55–56, 66–68; Anderson Humphreys, Curt Guenther, eds., *Semmes America* (Memphis: Humphreys Ink, Inc., 1989), 295–97.

52. The late Sister Mary Leonard Whipple, Georgetown Visitation Convent, to author, 14 December 1987; *DAB*, 8:579–82; Humphreys, *Semmes America*, 197, 309–10; Newman, *The Maryland Semmes* 64–65, 75–76; *National Cyclopedia of American Biographies*, 6:470. Newman gives Dr. Benedict Joseph Semmes of Piscataway as the guardian of young Raphael, but the *DAB* and family records assign this role to his uncle Raphael of Georgetown. The Trinity Baptismal Register 1805–1834, HTA, records Captain Alexander Semmes' son as Alexander Anthony Semmes, while Newman and the National Cyclopedia give his middle name as Alderman and Aldebaran, respectively.

53. *BDUSC*, 1788; Newman, *The Maryland Semmes*, 68–69; Humphreys, *Semmes America*, 296, 298–99; Edward C. Papenfuse, ed., *Archives of Maryland, New Series: An Historical List of Public Officials* (Annapolis: Maryland State Archives, 1990), 503; Joshua Civin, unpub. MS "Passage of the Maryland Jew Bill, 1797–1826," MSA; Governor and Council (Election Returns), 5 October 1829, AL-WO U.S. Representatives, 132–984, and 3 October 1831, 132–1044, 40 MSA. Benedict Semmes won by margins of 1,204 to 743 and 1773 to 1072 in the elections of 1829 and 1831, respectively. His district included Anne Arundel and Prince George's counties. *DAB* 8:578–79, 582; Robert S. O'Leary, "Doctors Afield: Alexander Jenkins Semmes," *New England Journal of Medicine*, 7 October 1954; *DAB* 8:578–79, 582.

54. *Official Register*, 1829, 1841; *Washington Directory, 1822*. The Trinity Baptismal (1795–1805, 1805–1834) and Marriage (1805–1875) Registers, HTA, reveal the Clementses as one of the parish's largest families.

55. Cordelia Jackson, "People and Places in Old Georgetown," *CHS* 33–34 (1932): 149–50; John Claggett Proctor, ed., *Washington Past and Present*, 5 vols. (New York: Lewis Historical Publishing, 1932), 5:1052–53; Georgetown College Ledgers, 1789–1793 and 1793–1796, GUA; William Wilson Corcoran, *A Grandfather's Legacy* (Washington: Henry Polkinhorn, 1879), 84, 164; Kelly, *History of Holy Trinity Parish*, 112; Charles Herbert Stockton, "Historical Sketch of George Washington University, D.C.," *CHS* 19 (1916):

112–13; Announcement Book, Holy Trinity Church, 6 December 1857, HTA. Corcoran purchased lots for his servants in the Trinity Church Cemetery and is also believed to have given much of the land for Holyrood Cemetery, to which grave sites from the Trinity and Georgetown College cemeteries were later transferred. He was a parishioner of St. John's Episcopal Church in Georgetown and both a founding member and contributor to Christ Episcopal Church of Georgetown, formed after a split in the St. John's congregation in 1817. His son William Wilson Corcoran made a "liberal aid . . . by a loan of money" toward the construction of the second Holy Trinity Church, as Trinity was by then known, in 1850, plus what Pastor William Mulledy called "a magnificent donation" in 1857. For St. John's Church see MS "Pew Diagram for St. John's," n.d., [prior to 1817], miscellaneous vestry papers, St. John's Church, Georgetown; Mitchell, *A Short History of St. John's Church*, 4, 6; Grace Dunlop Ecker, *A Portrait of Old Georgetown* (Richmond, VA: Garrett & Massie, 1933), 60, 174.

56. *Georgetown Metropolitan*, 28 April 1835.

57. *Ordinances of the Corporation of Georgetown*, 28 June 1823, 8, 29 March 1824. In 1823 the Georgetown Corporation authorized $2230 for building a municipal tobacco warehouse. Three years later the council voted to construct an additional warehouse. Constant dredging and channel marking kept the port of Georgetown open to ocean-going ships until well after the Civil War. But Baltimore was the much-preferred port, being easier for ships sailing the Chesapeake Bay to reach. From the mouth of the Potomac River to Georgetown ships sailed upstream 110 twisting nautical miles.

58. *Ordinances and Resolutions*, 8, 15 April 1837, 17 March 1838. See also n. 47 above. In the 1830s the mayor received $600 a year, while the clerk of the corporation, the highest salaried position, was paid $1,000. Some of the inspector positions were paid by piece work; e.g., so many cents per cask of liquor inspected by the gauger, or per barrel of meat or fish by the inspector of salted provisions. Many of the positions were part-time. For example, George Mahorney, the scavenger, was a bricklayer by profession; Ignatius Newton, weigher of hay, etc., a grocer.

59. Meeting, 27 January 1832, Corporation of Georgetown, "Journal of Board of Aldermen and Common Council," Manuscript Division, LC; Hennesey, *American Catholics*, 117–18, 121–22.

60. Meetings, 27 January, 24 February, 13, 16, 23, 30 March, 13 April, 1832, "Journal of Board of Aldermen and Common Council," LC; The Journal only summarizes the debates, but does give the complete text of committee recommendations and council resolutions. The portion quoted is from a Board of Aldermen minority committee report (13 April) by Henry Addison.

61. Ibid., 27 April 1832; "Journal of Stephen Dubuisson," 27 February 1832, 14C 1, MPA; Anthony Kohlman to John McElroy, Rome, 1 February 1836, 211 K 6, MPA. It is interesting to note that Mayor Cox, Samuel McKinney and Henry Addison were all Protestants. In fact, Bennett Clements was at the time the only Catholic member of the Council.

62. Hennesey, *American Catholics*, 118. In 1800 the total free population of Georgetown was approximately 3,600 and the City of Washington, 2,580. By 1820 Washington was 11,172 and Georgetown 5,993. Green, *Washington*, 1:21.

63. Rev. Stephen Dubuisson to Aloysius Young, 3 March 1827, 208 Z 12a. MPA; Robert Emmett Curran, S.J., *The Bicentennial History of Georgetown University, Volume 1: From Academy to University, 1789–1889* (Washington: Georgetown University Press, 1993), 208.

64. Anne Newport Royall, *Sketches of History, Life and Manners in the United States by a Traveller* (New Haven: for the author, 1826), 182.

65. "Journal of the Board of Aldermen," 13 April 1832.

NOTES TO CHAPTER 5

1. Rev. Edward I. Devitt, S.J., "Trinity Church, Georgetown: An Historical Discourse," *WL* 33 (1904): 314. Devitt knew McElroy during the latter's old age and heard the story directly from him.

2. Report of Georgetown Corporation for 1827, quoted in Jonathan Elliot, Jr., *Historical Sketches of the Ten Miles Square Forming the District of Columbia* (Washington: J. Elliot, Jr., 1830), 260 61; Green, *Washington*, 1:5 6. Washington City did not show appreciable growth until after 1810. By 1830 its total population was 18,800 or almost twice that of Georgetown, which by then was relatively stationary.

3. Baptism and Marriage Register 1795–1805, "Francis Neale to the Members of the R. C. Congregation of Trinity Church," 22 March 1806, HTA.

4. Roccofort, "Essai."

5. Baptism and Marriage Register 1795–1805, HTA; College Ledgers 1789–1793, 1793–1796; College Catalogues 1791–2—1803–4, 1804–5—1814–15, GUA. In the first ten years, the Trinity register lists 110 marriages and baptisms for Georgetown residents and 94 for out-of-town (including Washington City) residents. These figures do not include the black congregation, then largely slave and thus domiciled with their masters.

6. Margaret Bayard Smith, *The First Forty Years of Washington Society: Portrayed by the Family Letters of Mrs. Samuel Harrison Smith* (New York: Charles Scribner's Sons, 1906), 16; Frances Flaherty-Knox, genealogist and Queen family descendant to author, 4,18, February 1988; Mary Elizabeth Jensen and Henry Jerningham Queen, *The Ancestors and Descendants of Charles Jerningham Queen, Prince Georges County, Maryland, and His Wife, Lillian Ann Clark* (Syracuse, NY: privately printed, n.d.). Richard Queen (1705–?), the builder of Queen's Chapel, was the second son of Samuel and Katherine (Marsham) Queen. Katherine Marsham was the daughter of Richard and Katherine (Brent) Marsham. The latter was a sister of Giles Brent II and one of four surviving children of Giles Brent I and Mary Kittamaquand.

7. John Gilmary Shea, *Life and Times of the Most Rev. John Carroll* (New York: 1888), 89; Rev. James Redmond, S.J., to Archbishop Ambrose Maréchal, 8 December 1817, 20 B 2, AAB. Shea and others have suggested that Carroll had the chapel built sometime soon after his return from Europe. But in the letter cited above, James Redmond, the pastor of St. Mary's Church in Rockville, Maryland, answered one of Archbishop Maréchal's periodic diocesan surveys by stating that the chapel was "a frame building about 30 years or perhaps less old," which would date it 1787 or later. Unfortunately, there are no references to it in the papers of John Carroll himself, except for the will of his brother Daniel, who in 1796 gave "unto my brother John Carroll and his successors two acres of land comprehending and contiguous to the Roman Catholic Church erected upon my land." Montgomery County Registrar of Wills, *Estate Records* C 268–270, C 1138–4, 1–17–8–39, MSA.

8. Eberlein and Hubbard, *Historic Houses*, 392–93, 402–03; George C. Henning, "The Mansion and Family of Notley Young," *CHS* 16 (1912): 2–3. Henning visited the Young residence as a child. Father Bennett Neale (?–1787), Francis Neale's great uncle, left records of attending the Young mansion throughout much of the 1760s. Bennett Neale, "Sermons," American Catholic Sermon Collection, GUA.

9. Frances Flaherty-Knox to author, 20 January, 18 February, 1988; "History of St. Mary's Church, Alexandria," undated MS, 325 N 4–5, MPA. Richard L. Carne, *A Brief Sketch of the History of St. Mary's Church Alexandria, Virginia* (Alexandria: Catholic Benevolent Union of Virginia, n.d.) 4–5; "History of St. Mary's Church" states: "Two small mission churches are attended from Alexandria, viz. Falls Church, which is ten miles and Fairfax Station which is seventeen miles from Alexandria." The first Queen's Chapel, said to have been disguised as a smokehouse, burned down in 1774. The

254   second, a larger structure, was destroyed by fire during the Battle of Bladensburg in the War of 1812. It was rebuilt on the spot, only to be burned again fifty years later by Union troops from Fort Bunker Hill who mistakenly thought the Queens were southern sympathizers. In the 1890s Cardinal Gibbons refused a request from the Queen family descendants and former congregation members for funds to preserve the old chapel graveyard, but he did authorize the construction of St. Francis de Sales Church, finished in 1904, to serve the needs of the area.

   10. *DAB*, 9:406–07; Carroll, *Papers*, 2:108.

   11. Rev. William Matthews to Archbishop Carroll, 14 November 1809, 5 I 13, AAB; Rev. Notley Young, S.J., to Carroll, 13 April 1809, 8 R 3, AAB.

   12. Trustees of St. Mary's Church, Alexandria, to Archbishop James Whitefield, 2 November 1830, 209 H 1, MPA. For further difficulties at St. Mary's, see Chapter 6, n. 38.

   13. Rev. James Redmond to Archbishop Leonard Neale, 18 November 1816, 12 AL 6, AAB; Redmond to Archbishop Maréchal, 8 December 1817, 20 B 2, AAB; *WL* 34 (1905): 225–26. After serving the Montgomery County circuit for a year, Redmond proposed in 1816 that each of four congregations at "Rock Creek, Rockville (where the new church is now building), Lower Seneca, and Barnesville engage to pay a clergyman who will reside in the central part of the county $100 per annum." He also mentioned a small congregation at Holland's River, "commonly called Peter Gardiner's," which should contribute $16 to $20 a year. In the same year, in November 1816, he reported 140 to 150 regular communicants at Rock Creek, 60 to 70 at Rockville, 50 at Lower Seneca, 160 at Barnesville, and 35 at Holland's River.

   14. Rev. Frances Malevé, S.J., to Archbishop Ambrose Maréchal, 9 January 1818, Oversize 18 N 3, AAB; Rev. John Grassi, S.J., "The Catholic Religion in the United States in 1818," *WL* 11 (1882): 235; 30 (1901): 349–50.

   15. Carroll, *Papers*, 1:192.

   16. R. Emmett Curran, S.J. "Troubled Nation, Troubled Province, 1833–1880," MS, 3–6; Carroll, *Papers*, 1:192, 405.

   17. Rev. Robert Plunkett to Rev. Enoch Fenwick, 5 February 1813, Robert Plunkett Papers, GUA. Leonard Neale had previously served as pastor of St. Mary's in Philadelphia, but after Carroll chose him to be bishop coadjutor he moved to Georgetown and requested the regional assignment as he awaited ratification from Rome. He became archbishop of Baltimore upon Carroll's death in 1815. But by then Neale was advanced in years and in poor health, with the result that he remained almost in retirement at the Visitation Convent until his death two years later. Hennesey, *American Catholics*, 90.

   18. Grassi, "The Catholic Religion in the United States," 239–40.

   19. Ibid. 238–39; James Redmond to Francis Neale, 18 November 1816, 12 A L 6, AAB.

   20. Carroll, *Papers*, 1:180; Baptism and Marriage Register 1795–1805, HTA.

   21. "Jesuit Farms in Maryland: Facts and Anecdotes," unsigned, *WL* 41 (1912): 218. Apparently Francis Neale took these words from a retreat meditation or sermon given by Father George Hunter in 1749. The borrowing of sermons was then a common practice among priests.

   22. Grassi, "The Catholic Religion in the United States," 243.

   23. R. Emmett Curran, S.J., "'Splendid Poverty': Jesuit Slave Holding in Maryland, 1805–1838," in *Catholics in the Old South: Essays on Church and Culture*, ed. Randall L. Miller and Jon L. Wakelyn (Macon, GA: Mercer University Press, 1983), 312; Herbert P. Gutman, *The Black Family in Slavery and Freedom, 1750–1925* (New York: Vintage Books, 1976), 27; Gerald P. Fogarty, S.J., "The Origins of the Mission, 1634–1773," in *The Maryland Jesuits* (Baltimore: Maryland Province of the Society of Jesus, 1976), 18–19; Paul Kohlmann, S.J., "*Ex hortatio ad nigros servos*," White Marsh 1819, Rev. Paul Kohlmann Papers, GUA. As Gerald Fogarty points out the relatively liberal treatment

of Jesuit manor slaves was so well known in southern Maryland that the term "priest's slave" carried the meaning of "one who was granted a large measure of freedom of movement, did not work too hard, and was well cared for."

24. Peter Guilday, "The Priesthood of Colonial America," *WL* 63 (1934): 184.

25. *Baptism and Marriage Register, 1795–1805*, HTA; Margaret H. McAleer, "The Other Congregation: Patterns of Black Worship at Holy Trinity Church, Georgetown, D.C., 1795–1845," Georgetown University seminar paper, 1986, 26–27, 33–34.

26. Deposition of Samuel Abell, *Craig v. Mary Butler*, 27 May 1767, "C," June 1791 no. 3, Judgments, Court of Appeals, S 381–52, MSA.

27. Ibid.; Thomas Harris, Jr., and John McHenry, eds., *Maryland Reports: Being a Series of the Most Important Law Cases Argued and Determined in the Provincial Court and Court of Appeals of the Province of Maryland from the Year 1700 Down to the American Revolution* (New York: I. Riley, 1809), 371–84; Thomas Harris, Jr., and John McHenry, eds., *Maryland Reports: Being a Series of the Most Important Law Cases Argued in the General Court and Court of Appeals from May 1780 to May 1790* (New York: C. Wiley, 1812), 214–36.

28. Baptism and Marriage Register 1795–1805, Baptism and Confirmation Register 1805–1834 (see especially "Old Book Section"), Marriage Register 1805–1834, HTA; McAleer, "The Other Congregation," 32–33.

29. Ibid., 10–12, 18–19; Free Male School, Holy Trinity, List of Subscribers, 1831–1833, 57 R 2a and b, MPA.

30. Comparative study of Holy Trinity baptismal, marriage and confirmation registers, 1795 through 1905, HTA. Rev. Gerard A. McWilliams, "History of Epiphany Catholic Church," in *Epiphany Catholic Church Directory* (Georgetown: privately printed, 1967), 13–14.

31. See Chapter 1.

32. Allen C. Clark, "The Mayors of the Corporation of Washington: Thomas Carbery," *CHS* 19 (1916): 62–63, 88–90. Carbery's role in the construction of the capital is described in the next chapter. His brother Henry was also an officer during the Revolution and the War of 1812, attaining the rank of general. Carbery's sons and daughters who were prominent in Washington history are discussed in succeeding chapters.

33. Commissioners to William Prout, 3 August 1792, District Commissioners, Letters Sent, RDCC.

34. Benjamin Henry Latrobe, *The Papers of Benjamin Henry Latrobe* ed. Edward C. Carter II, et al., *Journals*, 3 vols., *Correspondence and Miscellaneous Papers*, 3 vols. (New Haven: Yale University Press, printed for the Maryland Historical Soceity, 1980–88); *Journals* 3:69–70.

35. Potomac Company Records, Proceedings of General Meetings, Letter Book A, 1785–1796, 1785–1826. The proceedings for August 1792 through August 1795 give a chronology of progress at Little Falls and those from January 1797 through August 1802 at Great Falls. For more concise accounts, see Walter S. Sanderlin, *The Great National Project: A History of the Chesapeake and Ohio Canal* (Baltimore: Johns Hopkins University Press, 1946), 32–36, and Wilbur E. Garret, "George Washington's Patowmack Canal," *National Geographic* 171 (June 1987): 717–53.

36. College Ledgers 1819–1822, 1822–1835, and 1846–1860, GUA. The accounts for these college employees suggest that most were single men for whom the college provided lodging. Their period of employment ranged from several months to several years, averaging approximately twelve months. Many had money deducted from their salaries to be sent home to relatives in Ireland.

37. Baptismal Register, 1805–1834, Pew Rental Diagram 1855, HTA; Rev. Stephen Dubuisson account book, 21 June 1832, 57 N 6, MPA; *Georgetown Directory* 1860.

38. *Georgetown Architecture—Northwest, Historic American Buildings Survey Selection No. 6* (Washington: Commission of Fine Arts, 1970), 206–07. Baptismal Register

1805–1834, Pew Rental Diagram 1855, HTA; *Georgetown Directory, 1834; Washington Directory 1822, 1834*. There are many spellings of the family name, which was not standardized as Donoghue until the 1830s.

39. Clarence S. Brigham, *History and Bibliography of American Newspapers, 1690–1820* (Worcester, MA: American Antiquarian Society, 1947), 258–61. The *Marylandische Zeitung* appears to have run from 1785 to 1789; the *General Staats-Bothe*, from 1793 on.

40. *Georgetown Directory 1830, 1834; Washington Directory 1834*.

41. Dolan, *The American Catholic Experience*, 111, 128–29; *NCE*, 14: 429–30.

42. William J. Bangert, S.J., *A History of the Society of Jesus* (St. Louis: Institute of Jesuit Sources, 1972), 413–14, 423–24. Neale's first efforts to reestablish the Society in America began as early as 1790.

43. Ibid., 424–25; Carroll, *Papers*, 1:319; Hughes, *History of the Society of Jesus, Documents*, 2:816. The seven other priests were Charles Sewall, Robert Molyneux, Sylvester Boarman, John Bolton, John Dubois, William Matthews, and Frances Beeston. Bishop Carroll and Leonard Neale wrote to Father General Gabriel Gruber on 25 May 1803. Their letter is partially preserved (Carroll, *Papers*, 2:412; *WL* 34 (1905): 214–15). Gruber's long-delayed reply, dated 12 March 1804, is found in its entirety in *WL* 34:215, 218. Carroll's continuing doubts about the canonical foundations of the Russian association are best found, inter alia, in his letters to Charles Plowden, 7 December 1804, and to Charles Neale, 11 September 1810; Carroll, *Papers*, 2:460; 3:120–21.

44. John McElroy, S.J., "An Account of the Reestablishment of the Society in the United States, and of Events Connected Therewith," *WL* 16 (1887): 161–62; Devitt, "History of the Maryland-New York Province: Holy Trinity Church," *WL* 64 (1935): 30–31; Rev. Anthony Kohlmann to Gruber, 25 November 1806, quoted in *WL* 34 (1905): 230; Grassi to Rev. William Strickland, 8 October 1811, extract, translated from the Italian, 4 S 3, MPA; Carroll, *Papers*, 2:465, 539; Louis Van Miert, S. J., "Some Historical Documents Concerning the Mission of Maryland, 1807–1820," *WL* 30 (1901): 346–50. In addition to Kohlmann and Grassi, priests coming from the Russian province to the United States included Francis Malevé, John Henry, Adam Britt, Peter Epinette, and Maximilian de Rantzau. Both Malevé and Epinette were initially assigned to Trinity. "Newtown Manor and Church," *WL* 14 (1885): 72–73.

45. *WL* 44 (1915): 12–13; *WL* 16 (1887): 161–62; *WL* 34 (1905): 229–30. Besides the Fenwick brothers and John McElroy, the novices included Charles Bolton, Leonard Edelen, Patrick McLaughlin, James Ord, William Queen, James Spinck, and Michael White. The two Fenwicks, Edelen, Queen, and Spinck were descendants of old southern Maryland families. McLaughlin and McElroy entered as lay brothers. James Ord is believed to have been the son by Morganatic marriage of King George IV and Maria Fitzherbert. He did not complete his noviceship, but stayed on in Georgetown as a member of the college faculty for a number of years. William Queen took his first vows in June 1809, but left the order soon thereafter to become a physician.

46. *WL* 34 (1905): 230. Benedict Fenwick was to become bishop of Boston and founder of Holy Cross; his brother Enoch, twelfth president of Georgetown Collge; and John McElroy, founder of Boston College.

47. *Catalogus Sociorum Misiones Americae Foederatoe Societatis Jesu, Ineunte Anno, 1809*, Woodstock, Ex Typis Collegii.

NOTES TO CHAPTER 6

1. Rev. Anthony Caffry to the District Commissioners, 14 April 1794; Letters Received, Commissioners to Caffry, 15–24 April 1794, Proceedings, RDCC. For the geographic boundaries of the City of Washington, see n. 29, Chapter 1.

2. Carroll, *Papers*, 2:109. For the Hoban tradition, see Virginia Frye, "St. Patrick's: First Catholic Church in the Federal City," *CHS* 23 (1920): 31, which is not without numerous errors. Caffry may have come to the United States on his own initiative, a not uncommon practice when the Dominican and other orders were suppressed in various countries in Europe. The cited Carroll letter has Caffry "settled and provided for" in Washington by January 1794.

3. Carroll, *Papers*, 2:122; Carroll to Commissioners, 14 December 1794, Letters Received, RDCC.

4. "An Unpublished Letter of Father Van Quickenborne," WL 30 (1901): 87; Joseph T. Durkin, S.J., *William Matthews: Priest and Citizen* (New York: Benziger Brothers, 1963), 12; Bryan, *History*, 1:605; Smith, *First Forty Years*, 13, 16; Van Quickenborne, in a letter to colleagues in the Netherlands, wrote in 1818 that "Twelve years ago in Washington, instead of the present church was a large room merely, and there were but twelve of the Catholic communion." Bryan sets the date for the frame church somewhat ambiguously as some thirteen years before the construction of the second St. Patrick's, which would make it 1796. Durkin, citing Margaret Bayard Smith, puts it at 1800.

5. Robert Plunkett to John Carroll, 10 April 1807, 6 V 10, AAB.

6. Caffry to Carroll, 29 August 1800, 8 A-C3, AAB.

7. Later Rev. Notley Young II also tried to obtain the St. Patrick's pastorate. Young to Carroll, 13 April 1807, 8 R 3, AAB; Matthews to Carroll, 14 November 1809, 5 I 13, AAB.

8. Durkin, *William Matthews*, 6–11; "Gonzaga College: A Sketch of Some of Its Residents," unsigned, *WL* 19 (1890): 19–20; Father Durkin's book remains the sole authoritative biography of Matthews.

9. Durkin, *William Matthews*, 13; Bryan, *History*, 1:160–61.

10. *National Intelligencer and Washington Advertiser*, 30 June 1809; James Goode, *Capital Losses: A Cultural History of Washington's Destroyed Buildings* (Washington: Smithsonian Institution Press, 1979), 106–07; Durkin, *William Matthews*, 14–15; Daley, *Georgetown University*, 154–55. Matthews was asked to take on the college presidency following the brief term of Robert Molyneux, who died in office. He so served for seven months, during which he strengthened and completed the college's Old North building. Daley has characterized Matthews as "one of the most outstanding maintenance men with whom the college was ever blessed." The brick church was replaced by the present St. Patrick's, completed in 1884.

11. Baptismal Register, vol. 1, 1811–1816, vol. 2, 1819–1836, St. Patrick's Church, Washington, D.C. Among Maryland families recorded are Daniel Carroll Brent (of the State Department) and his wife Eliza Walsh Brent, Mayor Robert Brent, Daniel Carroll of Duddington, William Dudley Digges and his wife Norah Carroll Digges, Nicholas and Eleanor Boyd Queen, Francis Fenwick, and Ann Young Casanave, the widow of Georgetown Mayor Peter Casanave. Interestingly, some Catholics who left Georgetown for Washington kept pews at both St. Patrick's and Trinity. Giuseppi Franzoni and Giovanni Andrei were the first Italian sculptors recruited to work on the Capitol by Thomas Jefferson. They were followed shortly by the painters Carlo Franzoni and Pietro Bonanni. James Alexander Simpson, Georgetown's first professor of art (see n. 29, Chapter 5) married Giuseppi Franzoni's daughter Juliana. Consentino and Glassie, *Capital Image*, 34–35, 54, 271.

12. Peter Kenney, S.J., to Rev. Robert Haley, 13 July 1832, 210 P 4a, MPA; Durkin, *William Matthews*, 110.

13. "Gonzaga College," *WL* 19 (1890): 16–17; Durkin, *William Matthews*, 122–23.

14. W. Dawson Johnston, "Early History of the Washington Library Company and Other Local Libraries," *CHS* 7 (1904): 22, 25, 30–31. Matthews served as president of the sponsoring organization, known as the Washington Library Company, for thirteen years. During this time it amassed more than 4,000 volumes and acquired space of its own in the Post Office Building. It became the prototype of a national library in 1823 when Congress, one of its principal users, asked that it be the repository for the journals of Congress and other state papers.

15. Samuel Yorke Atlee, *History of the Public Schools of Washington City, D.C., extracted and printed separately from the Twenty-Eighth Report of the Board of Trustees* (Washington: 1876), 023, 025–26. Sixty different trustees served on the board from its inception in August of 1805 to July of 1816. The bill with the amendment for St. Vincent's was first proposed in October of 1841.

16. Durkin, *William Matthews*, 83–87.

17. Ibid., 86, 87, 96–100; Daley, *Georgetown University*, 197–98; Edward L. Devitt, S.J., "History of the Maryland-New York Province," *WL* 64 (1935): 42–44.

18. *National Intelligencer*, 28 July 1825; "Gonzaga College," *WL* 19 (1890): 14.

19. Rev. Peter Verhaegen to Archbishop Eccleston, 16 April 1847, 215 G 3, MPA; Eccleston to Verhaegen, 17 April 1847, 215 G 4, MPA; Devitt, "History of the Maryland-New York Province," 45–46; "Gonzaga College," 166–67; Durkin, *William Matthews*, 100–03, 117–18.

20. Baptismal Registers, vol. 1, 1811–16, vol. 2, 1819–36, St. Patrick's Church.

21. "The Roman Catholics living on or near the Eastern branch in the City of Washington," n.d., 11 H 5, MPA. The document probably should be dated no later than 1802, since one of the principal subscribers, Notley Young, died in April 1802. Capt. Thomas Tingey is not known to have been a Catholic; he probably subscribed out of interest in the improvement of the nearby Navy Yard community and his friendship with the Carrolls and the Brents. Thirty-five donors pledged a total of $1,060.

22. Barry to Carroll, extract, n.d. but probably 1801, 11 S 2, AAB; Carroll to Barry, 16 September 1801, Carroll, *Papers*, 2:363. Barry is sometimes confused with the Revolutionary War hero, naval Captain (later Commodore) John Barry (no relation), probably because James Barry was a shipowner and sometimes addressed as captain. Carroll's letter to Barry states that Hoban estimated the cost of the chapel at $2,000. An account memorandum in the papers of Daniel Carroll of Duddington, who evidently helped defray the costs, shows "$70.00 paid Jas. Hoban, plan & attending building, St. Mary's Church," June 12–July 8, 1806, Daniel Carroll of Duddington Papers, Manuscript Division, LC [hereafter DCD Papers].

23. Margaret Brent Downing, "James and Joanna Gould Barry," *United States Catholic Historical Society Historical Records and Studies*, 15 (1921): 49–53; Allen C. Clark, "Captain James Barry," *CHS* 42–43 (1940–41): 5–12.

24. Clark, "Captain James Barry," 13–14.

25. Downing, "James and Joanna Gould Barry," 51–53; Clark, "Captain James Barry," 12–13. Downing calls James D. Barry an adopted son; Clark, a nephew. The latter appears to be correct, since James Barry himself refers to "my nephews James D. and David Barry" in his instructions regarding use of the chapel cited in n. 22 above. All persons buried in St. Patrick's and other city churchyards sold for development were supposedly reinterred at Mt. Olivet or St. Mary's Lincoln Road Cemetary, which were in part established by the Archdiocese in 1858 to meet this need. But no records are kept at St. Mary's, and the current staff at Mt. Olivet claims no knowledge of the burial site of the Barrys.

26. Clark, "Daniel Carroll of Duddington," 34; Rev. J. M. Lucas to Archbishop Ambrose Maréchal, 25 November 1823, 18 K 63, AAB. Carroll donated lots totalling approximately 11,000 square feet on Second and C streets, S.E., the church's present site.

27. Maréchal to Francis Dzierozynski, S.J., translated from the French, 13 July 1827, 208 T 3, MPA. At the time Dzierozynski was superior of the Maryland mission (later Province) of the Society of Jesus. Lucas was transferred to Trinity Church three years later.

28. Lucas to Maréchal, 25 November 1823, 14 July 1824, 18 K 69, AAB; "Maréchal Diary," 439. Nicholas Young gave Archbishop Maréchal a square of three acres in Washington City "in trust for the Congregation of St. Peter's." Lucas wrote of Matthews: "He much desires to remove [the Jesuits] a bit farther from him and to make them think he is their friend."

29. Goode, *Capital Losses*, 198–99; *National Intelligencer*, 7 September 1846; *A Short History: Saint Mary Mother of God*, current church pamphlet, Washington, D.C., n.d.; Rev. Peter Verhaegen to Archbishop Eccleston, 17 April 1847, 215 G 4, MPA.

30. *Young Ladies Academy of the Convent of the Visitation, in Georgetown, D.C.*, prospectus, circa 1819, Visitation Academy Students Lists, Archives of Visitation Academy, Georgetown, DC; Eleanor C. Sullivan, *Georgetown Visitation Since 1799* (Baltimore: French-Bray, 1975), 48–49, 51–54, 63, 68–73, 89, 94; *Historic American Buildings Survey, Georgetown Architecture—Northwest*, 400.

31. Rev. Theodore De Theux, S.J. to Maréchal, 2 April 1821, 15 p. 7, AAB; Julia Compton to Anne Martha Young, 21 March 1837, Willson-Compton Papers, M 1455, M 2640, MSA. Julia Compton was a school teacher and Trinity parishioner whose letters to her friend Anne Martha Young, later Mrs. Richard Bennett Willson of Rock Hall on Maryland's Eastern Shore, are a rich source of observations for Trinity parish and Georgetown society in general.

32. Roccofort, "Essai"; Robert Emmett Curran, S.J., ed., *American Jesuit Spirituality: The Maryland Tradition 1634–1900* (New York: Paulist Press, 1988), 193. Although McElroy was accepted in Neale's first novitiate as a temporal brother, his aptitude and talents for priestly ministry were so evident that he was soon made a scholastic. After serving as an assistant pastor at Trinity from 1818 to 1822, he was sent to Frederick, Maryland, where in the course of twenty-three years he founded both boys' and girls' schools, an orphanage, a convent, and a Jesuit novitiate. Following the Mexican War, he returned to Trinity as pastor for the years 1845–1846. McElroy was next appointed pastor of St. Mary's Church in Boston, where in 1863 he founded Boston College. *NCE* 9:15.

33. Data compiled from Trinity Church registers and the biographical notes on nineteenth-century Jesuit priests in the *Woodstock Letters*. One cause of the rapid turnover was Georgetown College's practice of assigning foreign-born priests to Trinity while receiving English instruction or serving short terms on the college faculty. The priests received a good introduction to American customs and American parish life before moving on, but it is doubtful that Trinity's congregation benefitted from the practice.

34. McElroy Diaries, entry for 19 March 1818, GUA. For a comprehensive study of the Catholic revival movement, see J. P. Dolan, *Catholic Revivalism: The American Experience, 1830–1900* (Notre Dame: University of Notre Dame Press, 1978). Dolan (17) states that "few references to parish revivals can be found prior to 1825." See also Curran, *American Jesuit Spirituality*, 27.

35. Grassi, "The Catholic Religion in the United States," 234; McElroy Diaries, 3, 4, and 5 July 1819, 3 October 1819. The outlines of the arches, long since bricked in, are still plainly visible on the church's west wall.

36. Devitt, "History of the Maryland-New York Province," 32; McElroy Diaries, 23 March 1819.

37. Ibid., 23 March and 5, 6, 8 April 1819.

38. St. Mary's first resident pastor, British-born James Fairclough, was a successful fundraiser and parish administrator, but his overbearing and sometimes aggressive approaches got him in such trouble that Archbishop James Whitfield ordered his removal. However, the St. Mary's lay trustees and most of the parish supported him, and Fairclough defied the archbishop's order, refusing to leave. He was eventually evicted by court order after staging what we today would call a sit-in at the rectory. The significance of this case and why it is mentioned here is that it represented a high watermark in trustee pretensions and the most serious outbreak of trusteeism in the capital area. At one point, in fact, the trustees informed Archbishop Whitfield that they wished Whitfield and his successors to "disclaim any intereference in the temporal concerns of the church." Rev. James Fairclough, S.J., to Archbishop Ambrose Maréchal, 1 March 1820, 16 M 15, AAB; Archbishop James Whitfield to Rev. Francis Dzieroznyski, S.J.; 10 October 1830, 209 K 8, MPA; Whitfield to Fairclough, 5 October 1830, 209 K 9, MPA; Whitfield to Dzierozynski, 14 October 1830, 209 K 15, MPA; Rev. Peter Kenney, S.J., to John McElroy, 23 November 1830, 209 H 12, MPA.

39. McElroy Diaries, 25 December 1819.

40. Ibid., 25 March 1819; *Association of the Confraternity of the Rosary, Established in Trinity Church, Georgetown, D.C.* (Washington: Printed by Dailes and Force, 1822), Rare Book Room, LC; Records of the Confraternity of the Living Rosary, HTA; Records of the Bona Mors Society, HTA; Dolan, *The American Catholic Experience*, 214. Dolan's studies have revealed that only two percent of all devotional societies were established before 1840. Their greatest rise took place after 1860.

41. Curran, *American Jesuit Spirituality*, 15; Julia Compton to Anna Young, 1 December 1839, Willson-Compton Papers.

42. Ibid., 22 June 1845; Roccofort, "Essai."

43. Jonathan Elliott, *Historical Sketches of the Ten Miles Square Forming the District of Columbia* (Washington: Printed by J. Elliott, Jr., 1830), 211–12; Julia Compton to Anne Young, 11 January 1840, Willson-Compton Letters; Holy Trinity Sunday Announcement Book, 3 September 1856, 18 April 1869, HTA. Another source for the size of the Trinity congregation is Archbishop Maréchal, whose 1820 report gave 800 as the number of parishioners making their Easter duty that year, which also saw 213 confirmations and "converts 60 at least." Maréchal, *Diary*, 437.

44. Diary of Rev. Stephen Dubuisson, S.J., 14 February 1825, Dubuisson-Feiner Collection; Dubuisson Journal, 8 February 1832, MPA 14 C 1, GUA.

45. The house was purchased by Neale in 1805 from a free black, Mann Butler, for $550. Following its use for the first Jesuit novitiate, it served alternately as the Free School schoolhouse and as a residence for Trinity's pastors and priests. College Ledger, 1803–13, Property Files, GUA; Old Account Books, HTA.

46. Brigden first appears in the college account ledgers in 1813 as a handyman. Following the founding of the Trinity Free School in 1818, a significant number of appropriate books are charged to his account. His position at the school is confirmed in Jonathan Elliott's *Sketches* (see n. 43 above), where the Free School is described as "under the direction of the zealous and indefatigable Mr. Brigden." College Ledger 1803–13, GUA; Elliott, *Historical Sketches*, 211–12; William Byrne, *History of the Catholic Church in the New England States*, 2 vols. (Boston: Hurd and Everetts Company, 1899), 2:3.

47. McElroy Diaries, 22 April 1819, 27 June 1819; U.S. House of Representatives, "Special Report of the Commissioner of Education on the Condition and Improvement of Public Schools in the District of Columbia," House Executive Document 315, 41st Cong., 2d sess., serial 1427; Charles Stonestreet, S.J., *Discourse on the Right Rev'd Benedict J. Fenwick, D.D.* (Frederick, MD: J. W. Baughmann, 1846), 23.

48. Free School accounts, December 1831-April 1833, 57 R, MPA; Minutes of the Meetings of Trustees of the Free School attached to Trinity Church, undated 57 R 4, MPA; Dubuisson Journal, 27 February 1832. President Thomas Mulledy of Georgetown College was instrumental in obtaining the support of the Society for the school, while Dubuisson formed a responsible board of lay trustees whose membership included Joseph Brooks, Henry Waring, Charles King, Ignatius Clarke, Peter O'Donaghue, Bernard Brian, Alfred Boucher, John Holtzman, Edward B. King, and John R. May.

49. Curran, "Troubled Nation, Troubled Province," 1–4, 16; Green, *Washington*, 21; Green, *The Secret City: A History of Race Relations in the Nation's Capital* (Princeton: University Press, 1967), 32–33, 38. Curran gives a lucid account of the debates over rural versus urban concentration of effort and the related problem of what to do with the rural missions' slaves. By 1840 the ratio of free blacks to slaves in Georgetown was even greater, or 1,403 to 785.

50. Archbishop Maréchal to Rev. Peter DeVos, S.J., 15 January 1827, Peter DeVos Papers, GUA; Curran, "'Splendid Poverty,'" 143; Curran, "Troubled Nation, Troubled Province," 6–10.

51. Stephen Dubuisson, "Commentary on the Maryland Province" [a report to the French Society for the Propagation of the Faith], quoted in Curran, "Troubled Nation, Troubled Province," 24.

52. The Proceedings of the Philodemic Society, October 1, 1837–November 28, 1848, GUA; *Baltimore Sun*, 13 May 1842; New York *Freeman's Journal*, 21 May 1842. The *National Intelligencer* estimated the crowd at 5,000. Congressman William Cost Johnson of Maryland also attended, and Henry G. S. Key, a cousin of Francis Scott Key, served as chief marshal. The organizers of the event appear to have made a conscious effort to give it an ecumenical character. Congressman Johnson and Kennedy were Protestants, as were Henry Key, Mayor Seaton, and G. W. P. Custis. Principal speaker William G. Reade was a convert to Catholicism, and Emily Harper was the youngest and only surviving daughter of a mixed marriage between Robert Goodloe Harper, a prominent Protestant attorney under whom William Reade studied, and Catherine Carroll, a daughter of Charles Carroll of Carrollton.

NOTES TO CHAPTER 7

1. "Diary of Mrs. William Thornton," *CHS* 10 (1907): 92. Thornton, Gustavus Scott, and Alexander White were the second trio of commissioners, replacing Thomas Johnson, David Stuart, and Daniel Carroll of Upper Marlboro in 1794–95. Unlike their predecessors, the second group were salaried and required to live in Washington City.

2. Ibid., 93.

3. Richard Henry Lee to Daniel Carroll of Duddington, 22 January 1800, DCD Papers.

4. Latrobe to Philip Mazzei, 29 May 1806, *Latrobe Papers*, 2:228.

5. Washington to Stuart, 8 March 1792, Washington, *Writings of Washington*, 31:504; Bowling, *The Creation of Washington, D.C.*, 212.

6. Working against Washington was the fact that sailing ships could take weeks to twist up the Potomac River to Washington or Georgetown, given contrary winds or rain-swollen currents, whereas those continuing north from the mouth of the Potomac up the Chesapeake Bay could make Baltimore in twenty-four hours in anything but strong headwinds or a flat calm.

7. Pierre L'Enfant, who came to Washington in March 1791, might be included among the builders of the capital but for the fact he had no opportunity to be one. During his first sojourn in Washington he was entirely occupied until his dismissal with his well-known and long-awaited plan for the city. He thus gave himself no time to practice architecture or supervise building construction, as he had done with some success in New York. Also, although born and baptized a Catholic in France, L'Enfant does not appear to have been an active or practicing Catholic during his years in the United States. (See H. Paul Caemmerer, *Life of Pierre Charles L'Enfant*, 98–103, for L'Enfant's close social and professional association with the Protestant Episcopal St. Paul's and Trinity

Churches during his sojourn in New York.) L'Enfant's closest friends in Washington, however, were the Catholics Thomas Atwood Digges and George Hadfield. The author is grateful to Philip Ogilvie, public records administrator of the District of Columbia, for the latter information.

8. Cora Belle Harbaugh, *Harbaugh History: A Directory, Genealogy and Source Book of Family Records* (Evansville, IN: privately printed, 1947), entries 1394, 1395, 1279, 2008, 2127; Rev. H. [Henry] Harbaugh, *Annals of the Harbaugh Family in America from 1736 to 1836* (Chambersburg, PA: M. Kieffe and Co., Printers, 1856), revised and illustrated by W. L. Harbaugh, privately printed, n.d.; Baptismal and Marriage Records, 1795–1805, 1805–1834, HTA; College Ledger 1793–1796, GUA; Baptismal Registers, 1811–1816, 1819–1836, St. Patrick's Church. Rev. Henry Harbaugh's *Annals* has both obvious errors and misprints. Cora Belle Harbaugh's *Harbaugh History* is a more serious genealogical effort, although it too contains gaps and errors, as its author forewarns. Known data from baptismal, marriage, and Georgetown College records is as follows: Leonard Harbaugh had at least two sons who remained in the Washington area. One, Leonard, Jr. (1775–1812), a grocer, married Mary Earp in the Trinity Church his father had built, 4 September 1803. They had two sons baptized at Trinity, Hiram Joseph and Edward Leonard, both of whom died young. Another, Joseph (1779–1864), a carpentry inspector and member of the Washington City Council from 1830 to 1837, married first Eleanor (last name not recorded) and second Rebecca Peters; Joseph's children were baptized both at Trinity and St. Patrick's and their children, in turn, for the most part remained Catholic. Two other sons, Thomas (1777–1857) and Samuel (1781–?), attended Georgetown College in 1794. Thomas served his father as an accountant for the Potomac Company and toll collector at Shenandoah Falls. He later moved to Harpers Ferry. Samuel is said to have lived mainly in Baltimore. Proceedings of the Board and President and Director of the Potomac Company, 10 February 1807, Potomac Company Records, Record Group 79, NA.

9. Proceedings, Potomac Company Records, 27 December 1794, 6 August 1795; Commissioners to Harbaugh, 18 August 1796, 9 May 1799, Letters Sent, RDCC. Harbaugh to Commissioners 23 August 1796, Letters Received, RDCC. Harbaugh was engaged to finish the locks at Little Falls in December 1794, which he did in six months, much to the company's pleasure. To save time and money the locks were made of timber, which later had to be replaced by stone.

10. Harbaugh to Commissioners, 18 April 1798, Letters Received, RDCC; Proceedings 20, 23 June 1798, RDCC.

11. John Walker, "The High Art of George Hadfield," *American Heritage* 37 (August-September 1986): 75–76; Roger Kennedy, *Architecture, Men, Women, and Money in America 1600–1860* (New York: Random House, 1985), 214, 221; George S. Hunsberger, "The Architectural Career of George Hadfield," *CHS* 51–52 (1951): 46, 47; *DAB*, 4:76–77; *Dictionary of National Biography* (London: Oxford University Press, 1917), 8:875–76, 1203–04. Walker offers a convenient summary of Hadfield's career in Washington, while Kennedy and to a lesser degree Hunsberger have more on Hadfield's family background. Maria Cosway met Jefferson during visits to Paris in 1786 and 1787, when he was American Minister there.

12. Walker, "High Art of George Hadfield," 75–76.

13. Ibid., 74–75; Hadfield's front elevation for the Treasury (74), is the only known representation of the building as Hadfield designed it. Modification of architects' plans by builders was not uncommon at the time. In the case of Harbaugh's half-story, however, the commissioners demanded that he count every brick used in the building and later the twin War Office in submitting his final accounts. They then refused to reimburse him for the bricks "as have been used in the third Stories of said buildings in Consequence of Alterations in the roofs made by Mr. Harbaugh which he agrees should occasion no additional Expence to the Public." This seems a harsh penalty, since the half-story provided much needed additional office or storage space, did not detract from the original design, and was incorporated first in the twin War Office (1802) and then in two more identical buildings for the State and Navy Departments (1819–1819). Proceedings, 15 December 1800, RDCC.

14. Commissioners to Washington, 31 January 1797, Letters Sent, RDCC; Washington to Commissioners, 21 October 1796, *Writings of Washington*, 35:250; Wilhelmus Bogart Bryan, "Why the City Went Westward," *CHS* 7 (1904): 138–41.

15. "Accounts of Divisions with Original Proprietors and the Commissioners of Public Buildings and Grounds of the City of Washington and the District of Columbia," Record Group 42, NA; Proceedings, 6 August, 26 September 1799, Letters Received, RDCC; Commissioners to Harbaugh, 9 May 1800, Letters Sent, RDCC; In the above-cited "Accounts," Uriah Forrest is recorded as co-signee for five of the lots purchased by Harbaugh. It is possible but unlikely that Harbaugh would have bought all of the remaining lots on his own account. During the same year Daniel Carroll of Duddington and James Barry, two of the capital's richest investors, bought properties totalling $3,859 and $4,658, respectively. Both the original Treasury and War Office Buildings were burned by the British in 1814 and rebuilt under the supervision of James Hoban, who is sometimes given credit as their architect, after Hadfield. The principal modifications (other than Harbaugh's half-story) were all in exterior detail, most notably in number of columns and a larger pediment for the portico. But whether these were originally introduced by Harbaugh or added by Hoban is impossible to determine, since there are no illustrations of the Treasury or War Office as they were actually built prior to 1814. The building's original dimensions were kept, however, and Hoban's modifications, may have been very minor or none, since George Hadfield's damage report of 1814 to the commissioners found the Treasury and the War office the least damaged of all Washington's public buildings and "easily repaired." Beginning in 1818 the buildings were again duplicated, to make four in all, housing the Treasury, State, War, and Navy Departments. Goode, *Capital Losses*, 292–94.

16. *Centinel of Liberty or Georgetown and Washington Advertiser*, 23, 27 May, and 3 June 1800; John Ball Osborne, "The Removal of Government to Washington," *CHS* 3 (1900): 138, 140–46; Noble Cunningham, *The Process of Government Under Jefferson* (Princeton: Princeton University Press, 1978), 32.

17. Cora Bacon-Foster, "Early Chapters in the Development of the Potomac Route to the West," *CHS* 15 (1912): 187, 189, 191; Commissioners to Harbaugh, 30 October 1800, 16 April 1801, Letters Sent, RDCC; *National Intelligencer*, 30 October 1800; *Centinel of Liberty*, 17, 21 October 1800; *National Intelligencer*, 3 November 1800; *Washington Federalist* 30 October 1800.

18. Proceedings, 4 October 1797, 6 January 1802, Report of the President and Directors, 2 August 1802, 12 December 1803, Records of the Potomac Company; Bacon-Foster, "Development of the Potomac Route to the West," 162–64. Among the visitors during construction and trials was the Duke de la Rochefoucalt-Liancourt, author of the well-known *Travels Through the United States*. Bryan, *History*, 1:272, 274–75.

19. The Potomac Company's objective was to make the river itself navigable, *not* to build a complete parallel system of canals and locks as the Chesapeake and Ohio Canal Company did later, commencing in 1828. George Washington and his Potomac company directors hoped "to improve" the river course for barge traffic by building wing dams, digging sluiceways and diversionary channels, and removing obstructive boulders during the lower water season. Locks were to be built only at such major impasses as the Little and Great Falls. But Washington's dream was illusory; the Potomac ultimately proved impossible to tame. Floods, high water, and more especially prolonged periods of summer low water rendered the river unnavigable for loaded barges for the greater part of every year. (A joint Maryland-Virginia commission in 1823 found that "the whole time when goods and produce could be stream borne on the Potomac in the course of an entire year did not exceed forty-five days.") Many of the down-river barges were so battered upon arriving in Georgetown that they were sold for firewood. Cora Bacon-Foster's "Early Chapters in the Development of the Potomac," cited above, offers a readable account of the company's trials, and Wilbur E. Garrett's "The Patowmack Canal: Waterway that Led to the Constitution," *National Geographic* 171 (June 1978), offers an excellent account of the engineering of the Great Falls locks and the achievement of Leonard Harbaugh. In addition Bryan's *History*, 1:69–70, offers the best account of the basic reasons for the project's ultimate failure.

20. William Seale, *The President's House*, 2 vols. (New York: Harry N. Abrams, 1986), 1:39–44; *National Cyclopedia of American Biography*, 24:85–86.

21. Seale, *The President's House*, 26–28; Commissioners to Thomas Jefferson, 14 March 1792, Letters Sent, RDCC.

22. Washington to Commissioners, 6 June 1792, Letters Received, Commissioners to Washington, 19 July 1792, Letters Sent, RDCC; Seale, *The President's House*, 29.

23. Foster, *Jeffersonian America*, 12; Latrobe to Philip Mazzei, 29 May 1806, *Latrobe Papers*, 2:228. Foster first served as secretary to British minister Anthony Merry from 1804 to 1807 and then as minister in 1811 and 1812.

24. Seale, *The President's House*, 44–48. Leinster House is now the Dail Eireann, or seat of Ireland's Parliament.

25. Commissioners to Washington, 19 July 1792, Letters Sent, RDCC; Washington to Commissioners, 3 August 1792, Letters Received, RDCC.

26. Seale, *The President's House*, 56–58.

27. Ibid., 50.

28. Bryan, *History*, 1:169. George Brent (1760–1803) was the oldest of Robert and Ann Carroll Brent's five sons. His brother Robert (1763–1819) soon took over the principal role in dealing with the commissioners for both the government-leased and Cooke-Brent quarries. William Brent (1775–1863) resigned as clerk to the commissioners in 1801 to become clerk for the District Court in Washington. See, for example, Robert Brent to Commissioners, 2 July 1792, Commissioners to Robert Brent, 6, 22 November 1792, Commissioners to William Brent, 12 May 1792, 11 May 1797, RDCC. The records of the commissioners have frequent exchanges with Robert Brent on the Cooke-Brent quarries beginning in the spring of 1795. Difficulties in the supply of stone were such that work on the Capitol was occasionally brought to a halt. For the relative importance of the various quarries, see Benjamin Latrobe's report of 1804, "Producing Stone for the U.S. Capitol," *Latrobe Papers*, 2:425–26.

29. Commissioners to James Fenwick, Commissioners to Municipality of Bordeaux, 4 January 1793, Letters Sent, RDCC; Proceedings, 3, 30 August 1792, 21 July 1797, RDCC.

30. Leonard Harbaugh to Commissioners, 22 May 1799, Letters Received, RDCC; Bryan, *History*, 1:300n. Fenwick served a second term as a surveyor, not noted in Bryan, beginning 1794.

31. Commissioners to Major Andrew Ellicott, 14 March 1792, to Benjamin and Joseph Ellicott, 28 January 1794, Letters Sent, RDCC; Andrew Ellicott to President Washington, 27 June 1793, 2 February 1794, Letters Received, RDCC; Proceedings, 10 April 1793, 25 March 1794, 15–20 April 1794, RDCC. Silvio A. Bedini, *The Life of Benjamin Banneker* (New York: Charles Scribner's Sons, 1972), 133–34; "The Planners of the City of Washington, L'Enfant, the French Catholic, and Dermott, the Irish Catholic," unsigned, *The American Catholic Historical Researches*, New Series, 2 (January 1906): 68–69.

32. Proceedings, 10, 12 November 1796; Thomas Carbery to Commissioners, 1 March 1797, 6 May 1797, Letters Received; Commissioners to Carbery, 3 May 1797, Letters Sent, RDCC.

33. Seale, *The President's House* 1:38; Daniel Carroll of Duddington to Commissioners, 10 June 1792, Letters Received, RDCC. Carroll himself later became one of the principal suppliers of bricks for the Capitol and Capitol Hill residences.

34. *BDML* 2:482; Proceedings, 26 September 1797, RDCC; Seale, *The President's House*, 1:75, 140; Mudd, *Mudd Family in the United States*, 593; Margaret Phelan, Kilkenny Archeological Society, Rothe House, Kilkenny, Ireland, to author, 29 June, 2 July, 1989. The author is grateful to William Seale for providing a list of contractors, suppliers, and laborers engaged in the construction of the President's House.

35. "Accounts of Divisions with Original Proprietors," Record Group 42, NA; Wilhelmus Bogart Bryan, "Hotels of Washington Prior to 1814," *CHS* 7 (1904): 78–83. The Hoban-Purcell purchases were made in the months of October and December of 1792. A year later Hoban alone, as though hedging his bets, bought lots near to and on Capitol Square. Frequent turnover of taverns and hotels was the rule, not the exception, both in Georgetown and Washington. The description of the Fenwick house is from an advertisement for its sale placed by Bennet Fenwick's widow Mary (*National Intelligencer*, 28 May 1802). The D. McClelland Map of the City of Washington of 1854, reproduced in a foldout in Varnum's *Seat of Government*, is a convenient source for locating the squares used in property sales.

36. Bryan, *History*, 1:187–89, 205–08, 228–29; Goode, *Capital Losses*, 160–61; Diary of Mrs. William Thornton, *CHS* 10 (1907): 193–94. The Great Hotel was probably the largest private structure of its day. After its use as a theater, it served as the Post Office Department, a temporary home for Congress, and the United States Patent Office. It was destroyed in a disastrous fire in 1839.

37. Proceedings, 15 January 1799, 16, 17, 23 April 1798, RDCC. After discharging the stonecutters, the commissioners gave their foremen authority to engage replacements or take back the dismissed cutters at reduced wages.

38. Proceedings, 15–24 August 1794, 13 August 1798, RDCC; Seale, *The President's House*, 67. A temporary hospital was first planned for the President's Square, but later built on Judiciary Square. Dr. Charles Worthington, a prominent Georgetown physician, first attended the workers, followed by Dr. John Crocker.

39. Seale, *The President's House*, 73–74.

40. *Centinel of Liberty*, 9, 12, 16 April 1799; Bryan, *History*, 1:315; Hunsberger, "The Architectural Career of George Hadfield," 55. The commissioners exonerated Hadfield of all of Redmond Purcell's charges, which they characterized as "malicious falsehoods and malevolent slanders." Purcell was subsequently discharged. Proceedings, 4 April 1799, RDCC.

41. Proceedings, 28 May 1798, RDCC.

42. Seale, *President's House*, 75; Bryan, *History*, 1:241. The other Mudd builders and craftsmen were Ignatius Mudd (1778–1851), who later became the District's commissioner of public buildings and Thomas James Mudd (1780–1846), who was also a Georgetown and Washington realtor. Baptismal and Marriage Register, 1794–1805, HTA; Mudd, *Mudd Family in the United States*, 593–99.

43. Washington to Commissioners, 15, 17 February 1797, *Writings of Washington*, 35:389–92.

44. Proceedings, 28 May, 21 August 1798, RDCC.

45. Baptism and Marriage Register, 1795–1805, HTA.

46. Hoban to Commissioners, 12 March 1799, Letters Received; Commissioners to Hoban, 11 April 1799, Letters Sent, RDCC.

47. Proceedings, 28 May 1798, RDCC; *Centinel of Liberty*, 11 February, 21 October 1800; *Washington Federalist*, 30 October 1800; Bryan, *History*, 1:375.

48. "Diary of Mrs. William Thornton," 207–08; Seale, *President's House*, 80–81.

49. *National Intelligencer*, 17, 19, 21 November 1800; "Diary of Mrs. William Thornton," 214; *Centinel of Liberty*, 24 November 1800; Bryan, *History*, 1:375.

50. *Annals of the Congress of the United States - Sixth Congress, 1799–1801* (Washington: Gales and Seaton, 1851), 723, 785–86; *National Intelligencer*, 28 November 1800.

NOTES TO CHAPTER 8

1. Quoted in Green, *Washington*, 1:39.

2. *Diary of William Dunlap, 1766–1839*, 2 vols. (New York: New-York Historical Society, 1930), 2:386, 381; Charles William Janson, *The Stranger in America 1793–1806* (1807; reprint, New York: Press of the Pioneers, 1935), 213; Gouverneur Morris to Princesse de la Tour et Taxis, 14 December 1800, in *The Diary and Letters of Gouverneur Morris*, ed. Ann Carey Morris, 2 vols. (New York: Da Capo Press, 1970), 1:394–95. For a full sampling of negative comments, unrelieved by any positive observations, see James Sterling Young, *The Washington Community 1800–1828* (New York: Columbia University Press, 1966), 22–26, 43–48.

3. Smith, *First Forty Years*, 1–3.

4. Ibid., 11. For an interesting account of a night of social rounds along a muddy Pennsylvania Avenue, see Clark, "Daniel Carroll of Duddington," 28–29.

5. *Centinel of Liberty*, 15 February 1800; Clark, "Captain James Barry," 5; Smith, *First Forty Years*, 14–15.

6. *National Intelligencer*, 19 November 1800; *DAB*, 9:343, 344; Allen C. Clark, "Joseph Gales, Jr.," *CHS* 23 (1920): 86–89.

7. Smith, *First Forty Years*, 94.

8. *DAB*, 9:318–19, 343–44.

9. Smith, *First Forty Years*, 29.

10. Foster, *Jeffersonian America*, 16; "Diary of Mrs. William Thornton," *CHS* 10 (1907): 91, 96–97, 99, 160, 176, 182; Downing, "James and Joanna Gould Barry," 48–49. In 1801 Congressman John Cotton Smith called the estates of Daniel Carroll of Duddington and Notley Young the only "two really comfortable habitations in all respects within the bounds of the city." Varnum, *Seat of Government of the United States*, 45–46.

11. "Diary of Mrs. William Thornton," 102, 104, 109, 111, 143, 146, 154, 157, 164, 166, 182–83, 201, 205–06, 209; James Dudley Morgan, "Robert Brent, First Mayor of Washington City," *CHS* 2 (1899): 236–37, 247; Smith, *First Forty Years*, 56.

12. Grassi, "Catholic Religion in the United States, " *WL* 11 (1882): 245.

13. Royall, *Sketches of History Life and Manners*, 182; Royall, *Letters from Alabama* (Washington, 1830), 199–200; Carter, *Latrobe Papers: Journals*, 3:69.

14. Smith, *First Forty Years*, 45, 53; "Diary of Mrs. William Thornton," 113, 114.

15. Ibid., 154, 222.

16. *BDML*, 2:507, 529; Carroll, *Papers*, 2:408, 3:430. In Bishop Carroll's branch of the family mixed marriages involved three of his nephews, William Brent (?–1786), Daniel Carroll Brent (1759–1814), and George Brent (1760–1803), who married Protestants Elizabeth J. Ambler, Ann Fenton Lee, and Molly Fitzhugh, respectively, and a cousin, Maria Digges, who married Protestant Congressman Robert Livingston of New York. Charles Carroll of Carrollton's only son, Charles Carroll of Homewood and his two surviving daughters, Mary and Catherine, all married Protestants. In the next generation all four of his granddaughters by Mary, who married Richard Caton of Baltimore, made interfaith marriages. (These included Elizabeth, Marianne, and Louisa Caton, known as "the three graces" for their great beauty; all three married British nobles.)

In addition, Charles Carroll of Belle Vue, brother to Daniel Carroll of Duddington, married Protestant Ann Sprigg; two of their sons and two of their daughters also had mixed marriages. Chief Justice Roger Brooke Taney's principal biographers have suggested that Anne Key and Taney may have made a pre-marital agreement that their children should be brought up in the faith of the parent of their own sex. Steiner describes this arrangement as "according to the rule of the day," and Robert McNamara, inclines to the same view. However, the author has found that within the limited sample of this study the faith of the mother was more often the determining factor. But the author would be the first to agree with McNamara that a thorough study remains to be done on this subject, which "given the delicacy of the subject . . . would probably be very difficult to research." *BDML* 1.197; Geiger, *Daniel Carroll II*, 300–01, and genealogical chart; Devanter, *Anywhere So Long As There Be Freedom*, 210, 214, 218, 221, 224, 231, 234, 242, 244, 250, 252, and genealogical charts; Carroll, *Papers*, 2:510, 514, 3:92; McNamara, "John Carroll and Interfaith Marriages," 28, 40–57. Carl Brent Swisher, *Roger B. Taney* (New York: Macmillan Company, 1935), 50; Bernard C. Steiner, *Life of Roger Brooke Taney* (1922; reprint, Westport, CT: Greenwood Press, 1970), 44.

17. Baptismal Registers, 1811–1816, 1819–1836; Marriage Register 1807–1852, St. Patrick's Church; Durkin, *William Matthews*, 37. James Ord completed his novitiate (see n. 45, Chapter 5,) and joined the Society of Jesus for the years 1806–1811. He then enlisted in the navy, but finally became an army officer. Ord married Rebecca Cresap; various of his children were baptized at St. Patrick's. Stephen Cassin appears in both the Trinity and St. Patrick's registers. For more on Ord see Curran, *Georgetown University*, 40, 343.

18. "Diary of Mrs. William Thornton," 129.

19. *National Intelligencer*, 25 March, 3 April 1801.

20. Bryan, *History*, 1:387ff, 399.

21. Proceedings, 5 February 1799, RDCC; *National Intelligencer*, 18 February 1800, 3 September 1802, 12 August 1808. Government property sales were often held at the Little Hotel, beginning in 1799. The *Intelligencer* issues cited above give typical announcements for assembly ball subscriptions and meetings of militia companies and volunteer fire brigades.

22. Dr. John Kearney, later a U.S. Navy surgeon, was an original member of James Hoban's Washington Artillery, one of the District's earliest volunteer militia companies. Its members were largely of Irish descent. His brother Colonel James Kearney, a topographical engineer with the U.S. Army, helped Hoban and his F Street friends organize the Union Fire Company in 1808 and later served as secretary of the Sons of Erin. Clotworthy Stephenson, also a neighbor of Hoban's, commanded another early militia company known as the Washington Grenadiers. Richard Forrest, a State Department clerk and another F Street neighbor, was the nephew of Georgetown's leading tobacco merchant, Colonel Uriah Forrest. The volunteer militia companies were chartered societies with a strong club-like character; their membership, especially their leaders, tended to be activists in the District's early affairs. After an act of Congress in 1802, the District's militia was organized into corps and regiments with commanding officers appointed by the President. Frederick R. Todd, "Militia and Volunteers of the District of Columbia, 1783–1820," *CHS* 50 (1948–50): 379–434; *Washington Directories*, 1822, 1834; *Centinel of Liberty*, 11 February 1800; *National Intelligencer*, 22 August 1804, 12 August 1808, 13 June 1810; Wilhelmus Bogart Bryan, "Sketch of Various Forms of Local Government in the District of Columbia; with a List of Washington City Officials," in *Celebration of the One Hundredth Anniversary of the Establishment of the District of Columbia*, H. Doc. 522 (Washington: Government Printing Office, 1901) [hereafter "Washington City Officials"], 298. Unless otherwise stated Bryan's list of city officials, the only compilation of its kind, serves as standard reference for all elected members of the Washington city council and some appointed municipal officials.

23. Bryan, "Washington City Officials," 286–87.

24. Bryan, *History*, 1:419–20; Eberlein and Hubbard, *Historic Houses of George-Town and Washington City*, 425–26.

25. *Washington Federalist*, 22, 25 March 1802; *National Intelligencer*, 24 March 1802. Other members of the committee were Benjamin Moore, Dr. Cornelius Coningham, and Thomas Tingey, commandant of the Navy Yard.

26. Bryan, *History*, 1:427–29, 441, 443–44, 494–95; Lee W. Formwalt, "Benjamin Henry Latrobe and the Development of Transportation in the District of Columbia," *CHS* 50 (1980): 48; *National Intelligencer*, 30 April 1802.

27. *Statutes at Large of the United States of America, Seventh Congress, Session I, Ch. 53*, ed. Richard Peters, 46 vols., (Boston: Charles C. Little and James Brown, 1845), 2:196, 197. Following the original models of Georgetown and Alexandria, the council members voted among themselves to elect five of their number to constitute a "second chamber," later the Board of Aldermen, while the remaining seven comprised the "first chamber," later the Common Council. Congress extended the two-year trial period to fifteen years in February 1804 and also freed the citizens of Washington from paying further taxes to the levy court of Washington County, which lay in the northern half of the District beyond the city line. (These county taxes had previously been used for county roads, bridges, and other public works of little direct interest to Washington City.) At the same time Congress changed the composition of the council to two chambers of nine men each, both popularly elected, and gave the council authority to "provide for the establishment and superintendence of public schools." Bryan, "Washington City Officials," 288; *Statutes at Large, Eighth Congress*, 1st sess., Ch. 15 (1804), 2:254–55.

28. Neither the mayor nor the council members received any pay for the first ten years of Washington's city government. Beginning in 1812 the mayor received a yearly salary of $400, and the council members, $2.00 per day when attending sessions. The mayor's salary was raised to $500 in 1813 by action of the council. Bryan, "Washington City Officials," 289.

29. Griffith Coombe was a property owner, builder, and general merchant associated with both Daniel Carroll of Duddington and James Barry. Thomas Herty appears in the records of both Trinity and, later, St. Patrick's Churches. Downing, "James and Joanna Gould Barry," 53. Baptismal Register, 1811–1816, St. Patrick's Church; Baptismal and Marriage Register, 1794–1805, HTA.

30. *National Intelligencer*, 7, 11, 12, 14, 27, 28 May 1802. Other members of Hoban's eight-man organizing committee included the Catholics Griffith Coombe and Thomas Herty. Robert Brent's east-side committee chose a ticket of James Barry, Daniel Brent of the State Department, George Blagden, Benjamin Moore, and Samuel H. Smith. The *Intelligencer* for May 7 carries typical notices from readers proposing candidates and an editorial expressing the conviction that "neither party nor local spirit will influence the selection." A May 28 *Intelligencer* editorial declared that "no part of the union is more exempt from party spirit; nor is there, perhaps, any part of the union in which social intercourse is less interrupted by a division of political statement." This proved generally to be true of subsequent local elections; "interruptions" did however occur during the partisan Jackson administration and later during the Know Nothing period, treated in a subsequent chapter. In the first municipal elections, the *Intelligencer* gave the party affiliation (Jeffersonian Republican or Federalist) of all candidates when publishing the results. It discontinued the practice in 1804 in an effort to keep national politics out of municipal affairs. *National Intelligencer*, 4 June 1804.

31. *National Intelligencer*, 16 June 1802; Bryan, "Washington City Officials," 298; Baptismal Register, 1795–1805, HTA; Baptismal Register, 1811–1816, St. Patrick's Church. The duties of the city Register may be found in the *Intelligencer* 23 July 1802 and, as they later evolved, in Delano's *Washington City Directory* of 1822. William and Susannah Hewitt are recorded at St. Patrick's as having a son, William Benjamin, baptized there in May 1814, but the author has been unable to find further verification. Notley Young's interment services were held at Georgetown's Trinity Church on March 25, 1802. His wife Mary Carroll Young, the Archbishop's sister, was also buried there; her gravestone is one of only two remaining in the original Trinity churchyard. *Washington Federalist*, 25 March 1802.

32. *National Intelligencer*, 23 May 1802; Bryan, *History*, 1:412; *BDML*, 2:510; *DAB*, 5:375. Holt, "Americans at St. Omers, Bruges and Liège," 245; The circuit court was established by act of Congress on 27 February 1801; its present-day equivalent is the Superior Court of the District of Columbia. The *DAB* entry errs in placing the date of Kilty's appointment as April 1801, by which time Adams was no longer in office. Kilty's brother John was also something of a literary figure and bibliophile. Both were among the founders of the Society of the Cincinnati.

33. William F. Carne, "Life and Times of William Cranch, Judge of the District Court, 1801–1805," *CHS* 5 (1902): 296–98. *BDML*, 1:258, 651.

34. *National Intelligencer*, 23, 25 March 1802; "Temporary Presidential Commissions, 1789–1901," 1:96; "Miscellaneous, Permanent and Temporary Presidential Commissions," March 26, 1801–November 7, 1812, vol. C, Record Group 346, NA; Dispatches from U.S. Consuls in Paris, 1790–1906, pari passim 1833–1841, Record Group 59, NA; Records of the D. C. Circuit Court, Record Group 21, NA; Frederick S. Calhoun, *The Lawmen: United States Marshals and Their Deputies* (Washington: Smithsonian Institution Press, 1989), 17–19. Daniel Carroll Brent, fourth son of Robert and Ann Carroll Brent of Woodstock, who served as the State Department's clerk, chief clerk, and consul to Paris, always signed his name Daniel Brent, as may be seen in the consular dispatches cited above. By contrast, Daniel Carroll Brent, the second son of William and Eleanor Carroll Brent of Richland, who served in the Virginia assembly and later as marshal of the District, signed his full name. Contemporary newspapers and other printed sources also usually made the same distinction. Nevertheless, the two are sometimes confused by local historians.

35. *National Intelligencer*, 4 June 1802; Bryan, *History*, 1:467; Morgan, "Robert Brent, First Mayor of Washington City," 235, 237.

36. Clark, "Mayoralty of Robert Brent," 270; Morgan, "Robert Brent, First Mayor of Washington City," 238; Jefferson to William Brent, Washington, 20 January 1804, Henry Hunt—William Chilton Collection, series 1, box 2, folder 5, GUA; Bryan, *History*, 1:455; Commissioners to William Brent, 19 December 1827, 5 January 1828, RDCC; Bryan, "Washington City Officials," 298, 303–06. William Brent was known as "Billy" to his family; official documents and other correspondence often refer to him as Colonel William Brent, in respect of his militia rank during the War of 1812. For a concise summary of his lengthy public service, see *Latrobe Papers*, 1:386n., 387.

37. *Annals of the Congress of the United States*, 7th Cong., 2d. sess. (Washington: Gales and Seaton 1851–), 486–90; William Tindall, *Origin and Government of the District of Columbia* (Washington: Government Printing Office, 1908), 77–78; Bryan, *History*, 1:440.

38. Seale, *President's House*, 1:91, 93; Goode, *Capital Losses*, 288, 296; Walker, "High Art of George Hadfield," 78.

39. "District of Columbia-City Council Proceedings 1803–1804," Manuscript Division, LC.

40. Bryan, "Hotels of Washington Prior to 1814," *CHS* 7 (1904): 82–91; Goode, *Capital Losses* 163–64, 167–68, 173; George Gibbs, ed., *Memoirs of the Administration of Washington and John Adams, Edited from the Papers of Oliver Wolcott, Secretary of the Treasury*, 2 vols. (New York: William Van Norden, 1846), 2:377; William Parker Cutler and Julia Perkins Cutler, *Life, Journals and Correspondence of Reverend Manasseh Cutler, LL.D.*, 2 vols. (1888; reprint, Athens, OH: Ohio University Press, 1987), 2:51–52, 143; Washington Topham, "Centre Market and Vicinity," *CHS* 26 (1924): 2, 7–11; Clark, "Mayoralty of Robert Brent," 273, 276–77, 294–95; *National Intelligencer*, 16 September 1803 and 7 September 1804; "Dr. Mitchill's Letters from Washington, 1801–1813," *Harper's New Monthly Magazine*, April 1879, 746–47. William Brent was treasurer and Hoban and Stephenson the supervisors of construction for the Centre Market. Robert Brent and Daniel Carroll of Duddington were original board members and directors of the Washington Theater Company; Herty served as its secretary. Gilbert Stuart was in Washington from 1803 to 1805. Rev. Cutler, a noted botanist and polymath, was a Congressman from Hamilton, Massachusetts; "Dr. Mitchill" was Dr. Samuel Latham Mitchill, congressman and later senator from Hempstead, New York.

41. Tindall, *Origins of Government*, 78; *Annals of Congress*, 8th Cong., 2d sess., 1804–1805, 864, 874–982.

42. Gibbs, *Memoirs of the Administration of Washington and John Adams*, 2:377.

43. *National Intelligencer*, 1 June 1803; Clark, *Mayoralty of Robert Brent*, 283–84; Green, *Washington*, 1:42.

44. *National Intelligencer*, 23 January 1805; Bryan, *History*, 1:541.

45. Charles Moore, ed., *Joint Select Committee to Investigate the Charities and Reformatory Institutions in the District of Columbia; Part III Historical Sketches* (Washington: Government Printing Office, 1898), 2, 3, 7; Bryan, *History*, 1:541–43; Green, *Washington*, 1:42.

46. Bryan, *History*, 1:475–84; Clark, "Mayoralty of Robert Brent," 287–90; *National Intelligencer*, 27 September 1805; Green, *Washington*, 1: 42–44; Durkin, *William Matthews*, 58–59, 63–65. The same act of Congress (February 24, 1804) that authorized the city to establish and superintend its public schools also extended the trial period for Washington's city government for another fifteen years. The idea of a national university was first advanced by President Washington and championed by Commissioner Thornton and Samuel Blodget.

47. Bryan, "Washington City Officials," 299–306. Only the journal of the first (1802–3) council is preserved, in the Library of Congress. The ordinances of all councils were printed annually.

48. Ibid., 298–303; Carroll, *Papers*, 2:363; Rev. John McElroy to Rev. Mr. Carey, 4 May 1815, 204 H 4, MPA; *National Intelligencer*, 22 August 1804, 13 June 1810, 17 September 1812; *Memorial of the Inhabitants of the District of Columbia Praying for the Gradual Abolition of Slavery in the District of Columbia*, H. Doc. 140, 23rd Cong., 2d sess., 1828. An undated account in the DCD Papers reads as follows:

St. Mary's Church   Dt. to James Barry
1806 June 12 paid for corner inscription and stones $17.38
July 8 paid Jas. Hoban, plan & attendg. building $70.00
July 8 paid G. Coombs bill of building church $820.00

There are no records concerning Hoban's role in the novitiate building other than the McElroy letter of May of 1815 cited above. The building was finished by spring 1817. Since Hoban was much occupied during this period with the rebuilding of war-damaged Federal structures, he probably only drew the plans. Durkin, *William Matthews*, 83–84.

49. Kennedy, *Architecture, Men, Women, and Money*, 218–20; Walker, "High Art of George Hadfield," 76–78; Maria Cosway's letter to Jefferson, 20 July 1801, is quoted in Helen Claire Bullock, *My Head and My Heart: A Little History of Thomas Jefferson and Maria Cosway* (New York: G.P. Putnam's Sons, 1945), 153. Maria's concern about Catholics in America may have been prompted by exaggerated reports of sectarianism in the 1801 presidential campaign.

50. *Daily National Journal*, 7 February 1826; Goode, *Capital Losses*, 288–89, 296; Bryan, *History*, 1:517, 2:5, 6; *DAB*, 4:76, 77; Walker, "High Art of George Hadfield," 78; Junior League, *Illustrated History*, 99, 307. Inaugural balls for Presidents Jackson, Van Buren and Tyler were held at the Assembly Rooms, and such well-known actors and actresses as Charles and Fanny Kemble and Edwin Booth performed there. The Carusis eventually married into the family of the naval hero and Trinity parishioner, Commodore Stephen Cassin. Mrs. Eugene Carusi, conversation with author, September 1987.

51. Kennedy, *Architecture, Men, Women, and Money*, 205–11. Consentino and Glassie, *Capital Image*, 56–57.

52. William Tindall, "Homes of the Local Government," *CHS* 3 (1900): 279–81; Bryan, *History*, 2:79–81; *American Commercial and Daily Advertiser*, 18 July 1820; *National Intelligencer*, 22 August 1820. The "Town House or City Hall" lottery was first authorized by the council in 1818; the ordinance of February 23, 1815 cited by Tindall authorized lottery managers and further implementation of the ordinance of 1818.

53. Walker, *High Art of George Hadfield*, 81. One of Hadfield's principal design elements, a dome above the central rotunda, was not retained. The city council moved into one wing of the City Hall well before completion; the circuit court subsequently occupied the other.

54. Latrobe to Col. William Tatham, 5 February 1810, *Latrobe Papers*, 2:836.

55. "Accounts of Divisions with Original Proprietors," Record Group 42, NA. The "accounts" list the sale of thirty lots for $7,647.27, with purchasers required to make a down payment of twenty-five percent, during four days in October 1791. These figures do not include lots said to have been purchased by the commissioners.

NOTES TO CHAPTER 9

1. Downing, "James and Joanna Gould Barry," 45; Bryan, *History*, 1:247, 434.

2. Downing, "James and Joanna Gould Barry," 47–48; Richard Mannix, "Albert Gallatin in Washington," *CHS* 48 (1971–72): 63; Allen C. Clark, *Greenleaf and Law in the Federal City* (Washington: W.F. Roberts, 1901), 245–46, 257; Bryan, *History*, 1:434, 525.

3. Clark, "Mayoralty of Robert Brent," 273–75; Bryan, *History*, 1:528–30; Downing, "James and Joanna Gould Barry," 45, 51.

4. Green, *Washington*, 36; Bryan, *History*, 1:526.

5. "Accounts of Divisions with Original Proprietors," Record Group 42, NA; Young, *The Washington Community*, 20. The "Accounts" list the sale of only eight privately held lots as against more than two hundred sold by the government during the period 1791–1795. Young's and other estimates of the early property sales are just that, since the records of the accounts are unfortunately not complete.

6. Robert Brent and Marsham Waring were directors of the Bank of Columbia. Chartered in December 1793, it was Georgetown's first and met for many years in Semmes Tavern. Adam King was one of the original subscribers to the Union Bank of Georgetown, founded in 1809 at the Union Tavern. Serving on the board of directors of the National Bank of Washington were Robert Sewall, Robert Brent, and Griffith Coombe; Daniel Carroll of Duddington was its founding president. William Brent and James D. Barry were board members of the Washington branch of the Bank of the United States, founded in 1801. Robert Brent was also president of the Patriotic Bank of Washington, established in 1815, and Daniel Carroll of Duddington was its major investor. Charles E. Howe, "The Financial Institutions of Washington City in Its Early Days," *CHS* 8 (1905): 10, 11, 21, 23, 29, 31; Fred A. Amory, "Banks and Bankers in the District of Columbia," *CHS* 46–47 (1944–45): 273–74.

7. Kate Mason Rowland, *Life and Correspondence of Charles Carroll of Carrollton*, 2 vols. (New York: G.P. Putnam's Sons, 1898), 1:106; Van Devanter, "*Anywhere So Long As There Be Freedom*," 220, Genealogical Charts I and III.

8. Charles Carroll of Carrollton to Captain Ignatius Fenwick, 13 May 1782, DCD Papers. In his letter to Fenwick, Carroll repeats what he had written the London factors, Wallace, Johnson, and Muir, asking them to take his cousin, Daniel, then eighteen years of age, to be "bound over to you for 3 years." Captain Ignatius Fenwick (?–1796), the second husband of Daniel's mother, Mary Hill, was Daniel's guardian and most dutiful adviser. He is the same Ignatius Fenwick who served as Trinity Church's first fund-raiser, not to be confused with Colonel Ignatius Fenwick (?–1784) of Wallingford, St. Mary's County.

9. Daniel Carroll of Duddington [hereafter DCD] to Captain Ignatius Fenwick, 2 October 1785, DCD Papers.

10. Ibid. Fenwick must have had some prior misgivings about Charles' temperament and ability. In his first letter to Daniel abroad, before he had heard anything of his brother's departure from Liège, Fenwick urged Daniel to speak with the Rector there and also "a Mr. Mattingly [Rev. John] and a Mr. Neale [Rev. Francis Xavier] with whom I have corresponded . . . [and] beg of them to inform you of all Charles' little foibles, and take some pains in talking with him yourself." Daniel eventually caught up with his wayward brother at Bornheim in Germany and apparently persuaded him to continue his studies at a Dominican academy there. Charles returned to the United States in February of 1787, after enduring a shipwreck in Ocracoke Inlet, North Carolina. He remained a thorn in his older brother's side through bad investments and land speculation, especially in western Maryland, upstate New York, and Missouri. Fenwick to DCD, 7 August 1785, 1 April 1787, DCD Papers.

11. Charles Carroll of Carrollton to DCD, 13 March 1787, in Rowland, *Life and Correspondence*, 2:104–05. Daniel subsequently married Anne Brent, daughter of William and Eleanor Carroll Brent of Richland.

12. Charles Carroll of Carrollton to DCD, 12 January 1799; "Agreement Between Notley Young and Daniel Carroll of Duddington," 19 May 1789, recorded at clerk's office, Prince George's County, 26 May 1789; Fenwick to DCD, 1 April 1789, DCD Papers. The "agreement" was contingent on a resurvey and re-examination of titles dating back to prior owners Thomas Jenkins and William Pierce.

13. "Daniel Carroll's Case," Commissioners' report to Washington, 8 January 1792; Commissioners to Washington, 25 November 1791; Commissioners to L'Enfant, 26 November 1791, Commissioners to Jefferson, 8 December 1791, Letters Sent, RDCC; Washington to DCD, 28 November, 2 December 1791, *Writings of Washington*, 31:429–30; L'Enfant to Commissioners, 21 November 1791, Letters Received, RDCC. In time President Washington became more concerned about the dates survey lines were run and when, how, and by whom Carroll and the commissioners were notified of L'Enfant's intentions. These lines of investigation ultimately led him to turn the dispute over to the Attorney General. Washington to Commissioners, 27 December 1791, Letters Received, RDCC.

14. Washington to L'Enfant, 28 November, 2 December 1791, *Writings of Washington*, 31:419–23; Commissioners to President Washington, 21 December 1791, forwarding memorial of same date from Georgetown proprietors to commissioners, Letters Sent, RDCC; Bryan, *History*, 1:179. Other of the memorial signatories were Overton Carr, P.R. Fendall (by Uriah Forrest), George Walker, Samuel Davidson, David Burnes, and William Prout (by Overton Carr). The commissioners' covering letter to the President expressed surprise that Uriah Forrest had signed the memorial, since he had previously professed himself to be displeased and alarmed at the way in which L'Enfant had acted independently of the commissioners. The commissioners somewhat cryptically concluded: "We have since reason to think that he [Forrest] has been the chief promoter of it." Promoter of what, the researcher is tempted to ask? Whether the commissioners were referring simply to Forrest's role in writing the memorial or possibly as the promoter of the L'Enfant-Carroll dispute in general is an interesting question. Whatever the answer, Forrest seems to have been designated by the group to placate L'Enfant following the latter's dismissal. See, for example, Forrest to L'Enfant, 21 March, 27 April 1792, Digges, L'Enfant, Morgan Family Papers, Manuscript Division, LC.

15. Washington to Commissioner David Stuart, 20 November 1791, Washington to Commissioners, 1 December 1791, *Writings of Washington,* 31:419–23, 430–34; Ellicott to Commissioners, 10 December 1791, L'Enfant to Commissioners, 6 December 1791, Letters Received, RDCC; "Daniel Carroll's Case," Commissioners report to Washington, 8 January 1792, Letters Sent, RDCC. Interpretations of the L'Enfant-Carroll confrontation are many and various. Among secondary sources see Elizabeth S. Kite, *L'Enfant and Washington* (Baltimore: Johns Hopkins Press and *Institut Francais de Washington,* 1929, with an introduction by Ambassador J.J. Jusserand) for the work of L'Enfant's chief apologist, notable for its omissions. H. Paul Caemmerer's *Life of Pierre L'Enfant* (Washington: National Republic Publishing Company, 1950) depends largely on Kite. Bryan's *History of the National Capital,* 1:166–69, 173–80, gives a brief and more balanced account. Among the primary sources cited above, Washington to Stuart, 20 November, best illustrates the President's great disappointment over L'Enfant's failure to provide the printed street map, likening the position of prospective lot purchasers as having to buy "A Pig in a Poke." L'Enfant to the commissioners of 6 December is the planner's lengthy defense of his actions. "Daniel Carroll's Case," or the commissioners' report of 8 January, is the most significant of the primary documents, based as it is on testimony from witnesses and supporting documents. In the Ellicott-Commissioners' correspondence, it is interesting to note that because L'Enfant made his claim of obstruction of government property to include a square in the diagonal avenue in question (the proposed New Jersey Avenue), the commissioners wrote to Ellicott after the destruction requesting surveyed locations of the square vis-à-vis the foundations of Carroll's house. Ellicott replied that that particular survey had not yet been done and would not be completed until the following spring. (Ellicott to Commissioners, 10 December 1791.) It should also be noted that Commissioner Daniel Carroll of Upper Marlboro stated that he would not act with the Board of Commissioners in the proceedings because of his relationship (uncle by virtue of his marriage to his cousin, Eleanor Caroll) to Daniel Carroll of Duddington. He would, however, "appear as an evidence, not as a commissioner," if the other commissioners so approved. "Daniel's Carroll's Case," 8 January.

16. L'Enfant to Commissioners, 22 December 1791, Digges, L'Enfant, Morgan Family papers, LC; Eberlein and Hubbard, *Historic Houses,* 400–01; Notley Young to Commissioners, 7 January 1792, Letters Received, RDCC; Washington to L'Enfant, 28 February 1792, *Writings of Washington,* 31:488–89. In the end, L'Enfant's insistence that the commissioners be replaced or that he be allowed to act independently was the principal factor leading to his dismissal. But his representations to Notley Young did not go unnoticed. It is not known if L'Enfant's December 22 letter to the commissioners was actually received by them. (The copy in the L'Enfant papers is a draft.) In any case two weeks later Young complained to the commissioners that L'Enfant had informed him that his house was an obstruction, even though Ellicott said otherwise, just as was the case with DCD. Notley Young to Commissioners, 7 January 1792, Letters Received, RDCC.

17. Proceedings, 4 June 1792, RDCC; Eberlein and Hubbard, *Historic Houses,* 392–93. No documentary evidence has been found on Latrobe's possible role in rebuilding Duddington Manor, although the conjecture appears in some historical accounts. There is no doubt, however, that Carroll and Latrobe were good friends and had some business association. See, for example, Latrobe to DCD, 20 September 1813, DCD Papers.

18. Bryan, *History,* 1:167n., 214–21; Green, *Washington* 1:15. The syndicate is more commonly referred to as the Greenleaf and Morris, or Greenleaf, Morris, and Nicholson syndicate. For convenience the names of all the major figures involved are included.

19. "Agreement with James Greenleaf," 26 September 1793, DCD Papers, Eberlein and Hubbard, *Historic Houses*, 396–97; Clark, *Greenleaf and Law*, 124–25, 179–80. Although the copy of the Greenleaf agreement in the DCD Papers obliges Greenleaf only to build "brick houses" of the stated dimensions, a copy used in a subsequent court case against Carroll required that he "erect a good *brick house* on each lot." Pratt, Francis, and Others vs. Daniel Carroll of Duddington, "Appeal from the Decree of the Circuit Court of the District of Columbia for the County of Washington Sitting in Chancery," (?) 1804, DCD Papers.

20. Clark, *Greenleaf and Law*, 125–27, 134, 140; Eberlein and Hubbard, *Historic Houses*, 396–97; Bryan, *History*, 280. The agreement as amended permitted the houses to be of any dimensions, including height, as long as they covered the same amount of ground. Clark, as well as Eberlein and Hubbard, have it that six of the buildings were completed. Bryan states that none was ever finished.

21. Bryan, *History*, 1:298, 321; Robert Morris to Governor Thomas Sim Lee, Philadelphia, 18 August 1793; SCM 2361/2364, 1006–44, HLC Papers. Nicholson died in prison. Greenleaf was released after one year, while Robert Morris, whose notes were once used as currency during the Revolution's fiscal crisis, endured three and a half years of debtor's prison. He died on May 7, 1806, five years after gaining his freedom.

22. DCD to James Greenleaf, (?) October 1795, quoted in Eberlein and Hubbard, *Historic Houses*, 397; Richard Brent to DCD, 16 August 1791, 16 March 1792, "A List of Bonds Belonging to Danl. Carroll of Dudd. Esq.," 27 March 1791, William Hammond to DCD, 25 April 1793, DCD Papers.

23. "Daniel Carroll of Duddington in account with the Commissioners of the Federal Buildings," 20 March 1800, DCD Papers. By their own account the District Commissioners had appropriated 248 acres and 24 perches [one square perch = 1/100th of an acre] of Carroll's land for public use and owed him $16,543, plus $5,707 in interest accumulated since June 21, 1794. The commissioners' account was apparently sent with a covering note by William Brent ("Enclosed is a copy of your account with the Commissioners, which during this gloomy weather, you will have the more leisure to pursue. . . ."), undated and in a separate file in the DCD Papers.

24. Ibid., Charles Carroll of Carrollton to DCD, 18 November 1793, 26 October 1797, 11 September 1805, DCD Papers. In 1793 Charles Carroll complained that he, too, had met with "such disappointments in the receipt of monies," that it was simply not in his power to loan any more. He refused Daniel's request for $5,000 in 1805 giving much the same reason.

25. For Carroll's purchases and exchanges see Proceedings for 30 January, 19 March, 21 March, 3 September 1799, 27 January, 15 February and 10 March 1800, RDCC. For Barry see 20 November 1798, 26 March, 29 August, 12 November 1799. For the price range of lots sold at the auctions of 1791 and 1792, see "Accounts or Divisions with Original Proprietors," Record Group 42, NA. Barry continued to purchase more property in the years immediately following the turn of the century.

26. Bryan, *History*, 1:433, 444; Bryan, "Hotels of Washington Prior to 1814," 80–83; Holmes, "City Tavern," 11, 18, 25; Articles of Agreement between Daniel Carroll of Duddington and Nicholas L. Queen, 19 December 1815, DCD Papers, Bennett Fenwick and later his widow were the proprietors of the Little Hotel-Rhodes Tavern, which saw a number of management turnovers. After his tenancy at the Indian King (City Tavern) in Georgetown, Joseph Semmes leased the Rhodes Hotel from 1804 to 1807. Nicholas L. Queen, a city councilman and member of the Queens Chapel family (see Chapter 5), rented what was formerly Stelle's Tavern on Carroll Row from Daniel Carroll of Duddington at $1,000 a year.

27. Clark, *Greenleaf and Law*, 188–93. The author is unable to verify Clark's contention that Greenleaf managed to have the trial conducted in Alexandria because there was "no reasonable prospect of unprejudiced hearing in Washington." It is more likely that the rotating circuit court of the District held its scheduled session there at the time. Judge Cranch, a nephew of Abigail Adams, came to Washington from Massachusetts in 1794 to serve as Greenleaf's financial agent. He married Greenleaf's sister the following year and was appointed chief justice of the circuit court in 1806.

28. Proceedings of the General Meetings of the Potomac Company, May 17, 1785—August 1, 1796, Letter Book "A"; Clark, "Mayoralty of Robert Brent," 293–94; Lee W. Formwalt, "Benjamin Henry Latrobe and the Development of Transportation in the District of Columbia, 1802–1817," *CHS* 50 (1980): 39–40, 48; Bryan, *History*, 1:506–07. Other Catholics on the board of the Washington Assembly were Mayor Robert and William Brent. The Brent brothers were also directors of the Washington Theater Company, and Thomas Herty was its secretary. Clark, "The Mayoralty of Robert Brent," 293–94.

29. Petition of the President and Directors of the Bank of Washington to the United States Senate and House of Representatives for a charter, unsigned draft, December 1809, Record of meeting, Bank of Washington, Tomlinson's Hotel, 3 January 1814, DCD Papers; Howe, "Financial Institutions of Washington," 17–21; Bryan, *History*, 1:535–36; William Yowell, "Historical Highlights of Washington's Oldest Bank," *CHS* 43 (1957–59): 60–62. Carroll resigned from the presidency of the Bank of Washington in September of 1819. Frances Corbin to DCD, 20 September 1819, DCD Papers.

30. Formwalt, "Latrobe and the Development of Transportation," 41–46. Coombe, along with Latrobe and Joseph Forrest, a nephew of Georgetown's Colonel Uriah Forrest, was one of three commissioners charged with laying out the turnpike routes.

31. Ibid., 46–51; Green, *Washington*, 1:28–29; Junior League, *City of Washington*, 122; Bryan, *History*, 1:497–98; Anonymous (attributed to Thomas Law), *Observations on the Intended Canal in Washington City* (Washington, 1804), reprinted in *CHS* 8 (1905): 159–68. See Chapter 5, n. 19, for causes of the Potomac Company's low volume of traffic. In order to pass through the locks at Great Falls, the Potomac Company's barges and rafts had to have beams of seven feet or less. Loaded down, they were unstable and subject to capsize on the broader waters of the Potomac below Georgetown as they attempted to reach Washington Harbor, or the Eastern Branch east of Greenleaf Point, where deeper draft vessels usually anchored. ("The boatmen, I understand, positively refuse to go around Turkey Buzzard's [Greenleaf] Point," Thomas Law wrote to Carroll in his proposal for the canal, Law to DCD, n.d., probably 1806, DCD Papers.) For ocean-going ships the problem was just the opposite. The ship channel upstream to Georgetown was silting up so much that the larger sailing vessels were unloading part or all of their cargo at Alexandria. Ideally, given sufficient commerce, the Washington Canal would have helped solve both these problems.

32. Formwalt, "Latrobe and the Development of Transportation," 55–61; Green, *Washington*, 1: 134–35; Report of the Board of Health, September 18, 1832, printed in *National Intelligencer*, 20 September 1832. Formwalt's article gives a good synthesis of the restrictions placed on Latrobe, against his professional judgment, that led to the technical failures of the canal. The citizen movement to drain the canal began in the 1820s, but was long delayed by Congress' refusal to approve funds for this purpose. The canal was not fully drained until after the Civil War and parts were not filled in until early in this century.

33. *Annals of the Congress of the United States, Twelfth Congress, 1st Session, 1811–1812* (Washington: Gales and Seaton, 1854), 2:2290; Bryan, *History*, 1:469–70; Bryan, "Washington City Officials," 301; Joseph King to DCD, House of Representatives, Washington, 1 February 1820, DCD to Mayor William A. Bradley, Washington, 9 January 1836, DCD Papers. Carroll's property assessments were constantly being increased by the Washington city government, with whom he had long-standing arguments about the use of unimproved property, well before the act of May 4, 1812. In 1810, for example, he complained to the city's Board of Appeals that one of his 1808 assessments of

$190,285 was increased to $348,250 in 1809, for the identical property. "Is there any reason for this unheard of increase, or is it possible in the whole world, except in this place, men could be found who would lay such a valuation on a drear waste?" protested Carroll. The act of May 12 gave the original proprietors two years following the public sale of their property in which to buy it back at the price of the taxes due, plus ten percent interest per year and the costs of advertising the sale. The War of 1812 and the rebuilding of the city, in addition to Carroll's efforts, apparently delayed any application of the act's seizure provision. But by 1829, if not earlier, some of his lands were advertised for sale in default of taxes. In September of that year, William Seaton and Joseph Gales, Jr., publishers of the *Intelligencer*, sent Carroll a considerate note expressing their anxiety at having to print the public notice and hoping somehow he could avoid the sheriff's order. Later, some of Carroll's property in Baltimore County was similarly seized and sold for taxes. DCD to Board of Appeals for Washington City, 28 November 1810; Gales and Seaton to DCD, 21 September 1829; John S. Gittings to DCD, 4 January 1835; John Merryman to DCD, 16 June 1830; DCD Papers.

34. John Mason to DCD, Bank of Columbia, 18 June 1819; President, Bank of the United States to Charles Carroll of Bellevue and Daniel Carroll of Duddington, Esq., Washington, 8 September 1819; Thirty-day promissory note, Office of Discount and Deposit, Washington, H. Carroll to DCD, 8 September 1818, assumed by DCD in October 1819; Charles Carroll of Carrollton to DCD, 9 January 1820; DCD to Charles Carroll of Carrollton, 15 January 1820; Bank of Washington to DCD (?) 1835; DCD Papers. Clark "Daniel Carroll of Duddington," 35. Carroll's loans to his family represented only a small part of his banking transactions. Obviously the many unrecovered family loans (the text gives but a sampling) caused Carroll the greatest distress and were certainly a factor in his disillusionment and gradual withdrawal from public service. A full study of Carroll's voluminous financial papers at the Library of Congress represents a major research project, yet to be undertaken.

35. Richard Caton to DCD, 11 May 1829; DCD to Caton, 18 May, 29 May, 1829; draft of newspaper advertisement in Carroll's hand, March 1824, DCD Papers.

36. DCD to Henry J. Brent, 24 July 1837, DCD Papers.

37. Eberlein and Hubbard, *Historic Houses*, 398–99; Baptismal Registers, 1811–1816, 1819–1836, St. Patrick's Church; Rev. Robert J. McNamara, S.J., Rochester, NY, to author, April 9, 1991; Clark, "Daniel Carroll of Duddington," 34; Bryan, *History*, 2:189. Carroll first married Anne Brent (1768–1805), a daughter of William and Eleanor Carroll Brent of Richland, by whom he had one daughter, Norah, who married William Dudley Digges of Warburton and Green Hill, and a son, Charles, who died in his youth. Carroll's second wife was Ann Rebecca Boyce, who gave him his remaining daughters. On St. Mary's see Chapter 6, n. 22, and Chapter 8, n. 47.

38. Latrobe to DCD, 20 September 1815, DCD Papers; Green, *Washington*, 1:51; Eberlein and Hubbard, *Historic Houses*, 398–99.

39. Quoted in Clark, "Daniel Carroll of Duddington," 45.

40. *National Intelligencer*, 15 May 1849.

41. Walter Lord, *The Dawn's Early Light* (New York: W.W. Norton & Co., 1972), 19–20.

42. John Lucas to Stephen Dubuisson, 25 July 1834, 57 M 1, MPA; Theodore Roosevelt, *The Naval War of 1812*, 2 vols. (New York: G. B. Putnam's Sons, 1910), 2:132; *National Cyclopedia of American Biography*, 13:263. When forming a new choir Lucas told Dubuisson he would not "admit any of the young *Beaux* who with Commodore Cassin himself used to scandalize the congregation." Roosevelt describes Cassin's actions aboard the *Ticonderoga* as a key factor in the battle's outcome. Cassin later distinguished himself in routing pirate ships and resorts in Florida and the West Indies. He was promoted to commodore in 1830.

43. Frederick Todd, "The Militia and Volunteers of the District of Columbia," *CHS* 50 (1948): 379–80, 385, 388, 393, 401–02, 410–11, 426–27, 429, 431–433; Selden Marvin Ely, "The District of Columbia in the American Revolution and Patriots of the Revolutionary Period Who Are Interred in the District or in Arlington," *CHS* 21 (1918): 147–48. Todd's work provides general background on the origins and differences of the volunteer companies and the enrolled militia, as well as the composition of the Washington area companies, to the degree that fragmentary records permit. Daniel Carroll Brent was a lieutenant colonel in the Columbian Brigade from 1802 to 1804, if not longer. William Brent began as a captain of the Washington Light Horse Company in 1807 and was colonel of the 2nd Regiment of the First Columbia Brigade by the outbreak of hostilities. As mentioned earlier James Hoban founded the Washington Artillery Company, which Todd describes as composed mainly of Irish American volunteers, as early as 1796. In 1808 its command changed from Hoban to Benjamin Burch, who remained in charge throughout the war. Adam King of Georgetown, although himself a volunteer, was made a major in command of the first Regiment of the Columbia Division, which was a unit of enrolled militia encamped to guard the President's House. Joseph Cassin was the younger brother of Commodore Stephen. He was long a Washington alderman and later joined the Navy, dying aboard the U.S.S. *Porpoise* at Pensacola, Florida, in 1821. Bryan, "Washington City Officials"; Frances Flaherty-Knox to author, 4 February 1988.

44. Lord, *Dawn's Early Light*, 62, 93–94, 104–05, 114, 128–29, 135–38; Martin Kenneth Gordon, "The Military of the District of Columbia," Ph.D. diss., George Washington, University, 1975, 340–42.

45. Robin Reilly, *The British at the Gates: The New Orleans Campaign in the War of 1812* (New York: G.P. Putnam's Sons, 1974), 148–49. McElroy Diaries, 29 August 1814; Durkin, *William Matthews*, 16.

46. Lord, *Dawn's Early Light*, 196–97; Smith, *First Forty Years*, 101. Fort Warburton was blown up because the American commander mistakenly thought he was being attacked both by land and water when the British fleet, long delayed by contrary winds, arrived there the same day President Madison was re-entering Washington. The explosion is said to have rattled windows in the city, twelve miles up the river.

47. George Hadfield, "Report to the Commissioners," 13 October 1814, Letters Received, RDCC.

48. *Annals of the Congress, Thirteenth Congress-3rd Session*, 1814–1815, 3:311–12, 342–346, 375, 395; Resolution by the Board of Alderman and Board of Common Council of the Corporation of Georgetown, September 28, 1814, reprinted in *National Intelligencer*, 5 October 1814; Most of the resolutions and the Committee bill reported to the House spoke of "temporary" removal, but the tenor of the debate and various amendments make it clear that the definitive choice of another site was the ultimate goal. On September 30, or two days after the Georgetown Corporation's offer of the college to Congress, Archbishop Carroll wrote to the college's president, Father John Grassi, advancing some reasons why he doubted the government would accept the offer, but also advising him that "if a decision should be formally called for, the Trustees must be called to determine on the answer." Carroll, *Papers*, 3:297.

49. *Philadelphia True American*, quoted in *National Intelligencer*, 13 October 1814; Bryan, *History*, 1:630; Hadfield, "Report to the Commissioners." In the final House vote (see n. 50 below) the New York, New England, Pennsylvania, and New Jersey delegations produced large blocs for removal, while the southern and western states, with the exception of Kentucky, were almost solidly against it. By party the Federalists voted 44 for removal and 9 against; the Republicans, 30 for removal and 74 against. *National Intelligencer*, 18 October 1814.

50. *Annals of Congress, Thirteenth Congress-3rd Session*, 1814–1815, 3:387–96; *National Intelligencer*, 18 October 1814; Bryan, *History*, 1: 635n. Bryan incorrectly tran-

278   scribed the final House vote from the *Intelligencer*'s report as 83 to 54. Constance McLaughlin Green, James Goode, and others have repeated or magnified the error (Green, *Washington*, 1:65; Goode, *Capital Losses*, 291). Both the *Annals* and the *Intelligencer* record the vote of each member and give the result as 83 to 74. See also Tindall, *Origin and Government of the District of Columbia*, 80, for an interesting commentary on the sectional character of the vote.

51. *Annals of Congress, Thirteenth Congress-3rd Session*, 1814–1815, 3:216–223, 1122, 1131–1142.

52. Seale, *The President's House*, 1:139–41.

53. Bryan, *History*, 1:631–32; Goode, *Capital Losses*, 161, 291; *Annals of Congress, Thirteenth Congress-3rd Session*, 1814–1815, 3:353–54.

54. Goode, *Capital Losses*, 290–92; Bryan, *History*, 1:637, 2:33. Bryan sets the cost at $25,000, of which sum $5,000 was provided by the Congress for interior fittings. From contemporary comments, there is little doubt that the building put a halt to any dissatisfaction by Congress. The building was subsequently used as a temporary school following the closing of the Washington Catholic Seminary, a boarding house for congressmen, the home of the Circuit Court, the notorious Capitol Prison during the Civil War, and, finally, conversion into town houses. Bryan, *History*, 2:40, 81.

55. Bryan, *History*, 1:637; DCD, Thomas Law, and Frederick May to the Commissioners, ? May 1815. The date may be established as early May since Law sent a copy of the letter to President James Madison with a covering letter dated 7 May 1815 (see James Madison Papers, vol. 59, 1815, Manuscript Division, LC). Carroll and Law took the lead in petitioning the commissioners and President Monroe for approval of the temporary capitol plan. They, along with Frederick May, were appointed as a committee to this purpose "at a general meeting of citizens held on Capitol Hill" (Clark *Greenleaf and Law*, 293–94). Carroll purchased stock to the value of $2,000; Thomas Law, $1,500. The next highest shareholders were Griffith Coombe and William Brent. The Brick Capitol was the largest privately constructed building in Washington in its time and also set a record for speed of development and construction, from stock subscription and cornerstone laying to occupancy by Congress in seven-and-a-half months.

56. *Annals of Congress, Sixteenth Congress-1st Session*, 1819–1820, 1:878. Many other proposals to relocate, including a bill to move the capital to Fort Leavenworth, surfaced again after the Civil War while Washington was still suffering the scars of the conflict. Prominent among these was Illinois Congressman John Logan's campaign for St. Louis in 1869, which gained some momentum from press support led by Horace Greely in the New York Tribune. But Congress was largely indifferent to the various proposals and President Grant insisted that any move would require a constitutional amendment. Bowling, *The Creation of Washington*, 244; Bryan, *History* 2:565.

NOTES TO CHAPTER 10

1. Bishop Benedict Fenwick to Rev. Mother Superior of the Ursulines, Boston, 10 February 1837, in *U.S. Catholic Historical Society Historical Records and Studies* 9 (June 1916): 187–90; Hennesey, *American Catholics*, 121–22.

2. Hennesey, *American Catholics*, 122–24; Ray Allen Billington, *The Protestant Crusade, 1800–1860* (1938; reprint, New York: Rinehart, 1952), 220–30; Rev. James Ryder to John McElroy, Georgetown College, 12 May 1844, 214 M 4, MPA.

3. Dolan, *The American Catholic Experience*, 128–30, 160–61; Green, *Washington*, 1:183.

4. Charles van Quickenborne to Colleagues Abroad, 16 January 1818, *WL* 30 (1901): 87. Van Quickenborne would later form part of the first Jesuit mission to Missouri. Bangert, *History of the Society of Jesus*, 480.

5. McElroy Diaries, 25, 26 July 1817, 2 February 1819, 2 February 1820, Sister Laurita Gibson, *Some Anglo-American Converts to Catholicism Prior to 1829* (Washington: The Catholic University of America, 1943), 206–09, 211–12; Rev. Hudson Mitchell, S.J., "Virgil Horace Barber," *WL* 79 (1950): 303–11, 321–28.

6. Gibson, *Some Anglo-American Converts*, 209, 211–17; Eleanore C. Sullivan, *Georgetown Visitation Since 1779* (Baltimore: French-Bray Printing Company, 1975), 84–86; *NCE*, 2:90; Mitchell, "Virgil Horace Barber," 321, 325–27; 313–15, 318.

7. Gibson, *Some Anglo-American Converts*, 202–05, 216–17; *NCE*, 5:884–85. Barber's conversion is said to have started after reading a novena to St. Francis Xavier belonging to an Irish servant girl. He then began systematic studies and sought out Benedict Fenwick when the latter was pastor of St. Peter's Church in New York. Understandably, as a wife and mother, Jerusha experienced a more difficult journey before entering the religious life.

8. McElroy Diaries, 22 January 1820; Journal of Stephen Dubuisson, entry for 25 June 1831, 14 C 1, MPA; James A. Ward to Samuel Barber, (?) 1835, 21 N 12, MPA; "Diary of Archbishop Maréchal 1818–1825," 437.

9. Robert Emmett Curran, S.J., "'The Finger of God Is Here': The Advent of the Miraculous in the Nineteenth Century American Catholic Community," *Catholic Historical Review* 73 (January 1987): 42–44. For those interested in a fuller account of the miracle and its subsequent effects, Father Curran's article is an excellent source.

10. Ibid.

11. *A Collection of Affidavits and Certificates Relative to the Wonderful Cure of Mrs. Ann Mattingly* (Washington: privately printed, 1824), 1–9, 11–14, 16, 18–25, 33, 35–36; Clark, "Mayors of the Corporation of Washington: Thomas Carbery," 82–83. Along with Father Dubuisson and Anne Fitzgerald, the other witnesses were Mrs. Mattingly's sisters Ruth and Catherine, her aunt Sybilla Carbery, and her sister-in-law Mary Susan Mattingly. Others making depositions included chief of the city post office George Sweeney, Dr. William Jones, Dr. Alexander McWilliams, Dr. N. P. Causin, Dr. George A. Carroll, Dr. Thomas Scott, and Mrs. Mattingly's three brothers, James, Rev. Joseph, and Lewis Carbery.

12. *Collection of Affidavits*, deposition of Mrs. Mattingly, 7; Curran, "'The Finger of God,'" 44–47.

13. *National Intelligencer*, 30 March 1824; Curran, "'The Finger of God,'" 45–53.

14. *Collection of Affidavits*, depositions of Dr. William Jones and Dr. Alexander McWilliams, 22–24; Curran, "'The Finger of God,'" 59.

15. Curran, "'The Finger of God,'" 51, 53–55; "Sister Mary Apolonia's Cure," 16 February 1831, 19 A 2, MPA. The latter document is a lengthy account of the event, complete with the physician's report and the testimony of many witnesses, sworn before Mayor John Cox of Georgetown. Since so many of the alleged cures took place at Visitation, the sisters of the convent became the most frenzied advocates of the cause. In 1831 the visiting Irish Jesuit Peter Kenney wrote to Dubuisson to say the sisters were likely "to plague him [the archbishop] to death. . . . Some of them I hear are more like furies, than Christians!!" (Kenney to Dubuisson, 5 April 1831, 210 W 1, MPA.) The attending physician, Dr. Benjamin Bohrer, is said to have been so awed by Sister Mary Apolonia's recovery that he vowed to become a Catholic. Visitation historian Rose Hawthorne Lathrop (see n. 17 below) has it that he remained a Protestant, but other sources suggest that he became a Catholic after the death of his first wife, Eliza Loughborough, in 1831. For more on Bohrer see n. 21 below.

16. Curran, "'The Finger of God,'" 59, 61.

17. *DAB*, 5:176–77; Diary of Stephen Dubuisson, entry for 23 March 1825; George Parsons Lathrop and Rose Hawthorne Lathrop, *A Story of Courage: Annals of the Georgetown Convent of the Visitation of the Blessed Virgin Mary* (Cambridge: Riverside Press, 1895), 247, 252–259. George Parsons Lathrop was a noted literary figure of his time and the editor of the first *Complete Works of Nathaniel Hawthorne* (1883). His wife Rose was the youngest of Nathaniel and Sophia Peabody Hawthorne's three children. Although occasionally written in the hagiographic manner of much nineteenth-century Catholic history, their work is for the most part an accurate history of the convent and the academy based on the convent archives, to which the Lathrops had access. Both the Lathrops converted to Catholicism in 1891. Following her husband's death in 1898, Rose became a Dominican sister. *DAB*, 6:15–16.

18. Charles Francis Adams, ed., *Memoirs of John Quincy Adams* (Philadelphia: J.B. Lippincott, 1876), diary entry for 30 July 1828, 72; Sister Catherine McSherry to William McSherry, S.J., 14 September 1825, 207 P 24, MPA.

19. Susan Decatur to Rev. John Beschter, 3 December 1828, 18 H 4, MPA; Decatur to Rev. Benedict Fenwick, 8 December 1838, 18 H 5, MPA; Royanna Baily Redon, "Mrs. Susan Wheeler Decatur," in *Decatur House*, ed. Helen Duprey Bullock (Washington: National Trust for Historic Preservation, n.d.), 49–52. As a young girl Susan Decatur was a favored visitor at the home of an aging Charles Carroll of Carrollton and a close friend of his daughters. She was baptized in the students' chapel at the college, November 25, 1828, and received her first communion at Trinity Church, December 31, 1828.

20. Geiger, *Daniel Carroll II*, 62–63; Thomas Clagett, son of Thomas Clagett and Rachel Offutt Clagett married Jane Maria Offutt, daughter of Reason Offutt and Catherine Knott Offutt on March 11, 1834, "dispensation being obtained," Marriage Register, 1805–1835, HTA; J. Herman Schauinger, "The Domestic Life of William Gaston," *Catholic Historical Review* 30 (January 1945): 405–08.

21. Margaret C. Loughborough to President John B. Creeden, S.J., Georgetown University, 28 March 1917, Francis C. Brown to James S. Ruby, Georgetown University Alumni Association, 29 March 1957, Loughborough Family Papers, GUA; Stuart C. Loughborough conversations with author, September 1989; *History of the Medical Society of the District of Columbia, 1817–1909* (Washington: Medical Society of the District of Columbia, 1909), s.v. "Benjamin Schenkmeyer Bohrer," 217; Pew Rent Petition, Christ Episcopal Church Georgetown; Rose Hawthorne Lathrop, *Story of Courage*, 238–39, 241; "Sister Mary Apolonia's Cure," 19 A 2, MPA; The Loughborough family papers refer to Eliza's marriage to Dr. Bohrer and also contain a statement by a nineteenth-century descendant that "Mrs. Bohrer became a Catholic and the whole family later followed suit." Another source is the correspondence of Julia Compton, who in the 1840s referred to "the Misses Loughborough, who have all become Catholics since the death of their mother. . . ." Julia Compton to Anna Young, 22 June 1845, Willson-Compton Papers, MSA. One of Eliza's brothers, Hamilton, is known to have converted, but the possible conversion of the other siblings is difficult to verify. Dr. Benjamin Bohrer, one of the founding members of the Medical Society of the District of Columbia and originally a parishioner at Christ Episcopal Church in Georgetown, is known to have been the attending physician of Visitation Convent and Academy and is also recorded as attending Georgetown College temporary infirmary during the cholera epidemic of 1832. He may well have become a Catholic during or more likely after his marriage to Eliza Loughborough, for whom he purchased a burial lot in the Trinity Church graveyard circa 1828. Eliza died on Christmas Day 1832, probably of cholera. Various of the Bohrer girls attended Visitation Academy early in its history. Mary Bohrer, listed as completing classes in 1829, is probably the daughter of Benjamin and Eliza. Records of the Trinity Church Graveyard ("Account Book") 1817–1833, GUA; Death Register, Holy Trinity Church 1818–1867, HTA; Student Lists, Visitation Convent and Academy Archives.

22. Margaret K. Fresco, *Marriages and Deaths, St. Mary's County Maryland 1634–1900* (privately printed, 1984), 107; Guy Castle, "Life in Georgetown, 1819–1841, as Told in the Personal Correspondence of Ann Shaaff," *CHS* 44 (1960–62): 79–80; William Beschter, S.J., to Francis Dzierozynski, S.J., 14 September 1826, 207 G 4, MPA; House Diaries, Georgetown College Jesuit Community, Jesuit House Archives, entries for 23 August, 12 October, and 7 November 1826; Sabina de Iturbide to Angel de Iturbide, Philadelphia, 8, 18 June 1855, Iturbide Papers, Manuscript Division, LC. The Empress Iturbide, as she was called by some, arrived in Georgetown in August 1826. Soon to follow were her five children, a family priest, and a retinue of servants. Her opposition to her son Angel's marriage to Alice Green is manifest in the letters to Angel from his sister Sabina, cited above. The Forrest family's reaction to Maria's marriage is vividly described in the letters of Ann Shaaff. (Shaaff correctly identifies Maria Forrest as Mrs. John Tayloe, since she was a widow of navy Lieutenant John Tayloe at the time of her marriage to Dr. Bohrer in 1834, but incorrectly calls the latter Dr. John Bohrer, probably confusing him with one of his brothers or cousins.) The Forrest family's disapproval of Ann's conversion to Catholicism, as well as Maria's marriage, has mute testimony in the form of a long history of blanks or incomplete information about Ann, Maria, and their descendants in standard genealogical and biographical reference works, extending even to the recently published *BDML* (see *BDML* 2:324). An exception is Louise Mann-Kenney's *Rosedale: The Eighteenth Century Estate of General Uriah Forrest* (Washington: privately printed, 1989), 49–50, which gives some attention to the Iturbides and much to the Green family, including Ann Forrest Green's role in founding St. Ann's, the first Catholic church in what is now the Tenley Circle area of Northwest Washington.

23. Thomas Carbery, Sr., was the timber and building materials supplier mentioned in Chapter 7. His wife was Mary Asonath Carbery, by whom he had all his children. The principal secondary source for the Carbery family is Allen C. Clark's, "The Mayors of the Corporation of Washington: Thomas Carbery," *CHS* 19 (1916): 61–98. Primary sources are mainly the baptism and marriage registers of Trinity and St. Patrick's. The St. Patrick's records include the baptism of Henry Carbery (died young), son of Thomas and Mary Manning Carbery, 11 October 1827; adult baptism of Euphemia Manning (Mayor Thomas Carbery's mother-in-law), 15 October 1827; baptism of Ann Asonath Carbery, daughter of James and Emza Cloud Carbery, 5 April 1820, and the marriage of Lewis Carbery and Artemesia Cloud, 9 September 1817 and the baptism of their daughter Mary Susannah, 21 May 1819. Trinity Church records include the adult baptisms of Artemesia Cloud Carbery, born of Abner and Susan Cloud, and her sisters Mary, Noemy, and Susannah Cloud, 15 February 1820; baptism of Martha Louisa Carbery, daughter of Lewis and Artemesia Carbery, 30 October 1827; and the marriage of Martha Louise Carbery and Aloysius Peirce Shoemaker. St. Patrick's Church Baptismal Register 1819–1836, Marriage Register 1813–1817; Baptismal Register, 1805–1834, Marriage Register, 1805–1875, HTA. The author is grateful to Margaret DuVivier, a descendant, for first pointing out the relationships of the Cloud, Carbery, Peirce, and Shoemaker families.

24. Roccofort, "Essai"; Edward I. Devitt, S.J., "Holy Trinity Church, Georgetown," *WL* 64 (1935): 320.

25. Fresco, *Marriages and Deaths St. Mary's County Maryland 1634–1900*, 107; Baptismal Register, 1835–1858, HTA; Goode, *Capital Losses*, 451; Christopher Johnston, "Lowndes Family," *MHM* 12 (1907): 276–79; Pew rental and vestryman lists, 1802–1828, St. John's Episcopal Church, Georgetown, Record Group 1-A; Pew Diagram, Holy Trinity Church, 1859, HTA; Baptismal Register, 1835–1858, HTA; *BDML*, 2:780; *DAB* 9:62–63. Bladen Forrest, the grandson of Col. Uriah Forrest's brother Zachariah, was the brother of naval officer French Forrest, who distinguished himself in the war of 1812 as a midshipman aboard the *Hornet* and later in the Mexican-American and Civil Wars. Bladen

Forrest apparently converted following his marriage to Helen Keith of Georgetown, conducted by Trinity Pastor Peter O'Flanagan in August of 1844, after which he appears in the front row of the Trinity pew diagram cited above. They had three children, Bladen Ignatius, Joseph, and Mary Helen, all baptized at Holy Trinity. Francis Lowndes (1784–1867) was the grandson of Christopher (1713–1785) and Elizabeth Tasker Lowndes, a leading merchant family of early Bladensburg, and a nephew of Rebecca Lowndes who married Georgetown's Benjamin Stoddert of Forrest, Murdock, and Stoddert. Francis received adult baptism at Trinity Church on 10 July 1843. Unlike his father and grandfather, who were among the wealthy tobacco merchants of Bladensburg and Georgetown, Francis Lowndes entered government and served as clerk in the Treasury Department. He married Angelletta Craighill of Jefferson County, Virginia, and died without issue in 1867.

26. Benjamin Stoddert to the Right Rev. Dr. Carroll, Georgetown, 3 September 1804, 7 U 9, AAB; Sister Mary Leonard Whipple, Visitation Convent, interview with author, November 1986; Russel J. Quandt, treatment report of Peale portrait of Stoddert children for National Society of Colonial Dames of America, Dumbarton House, 5 November 1969; Charles Coleman Sellers, *Portraits and Miniatures by Charles Willson Peale* (Philadelphia: American Philosophical Society, 1952), 202–03. Appraisal of estate of Elizabeth Stoddert Ewell, 11 February 1901, Register of Wills, District of Columbia, Court Records, Record Group 21, NA; Baptismal Register, 1835–1858, HTA. Stoddert's land offer was not entirely philanthropic. As he said of it, the land included some "To be equal to any land in Kentucky" and some to be "level and free of stone, but not what is called the first quality in Kentucky." He then stated that he hoped Bishop Carroll would direct a Roman Catholic College or "seminary of learning" to be built upon it. This done, he would then endeavor "to lease out the rest of the land (i.e., land adjoining the 5,000-acre tract he was offering, since Stoddert owned 10,000 acres in all) on very moderate terms—or to sell it on terms still more moderate to the Roman Catholic settlers." Still and all, it was a gift, none of the above conditions being firm stipulations. There is no record that it was accepted. The restorer of the Charles Willson Peale portrait cited above found a T-shaped tear in the neck of daughter Elizabeth which was covered over with hard oil paints, early in the painting's history. If not accidental, the T-shaped tear would certainly suggest the excision of a necklace and pendant. The estate appraisal made in 1901 included objects that represented a household accumulation of more than a century.

27. Green, *Washington*, 1:71–72; Rev. Peter Kenney to Francis Neale, 16 September 1832, 207 G 4, MPA; Baptismal Register, 1835–1858, HTA; Death Register, 1818–1867, HTA.

28. Board of Health Committee Report on Epidemic Cholera, *National Intelligencer*, 8 January 1833; Rev. Francis Barnum, College Archivist, 7 March 1832, Chronological Notes, GUA.

29. *Washington Federalist*, 14 April 1802.

30. Richard B. Morris, "Andrew Jackson, Strikebreaker," *American Historical Review*, 55 (October 1949): 54–64; W. David Baird, "Violence Along the Chesapeake and Ohio Canal: 1839," *MHM* 66, no. 2 (Summer 1971): 121–27. The latter article concerns the violence that broke out again in 1839, this time mainly between Irish and German laborers.

31. *Washington Metropolitan*, 29 August 1835.

32. Ibid., 8 August 1835.

33. Bryan, "Principal City Officers," 298–306; *Latrobe Papers*, 1:387n.; Baptismal Register, 1811–1816, St. Patrick's Church. Brent was elected to the Common Council in 1802 and again in 1828, 1829, and 1830; he then was elected to the Board of Aldermen continuously from 1831 through 1840, for a total of fifteen years service. Queen served one term on the Common Council in 1809 and two on the Board of Aldermen in 1812 and 1819; Coombe, four on the council in 1805, 1822, 1823, 1824, and one on the aldermen in 1825; Barry, one on the council in 1819; and Cassin, five on the aldermen from 1809 to 1822.

34. Bryan, *History*, 2.161–62; Clark, "The Mayors of the Corporation of Washington: Thomas Carbery," 85–88, 93–94. Following his mayoralty Carbery was long a justice of the peace, a member of the board of managers of the Washington Monument Society, and from 1855 until his death, president of the Bank of the Metropolis. His house has been described as having an extensive library and a large collection of seashells and insects.

35. Bryan, "Principal City Officers," 301–02; Baptismal Registers, 1811–1816, 1819–1836, St. Patrick's Church; *Washington Directory*, 1832; Frances Flaherty-Knox to author, 4 February, 1988; *Washington Directory, 1822*. George Sweeney (also spelled Sweeny) was first appointed chief clerk of the city post office in 1822 during the administration of Mayor Carbery, with whom he had lifelong associations. He ran for mayor as a Jacksonian Democrat but was defeated by the popular John Van Ness (Bryan, *History*, 2:165).

36. *DAB*, 9:289–93; *BDUSC*, 1492, 1789; Eisenberg, *Marylanders Who Served the Nation*, 148–49, 189–90; Magdalen McWilliams Mackall, *The Neales of Maryland and Their Descendants* (for private distribution, 1965), 41; Newman, *The Maryland Semmes and Kindred Families*, 68. Taney was a native of Frederick, Maryland, but long a resident of the capital as a result of his various government appointments. He is believed to have worshipped at Trinity, where his brother Augustus was a parishioner, as well as at St. Patrick's.

37. Bryan, "Principal City Officers," 304–09; Bryan, *History*, 2:254n., 297, 387n.; Baptismal and Marriage Register, 1795–1805, HTA; *Washington Directory, 1834*; Cooprider, *Harbaugh Family History*, 241–60; Clark, "Mayors of the Corporation of Washington: Thomas Carbery," 89–90; Richard H. Mudd, *The Mudd Family of the United States* (Ann Arbor, MI: Edward Brothers, Inc., 1951), 474–76; Seale, *The President's House*, 1:140; Cooprider shows Joseph Harbaugh as the fourth of Leonard Harbaugh's numerous sons. The first Trinity baptismal register records the baptism of William Harbach, "son of Joseph and Elinor Harbach living in Washington," October 7, 1801. Cooprider erroneously lists Joseph's wife's name as Elizabeth.

38. Billington, *The Protestant Crusade*, 98–108.

39. Curran, *Georgetown University*, 1:162; Sister M. Eulalia Teresa Moffatt, M.A., "Charles Constantine Pise (1801–1866)," *U.S. Catholic Historical Society Historical Records and Studies* 20 (1931): 79; *NCE*, 11:387. The college's first grant, 1833, was for Washington City lots valued at $25,000.

40. Julia Compton to Anna Young, 22 June 1845, Willson-Compton Papers, MSA; Bishop Benedict Fenwick to Rev. George Fenwick, 20 October 1830, 210 S 1a, MPA; Stephen Dubuisson, Commentary on the Maryland Province to the French Society for the Propagation of the Faith, 1841, quoted in Curran, "Troubled Nation, Troubled Province," 24.

41. *National Intelligencer*, 15 July 1837; *The Native American*, 10, 11, 19 August, 14 October 1837; Chester Horton Brent, *Descendants of Coll⁰ Giles Brent*, 137–38, 149; *Washington Directory, 1822*; *Native American*, 24 February, 7 July 1838; John B. Blake, *An Address on the Life and Character of John Carroll Brent Before the Society of the Oldest Inhabitants of the District of Columbia* (Washington: R. O. Polkinhorn, 1876), 9. *The Native American* preceded by some seven years the publication of Philadelphia's *Native American*, first issued in April of 1844. Billington, *Protestant Crusade*, 210.

42. *Native American*, 23 September 1837; Dolan, *The American Catholic Experience*, 128.

43. *Native American*, 10 August 1837.

44. The 1850 Census was the first to distinguish between the native and foreign born, at which time the foreign born constituted sixteen percent of Washington's total white population of 29,730. Green, *Washington*, 1:183.

45. *National Intelligencer*, 21 July 1837; *Native American*, 10 August 1837.

46. *National Intelligencer*, 21, 24 July 1837. By August 15 the *Intelligencer* announced it would no longer print reports of the association or articles from the *Native American*, since "they had a tendency to produce ill blood more than either instruct or amuse."

47. *Native American*, 19 August 1837.

48. Ibid., 19 August 1837. Ironically, Sweeney was later named a member of the committee to present the memorial to Congress. He was also elected the association's treasurer and, by the summer of 1839, its president. *Native American*, 2 December 1837, 7 July 1839.

49. *Native American*, 7, 10 August and 7, 14 October 1837.

50. *National Intelligencer*, 15 July, 10 August 1837; *Native American*, 17 March, 7 April 1838. For the association's constitution, see *National Intelligencer*, 15 July 1837.

51. *Native American*, 6, 20 January 1838.

52. Ibid., 13 October 1838, 16 March 1839, 31 March 1838, 14 September 1839. In time the nativists' concept of what constituted "equal political footing" took a bizarre turn. Since native-born Americans had to wait until they were twenty-one years old to achieve full citizenship with voting rights, the nativists maintained that the same period of time—that is, twenty-one years of residence—ought to pass before the foreign born could be naturalized. During the Know Nothing era, in fact, bills were introduced in Congress to this effect.

53. Ibid., 26 January 1839.

54. Ibid., 24 February 1838, 14, 21 April 1838; 13 October 1838, 22 June 1839, 13 July 1839, 28 November 1840. Henry J. Brent went on to become a judge of the District Circuit Court (*National Intelligencer*, 7 June 1858), while John Carroll Brent, returned from Paris to pursue his literary career.

NOTES TO CHAPTER 11

1. Ellis, *American Catholicism*, 68; Billington, *Protestant Crusade*, 197–98.

2. Ellis, *American Catholicism*, 69; *NCE*, 12:454. At the time Father McElroy was the pastor of St. John's Church in Frederick, Maryland, and Rey was both pastor of Trinity and a vice president of Georgetown College. McElroy remained a chaplain for approximately three years, after which he began his career in Boston.

3. *National Intelligencer*, 1 June 1853.

4. *Daily Evening Star*, 28 May 1853.

5. An exception was the quasi-political American Republican Party, which elected officials in both New York and Philadelphia in 1844. Statement of purpose by Henry J. Brent, first issue of the Washington *Native American*, 10 August 1837.

6. William J. Evitts, *A Matter of Allegiances: Maryland from 1850 to 1861* (Baltimore: Johns Hopkins University Press, 1974), 64–66; Jean H. Baker, *Ambivalent Americans: The Know-Nothing Party in Maryland* (Baltimore: Johns Hopkins University Press, 1977), 6–7, 108–18; Billington, *Protestant Crusade*, 200–01, 380–86. The principal success of the American Republican Party was the election of James Harper as mayor of New York in 1844. But the party's main effort was directed to pressuring Congress for reform of the naturalization laws, the eventual failure of which led to its disintegration in 1846. Baker and Evitts are both excellent sources for the underground fraternal orders and how the

American Party sprang from them. Members of the orders indulged in such practices as ritual handshakes, code numbers for identification, and the swearing of oaths. Some oaths obliged members to do all in their power to prevent the election of Catholics to public office, or failing that, "if it may be done legally you will when elected or appointed to any official station . . . remove all foreigners, aliens, or Roman Catholics from office." (Baker, 113) Authorities believe the "I know nothing" or "I don't know" comment began with the Order of the Star Spangled Banner. In any case, the existence of the American Party was first noted in the Baltimore press by the fall of 1853 (Evitts, 65) and the term Know Nothing was first widely used by the Washington press during the municipal elections in the spring of 1854.

7. The identity of Know Nothings in this election, well before their victories forced public disclosure, is admittedly problematic. But a good indication of who their candidates were can be made by comparing the results of the 1853 elections with those of 1855 and 1856, when the Washington press began listing party affiliations. In some few cases membership in the older Washington Native American Association and the names of the officers and board of managers involved in the Know Nothing takeover of the Washington Monument Society have also provided clues. In addition to the newly elected members of the Board of Aldermen in 1853, two members not up for re-election can be identified as probable Know Nothings, for a total of five. Similarly, in the Common Council, three members returned from the previous year can be so identified, for a total of five also. In the same elections, John T. Towers, who became mayor in 1854, was voted president of the Board of Aldermen, after long service in both that body and the Common Council. Although he was elected mayor on the Know Nothings' 1854 ticket, Towers was a well-known Whig (see n. 11 below) who accepted the Know Nothing endorsement, but was probably not himself a member of the party. *National Intelligencer*, 5 June 1855, 3 June 1856; *Star*, 29 May 1855; Washington *Native American*, 19 August 1837; Bryan, *History*, 2:282.

8. Hennesey, *American Catholics*, 124–25; NCE, 2:218–19.

9. *Star*, 6, 13 March 1854; *National Intelligencer*, 8 March 1854.

10. *National Intelligencer*, 25 May, 3 June 1854; *Star*, 2, 3, June 1854. Interestingly, in the Baltimore city elections the following October, the Know Nothings employed the same strategy of not publicly acknowledging their candidate for mayor until shortly before the election. Evitts, *A Matter of Allegiances*, 66.

11. *National Intelligencer*, 6 June 1854; *Star*, 6 June 1854. Allen Clark, "John Thomas Towers—Mayor and Printer," *CHS* 25 (1923): 90–91. The vote for Towers was reported as 3,000, with 2,561 for Maury. The Know Nothings probably accounted for all sixteen of the newly elected Common Council members; at least six who cannot positively be identified as party members were elected from the two wards that gave the Know Nothings their greatest majorities. By the same standards the party's strength in the Board of Aldermen was probably seven or eight.

12. *Star*, 6 June 1854. "Sentinels" was the code word for a position of rank given to first-degree Know Nothing party members (Baker, *Ambivalent Americans*, 115–16). Thus Mr. Wilmot was in effect telling the crowd that Towers had promised to consider only Know Nothings for appointive positions in the new city government.

13. Billington, *The Protestant Crusade*, 388–89. The Know Nothings also made strong showings in 1854 and 1855 in Alabama, Louisiana, Mississippi, Tennessee, and Virginia.

14. Bureau of the Census, *Historical Statistics of the United States, Colonial Times to 1970*, Bicentennial Edition, pt. 1 (Washington: U.S. Department of Commerce, 1975), 14; Green, *Washington*, 1:183. For overall estimates of Irish and German immigrants and the percentage of Catholics among them, see Dolan, *The American Catholic Experience*, 128–30.

15. Billington, *The Protestant Crusade*, 325–27.

16. See especially Evitts, *Matter of Allegiances*, 73–74; Baker, *Ambivalent Americans*, 45–47.

17. The mass meeting was held at Carusi's Saloon, 19 September 1854; its resolutions and proceedings were later published in the first issue of the *Daily American Organ*, 13 November 1854.

18. Ibid., 16 November 1854. For similarly convoluted statements, see the Know Nothings' first national platform of 1855, quoted in Baker, *Ambivalent Americans*, 46.

19. The *Whig Standard* ran from 6 November 1843 to 16 November 1844. Its main purpose was all-out support for Henry Clay, then the Whig candidate, in his unsuccessful bid for the presidency. Issues from its first months are preserved in the Library of Congress.

20. *National Intelligencer*, 30 May 1854.

21. Ibid., 29 May 1854.

22. *Star*, 2 June 1854.

23. *National Intelligencer*, 3 June 1854.

24. See especially "A Citizen of Washington," *National Intelligencer*, 31 May 1854. Another defender wrote, "If there *is* a Know-Nothing Society whose principles are a *secret*, how do men not of that order know what these principles are . . . ?" Ibid., 5 June 1854.

25. *Star*, 2 June 1854; *National Intelligencer*, 29 May 1854.

26. *National Intelligencer*, 6 June 1854; *Star*, 6 June 1854.

27. Bryan, *History*, 2:425–26. The loss of the city council printing contract contributed to the *Intelligencer*'s decline. In the 3 June 1854 issue, the editors of the *Daily Evening Star* claimed they had gained top circulation only three months after they had purchased the paper a year earlier. The *Intelligencer*, nevertheless, lasted until 1869.

28. *Daily American Organ*, 13, 15, 16 November 1854. For readers familiar with the general run of nativist tracts and the Know Nothing press in other cities, the *Organ's* initial attacks on the church appear relatively mild. In time, however, its tone became more strident.

29. Devitt, "History of Holy Trinity Church," *Holy Trinity Monthly Bulletin*, 13 July 1918, HTA; Anonymous, "Gonzaga College: A Sketch of Some of Its Presidents, Professors, and Students," *WL* 19 (1890): 7. For the name change to Holy Trinity see Chapter 1, n. 16.

30. Bryan, *History*, 2:189–90; Goode, *Capital Losses*, 198–99; Sister Marie Perpetua Hayes, "Adele Cutts, Second Wife of Stephen A. Douglas," *Catholic Historical Review* 31 (July 1945): 181–83.

31. Durkin, *William Matthews*, 1–3; *Star*, 1 May 1854.

32. Curran, *Georgetown University*, 1:131–33, 138–43.

33. Sullivan, *Georgetown Visitation*, 100–01; *Georgetown College Journal*, 8, no. 3 (January 1880): 26.

34. The fraudulent meeting announcement, signed by "F.W. Eckloff, Clerk, WNM Society" was published only in the *Daily Evening Star* the day before the meeting and in the *Intelligencer* on the same day. The *Star* of 29 and 30 May 1855 carries the most complete report of the Know Nothing takeover and ensuing events, written by the society's secretary, John Carroll Brent. Its prestigious membership notwithstanding, the society had not been very effective in fund-raising and was slow to react and take action against the Know Nothings. The two boards co-existed for more than three years, as the Know Nothings' putative board tried to show it should rescue the fund-raising operation. It did not give up until 1858.

35. Select Committee on the Monument to the Memory of Washington, *Select Committee Report*, 33rd Cong., 2d sess., February 22, 1855, H. Rep. 94, 2–6; *National Intelligencer*, 20 June 1854; *Star*, 29 May 1855. At the time of the takeover the monument had

reached 150′ of its projected 517′ height, and $230,000 had been expended in its con-
struction, with $320,000 estimated to complete the obelisk's shaft. All funding for the
monument from Congress and the public came to a halt immediately after the Know
Nothing takeover, with the unfortunate effect that almost four years passed before the
regular board regained control of the society and twenty-four years before sufficient
funds were on hand to resume construction. The monument's capstone was set on 6 December 1884. For interesting illustrations of the monument at different stages of construction, see Junior League, *City of Washington*, 192–93, 263.

36. *Star*, 21, 23 September 1854, 30 May, 5 June 1855; *National Intelligencer*, 5,7,8
June 1855; Bryan, "Washington City Officials," 310–11. Before the 1855 election an Anti-
Know Nothing request that an observer be allowed to witness the voting in each ward
was denied by the Common Council. (The request certainly was reasonable since election commissioners in each ward had been appointed by the Know Nothings.) After the
election the *Star* calculated that some 725 legal votes had been refused by the Know
Nothing commissioners and claimed that the Antis might have carried three additional
wards (3rd, 4th, and 5th) but for the Know Nothings' "deliberate and palpable frauds."
The claim appears to have some basis since the Know Nothing council members in
those wards were listed as winning by such slender margins as 310 to 298, 535 to 501,
and 320 to 303.

37. Clark, "John Thomas Towers," 93–98.

38. Billington, *Protestant Crusade*, 427–28.

39. *Statutes at Large of the United States of America*, vol. 11, December 3, 1855 to
March 3, 1895 (Boston: Little Brown, 1859), 15. National legislation to put the foreign-
born on "equal footing" with native-born Americans by extending the naturalization
period to twenty-one years had been unsuccessfully introduced in Congress twice before in the preceding year (Billington, *Protestant Crusade*, 440–41). Thus this act was a
thinly concealed attempt to achieve locally what could not be done nationally.

40. Robert H. Harkness, "Dr. William B. Magruder," *CHS* 16 (1913): 152–55; *Daily
American Organ*, 17 May 1856; Clark, "John Thomas Towers," 103–04. Towers may have
declined to run because of disenchantment with the Know Nothings or ill health. He
died a little more than a year later at the age of forty-seven.

41. Billington, *The Protestant Crusade*, 305–06; Harkness, "Dr. William B. Magruder," 168.

42. *National Intelligencer*, 3 June 1856; *Star*, 30 May 1856. Some election disorders
occurred in the northern precinct of the Fourth Ward, the city's most populous. Generally speaking, the Anti-Know Nothings' greatest strength was in the First and Second
Wards in the northwestern section of the city, while the Know Nothings were strongest
in the Sixth and the Seventh in Southwest and Southeast. At the time, the Fourth, Second, and First had the highest property assessments, in that order, and the Sixth, Seventh, and Fifth, the lowest. See *National Intelligencer*, 8 June 1854, and Lawrence F.
Schmeckebier, "Ward Boundaries of Washington and Georgetown," *CHS* 51–52 (1955):
74–75.

43. Evitts, *Matter of Allegiances*, 113–17; Baker, *Ambivalent Americans*, 121–23,
131–32. Some of the clubs' names reflected their tactics. The Blood Tubs are said to have
been named after their practice of throwing blood on voters, whose appearance of being
severely wounded would scare other voters from the polls; another club, the Plug
Uglies, from a plug on the toe of their boots with which they kicked opponents. One of
the most common tactics was "cooping," or the kidnapping of prospective voters and
keeping them hidden in "coop houses" until well after the elections.

44. *National Intelligencer* 2, 3, 4, 8, 15 June 1857. The *Intelligencer's* day-after re-
portage (June 2) and Major Tyler's official report forwarded by the commandant of the
Marine Corps (June 15) give the most complete pictures of the day's events. The press,
including Know Nothing papers in Alexandria, Baltimore, Albany and New York City,

288   universally condemned the Plug Ugly incident. A number of Washington papers, including the *Intelligencer* (June 3), concluded there was no reason to doubt "that the 'Plug
Ugly' bands were imported by prior engagement from Baltimore," witness the fact they
were provided with railroad tickets and food for the day. There is also the fact that they
knew to go directly to the populous Fourth Ward, which had switched to the Anti-
Know Nothing side and been the scene of some disorders the year before.

46. *National Intelligencer*, 2 June 1857. The Anti-Know Nothing or Union Party
made a clear sweep of all seats in the First through the Fifth Wards, with the exception
of an alderman in the Fourth. This gave them a two-to-one majority in the City Council.

46. An augmented police force and citizen volunteers commissioned as special
police for the day won praise for the generally peaceful day. *National Intelligencer*, 5, 8
June 1858; Bryan, *History*, 2:430. Eight of the Independent party candidates can be identified as having run as Know Nothings in the previous two years. James G. Berret, who
headed what was now called the Democrat-Anti-Know Nothing ticket, was elected
mayor.

47. *National Intelligencer*, 6, 7 June 1859. The *Intelligencer* (7 June) reported: "All
the successful candidates with the exception of Mr. Given, were the candidates of the
Anti-Know Nothing Party, their opponents generally declining a contest."

48. Baker, *Ambivalent Americans*, 2, 130.

49. Ibid., 47; Evitts, *Matter of Allegiances*, 89–93; *Daily American Organ*, 30 May
1856. Baker gives an interesting statistical table on the decreasing references to anti-
Catholicism in Maryland Know Nothing speeches, platforms, and pamphlets, from 1854
to 1859. Evitts provides an excellent overview of the state party's changing strategy
after coming to power, including examples of the Know Nothing press in various localities. Unionism, or the necessity of preserving national unity in the approaching North-
South conflict, replaced anti-Catholicism and repeal of the naturalization laws as the
party's main theme, although not without considerable discord.

50. *National Intelligencer*, 29 May 1854.

Bibliography

PRINCIPAL ARCHIVAL SOURCES AND COLLECTIONS

"Accounts of Divisions with the Original Proprietors and the Commissioners of Public Buildings and Grounds of the City of Washington." Record Group 42, National Archives.

Alumni Files. Georgetown College, Special Collections Division, Georgetown University Library.

Archives of the Archdiocese of Baltimore.

Brown, William Hand, ed. *Archives of Maryland, Proceedings of the General Assembly, Proceedings of the Provincial Court of Maryland.* 72 vols. Baltimore: Maryland Historical Society, 1883–1972.

Carroll, Daniel of Duddington. Papers. Manuscript Division, Library of Congress.

Carroll, John, S.J. *The John Carroll Papers, 1755–1815.* Ed. Thomas O'Brian Hanley, S.J. Notre Dame, Ind.: University of Notre Dame, 1976.

Catholic Historical Manuscripts Collection. Special Collections Division, Georgetown University Library.

Digges, L'Enfant, Morgan Family Papers, 1674–1923. Manuscript Division, Library of Congress.

Digges of Warburton. Papers, 1680–1810. Maryland Historical Society.

Dubuisson, Stephen, S.J. Diary of Rev. Stephen Dubuisson, S.J., 1820–24, Dubuisson-Feiner Collection, and Journals, 1830–33. Society of Jesus Maryland Province Archives, Special Collections Division, Georgetown University Library.

Fenwick, George. Papers. Society of Jesus Maryland Province Archives, Special Collections Division, Georgetown University Library.

Georgetown College Catalogues, 1791–1835; Ledgers [account books], 1789–1803; Property Files. Special Collections Division, Georgetown University Library.

Holy Trinity Church. Baptismal and Marriage Registers, 1795–1875; Pew Rents; and Miscellaneous Correspondence. Holy Trinity Church Archives, Special Collections Division, Georgetown University Library.

———, Free Male School Accounts, Property Deeds, and Miscellaneous Correspondence. Society of Jesus Maryland Province Archives, Special Collections Division, Georgetown University Library.

Horsey, Lee, Carroll Family Papers. Maryland Historical Society.

Henry Hunt-William B. Chilton Collection. Special Collections Division, Georgetown University Library.

Maryland Governor, Council, and U.S. Representative Election Returns. Maryland State Archives, Annapolis.

McElroy, John, S.J. Diaries of Rev. John McElroy, S.J., 1813–21, 1834–36. Special Collections Division, Georgetown University Library.

Montgomery County Court Land Records. Commissioners of the Tax Assessment Records. Maryland State Archives, Annapolis.

Records of the District of Columbia Commissioners and of the Offices Concerned with Public Buildings, 1791–1867. Record Group 42, National Archives

Records of the Potomac Company. Record Group 29, National Archives.

Roccofort, Rev. Aloysius, S.J. "An Essai on the History of Trinity Church in Georgetown, D.C." Society of Jesus Maryland Province Archives, Special Collections Division, Georgetown University Library.

290 St. Patrick's Church, Baptismal and Marriage Registers, 1811–1857. St. Patrick's Church, Washington, DC.

Visitation Convent and Academy. Archives. Georgetown, DC.

Willson-Compton Papers. Maryland State Archives, Annapolis.

The Woodstock Letters. 98 vols. Woodstock, MD: Woodstock College Press, 1872–1969.

OFFICIAL AND OTHER PUBLIC DOCUMENTS

Register of Officers and Agents, Civil, Military and Naval in the Service of the United States, 1819–1830. Washington, DC: Davis and Force, 1822–30.

Annals of the Congress of the United States, 1789–1824. 42 vols. Washington, DC: Gales and Seaton, 1834–1856.

Statutes at Large of the United States of America. 17 vols. Ed. Richard Peters. Boston: Charles C. Little and James Brown, 1845–1873.

Bureau of the Census. *Historical Statistics of the United States, Colonial Times to 1970, Bicentennial Edition.* Part 1. Washington: Government Printing Office, 1975.

Ordinances of the Corporation of Georgetown, D.C. Georgetown: James C. Dunn, 1821.

Ordinances and Resolutions of the Georgetown Corporation from the Year 1751 to the Year 1858. Georgetown: E. Hughes, 1858.

Georgetown, DC. Corporation Records 1751–1881. Manuscript Division, Library of Congress.

District of Columbia. Proceedings of the [Washington] City Council, 1803, 1804. Manuscript Division, Library of Congress.

NEWSPAPERS AND OTHER PERIODICALS

Centinel of Liberty, or Georgetown and Washington Advertiser

Columbian Chronicle [Georgetown]

George-town Weekly Ledger

The Times and the Patowmack Packet [Georgetown]

Impartial Observer and Washington Advertiser [Washington]

Washington Federalist

National Intelligencer and Washington Advertiser

Daily Evening Star [Washington]

Washington Metropolitan

The Native American [Washington]

Daily American Organ [Washington]

Georgetown College Journal

Records of the American Catholic Historical Society [Philadelphia]

Records of the Columbia Historical Society (continued as *Washington History: The Magazine of the Historical Society of Washington, D.C.*)

Maryland Historical Magazine

Southern Literary Messenger

United States Catholic Historical Society Records and Studies

Catholic Historical Review

Virginia Magazine of History and Biography

SELECTED PUBLISHED SOURCES

Anonymous. "Gonzaga College: A Sketch of Some of Its Presidents, Professors, and Students." *Woodstock Letters* 18 (1889): 269–84; 19 (1890): 7–22.

Adams, John Quincy. *Memoirs of John Quincy Adams*. Ed. Charles Francis Adams. Philadelphia: J. B. Lippincott, 1876.

Askling, John, ed. "Autobiographical Sketch of Antony Charles Cazenove: Political Refugee, Merchant and Banker, 1775–1852." *Virginia Magazine of History and Biography* 78 (July 1970): 295–307.

Atlee, Samuel Yorke. *History of Public Schools of Washington City, D.C.* Washington: Board of Trustees, Public Schools, 1876.

Bacon-Foster, Cora. "Early Chapters in the Development of the Potomac Route to the West." *Records of the Columbia Historical Society* 15 (1912): 96–322.

Baker, Jean H. *Ambivalent Americans: The Know-Nothing Party in Maryland*. Baltimore: Johns Hopkins University Press, 1974.

Balch, Rev. Thomas Bloomer. *Reminiscences of Georgetown*. Washington: Henry Polkinhorn, 1859.

Bangert, William J., S.J. *A History of the Society of Jesus*. St. Louis, MO: Institute of Jesuit Sources, 1972.

Bedini, Silvio A. *The Life of Benjamin Banneker*. New York: Charles Scribner and Sons, 1972.

Beitzell, Edwin W. *The Jesuit Missions of St. Mary's County, Maryland*, 2nd edition. St. Mary's: privately printed, 1976.

Billington, Ray Allen. *The Protestant Crusade*. 1938; reprint New York: Rinehart, 1952.

Biographical Directory of the United States Congress, 1774–1989, Bicentennial Ed. Washington: Government Printing Office, 1989.

Blake, John B. *An Address on the Life of John Carroll Brent before the Society of the Oldest Inhabitants of the District of Columbia*. Washington: R. O. Polkinhorn, 1875.

Boarman, Rev. C. F. *The Boarmans*. Washington: privately printed, 1934.

Bowling, Kenneth R. *The Creation of Washington, D.C.: The Idea and Location of the American Capital*. Fairfax, VA: George Mason University Press, 1991.

Brent, Chester Horton. *The Descendants of Coll*[o] *Giles Brent and Cap*[t] *George Brent and Robert Brent,* [Gent] *Immigrants to Maryland and Virginia*. Rutland, VT: privately printed, 1946.

Brent, John Carroll, ed. *Biographical Sketch of the Most Reverend John Carroll, First Archbishop of Baltimore*. Baltimore: John Murphy, 1843.

Brigham, Clarence S. *History and Bibliography of American Newspapers, 1690–1820*. Worcester, MA: American Antiquarian Society, 1947.

Bryan, Wilhemus Bogart. *A History of the National Capital*, 2 vols. New York: Macmillan, 1914, 1916.

———. "Hotels of Washington Prior to 1814." *Records of the Columbia Historical Society* 7 (1904): 71–106.

———. "Sketch of Various Forms of Local Government in the District of Columbia; with a List of Washington City Officials." *Celebration of the One Hundredth Anniversary of the Establishment of the District of Columbia*. House of Representatives Doc. 522. Washington: Government Printing Office, 1901.

———. "Why the City Went Westward." *Records of the Columbia Historical Society* 7 (1904): 135–45.

Bullock, Helen Claire. *My Head and My Heart: A Little History of Thomas Jefferson and Maria Cosway*. New York: G. P. Putnam's Sons, 1945.

Bullock, Helen Duprey, ed., *Decatur House*. Washington: National Trust for Historic Preservation, n.d.

292   Byrne, William. *History of the Catholic Church in the New England States*, 2 vols. Boston: Hurd and Everetts, 1899.

Carne, Richard L. *A Brief Sketch of the History of St. Mary's Church, Alexandria, Virginia.* Alexandria: The Catholic Benevolent Union of Virginia, n.d.

Carne, William F. "The Life and Times of William Cranch." *Records of the Columbia Historical Society* 5 (1902): 294–309.

Carr, Lois Green. *Colonial Chesapeake Society*. Chapel Hill: University of North Carolina Press, 1988.

_____. "The First Expedition to Maryland." *A Relation of the Successfull beginnings of the Lord Baltemore's Plantation in Mary-land.* Ed. Edward C. Papenfuse and Lois Green Carr. Annapolis: Maryland Hall of Records 350th Anniversary Document Series, 1984.

_____ and David W. Jordan. *Maryland's Revolution of Government*. Ithaca, NY: Cornell University Press, 1974.

Chinnici, Joseph P. "Organization of the Spiritual Life: American Catholic Devotional Works 1791–1866." *Theological Studies* 40 (June 1979): 229–55.

Clark, Allen C. "Daniel Carroll of Duddington." *Records of the Columbia Historical Society* 39 (1938–39): 1–48.

_____. *Greenleaf and Law in the Federal City*. Washington: Press of F. W. Roberts, 1901.

_____. "The Mayors of the Corporation of Washington: Thomas Carbery." *Records of the Columbia Historical Society* 19 (1916): 61–98.

_____. "The Old Mills." *Records of the Columbia Historical Society* 31–32 (1930): 81–115.

_____. "John Thomas Towers—Mayor and Printer." *Records of the Columbia Historical Society* 25 (1923): 87–104.

_____. "Joseph Gale, Jr." *Records of the Columbia Historical Society* 23 (1920): 86–146.

Clay, Henry. *The Papers of Henry Clay*. 8 vols. Ed. James F. Hopkins. Lexington: University of Kentucky Press, 1959.

Coakley, Thomas M. "George Calvert and Newfoundland: 'The Sad Face of Winter.'" *Maryland Historical Magazine* 71 (Spring, 1976): 9–18.

Cohen, E.A., comp. *A Full Directory for Washington City, Georgetown, and Alexandria, 1834.* Washington City: E.A. Cohen.

A Collection of Affidavits and Certificates Relative to the Wonderful Cure of Mrs. Ann Mattingly. Washington: privately printed, 1824.

Consentino, Andrew J. and Henry H. Glassie. *The Capital Image: Painters in Washington, 1800–1915.* Washington: Smithsonian Institution Press, 1983.

Cunningham, Noble. *The Process of Government Under Jefferson*. Princeton: Princeton University Press, 1978.

Curran, Francis X. *Catholics in Colonial Law*. Chicago: Loyola University Press, 1962.

Curran, Robert Emmett, S.J. *American Jesuit Spirituality: The Maryland Tradition.* New York: Paulist Press, 1988.

_____. *The Bicentennial History of Georgetown University, Volume 1: From Academy to University.* Washington: Georgetown University Press, 1993.

_____. "'The Finger of God Is Here': The Advent of the Miraculous in the Nineteenth Century American Catholic Community." *Catholic Historical Review* 73 (January 1987): 41–61.

_____. "'Splendid Poverty': Jesuit Slave Holdings in Maryland, 1805–1838." *Catholics in the Old South: Essays on Church and Culture.* Ed. Randall L. Miller and Jon L. Wakelyn. Macon, GA: Mercer University Press, 1983.

_____. "Troubled Nation, Troubled Province, 1833–1880," Georgetown University Archives.

Cutler, William Parker and Julia Perkins. *Life, Journals, and Correspondence of Reverend Manasseh Cutler, LL.D.* 1888; reprint Athens, OH: Ohio University Press, 1947.

Daley, John M., S.J., *Georgetown University: Origin and Early Years.* Washington: Georgetown University Press, 1957.

Davis, Deering, Stephen P. Dorsey, and Ralph Cole Hall, eds. *Georgetown Houses of the Federal Period.* New York: Bonanza Books, 1946.

Decatur, Stephen, Jr. *Private Affairs of George Washington: From the Records and Accounts of Tobias Lear, Esquire, his Secretary.* Boston: Houghton, Mifflin, 1933.

Delano, Judah, ed. *The Washington Directory,* 1822. Washington: 1822.

Devanter, Ann C., ed. *"Anywhere So Long As There Be Freedom": Charles Carroll of Carrollton, His Family and His Maryland.* Baltimore: Baltimore Museum of Art, 1975.

Devitt, Edward L., S.J., "History of the Maryland-New York Province." *Woodstock Letters* 64 (1935): 24–57.

_____. "Trinity Church, Georgetown: An Historical Discourse." *Woodstock Letters* 33 (1904): 303–24.

_____. "History of Holy Trinity Church." *The Church Bulletin of Holy Trinity Church, Georgetown, D.C.* January 1917–July 1918.

Dolan, Jay P. *The American Catholic Experience.* Garden City, NY: Doubleday, 1985.

_____. *Catholic Revivalism: The American Experience, 1830–1900.* Notre Dame, IN: University of Notre Dame Press, 1978.

Downing, Margaret Brent. "James and Joanna Gould Barry." *Historical Records and Studies, United States Catholic Historical Society* 15 (1921): 45–54.

Durkin, Joseph T., S.J. *William Matthews: Priest and Citizen.* New York: Benziger Brothers, 1963.

Eberlein, Harold D. and Cortlandt Van Dyke Hubbard. *Historic Houses of George-Town and Washington City.* Richmond, VA: The Dietz Press, 1958.

Eisenberg, Gerson G. *Marylanders Who Served the Nation: A Biographical Directory of Federal Officials from Maryland.* Annapolis: Maryland State Archives, 1992.

Elias, Robert H. "The First American Novel." *American Literature* 12 (January 1941): 419–34.

_____ and Michael N. Stanton. *Letters of Thomas Atwood Digges.* Columbia, SC: University of South Carolina Press, 1982.

_____. "Thomas Digges and 'Adventures of Alonso': Evidence from Robert Southey." *American Literature* 44 (March 1972): 118–22.

Ellis, John Tracy. *American Catholicism,* 2nd ed. Chicago: University of Chicago Press, 1969.

Elliott, Jonathan, Jr. *Historical Sketches of the Ten Miles Square Forming the District of Columbia.* Washington: 1830.

Elliott, S.A. *The Washington Directory, 1827.* Washington: 1827.

Ely, Selden Marvin. "The District of Columbia and the American Revolution and Patriots of the Revolutionary Period Who Are Interred in the District or in Arlington." *Records of the Columbia History Society* 21 (1918): 129–54.

Estelle, Helen and Imogene Philbert. *Saint Matthews of Washington.* Baltimore, MD: A. Hone and Co., 1945.

Evitts, William J. *A Matter of Allegiances: Maryland from 1850 to 1861.* Baltimore: Johns Hopkins University Press, Studies in Historical and Political Science, 92nd Series, 1974.

Flexner, James Thomas. *Washington, the Indispensable Man.* Boston: Little, Brown and Company, 1974.

Fogarty, Gerald P., S.J. "The Origins of the Mission, 1664–1773." *The Maryland Jesuits.* Baltimore: Maryland Province of the Society of Jesus, 1976, 9–27.

_____. "Property and Religious Liberty in Colonial Maryland Thought." *Catholic Historical Review* 72 (October 1986): 577–600.

Formwalt, Lee W. "Benjamin Henry Latrobe and the Development of Transportation in the District of Columbia." *Records of the Columbia Historical Society* 50 (1980): 36–66.

294 Foster, Augustus John. *Jeffersonian America: Notes on the United States of America Collected in the Years 1805–6–7 and 11–12.* San Marino, CA: Huntington Library, 1954.

Garrett, Wilbur E. "George Washington's Patowmack Canal." *National Geographic* 171 (June 1987): 717–53.

Geiger, Sister M. Virginia. *Daniel Carroll II: One Man and His Descendants, 1730–1978.* Baltimore: privately printed, 1979.

Georgetown Architecture—Northwest. Historic American Buildings Survey Selections Number 6. Washington: Commission of Fine Arts, 1970.

Gibbs, George, ed. *Memoirs of the Administration of Washington and John Adams, Edited from the Papers of Oliver Wolcott, Secretary of the Treasury.* New York: William Van Norden, 1846.

Gibson, Sister Laurita. *Some Anglo-American Converts to Catholicism Prior to 1829.* Washington: Catholic University of America, 1943.

Goff, Frederick R. "Early Printing in Georgetown (Potomak), 1789–1800, and the Engravings of L'Enfant's Plan of Washington, 1792." *Records of the Columbia Historical Society* 50–51 (1950–51): 103–19.

Goode, James M. *Capital Losses: A Cultural History of Washington's Destroyed Buildings.* Washington: Smithsonian Institution Press, 1979.

Graham, Michael. "Meeting House and Chapel: Religion and Community in Seventeenth Century Maryland." *Colonial Chesapeake Society.* Ed. Lois Green Carr, et al. Chapel Hill: University of North Carolina Press, 1988.

Grassi, John, S.J. "The Catholic Religion in the United States in 1818." *Woodstock Letters* 11, no. 3 (1882): 229–46.

Green, Constance McLaughlin. *Washington: A History of the Capital 1800–1950,* 2 vols. Princeton: Princeton University Press, 1976.

_____. *The Secret City: A History of Race Relations in the Nation's Capital.* Princeton: Princeton University Press, 1967.

Griffin, A. P. C. "Issues of the District of Columbia Press in 1800–'01–'02." *Records of the Columbia Historical Society* 4 (1901): 32–74.

Guilday, Peter. "The Priesthood of Colonial America." *Woodstock Letters* 63 (1934): 169–90.

Gutman, Herbert P. *The Black Family in Slavery and Freedom, 1750–1925.* New York: Vintage Books, 1976.

Hamlin, Talbot. *Benjamin Henry Latrobe.* New York: Oxford University Press, 1955.

Harbaugh, Cora Belle (Cooprider). *Harbaugh History: A Directory and Source Book of Family Records.* Evansville, IN: privately printed, 1947.

Harkness, Robert H. "Dr. William B. Magruder." *Records of the Columbia Historical Society* 16 (1913): 150–87.

Hennesey, James, S.J. *American Catholics: A History of the Roman Catholic Community in the United States.* New York: Oxford University Press, 1983.

_____. "Several Youth Sent from Here: Native-Born Priests and Religious of English America, 1634–1776." *Studies in Catholic History in Honor of John Tracy Ellis.* Ed. Nelson H. Minnich, Robert B. Eno, S.J., and Robert F. Trisco. Wilmington, DE: M. Glazier, 1985.

Henning, George C. "The Mansion and Family of Notley Young." *Records of the Columbia Historical Society* 16 (1913): 1–24.

Holmes, Oliver W. "The City Tavern: A Century of Georgetown History, 1796–1898," *Records of the Columbia Historical Society* 50 (1980): 1–35.

_____. "Suter's Tavern: Birthplace of the Federal City." *Records of the Columbia Historical Society* 49 (1973–74): 1–34.

_____. "Stage Coach Days in the District of Columbia." *Records of the Columbia Historical Society* 50 (1948–50): 1–42.

Holt, T. Joffrey. "Americans at St. Omers, Bruges and Liège." *The Stonyhurst Magazine* 39 (Summer 1976): 243–47.

Homans, Benjamin. *The Georgetown Directory for the Year 1830*. Georgetown, DC: 1830.

Howe, Charles E. "The Financial Institutions of Washington City in Its Early Days." *Records of the Columbia Historical Society* 8 (1905): 1–42.

Hughes, Thomas S.J. *History of the Society of Jesus in North America, Colonial and Federal*. London: Longmans, Green, 1907.

Humphreys, Anderson. *Semmes America*. Memphis, TN: Humphreys Ink, Inc., 1989.

Hunsberger, George S. "The Architectural Career of George Hadfield." *Records of the Columbia Historical Society* 51–52 (1955): 46–65.

Inventory of the Diocese of Washington Archives: Vol. I; The Protestant Episcopal Church. Washington: Historical Records Survey, Works Progress Administration, 1940.

Irving, Washington. *Life of George Washington*, 2 vols. New York: G. P. Putnam and Sons, 1876.

Jefferson, Thomas. *The Papers of Thomas Jefferson*. 24 vols. Ed. Julian P. Boyd, et al. Princeton: Princeton University Press, 1950– .

Johnson, Allan and Dumas Malone, eds. *Dictionary of American Biography*. New York: Charles Scribner's Sons, 1957.

Johnston, Christopher. "The Brooke Family." *Maryland Historical Magazine* 1 (1906): 66–73, 184–88, 284–89.

_____. "Lowndes Family." *Maryland Historical Magazine* 2 (March 1907): 276–79.

_____. "Neale Family of Charles County." *Maryland Historical Magazine* 7 (1912): 201–18.

Jordan, David W. "Maryland's Privy Council." *Law, Society and Politics in Early Maryland.* Ed. Aubrey C. Land et al. Baltimore: Johns Hopkins University Press, 1977, 65–87.

Junior League of Washington. *The City of Washington: An Illustrated History*. New York: Alfred A. Knopf, 1981.

Kelly, Laurence J., S.J. *History of Holy Trinity Parish: Washington, D.C. 1795–1945*. Baltimore: J.D. Lucas, n.d.

Kennedy, Roger. *Architecture, Men, Women, and Money in America 1600–1860*. New York: Random House, 1985.

Land, Aubrey C. "Provincial Maryland." *Maryland, A History.* Ed. Richard Walsh and William Lloyd Fox. Annapolis: Maryland Hall of Records Commission, Department of General Services, 1983.

Lathrop, George Parsons and Rose Hawthorne. *A Story of Courage: Annals of the Georgetown Convent of the Visitation of the Blessed Virgin Mary.* Cambridge, MA: Riverside Press, 1895.

Latrobe, Benjamin Henry. *The Papers of Benjamin Henry Latrobe*. Ed. Edward C. Carter III et al. *Journals*, 3 vols. *Correspondence and Miscellaneous Papers*, 3 vols. New Haven: Yale University Press for the Maryland Historical Society, 1980–88.

[Law, Thomas]. "Observations on the Intended Canal in Washington City." 1804; reprint *Records of the Columbia Historical Society* 8 (1905): 159–68.

[Lear, Tobias.] *Observations on the River Potomack, the Country Adjacent, and the City of Washington.* New York: 1793.

Lord, Walter. *The Dawn's Early Light*. New York: W. W. Norton & Co., 1972.

Malone, Dumas. *Jefferson and the Ordeal of Liberty*. Boston: Little, Brown, 1962.

Mann-Kenney, Louise. *Rosedale: The Eighteenth Century Country Estate of General Uriah Forrest.* Washington: privately printed, 1989.

Maréchal, Archbishop Ambrose, S.S. "Diary of Archbishop Maréchal 1818–1825." *Records of the American Catholic Historical Society of Philadelphia* 11 (1900): 417–39.

Mayo, Bernard. *Henry Clay: Spokesman of the New West*. Boston: Houghton, Mifflin and Co., 1937.

_____. "Bishop Flaget and Henry Clay." *Catholic Historical Review* 27 (July 1941): 210–13.

McAleer, Margaret H. "The Other Congregation: Patterns of Black Worship at Holy Trinity Church, Georgetown, D.C., 1795–1845." Unpub. Georgetown University seminar paper, 1986.

McElroy, John, S.J. "An Account of the Re-establishment of the Society in the United States, and Events Connected Therewith." *Woodstock Letters* 16 (1887): 161–72.

McMaster, Richard K., S.J. "Benedict Fenwick, Bishop of Boston, American Apprenticeship (1782–1817)." *U.S. Catholic Historical Society Records and Studies* 47 (1959): 78–139.

_____. "The Tobacco Trade with France: Letters of Joseph Fenwick, Consul at Bordeaux." *Maryland Historical Magazine* 60 (March 1965): 26–55.

McNamara, Robert F. "John Carroll and Interfaith Marriages: The Case of the Belle Vue Carrolls." *Studies in Catholic History in Honor of John Tracy Ellis.* Ed. Nelson Minnich et al. Wilmington, DE: M. Glazier, 1985.

McNeil, Priscilla. "Map Showing Tracts and Lands in Prince George's County, Maryland, Conveyed for the Federal City & Ownership of the Land on June 28 & 29, 1791, When the First Trust Deeds were signed." *Washington History* 3, no. 1 (Spring-Summer 1991): 42–43.

Menard, Russell R. "Maryland's 'Time of Troubles': Sources of Political Discord." *Maryland Historical Magazine* 76 (June 1981): 124–140.

_____. "British Migrations in the Chesapeake Colonies in the Seventeenth Century." *Colonial Chesapeake Society.* Ed. Lois Green Carr, et al. Chapel Hill: University of North Carolina Press, 1988.

The Metropolitan Catholic Almanac and Laity's Directory, 1838 to 1857. 19 vols. Baltimore: F. Lucas, Jr.

Mitchell, Rev. Hudson, S.J. "Virgil Horace Barber." *Woodstock Letters* 79 (November 1950): 297–334.

Mitchell, Mary. *A Short History of St. John's Church Georgetown from 1796–1968.* Privately printed, 1968.

_____. "The Thomas Sim Lee Corner in Georgetown and Its Preservation." *Records of the Columbia Historical Society* 73–74 (1969–70): 510–16.

Mitchill, Samuel Latham. "Dr. Mitchill's Letters from Washington, 1801–1813." *Harper's New Monthly Magazine* 58 (April 1879): 740–55.

Moffatt, Sister Eulalia Teresa, A.M. "Charles Constantine Pise (1801–1866)." *U.S. Catholic Historical Society Records and Studies* 20 (1931): 78–97.

Monroe, James. *The Writings of James Monroe.* 5 vols. Ed. Stanislaus Murray Hamilton. New York: G.P. Putnam's Sons, 1893–1903.

Morgan, James Dudley. "Robert Brent, First Mayor of Washington City." *Records of the Columbia Historical Society* 2 (1899): 236–51.

Morris, Gouverneur. *The Diary and Letters of Gouverneur Morris.* 2 vols. Ed. Ann Carey Morris. New York: Da Capo Press, 1970.

Morris, Richard B. "Andrew Jackson, Strikebreaker." *American Historical Review* 55 (October 1949): 54–68.

Mudd, Richard D. *The Mudd Family of the United States.* Ann Arbor, MI: Edwards Brothers, Inc., 1951.

National Cyclopedia of American Biography. 61 vols. James T. White, 1898.

New Catholic Encyclopedia. 15 vols. New York: McGraw-Hill, 1967.

Newman, Henry Wright. *The Maryland Semmes and Kindred Families.* Baltimore: Maryland Historical Society, 1956.

Osborne, John Ball. "The Removal of Government to Washington." *Records of Columbia Historical Society* 3 (1900): 136–60.

Papenfuse, Edward C., ed. *Archives of Maryland, New Series I: An Historical List of Public Officials of Maryland.* Annapolis: Maryland State Archives, 1990.

Papenfuse, Edward C., et al., eds. *A Biographical Dictionary of the Maryland Legislature, 1635–1789.* 2 vols. Baltimore: Johns Hopkins University Press, 1979, 1985.

Reintzell, Anthony, ed. *The Washington Directory and Governmental Register for 1843.* Washington: 1843.

Rowland, Kate Mason. *Life and Correspondence of Charles Carroll of Carrollton.* 2 vols. New York: G.P. Putnam's Sons, 1898.

Royall, Anne Newport. *Sketches of History, Life and Manners in the United States by a Traveller.* New Haven: privately printed, 1826.

———. *Letters from Alabama.* Washington: 1830.

Sanderlin, Walt S. *The Great National Project: A History of the Chesapeake and Ohio Canal.* Baltimore: Johns Hopkins University Press, 1946.

Scharf, J. Thomas. *The Chronicle of Baltimore: Being a Complete History of "Baltimore Town" and Baltimore County from the Earliest Period to the Present Time.* Baltimore: Turnbull Brothers, 1874.

Schmeckebier, Lawrence F. "Ward Boundaries in Washington and Georgetown." *Records of the Columbia Historical Society 51–52* (1955): 66-77.

Seale, William. *The President's House.* 2 vols. New York: Harry N. Abrams, 1986.

Sellers, Charles Coleman. *Portraits and Miniatures by Charles Willson Peale.* Philadelphia: American Philosphical Society, 1952.

Semmes, John E. *John H. B. Latrobe and His Times, 1803–1891.* Baltimore: Norman Remington, 1917.

Shea, John Gilmary. *Memorial of the First Century of Georgetown College, D.C., Comprising a History of Georgetown University.* Washington: P. F. Collier, 1891.

———. *The Life and Times of the Most Reverend John Carroll.* New York: 1888.

Smith, Margaret Bayard. *The First Forty Years of Washington Society: Portrayed by the Family Letters of Mrs. Samuel Harrison Smith.* Ed. Gaillard Hunt. New York: Charles Scribner's Sons, 1906.

Spalding, Thomas W. *The Premier See: A History of the Archdiocese of Baltimore 1789–1989.* Baltimore: Johns Hopkins University Press, 1989.

Steiner, Bernard C. *Life of Roger Brooke Taney.* 1922; reprint Westport, CT: Greenwood Press, 1970.

Steiner, Bruce E. "The Catholic Brents of Colonial Virginia," *Virginia Magazine of History and Biography* 70 (October 1962): 387–409.

Stockton, Charles Herbert. "Historical Sketch of George Washington University, D.C." *Records of the Columbia Historical Society* 19 (1916): 99–139.

Stonestreet, Charles, S.J. *Discourse on the Right Rev'd Benedict J. Fenwick, D.D.* Frederick, MD: J. W. Baughmann, 1846.

Sullivan, Eleanor C. *Georgetown Visitation Since 1799.* Baltimore: French-Bray Printing Company, 1975.

Taggert, Hugh T. "Old Georgtown." *Records of the Columbia Historical Society* 11 (1908): 120–224.

Thompson, Henry F. "Richard Ingle in Maryland." *Maryland Historical Magazine* 1 (1905): 125–40.

Thornton, Anna Marie. "Diary of Mrs. William Thornton," with an introduction by C. Worthington Ford. *Records of the Columbia Historical Society* 10 (1907): 88–226.

Tindall, William. *Origin and Government of the District of Columbia.* Washington: Government Printing Office, 1908.

———. "The Executive and Voters of Georgetown, District of Columbia." *Records of the Columbia Historical Society* 24 (1922): 87–117.

———. "Homes of the Local Government." *Records of the Columbia Historical Society* 3 (1900): 279–302.

Todd, Frederick. "The Militia and Volunteers of the District of Columbia." *Records of the Columbia Historical Society* 50 (1948–50): 379–434.

298   Van Miert, Louis, S.J. "Some Historical Documents Concerning the Mission of Maryland, 1807–1820." *Woodstock Letters* 30 (1901): 346–50.

Varnum, Joseph B., Jr. *The Seat of Government of the United States.* Washington: R. Farnham, 1854.

Walker, John. "The High Art of George Hadfield." *American Heritage* 37 (August–September 1986): 74–81.

Walsh, Lorena S. "Servitude and Opportunity in Charles County, Maryland." *Law Society, and Politics in Early Maryland.* Ed. Aubrey C. Land et al. Baltimore: Johns Hopkins University Press, 1977.

Washington, George. *The Writings of Goerge Washington from the Original Manuscript Sources, 1745–1799.* 3 vols. Ed. John C. Fitzpatrick. Washington: Government Printing Office, 1931-44.

_____. *The Diaries of George Washington, 1748-1799.* 4 vols. Ed. John C. Fitzpatrick. Boston: Houghton Mifflin, 1925.

Young, James Sterling. *The Washington Community, 1800-1828.* New York: Columbia University Press, 1966.

Index